CLIO ENTHRONED

T0381787

CAMBRIDGE
UNIVERSITY PRESS

University Printing House, Cambridge CB2 8BS, United Kingdom

Published in the United States of America by Cambridge University Press, New York

Cambridge University Press is part of the University of Cambridge.

It furthers the University's mission by disseminating knowledge in the pursuit of
education, learning and research at the highest international levels of excellence.

www.cambridge.org
Information on this title: www.cambridge.org/9781107634572

© Cambridge University Press 1914

This publication is in copyright. Subject to statutory exception
and to the provisions of relevant collective licensing agreements,
no reproduction of any part may take place without the written
permission of Cambridge University Press.

First published 1914
First paperback edition 2014

A catalogue record for this publication is available from the British Library

ISBN 978-1-107-63457-2 Paperback

Cambridge University Press has no responsibility for the persistence or accuracy of
URLs for external or third-party internet websites referred to in this publication,
and does not guarantee that any content on such websites is, or will remain, accurate
or appropriate.

CLIO ENTHRONED

A STUDY

OF

PROSE-FORM IN THUCYDIDES

BY

WALTER R. M. LAMB, M.A.

LATE FELLOW OF TRINITY COLLEGE, CAMBRIDGE

CAMBRIDGE

AT THE UNIVERSITY PRESS

1914

Τίν γε μέν, εὐθρόνου Κλεοῦς ἐθελοίϲαϲ...
Δέδορκεν φάοϲ.

PINDAR, *Nem.* III. fin.

PREFACE

WHEN it occurred to me, some eight years ago, to write an essay on the style of Thucydides, my object was to examine the literary influences under which the History was composed, and so to gain what seemed to me the necessary position for estimating its author's peculiar genius. In composing the study which I now venture to publish, I have had the same object always in view. It is usual to speak of Thucydides as the inventor of scientific history, and then to wonder at the ornaments and intricacies of his style : I have tried to show what is the connection between the uneven surface of his book and the high intelligence which rules its content. For this purpose I have drawn what appeared to be the most useful illustrations both from the History itself and from other literary performances of the time. The effect of this comparison is, I think, to reveal with a certain progressive clearness the artistic invention of Thucydides, and his whole ambition of producing not merely a truthful document but a vigorous and impressive witness of the truth. In the end and altogether, I found that I was concerned with his aim and method of setting the Muse of history upon her rightful throne.

The modern world is fairly well provided with information about the Greeks of the fifth century B.C. It is possible, indeed, that the character of that ancient

culture has now been made as familiar to educated
Englishmen as they could reasonably desire. They do
not, and perhaps never will, regard sculpture as a means
of expressing either national or personal feelings. Their
interest in architecture is very fitful : when aroused, it
looks for a practical utility, or else a monumental display,
which are Roman ideals rather than Greek. They
inherit a native poetry of marvellous excellence and
variety ; yet they have no time to take any real
possession of its treasures. Trade, finance, sport, and
the sciences which promote or secure these pursuits, take
up the best of their energies ; and here the ancient world
has little or nothing to teach them. But the great movements of life and thought are now forcing them to make
experiments in adjusting civic cohesion to the rights and
needs of the individual ; democracy is faced with the
problem of empire ; and there is a keen appetite for
well-informed theory on the growth of political ideas and
institutions.   The records of civilisation are being
searched for examples and contrasts. While modern
history is attaining, under this new stimulus, some of its
proper importance in education, the public curiosity is
evidently willing to travel up above this diverse and
indeterminate stream to its simpler sources in antiquity.
    The most notable of such sources is the History of
Thucydides. It shows the Athenian state contending
with her neighbours for the supremacy of Greece, and
asserting the strength that underlay the brilliance of her
culture. It is the scrupulous testimony of a man who,
after holding high military command, became a detached
observer of many phases in the course of the struggle.
It pictures a fierce effervescence of political movements,
and shows such a management of light and shade, of line
and colour, that, while every feature is distinct, the

whole is astir with suggestions for our thought and
imagination. It is a book that must ever attract and
inspire the serious student of mankind. Hence an essay
which draws attention to the framework as well as the
complexion of such a work may fairly appropriate some
of the interest attaching to that intrinsic value. Even
without this claim, a fresh discussion of the document
which revives for us in such powerful tones the activities
of a long-vanished age may obtain from it some hints for
the history of language—the instrument and auxiliary of
the highest human faculties.

For, in fact, if we hear much of the imaginative
achievements of the Greeks, their invention of prose-
writing has been—at any rate in England—but scantily
noticed. In Germany, Blass[1] and Norden[2] have exhibited the main stages in the evolution of Attic prose :
yet their treatises, though very useful and important, are
apt to embarrass an ordinary student with the task of
wading through the numerous and often chilly pools of
ancient, mediæval and modern opinion. In France,
Alfred Croiset[3] prefixed to his edition of part of the
History an account of Thucydides' style which has the
French virtues of arrangement and precision : but it
clings too religiously to the lines of the ancient critics,
especially in regarding Thucydides and other writers of
his time as obedient or antagonistic to certain rules and
schemes of writing, which are largely the fond discoveries
of pedants among the boughs that have spread in all
directions from those early shoots. The only regular
treatment of the subject in English is that of the late
Sir Richard Jebb[4]; which, in the first place, confines its

[1] *Attische Beredsamkeit*, 1868.   [2] *Antike Kunstprosa*, 1898.
[3] *Thucydide*, I–II, 1886.
[4] *Attic Orators*, 1876, and more fully, *Speeches of Thucydides*, Hellenica,
1879.

scope to the rhetorical parts of the History, and secondly, aims at little more than a lucid statement of the views of Dionysius and other ancient writers on style. The method of my study will be to watch the beginnings of formality in the fragments of the early chroniclers ; then to examine its fuller developements in various writers of the fifth century, including Thucydides ; and finally to distinguish and discuss the chief effects of literary art in the History of the Peloponnesian War[1].

In England the modern art of prose-writing is usually regarded either as the humble drudge of truth or as the seductive minister of error. But the Greek intelligence, whose freedom and clarity we are so wont to admire, sought its expression in a language of frankly formal elevation and grace. In designing a statue or a poem, the Greek genius was able to select as symbols from the visible world, and then to combine in the needful relations, a number of shapes and gestures which had to be sensuously attractive before they could hope to be significant. This general motive of all the artistic achievements of the Greeks is connected with the special character of their paganism. Aware of vague forces in nature which refused to be brought under human control, they did not prostrate their thought in a blind, inert awe, but tried to delimit and fix their conceptions of those forces with some outlines of humanity; which then excited their sense to a deeper enjoyment of life, and urged their keenest minds to speculate upon the personal and social interests of man. This ardour of contemplation appears at its strongest in Thucydides, whose creative impulse, working to some extent together with the public arts of his time, moved him to mould and polish such an art of

[1] Thus I shall proceed for some distance in the direction indicated by the late Mr Forbes' illustrations, *Thuc.* Bk I, 1895, pp. xli–lxxx.

prose-style as should meet the demands of a genuine historical research. Hence we may expect to find that the particular embellishments by which he hoped, in narrative as well as harangue, to impress and stir his readers are full of meaning for those of them who would really grasp the intention of his work.

His artistic effort shows him to have reached only that stage of imperfect skill which invites and permits analysis. A great writer has remarked of Plato that 'his dramatic art and verbal argumentation appear to be indissolubly mingled with the grace and perfection of his Attic style[1]': his accomplishment, for the most part, is so easy and unobtrusive, that the literary critic can tell us of little else than either himself or philosophy. But Thucydides has a manner of writing that continually confesses him a self-conscious adventurer. Direct or involved, restrained or expansive—he is all these by turns—he seems to launch one expedient after another with a fresh ingenuous pride; so that he may be said to stand, as artist, on the way from archaic to classic. This position is likely to reward the zeal of a modern dissector; and if, in following out the peculiarities of the style, we can light upon some rare quality in the man which will connect his intellectual acumen with his pursuit of ideal form in art, we may see ourselves on the way to a better understanding of the whole tradition of eloquent prose.

I make no attempt, in a survey which already has to neglect or touch but lightly upon many points more closely related to its main subject, to apply my method or results to the styles of Andocides, Lysias, Isocrates, Isæus, Xenophon, Plato and Demosthenes. More than one of these could be shown to have been influenced in

---

[1] Gibbon, *Decline and Fall*, xlii.

their writing by Thucydides : but a satisfactory explanation would need a disproportionate increase of space.   I
only glance at Plato, and one or two of the others, where
they can supply me with a useful illustration.   Still less
do I concern myself with tracing the effects of Thucydides' great example in the aims of later historians[1].   My
range is bounded by his literary achievement, as the
range of that was by the Peloponnesian War.   The
preliminary and outlying ground over which I have to
hasten presents a variety of curious problems: only a
very few of these will be considered ; scarcely any,
perhaps, completely solved[2].   In many cases the nature
of the evidence provides me with the fitting excuse of
Thucydidean caution.   As to the rest, I can only urge
the claims of my central and predominant theme—
Thucydidean style.

The success of such studies must in great measure
depend on the number of persons who feel a definite
affection for literature as an art ; and these, on their side,
should be able to rely on classical scholars as responsible
to the present-day world for the life-breath of departed
cultures.   In the course of composing my original essay,
I was met by the appearance of Mr F. M. Cornford's
Thucydides Mythistoricus[3], and found that I must consider his view of the History before proceeding on my
way.   It did not take me long to perceive that, by formul-
ating my grounds for disagreement with that view, I was
making my own investigation more definite and thorough;
so that, if this controversy seems to make, as I fear it
does, a rather tiresome noise in some pages of my book,

[1] For this subject, especially on its historical side, see the lectures of
J. B. Bury, *Ancient Greek Historians*, 1909.
[2] Since my remarks on the Hippocratean *De Arte* (pp. 142–4) were written,
I find that Diels (*Hermes*, 1913, pp. 378–407) has set forth in detail the kind
of considerations on which I based my judgement.   [3] 1907.

my defence must be that I have found Mr Cornford's
assertions not only too dangerous but too useful to
be ignored. An alarm has been raised, and with some
reason, that the enthusiasms of anthropology are likely
or even eager to obscure the front of the classical temple
with the distresses and nostrums of primitive savagery.
Some readers, indeed, will think that I have myself
discounted the merit of combating the theory of a mythic
design in the History by straying too far, in another
chapter, towards the childish origins of personification.
Yet this latter attempt cannot be charged with more
than a few passing conjectures. It would be sad if taboo
and totem, dream-pedlary, and the ubiquitous snake,
were the best harvest that we could reap from the
laborious fields of learning. But wisdom and elegance
are not yet effete, nor even grown up. If Hume is as
dead as Rousseau, it is known who had the better
ending. When Anacharsis[1] had travelled through Greece,
and had enlarged his mind by conversing with its people,
he turned his steps at length to his home in Scythia.
He crossed the Hellespont: resolving to visit Cyzicus,
he happened there upon the celebrations in honour of
the Mother of the Gods. At once he was caught by the
contagion of the rites ; and vowed that, if he reached his
home in safety, he would worship Cybele with similar
orgies in the Scythian groves. He arrived safe in his
native land. Instead of hastening to give his countrymen
the benefit of the lore that he had gathered from the
Greeks, he proceeded to enact those frenzied rites in
the wild recesses of a wood, with the kettle-drum in his
hand, and the string of holy images round his neck.
In this condition he was discovered by a Scythian, who
promptly fetched the king ; and he, on observing the

[1] Herodotus, IV, 76.

indecency for himself, cut short the great scholar's aberration with an arrow. Perhaps this comment was too severe. But an admirer of Thucydides may be forgiven for protesting against all who would set out on rainbow-bridges for the truth.

I have to thank Mr Ernest Harrison, Fellow and Lecturer of Trinity College, for many useful remarks on my proofs. I am also much indebted to the vigilant care of the University Press.

W. R. M. LAMB.

5, CAMBRIDGE TERRACE,
   KEW GREEN,
      April, 1914.

ERRATUM, p. 227, n. 3—for 'MacCulley...1896' read 'MacCauley...1897.'

CONTENTS

CHAPTER I

THE GENERAL AIM OF THE HISTORY

CHAPTER II

ALLUREMENTS OF DRAMA

CHAPTER III

THE MIND OF THE WRITER

CONTENTS

CHAPTER IV

NARRATIVE PROSE

CONTENTS XV

CHAPTER VIII

INTONATION

CHAPTER IX

INTERPOLATION

CHAPTER X

CONCLUSION

CHAPTER I

THE GENERAL AIM OF THE HISTORY

§ 1

IF the views held of Thucydides by the majority of scholars to-day could be reduced to a summary consensus, it would be something of this sort :—that he is a great observer, a great thinker, a great historian, and a great writer; but that his work is strangely disfigured with obscurities and ambiguities, and especially with crabbed or garish freaks of phrase. The long and illustrious line of his editors, translators and commentators bears witness both to the importance of what he says and to his magnificent, yet often perplexing, manner of saying it. Baptised by Valla and nurtured by Stephanus, he was handed on by Hudson, Wasse, Duker, Gail and Haacke to Bekker, and by him to the encyclopædic Poppo. Thus plentifully equipped, he had further attentions from Goeller, Bloomfield, Arnold, Krüger, Boehme, Donaldson, Classen, Shilleto, Stahl, Herwerden, Croiset and Hude. These are the chief of his editors: while numerous advances in his study were made, among others, by Reiske, Herbst, Badham, Meineke, Dobree, Cobet, Müller-Strübing, Steup and Wilamowitz-Moellendorff. In England his fame has steadily increased, ever since Thomas Nicolls, 'Citezeine and Goldesmyth of London,' put forth his translation in 1550 under privilege from Edward the Sixth. The

account 'of the Life and History of Thucydides' prefixed
by Thomas Hobbes to his version in 1628 is full of
admiration directed by fine and solid sense : some of the
short-sighted criticisms of Dionysius are there disposed
of as fitly and firmly as could be wished. It is remarkable that Alfred Croiset, who has no reason to be partial
to England, picks out Macaulay as the best panegyrist
of Thucydides in recent times. A few sentences of
the English historian and critic may be repeated here[1].
In a letter of August 25, 1835, he says :
  'I do assure you that there is no prose composition
in the world, not even the De Corona, which I place so
high as the seventh book of Thucydides. It is the
ne plus ultra of human art. I was delighted to find in
Gray's letters the other day this query to Wharton :
"The retreat from Syracuse—Is it or is it not the finest
thing you ever read in your life ? " '
  On February 27 of the same year he had scribbled at
the end of a volume :—'This day I finished Thucydides,
after reading him with inexpressible interest and admiration. He is the greatest historian that ever lived.'
  Another of these notes, on May 30 of the next year,
declares him to be 'still of the same mind.' At the age
of twenty-seven (1827) he had set forth, in an essay on
History, his connected views on the Greek historians ;
and, though he has some strictures on his favourite's
method, it is Thucydides who comes nearest to his
ideal. This opinion, like the others quoted, can remain
important, whatever be our estimate of his own practice
later on ; though indeed there can be little doubt that
the obvious effects of his keen partisan spirit would
provide a further compliment to Thucydides' greatness
as distinguished as it was unintentional.

  [1] Macaulay's several references to Thucydides are collected at the
beginning of Jowett's Translation, 1881 and 1900.

As soon, however, as we meet with more thoroughly critical views, the discrepancy between the man and his language, and, of the latter, between the plain sort and the twisted, has to be faced. Perhaps the reputed faults of Thucydides have been most usefully stated by Colonel Mure in his judicious and lively survey of Greek literature[1]. Of the narrative style he speaks in terms of the highest praise : 'in no other author do we find the same combination of fluency and compression, of copiousness and clearness of matter with rapidity of manner'; and he cites 'as a fair general specimen' the account of the last days and death of Themistocles[2]. But he enters forthwith upon a lengthy indictment of the rhetorical parts of the History : his main accusations are the following :—'The principal defects in the genius of Thucydides are an over-subtlety of the Intellectual faculty, and a deficiency in the faculty of Taste ; or at least in that more delicate ingredient of the latter, which acts as a safeguard against popular mannerism and affectation in literature or art.' Many of the rhetorical passages 'are so laboured, sophistical and obscure, that it may be doubted whether any reader can honestly say, that he has read them with feelings of satisfaction'; and he shows how his opinion agrees on the whole with those of Cicero, Dionysius, Hermogenes and Tzetzes. The particular faults are stated as 'a studied antithetical arrangement of opinions and arguments; the unseasonable interspersion, or undue accumulation, of abstract and far-fetched maxims ; subtle definitions of obvious things ; wire-drawn distinctions between palpably different things ; and elaborate demonstrations of propositions which no reasonable man would ever think

[1] *Critical History of the Language and Literature of Antient Greece*, 1857, vol. v.
[2] Thuc. I, 135-139.

of disputing.' He adds an enumeration of grammatical
peculiarities, and mentions some curious tricks of sound
whose effect is 'to secure a certain uniformity of compass
or cadence, similar to metre in blank verse, to the
sentences composing each pair of antithetical categories,'
or else to produce alliteration or rhyme. These latter
points are illustrated with an English version of
Alcibiades' speech to the Lacedæmonian Council[1], a
list, in Greek, of assonant antitheses, and a few cases
of play upon words. He sums up as follows :—'The
excellence of his composition, the graphic precision of
his narrative, his spirited descriptions and penetrating
judgements on men and things, are the fruit of his own
better genius. His rhetorical mannerism reflects the
vicious taste of his age, working on his own natural
turn for nice distinctions and logical refinements....
His appeals are to the head rather than the heart ;
to the judgement rather than the sympathies ; scarcely
ever to the fancy or imagination.' In conclusion, we
are asked to be patient with Thucydides, for he
'improves on better acquaintance' ; we must try and
get over the harshness of 'the contrast between the
enigmatical subtlety of thought and expression that
pervades one large portion of his text, and the clear
common sense and sound judgement which animates the
remainder.'

From this precise and weighty expression of what
the best critics have felt, we may pass on to where
the problem contracts into a pitched battle, and at
times a hand-to-hand fight. Professor Gilbert Murray[2]
gives a striking sketch of the fray :—'Thucydides' style
as it stands in our texts is an extraordinary phenomenon. Undeniably a great style, terse, restrained,

[1] Thuc. VI, 92 ; Mure, vol. v, App. G, IX.
[2] *Ancient Greek Literature*, 1898, pp. 190 foll.

vivid, and leaving the impression of a powerful intellect. Undeniably also an artificial style, obscure amid its vividness, archaistic and poetic in vocabulary, and apt to run into verbal flourishes which seem to have little thought behind them.' There is mention of Gorgias, Antiphon and Prodicus in connection with the structure of the style; two features of which, however,—the inverted order of words, and the violent relief thus given to separate details,—are singled out as 'evidently part of the man's peculiar nature.' On the narrower question of the text we read :—'but what is not explicable is that he should have fallen into the intermittent orgies of ungrammatical and unnatural language, the disconcerting trails of comment and explanation, which occur on every third page.' We review the various answers that have been made to this riddle. Cobet and Rutherford preached the doctrine of foreign cross-references, explanatory interpolations and deliberate forgeries. To the last item Müller-Strübing gave the support of violent abuse. Wilamowitz holds that the book was edited after the author's death by another. Schwartz gloomily declares that 'the unity of authorship is as hopelessly lost in the Thucydidean question as in the Homeric.' After glancing at the conservative attitude of Herbst, Mr Murray confesses his sympathy with the general line of Cobet followed by Rutherford—'that the text is largely defaced by adscripts and glosses, and that Thucydides, a trained stylist at a time when style was much studied, did not, in a work which took twenty-nine years' writing, mix long passages of masterly expression with short ones of what looks like gibberish.' Unfortunately, ' Dr Rutherford's valuable edition of Book IV[1], attempting to carry these results to a logical

[1] 1889.

conclusion, has produced a text which hardly a dozen scholars in Europe would accept.'

Mr Marchant, after subjecting Book II[1] to an elaborate treatment after the methods of Rutherford, in a more recent edition of Book I[2] retreated altogether from the position he had so forcibly maintained. In the meantime, Professors Tucker[3] and Goodhart[4], in their editions of Book VIII, had shown good reasons for caution. Mr Stuart Jones[5], the last English editor of the whole text, announced, and in general pursued, a conservative policy. The latest and best equipped text is that of Dr Hude who[6], recognising that the style varies in character, professes to have taken the middle course of leaving unchanged any oddities of expression which seem to arise from the prevailing tone of the context, while smoothing away such harshnesses as may be cured by a ready emendation. He follows, therefore, what can be called a 'rule of exception,' under guidance from the author's shifting moods; and thus, after taking full account of the remedies offered by the whole succession of Thucydidean scholarship, leaves the field open for arguments based on literary habit. The need of obtaining some definite views in this direction becomes all the more obvious and urgent when we come to observe the particular corrections which this editor has made in his text. For the old question only grows more acute,—Is your historian so great in intellect and art, and yet tells his story *thus* and *thus*?—and definite reasons for rejecting or accepting, not merely a remedial policy, but each several suggestion, are required. Merely for this practical business, a clear sense of Thucydides' habits and moods must be helpful; and if, instead of vague disapproval, we can offer something like a

---

[1] 1891.   [2] 1905.   [3] 1892.   [4] 1893.
[5] Oxford Class. Ser. 1898.   [6] Leipsig, 1898–1901.

demonstration that Cobet and other fine masters of idiom were short-sighted in their own province, some tangible gain may be within our reach. But in the larger aspect of the matter, an examination of the literary movements of the fifth century should throw some fresh light, not only on the works of Thucydides and his contemporaries, but also, perhaps, on some of those discussions in which the eloquence of Plato appears as the genuine, if rather ungrateful, heir of the sophistic inventions.

'A trained stylist at a time when style was much studied'—is a phrase that alone should prompt some search among the fragmentary relics of the early prose-writers for the steps by which the style of Thucydides was formed. This, in brief, is what we shall attempt. The best method will be to set up a rough sketch of Thucydides' mind for the needs of immediate reference; and then, by filling it in, as we proceed, with such features as may be gathered from a more particular inspection of his work, to apply this surer criterion of his literary character to the more doubtful parts of the problem. Even in the minutest search for artistic influences in the various fabric of his book, it would be utter folly—too plain already in the fate of some censures—to lose sight of the man, and the ideas that he shared or did not share with the world around him.

§ 2

The words in which Thucydides introduces his account of the great plague—αὐτός τε νοσήσας καὶ αὐτὸς ἰδὼν ἄλλους πάσχοντας[1]—might well be taken as the

---

[1] Thuc. II, 48 fin.—'Having had the disease myself, and myself seen the suffering of others.'

motto of his whole life and work. He had bitter
personal experience of the war, and a strong personal
sense of its effect on the Greek world. The usual
modern astonishment at his impartial, impersonal tone
is too apt to overlook this rare merit of the History,—
that it was intended to be, and very largely is, a record
of such matters as he knew by personal contact. He says
he began to write it at the first approach of hostilities.
His words—'composed it...beginning as soon as hostilities
were coming on[1]'—may not imply more than the collection
of notes: but it is safe to assume that he formed the
plan of a record at the time when the Corcyræan and
Corinthian envoys came to Athens[2]. His design was
to relate the story of the war between the Peloponnesians
and the Athenians, detailing the operations on both
sides[3] in chronological order; and this not only year
by year, but 'by summers and winters.' Mr Grundy's
elaborate scrutiny of the best modern discussion[4] leaves
little doubt that Thucydides' view of his subject, and
his ambition as a writer, underwent considerable change
as he pursued his task. But we must remember that,
as is not uncommon in the survivals of old-fashioned
things, the interest we attach to some parts of the
book which finally appeared under his name has grown
out of all proportion to the author's discernible scheme.
It is likely, of course, that strategy, and violent encounters of rival states, will continue for some time
yet to be eagerly studied: but the progress of ages
has fixed our attention on political, anthropological and
other more humane and private questions which, though
they entered increasingly, as he advanced, into the scope
of his design, cannot be said to have originally prompted

---

[1] I, I. I—ξυνέγραψε...ἀρξάμενος εὐθὺς καθισταμένου.
[2] 433 B.C.   [3] I, I. I—ὡς ἐπολέμησαν πρὸς ἀλλήλους.
[4] *Thucydides and the History of his Age*, 1911.

the historian to his undertaking, or to have been at any time the main object of his research.

His choice of an annalistic method should of itself assert the military character of his book. That the history of a great war should be written by an experienced general is very desirable : yet, is it possible for him to make a satisfactory survey of events which extend through his own life, and in some of which he has played an active part himself ? Sir Walter Raleigh excused his concernment with remote antiquity in words that are now famous :—'Whosoever in writing a moderne History shall follow truth too neare the heeles, it may happily strike out his teeth[1].' A clear view of a great multitude of events, a sure grasp of their connection and meaning, is impossible to him who watches them passing close to his eyes ; and a journal, or register of each incident as it comes into sight, is the most he can usually hope to achieve. But a regular warfare, which is accepted and conducted as part of the common business of life, must be allowed an obvious exception. Not only is a close spectator able, in this case, to give a satisfactory account of a series of military operations, but he is the person best qualified for the work. A single campaign, or group of campaigns, unless the war proceeds in some very extraordinary fashion, can only be described in its actual stages of time ; and in cases where weather and temperature are decisive for the movements of troops—and particularly in naval affairs—it is important to keep continual note of the season of the year. It was natural, therefore, that Thucydides, as an active general, should compile his memoirs in the form of annals. For large portions of the narrative, as we possess it, this form was clearly the most expedient. But when his exile brought him

[1] *History of the World*, Pref.

larger opportunities of information, and at the same time a far more detached and critical standpoint, he widened his scope to an extent which he had not at first intended. Furnished with the time and means for observing the campaigns from more sides than one, he began, without as yet passing the bounds of military history, to incorporate in his work some account of plans and movements which the narrower scheme of a combatant on the Athenian side could not have included.

It will be worth while here to glance at the attack made by Dionysius—with more warmth than befits his own ideal and performance in history—on Thucydides' 'economy' (οἰκονομικόν) and, more especially, on his 'division' (διαίρεσις). He pitches on the narrative of Book III, cc. 2–114, and complains that it is 'broken up into mere small change[1]' by the conventional divisions of time. First we have the Mytilenæans, then the Lacedæmonians; their doings are only partly treated, and we pass on to the siege of Potidæa: in the middle of this we return to Mitylene; thence to Corcyra, and so on. The accusation, so far, is just: the comprehensive story is beginning to include motives and negotiations which will not fit comfortably on to the military framework. The author is finding some difficulty in bringing his settled method of accuracy to terms with his larger vision of events. In some instances, however, where the affairs are more purely military, such complaint is misplaced. The narrative of the Sicilian Expedition proceeds, quite properly, in chronological order; and if it is interrupted, for example, by a note on Agis' invasion of Attica[2] and the momentous fortification of Decelea, the reader's thoughts are held safely on the track by a strong guiding-line,—the letter which brings

---

[1] *De Thuc.* 826 foll.—εἰς μικρὰς κατακερματιζομένη τομάς.
[2] Thuc. VII, 19.

out, with such impressive simplicity, the embarrassments
of Nicias[1]. A little further on in the same Book there
is another break in the story; the Decelean War[2] comes
in again. This, so far from making a flaw in historical
continuity, is an intensifying touch added to the picture.
It may be called a digression; but it more than justifies
itself by the sudden revelation which heightens our sense
of the difficulties and dangers besetting the Athenians
at this particular moment. However, there is enough
reason in part of Dionysius' accusation to put us on
the alert for the beginning of a struggle between two
separate designs, one narrow and one wide, for which
no compromise has been discovered, or at any rate
perfected. We need not consider at this stage how
far Thucydides was ever conscious of the problem.
For the present it is enough to state, what must have
been his feeling for many years after he left the service
of Athens, that he was writing a military history, and
that his exile enabled him to make it more ample and
interesting than he had at first expected[3].

Still, in guessing at his personal inclinations, we
should not forget to add the circumstances of his child-
hood and upbringing to the leisure of his riper years.
Beyond the facts of his strategic failure to relieve
Amphipolis in 424, and his banishment from Athens
thereafter for twenty years, we know nothing important
about his life. Mr Forbes[4], whose cautious estimate of
the evidence lifts his biographical sketch above the
ordinary level, reduces the various theories about the
date of Thucydides' birth to this:—'In any case his

---

[1] VII, 11-15.   [2] VII, 27-28.

[3] V, 26—καὶ γενομένῳ παρ' ἀμφοτέροις τοῖς πράγμασι καὶ οὐχ ἧσσον τοῖς
Πελοποννησίων διὰ τὴν φυγήν, καθ' ἡσυχίαν τι αὐτῶν μᾶλλον αἰσθέσθαι—as though
hinting, what Plutarch (De Exil. 14) has remarked, that his banishment has
not been without advantage to the world.

[4] Introduction to Book I (1895), p. xiii.

youth and early manhood were spent during the time when Athens, under the undisputed leadership of Pericles, was at the height of her political, intellectual, and artistic greatness.' The probabilities as to the stages by which the History was composed have been minutely discussed by Mr Grundy[1]. In the result, he inclines to the view that in the years between the Peace of Nicias (421) and the beginning of the Sicilian Expedition (415) Thucydides completed a history of the Ten Years' War (431–421); and thus, having written Books I–V, c. 20, without certain passages referring to later events, he may have regarded his book as a finished whole. Then, as the Sicilian Expedition proceeded (415–413), he undertook the history of this affair as a separate work : but while he was engaged on this, the Decelean War (413–404) appeared to him a real continuation of the Ten Years' War, and he resolved to make one history of the two ; and, besides narrating the new section, began collecting materials for the intervening ' Years of Peace.' This part he composed shortly before his return to Athens (404) ; after which he formed a third conception of his work, and intended, by incorporating the Sicilian Expedition and completing the Decelean War, to produce a history of the whole twenty-seven years' war (431–404). The book, as we have it, only brings the tale down to 411.

Mr Grundy's arguments for this view[2] have to start from evidence which is scanty and not very solid : but it is obtained, as is necessary and proper, from the historian's intellectual grasp, at different times, of certain matters of fact. There is no obvious sign which will help us to the date of the more ornamental parts of the

---

[1] *Thuc. and the History of his Age*, pp. 387–534.
[2] The main points coincide with those suggested by Mr Murray, *Lit. Anc. Gr.* p. 184.

book : besides the general likelihood that the rhetorical embellishment of speeches and descriptions would belong to a late stage of composition, there is merely some reason for regarding occasional patches—for instance, the Corinthian speech which expounds the designs of the Peloponnesians[1] (Book I, cc. 120–124), or the digression on Hippias and Hipparchus[2] (Book VI, cc. 54–59)—as fairly late insertions.   The author's situation is roughly summed up by Mr Murray:—'it is characteristic both of the man and of a certain side of Athenian culture, that he turned away from his main task of narrative to develop the style of his work as pure literature[3].' Still, it is almost as easy to believe that he composed many or even most of the speeches along with their context, in the long leisure of his exile ; and that the few cases where we find a speaker anticipating after-events are due to a few late touches, added when these rhetorical pieces had received their final form. Moreover, it has hardly ever occurred to those who have collected and discussed these prophecies, that some of them might be reasonably ascribed to the foresight of the speakers, if not to that of the author.

§ 3

It will be useful at this point, if we are to attain some notion of what was ' characteristic of the man,' to see his own account of the method he adopted.   After illustrating the indolence of ordinary report with the tradition about Hippias and Hipparchus, he proceeds thus[4]:—

' But error will be avoided by holding, on the evidence here adduced, an opinion such as that which I have set forth, and by withdrawing confidence from what poets

---

[1] Grundy, *l.c.* p. 449.   [2] *Ib.* p. 425.
[3] *Lit. Anc. Gr.* p. 185.   [4] Thuc. I. 21–22.

have sung with their enhancing art, or what prose-writers
have composed more attractively to our hearing than
suitably to truth,—things not tried and tested, that for
the most part have by lapse of time won over untrust-
worthily into the fabulous ; whereas here matters may
be accepted as made out from the most indubitable
signs, with such sufficiency as their ancient date allows.
And this war, if men will consider it directly in its events
—though they always judge a present one, so long as
they are fighting, to be the greatest, and then, when they
have done with it, marvel more at those of earlier times
—will nevertheless prove itself to have been greater than
any before. As for the speeches uttered by the several
parties, either when about to make war, or when already
in it, I was at a hard pass for the proper recollection of
their words in simple exactness, whether heard by myself
or by sundry others who recounted them to me: they are
here expressed according as I supposed each person
would have spoken what was most requisite for treating
the actual matters before him ; and I have adhered as
closely as I could to the general purport of what was really
said. For the facts of what was done in the war,
I thought fit not to write down anything I might obtain
from casual informants, nor to give my view of the
matter, but only those things at which I myself was
present, or which, if learnt from others, I could investigate
in all possible accuracy of detail. It was a heavy labour
to search them out, since the persons who were present
at each event did not tell the same tale about the same
things, but according as they were swayed towards either
side[1] by favour or memory. Perhaps my hearers will
find my avoidance of the fabulous a failure in delight :
yet all who may wish for a clear vision of what came
to pass and, in the order of human affairs, may well

[1] Reading ἑκατέρων.

befall again some day in a like or comparable sort,—that these should deem the work useful will be a satisfaction. It is compiled more as a possession for ever than as a prize-performance for the moment's hearing.'

In the original Greek of this passage, the author's sincerity is as clear as his general meaning : at the same time, the awkwardness of phrase—hardly to be represented in tolerable English—seems to betray an anxious hesitation over his choice of method. He has dismissed the fabulous as useless ; but in working up his version of the speeches so as to widen and deepen the interest of his picture, he hopes that he has not made it less trustworthy. His anxiety will be more vivid to us, if we remember that the artistic problem did not begin only here. In describing the bare facts, he had to select and classify them, as well as test their truth. The question is not so much —Am I to make my history artistic ? as—In this art of writing history, how artistic am I going to be ? If this point is not obvious enough already, the early stages of the problem are well illustrated by what the Duc de Sully says about the composition of his Memoirs[1]:—

'The public is to expect in these Memoirs only descriptions of such events as are of some consideration, and which I witnessed, or which befell the king himself.... With a view to refreshing my memory, I jotted down at the beginning some features which had struck me, and, in particular, those utterances which the king made to me, or which I had heard him make, upon the war or political matters....His Majesty observed what I was at, since I sometimes recalled to him, word for word, what had fallen from his lips ; and he commanded me to set my work in some order, and extend it. Here I found great difficulties ; not the least of them was that which arose from my style.'

[1] Init. ann. 1590 (*Mémoires de Sully*, 1778, vol. I, p. 333).

The simplest historian may be none the less an artist
for holding fast to a purpose of usefulness. But this
art is not learnt in a day; and in the mere outlines
of Thucydides' narrative it is curious to see his pride
of knowledge at odds with formal unity. He has some
special episodes or digressions, of which the first
three—recounting the conspiracy of Cylon, the end
of Pausanias, and the end of Themistocles—almost
give the impression that he is trying his hand at the
inconsequent ease of Herodotus. In describing how the
Lacedæmonians sought to get as much pretext for war
as they could on their side, he has to mention 'the curse
of the goddess[1]' which they bade the Athenians expel
from their midst. To explain this dark allusion, he
briefly recalls the affair of Cylon, which occurred about
two centuries before. He secures its connection with
the present by showing how the phrase was aimed at
Pericles; and then, to explain the counter-demand of the
Athenians[2], he enters upon the story of Pausanias' dishonour and death. Now Thucydides has already stepped
a little out of his way, in a previous sketch of the rise of
the Athenian empire, to connect the wane of Spartan
influence with the ingenuity of Themistocles and the
despotic behaviour of Pausanias[3]. That brief yet most
illuminating sketch concludes with some words of personal
justification[4]:—'My reason for describing these matters
and thus digressing from my story is that this passage
was to seek in all who have been before me; what they
composed was either Greek history before the Median
Wars, or those Wars themselves. Hellanicus did touch
on these matters in his Attic Records: but his mention
of them was brief, and inaccurate in their timing. And

[1] Thuc. I, 126. 2.
[2] Alluding in turn to 'the curse of the goddess of the Brazen House,'
I, 128.   [3] I, 89–96.   [4] I, 97. 2.

besides, my account exhibits the manner in which the Athenian empire was founded.' The gist and tone of this excuse are neatly phrased by Cicero[1],—'ut ait Thucydides, ἐκβολὴ λόγου non inutilis.' But in treating this matter of the curse, it seems as though he were growing bolder with each step out of his measured path. He does not take so much pains to keep the whole story[2] pertinent to his main business: on the contrary, he indulges in a striking elaboration of detail; and the same minuteness appears in the ensuing story of Themistocles[3], who is immediately linked to Pausanias by his implication in the intrigue with Persia.

The setting and character of these episodes declare, not only that the author is conscious of the difference between the strict method which he had originally chosen for himself and the looser schemes of Herodotus[4] and other entertaining writers, but that he will now and then apply some special information, so as to relieve and brighten the orderly progress of his summers and winters with some glimpses of biography. Their true significance is overlooked if we merely note that one of them deals with matter 'which is quite irrelevant to the main purpose of the history,' and that the presence of the other (about Themistocles) 'can only be attributed to some special interest which the historian took in that great personality[5],' or perhaps to the design of correcting a false impression created by Herodotus[6]. 'Pausanias the Lacedæmonian and Themistocles the Athenian, the most distinguished Hellenes of their day[7]'—there is an obvious appeal to the imagination, for the larger understanding of the History, in this concluding sentence, which leaves the two leading

---

[1] *Ep. ad Att.* VII, i, 6.   [2] Thuc. I, 128–134.   [3] I, 135–138.
[4] 'Additions (προσθῆκαι) are what my story from the first affected'—is the genial confession of Herodotus, IV, 30.
[5] Grundy, p. 407.   [6] Grundy, p. 451.   [7] Thuc. I, 138 fin.

2

figures of that former generation face to face, as it were,
in the misty beginnings of the quarrel. The careful
completeness with which the fate of the one and the
character of the other are presented amounts almost to a
confession of faith in the uses of literary art, beyond the
work-a-day plodding of a log-book ; a confession which
meets us again in the more familiar, though very variously
and falsely estimated, association of imaginative rhetoric
with his pursuit of realistic fidelity.

At any rate, these hints are clear enough to prepare
us for the account of Theseus' formation of the capital of
Attica[1], and the archæological note on the ancient city
and its inhabitants[2]; the pleasant piece of myth about
Alcmæon's settlement in Acarnania[3]; the remarks on the
Delian festival and its literary associations[4]; and the discussion of Hippias and Hipparchus[5]. This last digression
stands out in more striking colours, not only because of
its length and its rather forced connection with the
mutilation of the Hermæ, but also because it looks like a
restatement, on a larger scale, of a passage on the same
subject in the first Book[6]. As it will be more convenient
to examine the intention of this emphasis elsewhere, in a
closer approach to Thucydides' mind, we may pass on to
a further point in his main design which modern critics
are apt to ignore.

§ 4

The History is commonly treated in terms which
seem to assume that Thucydides did not conceive of his
book being read by other than Hellenic students near to
his own time. This belief led Rutherford to condemn a
number of explanations which we find appended to what
must have been well-known places, customs and things ;

[1] Thuc. II, 15–16.   [2] II, 17.   [3] II, 102.
[4] III, 104.   [5] VI, 53–59.   [6] I, 20.

and, though few critics have expressly agreed with him, a definite answer is desirable. To suppose that the author did not contemplate being read by persons who might be ignorant of the sites not merely of Rhegium and Messene[1], but of the Piræus[2] and Acharnæ[3], is to overlook one of the most remarkable features in the purpose of the History. Thucydides is unique among the observers and thinkers of ancient Greece in his vivid sense of the instability of human institutions. One of the sayings that make his Introduction the first gateway of archæology is that which notes the discrepancy between the traditional fame of a city and the evidence appearing, to the eyes of a later age, in its desolate ruins[4]: he foresees far-distant speculations upon the ruins of Athens as well as of Sparta. Merely from the hint of this one passage, we might expect him to mark geographical positions which were familiar to Athenians of his own day. But there are signs that he even looked forward to a foreign domination of Greece. Describing the part played by Tissaphernes in the events of 411, he says[5]:—'To my mind, however, it is perfectly clear that his motive for not bringing the ships was that of wasting time and keeping the affairs of Hellas in suspense,—to damage them by loitering in his advance thither[6], and to hold them at balance by refusing to give superior strength to either side in the addition of his own: for I take it that, if he had so wished, he could have brought the war, by appearing on the scene, to a decisive end.' This opinion is expressed in a deliberate, controversial manner: other explanations have been offered; but Thucydides perceives that the King holds the Greek combatants in the hollow of his hand. Surely, then, it is rash to assume that the historian had no view of a possible inundation of Greece by foreign populations.

[1] IV, 24. 4–5. [2] II, 93. 1. [3] II, 19. 2.
[4] I, 10. 2. [5] VIII, 87. 4. [6] To Aspendus.

Mr Forbes[1] just touches on 'the elaborate and almost humorous study of the character of the Persian "pacha," Tissaphernes.'   Thucydides may intend us to be amused at the vacillations of the 'pacha'; but the account of the conferences between him and Alcibiades[2] is based on more than a tacit recognition of the power he represents. Alcibiades, anxious that the heavy foot of Persia shall not trample either side, works upon Tissaphernes' personal indecision, and gives him the cue of 'not being in too great a hurry to abolish the war[3].'

It may, of course, be urged that Thucydides only came to perceive the insecurity of Greek civilisation when he had reached the last stages of his work, and that this would account for his remark on the ruins of Athens in his Introduction.   Yet it may be argued from other evidence that the possibility of an overwhelming invasion was present to his mind at an early period of the war, or at least, of his exile.   Towards the end of the second Book[4] he takes some special pains to describe the size and resources of Macedonia; as though, possessing some unusual knowledge of the conquests of the Temenidæ, he was impressed with the steady consolidation of this great neighbouring power.   One particular point he seems anxious to enforce.   Although hopelessly outnumbered, the Macedonians were able to pierce the vast array of the Thracians with a small body of first-rate cavalry.   The incident is thrown into sharper relief by what he has previously observed of the strength of the Odrysian empire[5]:—'So the kingdom attained great power; for of all those in Europe, between the Ionian Gulf[6] and the Euxine, it became the greatest in respect of revenue and general prosperity, though in valour and number of

---

[1] Bk. I, Intr. p. xxv.   [2] Thuc. VIII, 45 ff.
[3] VIII, 46. 1—μὴ ἄγαν ἐπείγεσθαι τὸν πόλεμον διαλῦσαι.
[4] II, 99-100.   [5] II, 97. 5-6.   [6] I.e. the Adriatic.

soldiers a good way behind that of the Scythians. This latter is a nation that cannot possibly be matched by any in Europe: not even in Asia is there one which could stand against them, nation to nation, if only they held together unanimously. Not that they can be compared with other nations for general wisdom of policy, or for intelligence in dealing with the common requirements of life.' The implication is plain enough, though a modern historian would have set it forth in full. The intellectual civilisation of Greece will probably have to reckon with these three solid masses of barbarians. The expedition of Sitalces has furnished an opportunity of judging their strength, and they may easily grow stronger. At present they are ill-organised, and Brasidas[1] can speak slightingly of these foreign hordes—according to tradition since the Persian Wars—in order to encourage his men. But a sense of their possible predominance in Greece seems to stir beneath the thoughts of Thucydides.

And indeed, is it not strange that, if he is addressing himself to Greeks whose sum of knowledge was that of the average Athenian of his day, he should describe in such detail the ceremony with which the Athenians perform the funeral of their dead warriors[2], or the method of distributing the commands of the Spartan kings in the field[3]? Surely his tone here, as in what he says about the visitation of plagues[4] and the recrudescence of re-volutionary faction-strife[5] ('as long as human nature remains the same'), is that of a man who expects either a very different organisation of Greece in another age, or else a foreign audience for his words. Nor should we forget that the opening sentences of his book, which give reasons for considering the Peloponnesian War more im-portant than the Persian, are clearly intended for persons

[1] IV, 126. 3.   [2] II, 34.   [3] V, 66. 3.
[4] II, 48. 3.   [5] III, 82. 2.

who shall be remote in time from both conflicts, and whose interest shall extend to all the surrounding nations.

§ 5

But the most important excrescence upon the scheme of bare military annals appears in the speeches. What are we to think of these deliberate portraitures, of whose artificial complexion their author has not failed to inform us, and which, though he, and some of his critics, may justify their inner pertinence to a true and useful history, are bound to be suspect in the eye of modern disillusion ? Why does he colour or engrave the glass through which we are to behold the mental, the moral, and, above all, the political workings of the war, while its material activities are to be viewed through more ordinary windows? The answer, if it were to be complete, would have to consider all the outstanding features of the Hellenic mind, and of its various expression in all the Hellenic arts ; this done, it would have to place the mind of Thucydides in the proper relation to these tendencies or influences. As we shall presently have to estimate in some detail how far this mind is reflected in the speeches themselves, we need only fix here a few more of its outlines with some obvious hints appearing in the main body of the book.

It is plain that his hopes of making history useful are based on a calm confidence in the human intellect. Men have been too long contented, in his view, to take a childish delight in the past, regarding it merely as a storehouse of the marvellous : 'they accept from one another the rumours of former times, even those that concern their own country, with no discriminating test[1].' Let them grow up, and try what a trained intelligence

[1] Thuc. I, 20. I.

can do, first in marking off the known from the unknown, and then in perceiving some order and connection within the borders of its conquest. Tales of miracles old or new, popular superstitions, and the time-honoured pretensions of oracles, are vagaries of feeling or imagination which history must record, if they throw any light on the thought that moved behind this or that series of events : but nature is governed by inviolable laws, some of which have been or may be discovered, while many more remain hidden, and may be conveniently called by the common names of Fortune, Chance, Necessity or Divinity. Thucydides has been well likened to Socrates[1] for this insistence on the duty of intelligence,—an insistence whose moral fervour is more devoted to clear thought and experienced insight than to a revision of the usual sentiments of morality. On the appeal of these last he occasionally relies, as in his special study of the evils of faction-strife[2]: but even so, their office is simply to emphasise the troubles of ill-ordered reason. To see men at the mercy of old prejudice or of sudden impulse arouses in him something like a reprobation of sin, though it is principally a prevision of disaster. And, finding so often that wrong or confused thought is at the sources of political movements, he trusts that a convincing exposure will help to provide a remedy.

Perhaps he despaired of any direct instruction of the unthinking, passionate mass of men : but it would need only a few meetings of the Assembly to impress his keen observation with the decisive weight of one or two superior minds. So long as these could see straight and far, all must be well. But after the death of Pericles[3], who seems to have come very near to his ideal statesman, the leading spirits of Athens, while wielding great power

<hr>

[1] A. Croiset, *Notice sur Thucydide*, p. 48.
[2] Thuc. III, 83.   [3] 429 B.C.

over the people, were short-sighted, and soon got entangled in petty quarrels. 'More on a level with each other, and, grasping at their personal ascendancy, they went so far in gratifying the people as to surrender the public interests to them; and this, as might be expected in a great imperial state, produced a host of blunders[1].' The instance he gives is the Sicilian Expedition; which, however, might have succeeded, he says, if only the politicians at home had laid aside their little rivalries, and ensured a proper support to the armament that had been so gaily equipped and despatched. Accordingly, the virtues and vices of the statesman's mind have a high importance for the study of national conflicts; and Thucydides, in tracing the origins and sequences of the Peloponnesian War, has resolved to include the psychology of prominent persons as well as the more material causes. Further, he realises that such persons often owe their prominence to the fact that they express rather than control the prevailing spirit of the multitude, and that to present them clearly will often serve to reveal the ambitions or fears of the great majority of a whole people. But how has he chosen to present them? By making them speak, and often in the form of elaborate rhetoric. That we should hear their voices raised above the preparations and struggles of the war is, in a general view of the case, an admirable economy: for it not only opens to us the inner policy of each situation, but gives us a glimpse of the actual process by which that policy was formed and came to effect. Yet the real speeches, if kept in fit proportion to the scale of the book, would have to be reduced to summaries or abstracts that could stir no sense whatever of the living voice. Here, then, is a difficult problem for the sincere and zealous artist of useful history. We have noted his own rather uneasy

[1] Thuc. II, 65. 11.

confession[1]. It will be well, before we inspect his performance, to recall the chief suggestions or temptations that would meet him in the current literature of his country.

The popularity of the Homeric poems in the chief centres of fifth-century Greece is vividly attested by the *Ion* of Plato. In this little dialogue the professional reciter and expositor of Homer is shown to us in all the glitter of his ingenuous vanity, which, although it is doubtless exaggerated for the purpose of Socratic attack, must also, if that purpose is to be convincingly achieved, be characteristic of the masters of poetical education. The rhapsode tells of his triumph at Epidaurus, of the splendid costume he wore, of his golden wreath of victory, and of his audience amounting to more than twenty thousand persons[2]. His glorious success is due to his power of stirring a passionate excitement : at the pathetic passages in the epics his own eyes fill with tears ; where there is terror or awe, his hair stands on end, and his heart leaps ; immediately he sees the audience weeping, or otherwise responding to his emotions with their own, and often quite aghast at the tale they hear. So much for the powers of this enthusiastic recitation. But the profession had another side. By studying Homer to the exclusion of all other poets, the rhapsodes were able to interpret his thought and offer useful reflections upon it[3]. This kind of teaching is what we associate with the lecture-room : but, however it was given, we hear of one person who used to listen to rhapsodes 'almost every day,' and so maintained a fresh memory of both *Iliad* and *Odyssey* entire, which he had learnt by heart as a boy[4]. The first 'move' in the Socratic game is to class the rhapsode Ion with nature's privileged madmen : he is

---

[1] Above, p. 14.   [2] Plato, *Ion*, 535 D.
[3] *Ion*, 536 E.   [4] Xenoph. *Symp.* III, 6.

a mouthpiece of Homer, whose enchantment passes
through him to the audience, as a magnet's attraction
is transmitted by the ring that touches it to others more
remote[1]. Ion does not accept this dubious compliment.
What he claims is ability to give a reasoned exposition
of the poems; and he prefers to be trapped with the
admission that he is as well qualified to speak about
their military problems as to practise their recitation[2].

We need not suppose that Thucydides ever expected,
after reaching the years of his extraordinary discretion,
that he could acquire any practical knowledge from Homer
or his interpreters. As to the latter, most probably he
would agree with Euthydemus that they were block-
heads[3]. But it is too readily assumed that he was
insensible to the charm of poetry altogether. Jebb, in
summing up his literary character, remarks on 'a certain
hardness of temperament, such as is indicated by the
tone of his reference to the poets...he cites them simply
as authorities for facts, whose statements often require to
be modified. He makes a sort of apology for quoting so
equivocal an authority as Homer; and his extracts from
the fine passage in the Hymn to the Delian Apollo are
the briefest which could establish his two points,—that
there *was* an Ionian festival at Delos, and that it included
a musical contest[4].' Now if we are to arrive at any clear
notion of the artistic construction of the History, we
must shun this misconception. It is in the careful search
for truth that Thucydides weighs the evidence of Homer,
and the strict limits of the History have no room for the
expression of his own æsthetic tastes. Nevertheless, it
is possible and fair to detect, in places, a hint of the
personal sympathy which he has compelled to be dumb.
'Our glorious position,' he makes Pericles say, 'is secure:

---

[1] *Ion*, 533 E.   [2] 542 A.   [3] Xenoph. *Mem.* IV, 2. 10—ἠλίθιοι.
[4] Jebb, *Hellenica*, 'The Speeches of Thuc.,' fin.

we need no ornamental addition in the shape of a Homer's praises, nor of verses which will give pleasure for a time, yet cannot preserve their picture of the facts against the truth[1].' Of course the latter part of the sentence is meant to apply to the verses of Homer as well as to others ; but the mention of his name betokens a particular respect. Even he, the poet on whose eloquence they have all been nurtured, is for documentary purposes little better than others who have 'expressed themselves in song[2].' One of these, indeed, had spoken as severely of his own craft half a century before[3]:—'Verily marvels are many, and belike[4] the rumours of man exceed the true account, tales embroidered with ingenious lies, and strong to mislead. And the charm of verses, that accomplisheth all gentle joys for mortals, can so enhance them with honour, that many a time the incredible is made to have credit ; but the days that await us are the wisest witnesses.' Yet Pindar is not therefore to be considered any the less genuinely responsive to his Muse.

A plainer hint may be gathered from the digression on the Delian festival. Instead of merely referring to the evidence of the poet in the manner of the first Book, —'and we have the particular testimony of Homer[5],'— 'as Homer has declared, if any deem his evidence sufficient[6],'—'if here again we are to put any faith in the poetry of Homer[7],'—Thucydides, after describing the festival with some of the picturesque detail we have noticed in the episodes of this Book, proceeds to quote two passages—one of five, and the other of eight lines[8]— firstly, to support the statements he has just made not only about the existence of the Ionian festival, but also

---

[1] Thuc. II, 41. 4.   [2] I, 21. 1—ὡς ποιηταὶ ὑμνήκασι.
[3] Pind. *Ol.* I, 28 ff. (prob. 472 B.C.).
[4] καί πού τι καί—a phrase of personal guessing, used by Thuc. II, 87.
[5] I, 3. 3.   [6] I, 9. 3.   [7] I, 10. 3.   [8] III, 104.

about the way in which it drew all the Ionians, men, women and children alike, from all parts of Greece to attend or engage in the boxing and dancing and singing; and secondly, besides confirming the fact of a musical contest, to recall, *from a purely literary standpoint*, the curious mention which the poet makes of himself. It certainly is 'a fine passage'; but the whole tone of the digression can hardly leave a doubt that this was felt not least by Thucydides, who chooses to indulge for a moment his artistic admiration[1]. Mr Forbes[2] speaks of his 'somewhat prosy and unappreciative use of the Homeric and other legends; although, in quoting in full a passage from the Hymn to Apollo as proof of a small point about the history of the Ionian festival at Delos, he seems to be influenced by its poetic beauty.' These latter words, according as they approach nearer to the truth, leave the former in an increasingly awkward position. It would be more accurate and intelligible to say that in his archæological introduction he braces himself for the dispassionate treatment, in the service of history, of poems which in one place[3] he almost openly admires as art. His state of mind may perhaps be compared to the more familiar case of Plato: the ethical philosopher banishes the poets from his ideal state, which he actually cannot describe without betraying how much he owes to their imaginative strength and stately diction.

Hence, in accounting for the phenomenon of the speeches, we are not to exempt or exclude Thucydides

---

[1] It should be mentioned that G. Hermann (*Philologus*, 1846) proposed to cut out portions of this chapter, on the ground that the description of the ἀγών and the lengthy quotations are foreign to the style of Thucydides. Very few scholars have found any force in his arguments.

[2] Bk. I, Intr. p. xxii.

[3] The nearest thing in his book to the 'pleasant halting-places' of Livy IX, xvii 1 (deuerticula amœna).

from all feeling for the epics, merely because he is able
to take a critical view of some parts of them which
concern his History; and consequently, we ought to
attach rather more importance to the examples of rhetorical debate provided by Homer than critics have
generally allowed. Jebb[1] has himself given us a convenient statement of their qualities. He mentions the
ambition of the Greek epic 'to represent the energy of
the human spirit as much as possible in the form of
speech.... The Iliad and Odyssey accustomed the Greeks
to expect two elements in every vivid presentation of an
action,—first, the proofs of bodily prowess, the account of
what men did; and then, as the image of their minds, a
report of what they said.' He further reminds us of the
large part played in the affairs of states by public speech;
and observes that 'when Thucydides gave in full the
speeches made by Cleon and Diodotus, he was helping
his reader, the average citizen of a Greek republic, to do
on more accurate lines that which the reader would
otherwise have tried to do for himself.' We may be
fairly sure that he did not give those speeches in full,
and that he hoped that the rhetorical no less than the
narrative part of his book would be read by others
besides 'the average citizen of a Greek republic[2]'; but
we may agree that, for his immediate audience, eloquent
words ought to have as prominent a place as great actions
in any true memorial of that age.

The particular mode, however, in which he adapted
the Homeric tradition to his aim of presenting the
influence of speech, will become clearer if we look for
a moment at the more light-hearted acceptance of that
tradition in Herodotus. The History of the Persian
Invasions is the work of a strong poetic imagination

[1] *Hellenica*, 'The Speeches of Thuc.,' § 4.
[2] See above, § 4.

playing over a wide variety of characters and scenes. Built on the epic pattern, it shows a vast number of episodes and explanations[1], loosely strung upon the single central theme: the personality of the author is continually peeping out; we are not far from the tones and gestures of the minstrel. But suddenly, with the realistic abandonment of the rhapsode, he can make the figures of his story move and speak in individual life, and we find ourselves enthralled by the pathos of single utterances, or the tragic irony of conversations. The life of Crœsus might have been borrowed from among the lays of an epic cycle. Yet, as this example and the whole range of Herodotus' curiosity suggest, he loves to direct the conversation of distinguished persons to moral or religious questions: he is not concerned with the philosophy of history, but with the philosophy of life. The times and causes of events are little or nothing to him: what he loves is to trace and enlarge on the doings of crime, reverence and doom among the little days of men.

There is, however, one instance of a political debate in Herodotus, where Otanes, Megabyzus and Darius are heard discussing the comparative merits of democracy, oligarchy and monarchy[2]. Perhaps Herodotus was here working on a piece of model speech-writing from the pen of some ingenious rhetorician: it was not considered authentic even in his time. 'Many of the Greeks,' he says, 'do not believe in these speeches, but nevertheless, spoken they were[3]': and nevertheless, critics have long agreed to condemn them as wholly out of character. For us, the interesting point about them, and about his protestation, is that to the ears of many fifth-century Greeks this sort of talk would be the most natural thing in the world;

---

[1] Amounting almost to one half of the book.

[2] Herod. III, 80–82.

[3] III, 80 : cf. VI, 43.

and for Thucydides, the vogue of such discussions in
Athenian politics gave a new opportunity to the venerable
form of epic speech. This form is now to be applied to
the peculiar scheme of distinguishing the main threads
of thought in each momentous situation. We shall listen
not merely to heroes devising the course of action, but
to the ambitions of whole peoples made personal and
articulate; and this is the studious task of invention to
which Thucydides has so modestly, and perhaps diffidently,
confessed[1]. 'We are remarkable not least in this,' says
Pericles[2], 'that while we are ready to dare all, we are
equally ready to reason out the designs we are undertaking'; and it is the praise of both Themistocles[3] and
Antiphon[4], that they had tongues to recommend what
their brains had contrived. The History attempts to
show some typical examples of these public reasonings.
Herodotus had taken themes for debate from the region
of which Æschylus made himself the tremendous master:
Thucydides is exploiting the more practical disputations
which Sophocles and Euripides applied to the heroic
legends on the stage. He was not the only writer of
prose who pursued this art of arguing the chief considerations on each side of an actual difference or problem.
We possess, in the 'Tetralogies' of his elder contemporary
Antiphon, elaborate exercises for attaining proficiency in
debate, or supplying written speeches for plaintiff and
defendant in the law-courts. This project of drilling
Greek prose, as it were, for the battle of will and thought
seems to have received its first impulse from philosophic
and Sicilian rhetoric; whose obvious traces in the style
of Thucydides and other prose writers of his age we
shall have to inspect and appreciate. Suffice it here to
note that Thucydides is so anxious to set before us his

---

[1] Above, p. 14.   [2] Thuc. II, 40. 3.
[3] I, 138. 3.   [4] VIII, 68. 1.

penetrating vision of the principles that ruled each crisis of the war, and so careful of the proportions of his whole picture, that he leaves the methodical path of verified record, and boldly shows, in suggestive abstract, how he conceives the situation to have 'reasoned out' itself.

CHAPTER II

ALLUREMENTS OF DRAMA

§ 1

THE almost proverbial trustworthiness of the main features in the History has met with some vigorous attacks from the forces of scientific research. Suspicions of an artistic manipulation of the truth were first raised by Müller-Strübing[1], who saw, in the Theban surprise of Platæa[2] and the dating of the Peace of Nicias[3], clear marks of a poetic ambition which overrode the facts. In the former case, the historian was anxious to follow the advice of Pindar, and open the tale of war with a brilliant flourish; in the latter, he sought to emulate the bard of the Ten Years' War at Troy. It is hardly necessary to remark, when we bear in mind the character of the whole book and the difficulties to which its author confesses, that the small inaccuracies and omissions brought home to him by this and other critics can be explained more naturally than by the attractions of poetic design. Or again, if it be generally agreed that Thucydides seems to depart for a moment, in describing Cleon[4] and Hyperbolus[5], from his own high standard of impartiality, the search for the cause of such apparent lapses is best directed to the region of his political sympathies; though even there it is uncertain and delusive

---

[1] 'Das erste Jahr des Pelop. Krieges,' *Jahrb. für Philol.* vol. 127 (1883).
[2] Thuc. II, 2.   [3] V, 20.   [4] III, 36, IV, 39, V, 16.   [5] VIII, 73.

enough[1]. But these and graver historical failings have
recently been alleged against his reliability, and, in one
instance, have been made the matter of a comprehensive
theory concerning his mind and the artistic construction
of his book[2]. No account of Thucydides' style can
ignore the ingenuity and eloquence of this criticism,
which views the historian's thought and language in a
strange new light, reflected from archæological and
anthropological researches among the ideas of early
Greek drama. If we are to apply our notion of
Thucydides' mind to the task of judging him as a
writer, we must first consider fairly what title he has
to the character of tragedian.

The 'mythistorical' theory asserts that as the History
grew to its present shape from the jottings of a diary, it
was moulded, not merely in patches, but in the greater
part of its framework, by the author's habit of fitting
events to a certain tragic pattern. In the upshot, he
'turns the great moral of Æschylus' "Persæ" against
the Athenian Empire[3].' The process of suppression and
distortion is traced from the story of the occupation of
Pylos, throughout the treatment of Cleon, Alcibiades
and Nicias, to the fall of the deluded victims of Hope,
Desire and the like 'tragic passions' at Syracuse. 'A
mode of thought, which had grown without a break out of
a mythological conception of the world of human acts and
passions, has shaped the mass of facts which was to have
been shapeless, so that the work of science came to be a
work of art[4].' The outstanding sin against science is
detected in the account of the origin of the war, which
fails to fix attention on the commercial policy of the
Piræus: this, it is maintained, was tending at that time

---

[1] Cf. Forbes, *Intr.* Bk. I, p. cxxx.
[2] F. M. Cornford, *Thucydides Mythistoricus*, 1907.
[3] *Th. M.* p. 241.   [4] *Th. M.* p. ix.

towards Sicily and the West. Pericles was driven to
coerce Megara by the threats of a strong party whose
aim was to get possession of an 'isthmic route' to Sicily:
Thucydides, not perceiving this important movement,
erroneously sought the beginning of the friction among
the various pretexts alleged by the contending cities
before they came to blows. He thought he had set out
the causes and the differences sufficiently to meet the
question—'Whence arose this mighty war among the
Greeks[1]?'—but science is not satisfied.

Let us try to estimate whether or how far it is not.
First of all, we must remember that Thucydides knew
the dockyards and storehouses of the Piræus far better
than we can ever hope to know them ; and that he had
full opportunities, during the twenty years of his exile,
for understanding the policies and underlying interests of
the chief cities of Greece. 'I lived through the whole
time,' he says, 'using the perception of my manhood,
and applying the powers of my mind to the quest of
accurate knowledge[2].' That the study of real causes
received his long and serious attention seems probable
from both of his prefaces. His alternative use of two
words for 'reason' ($a\grave{\iota}\tau\acute{\iota}a$, $\pi\rho\acute{o}\phi a\sigma\iota\varsigma$) does not betray,
when the contexts are fairly read, any confusion of
'cause' with 'pretext[3].' Such a fault would be astonishing in the author of that careful Introduction, in which,
before entering on the story of the quarrel, he expounds
the causes, geographical as well as racial, of the different
developments of power in the Greek states. In the
first sentences of the History we read that the early
instability of these states was due chiefly to the lack
of commercial intercourse[4]. Athens got a start of the
rest because of the inferior quality of her soil; since

---

[1] Thuc. I, 23. 5.   [2] v, 26. 5.
[3] Cf. *Th. M.* pp. 57 ff.   [4] I, 2. 1—$\tau\hat{\eta}\varsigma$ $\grave{\epsilon}\mu\pi o\rho\acute{\iota}a\varsigma$ $o\grave{\upsilon}\kappa$ $o\check{\upsilon}\sigma\eta\varsigma$.

the inhabitants of Attica were unmolested by covetous intruders, and were able to consolidate their strength[1]. The occupation of an isthmus was important to a city for the control of trade[2]. As they became familiar with the sea, the people of a city like Corinth progressed from levying tolls on land-traffic to the creation of maritime power[3]. Yet this commercial growth, which brought the transition from hereditary rule to despotism[4], led eventually, by stages in the pursuit of gain, to external dominion[5]. This material basis of political influence is thus kept clearly before us: the formation of a fleet meant, first, increase of revenue, and then, empire[6]. When to these observations we add what the Corinthians say about the utility of dwellers by the sea to those of inland cities, as a means of export and import[7], it should not be easy to convince us that Thucydides overlooked the growth of trade as a cause of war, and that such remarks are due merely to a scrupulous but undiscerning fidelity. Yet it is asserted that economic tendencies had a far greater influence on politics than Thucydides would lead us to suppose; and we are warned against the 'modernist fallacy' of expecting from any mind of that period the thoroughness and

---

[1] I, 2. 5—τὴν Ἀττικὴν ἐκ τοῦ ἐπὶ πλεῖστον διὰ τὸ λεπτόγεων ἀστασίαστον οὖσαν ἄνθρωποι ᾤκουν οἱ αὐτοὶ αἰεί.

[2] I, 7. I—τοὺς ἰσθμοὺς ἀπελάμβανον ἐμπορίας ἕνεκα.

[3] I, 13. 5—οἰκοῦντες ἐπὶ τοῦ Ἰσθμοῦ αἰεὶ δή ποτε ἐμπορίαν εἶχον...ἐπειδή τε οἱ Ἕλληνες μᾶλλον ἔπλῳζον...ἐμπόριον παρέχοντες ἀμφότερα δυνατὴν ἔσχον χρημάτων προσόδῳ τὴν πόλιν.

[4] I, 13. I—τυραννίδες ἐν ταῖς πόλεσι καθίσταντο, τῶν προσόδων μειζόνων γιγνομένων.

[5] I, 8. 3—ἐφιέμενοι τῶν κερδῶν οἵ τε ἥσσους ὑπέμενον τὴν τῶν κρεισσόνων δουλείαν, οἵ τε δυνατώτεροι περιουσίας ἔχοντες προσεποιοῦντο ὑπηκόους τὰς ἐλάσσους πόλεις.

[6] I, 15. I—ἰσχὺν περιεποιήσαντο...χρημάτων τε προσόδῳ καὶ ἄλλων ἀρχῇ.

[7] I, 120. 2—τοὺς δὲ τὴν μεσόγειαν μᾶλλον καὶ μὴ ἐν πόρῳ κατῳκημένους εἰδέναι χρὴ ὅτι, τοῖς κάτω ἦν μὴ ἀμύνωσι, χαλεπωτέραν ἕξουσι τὴν κατακομιδὴν τῶν ὡραίων καὶ πάλιν ἀντίληψιν ὧν ἡ θάλασσα τῇ ἠπείρῳ δίδωσι.

precision of modern scientific thought. This warning is only too needful in many classical and historical studies: but the principle must apply to matter as well as to mind. It will bring us but little nearer to the truth, if we learn to regard ancient historians as children judging men[1]; we may be helped, in some cases, by viewing them as children judging children ; but even the boldest speculations on the character of Thucydides must recognise, and actually depend upon, the uncommon reach and maturity of his intelligence.

The historian has not confined his account of the origin of the war to a statement of material causes. Are we then to conclude that he did not investigate them fairly and thoroughly? We can only take this view by fallaciously assuming that the affairs he undervalued had passed through the complex development, and had settled into the systematic course, which economic science observes in its field to-day. It is very probable that trade, for a long time after the early stages described in Thucydides' Introduction, was conducted on such unstable terms as could only, or most accurately, be stated in the language of personal intercourse. 'Solon[2],' we are told, 'was on the verge of discovering' the law that exports must balance imports : and of this law 'we find Plato still ignorant[3].' But it may well be that Solon gives the right impression by speaking of 'the habits of merchants'; and that just as Plato found it best to describe the balance of trade, in its rudimentary form, by the instance of an agent who must take with him what is in demand elsewhere if he is to bring back what is in demand at home[4], so Thucydides gives us a reliable picture of the trade which founded the power of Athens or Corinth. In his account of the Congress at Sparta, he tells of the

[1] Cf. *Th. M.* p. 64.   [2] *Th. M.* p. 66.
[3] Plato, *Alcib.* i, 122 E.   [4] *Republ.* 370 E.

voting for and against war in this manner[1]:—'The ephor
could not decide which was the louder acclamation (their
decision being by acclamation, not by voting)...so he
said, "Let each Lacedæmonian who thinks that the
treaty has been broken, and that the Athenians are in
the wrong, leave his seat and go there" (pointing to a
particular spot), "and let all who do not think so go to
the other side." They arose and divided, and those who
held that the treaty was broken were in a large majority.'
Shall we blame Thucydides for not perceiving that the
ephor 'was on the verge of discovering' the method of a
Parliamentary division? But in approaching the state
of commerce which prevailed in his own time, Thucydides
can meet the facts with a general phrase which is not
beneath the dignity of modern science:—'If inland states
will not protect their neighbours on the coast, they will
find a corresponding difficulty in the conveyance of their
produce thither and in the return, by exchange, of what
the sea gives to the mainland[2]'; though the form of the
argument implies a simpler world than ours. It is surely
safer to imagine that the tavern-talk of the Piræus went
on lines like these, than to dream of a persistent and far-
reaching design debated by persons who must be the
more surprising masters of secret conspiracy, the more
numerous they are claimed to be. The commercial expansion of Athens in the fifth century proceeded by
rapid strides along with the imperialist spirit inaugurated
by Themistocles after Salamis: the outward splendours
of this spirit, as we see by the ostracism of its boldest
opponent[3], had gained a strong hold on the mass of the
citizens at least ten years before the war began. Exactly
how far and how quickly Pericles expected the trade of
the Piræus, as distinct from the funds of the anti-Persian

---

[1] Thuc. I, 87. 2.   [2] Thuc. I, 120. 2 (cited above, p. 36, n. 7).
[3] Thucydides, son of Melesias (442 B.C.).

confederacy, to support his ambition of setting up the power and glory of Athens to dominate the mind of all Greece, may be difficult to determine: but we can only limit that ambition to the scope of a 'School of Hellas' by ignoring this proud extravagance in the Funeral Oration[1]:—'Thereto be added that by reason of the greatness of our city there comes into her everything from every land, so that it is our fortune to gather for harvest, with no distinction of intimate enjoyment, the good things that other men produce as well as those that are put forth here[2]'; and by forgetting that, although the speech as a whole turns the eyes of the people from external prosperity to an inward spirit of lofty excellence[3], yet the ever-present necessity of war with their neighbours is continually kept in sight. Pericles was not solely devoted to an ideal of artistic refinement[4]: he was ready enough to strike wherever the imperial position of Athens was threatened by the jealous irritation of rivals. There is no evidence that the oppression of Megara was not his own policy, or that Thucydides did not intend us to regard the decree[5] which excluded it from the markets of the empire as one of his exemplary weapons. Current scandal is always difficult to explain, even five minutes after it is invented: but instead of using it to show that the people were in the dark as to the motives of the policy, we should start from the presumption that the gossip was set afoot by an outvoted opposition, whose aim was to obscure the true and popular motives; and that in the case of Aristophanes it was most amusing when it was recognised to be false. For that the blow

---

[1] Thuc. II, 38. 2.

[2] Cf. Pseudo-Xen. *Ath. Resp.* II, 7—ὅ τι ἐν Σικελίᾳ ἡδὺ ἢ ἐν Ἰταλίᾳ ἢ ἐν Κύπρῳ ἢ ἐν Αἰγύπτῳ ἢ ἐν Λυδίᾳ ἢ ἐν τῷ Πόντῳ ἢ ἐν Πελοποννήσῳ ἢ ἄλλοθί που, ταῦτα πάντα εἰς ἐν ἠθροῖσθαι διὰ τὴν ἀρχὴν τῆς θαλάσσης.

[3] Thuc. II, 36. 4. [4] Cf. *Th. M.* p. 12.

[5] 432 B.C.

struck at Megara was generally seen to be ominous and uncompromising is clearly represented by Thucydides in five passages[1] which are hardly to be dismissed as 'a few allusions[2].' Doubtless there were persons in the Piræus, and in Athens also, for whose private ends the decree was of deep importance: but there is no reason to suspect that the average citizen in the Ecclesia, after watching the traffic of the port as well as the plays in the theatre, would feel that there was anything inadequate to his own views in the words :—'This "small matter" involves the trial and confirmation of your whole purpose[3].' The meaning of the measure was well understood, and not least by Thucydides.

§ 2

Turning now to the Piræus party and its strong policy of expansion in the West, we are faced by the question of population. 'From 510 to 430 B.C., the population of Athens and the Piræus together is said to have increased from 20,000 to 100,000[4].' No authority is given for these figures. Another calculation gives an increase from '80,000 in the first quarter of the fifth century to 100,000 by the beginning of the war, counting both sexes and all ages. The metic class possibly reached the number of 30,000[5].' The most recent investigator sees 'no possibility of arriving at any definite conclusion as to the population of Attica in the time of Thucydides[6].' The first of these estimates, which belongs to the argument

---

[1] Thuc. I, 42, 67, 139, 140, 144.   [2] Th. M. p. 29.

[3] Thuc. I, 140. 4—τὸ γὰρ βραχύ τι τοῦτο πᾶσαν ὑμῶν ἔχει τὴν βεβαίωσιν καὶ πεῖραν τῆς γνώμης. The context shows that some 'little-Athens' aristocrats were inclined to murmur against going to war 'for such a trifle.'

[4] Th. M. p. 18.   [5] Bury, Hist. Gr. p. 408 (1900).

[6] Grundy, Thuc. and History of his Age, p. 89, n. 2. He is inclined to think with M. L. Gernet, L'approvisionnement d'Athènes en blé, 1909, that the total free population was 150,000, of whom 50,000 were metics.

we are discussing, seeks to suggest first, that about 80,000 traders and toilers flowed into the Piræus in those eighty years, and second, that the great majority of them received the citizenship; and so Pericles was intimidated into making war. But it is not credible that, if the influx of aliens came at such a rate, the phenomenon should have drawn no more attention than the indefinite sneers of Aristophanes and the 'Old Oligarch,' or the three 'rhetorical outbursts[1]' of Isocrates. It is still more questionable that such a huge proportion of metics should have obtained the franchise. Many of them were 'Phrygians, Lydians, Syrians and barbarians of every sort[2]'; they were permitted to reside, and in some cases to hold property, on condition of paying a special tax (μετοίκιον[3]), besides others on their sales, and of serving in the triremes. 'Their occupations excited the disgust of the true Athenian gentleman[4],'—and sometimes with good reason, as we learn from a case of 'cornering' wheat[5]: yet after all, it was in the hands of the Athenian gentlemen to give or withhold the citizenship; and if we have no means of telling even approximately what proportion of an ill-defined number of aliens ever did receive the franchise, it is not fair to salute them as 'the sovereign Demos' in order to discredit the perception or diligence of Thucydides. If there had been such a party, as an active political force, it is impossible that, realising the agricultural interest so clearly[6], he should have entirely missed the commercial.

No satisfactory evidence can be found to contradict his report. The only ancient treatise in our possession which deals with the commerce of this period is directed to exposing the obscure status of the metics in Athens[7],

---

[1] *Th. M.* p. 19. [2] [Xen.] *De Vect.* ii, 3.
[3] *De Vect.* ii, 1 ; Plato, *Leges*, ix, 850 B. [4] *Th. M.* p. 20.
[5] Lysias, *Orat.* xxii. [6] Cf. Thuc. II, 14. [7] *De Vect.* ii, iii.

and the undeveloped condition of mercantile organisation. The precise date and even the authorship of this tract are uncertain; but it seems to have been written by an aged Athenian who expects few besides himself to remember the time before the occupation of Decelea (413 B.C.); that is to say, when the revenue from the mines of Laurium had not lapsed owing to the desertion of slaves recorded by Thucydides[1]. It was probably about the middle of the fourth century that this careful review of the economic conduct of Athens was produced: it covers a period which overlaps, by a considerable space at each end, that of the Peloponnesian War. The author, after acknowledging that the character of a polity depends largely on the moral motives of its leading men, expresses his dissatisfaction with the financial methods of the government[2]. His complaint is that, instead of taking the easy way of taxing the confederate states, Athens ought to have cultivated her native and external resources on a sound basis of trade. The first improvement he suggests is relief from military service and personal protection for the aliens[3]: he goes on to urge that merchants and shipmasters should be given an honourable place in public assemblies[4]; that the money formerly swallowed up in expeditions of doubtful prospect should be applied to the formation of public capital[5]; and that this fund should be employed in building ships and warehouses[6], and in the (apparently new) experiment of acquiring merchant-ships for the state[7]. The only chance for these developments, and for the proper working of the mines, is shown by former experience to be a spell of settled peace. Trade cannot move freely unless the

---

[1] Thuc. VII, 27. 5; cf. *De Vect.* iv, 25.   [2] *De Vect.* i, 1.
[3] ii, 7—εἰ μετοικοφύλακάς γε ὥσπερ ὀρφανοφύλακας ἀρχὴν καθισταῖμεν. Cf. ii, 2.   [4] iii, 4.   [5] iii, 8.
[6] iii, 13.   [7] iii, 14.

seas are safe[1]. The error of Athens after the Persian
Wars was that she took too violent or tyrannous an
advantage of such prosperity as she had acquired[2]. The
whole essay is a Solonian attempt to set commerce on a
respectable and steady footing in Athens ; and it reveals,
among other interesting points, a striking difference
between ancient and modern trade, which can only be
explained by the facts of slave-labour, the slowness and
danger of sea-voyages, and almost incessant piracy and
warfare.

It will not be amiss to glance here at David Hume's
sagacious comments on this matter[3]. Of the inconveni-
ence felt by the Athenians when the land-route from
Euboea was stopped by the Lacedæmonian fortification of
Decelea[4] he says:—'a surprising instance of the imperfec-
tion of ancient navigation, for the water-carriage is not here
above double the land.' Perhaps for 'double' he had
better have said 'triple'; but his instance is still significant.
The dangers of a trading-voyage to Sicily were doubtless
reduced by using 'the isthmus of Corinth and Megara[5],'
but even so they were serious enough. Another observation of Hume's is worth recalling :—'Great interest of
money, and great profits of trade, are an infallible
indication, that industry and commerce are but in their
infancy. We read in Lysias[6] of 100 per cent. profit
made on a cargo of two talents, sent to no greater
distance than from Athens to the Adriatic ; nor is this
mentioned as an instance of extraordinary profit. The
most moderate interest at Athens (for there was higher
often paid) was 12 per cent., and that paid monthly.'

---

[1] *De Vect.* v, 12.

[2] v, 6—ὡμῶς ἄγαν δόξασα προστατεύειν ἡ πόλις ἐστερήθη τῆς ἀρχῆς.

[3] *Essay on the Populousness of Ancient Nations* (1742).

[4] Thuc. VII, 28. 1—ἡ τῶν ἐπιτηδείων παρακομιδὴ περὶ Σούνιον κατὰ θάλασσαν...πολυτελὴς ἐγίγνετο.

[5] *Th. M.* p. 33.   [6] Lys. *Orat.* xxxii, 25—ἐπεὶ δὲ ἐσώθη καὶ ἐδιπλασίασεν.

These well-known facts are enough to show that, when we speak of ancient and modern commerce, we are stretching a word to cover two things which are widely dissimilar in degree. Some of the principal merchants were probably known to have covetous designs upon Sicily before the war began. These wilder notions seem to be censured in the words of Pericles,—'if you will consent to seek no further accessions to your empire while you are carrying on the war[1].' His plan was to confine Athenian influence to the sphere of Greece proper; and if anything sure is to be inferred from a jest of Aristophanes, we know one alluding to the private intrigues of the filibusters at Ecbatana, Chaonia, and the Sicilian cities of 'Gela, and Catana, and Camarina and the Cata-mountains[2].' Nor is there any reason for thinking that the phrase, in which we are bidden to observe the blind fidelity of Thucydides revealing unawares the cloven hoof of the plot[3]—'or to help a fleet from here on its way thither[4]'—was not inserted by the historian, like that warning in Pericles' speech, with a full intention of showing that such schemes were in private heads, though they did not amount to anything like a formal policy. That there was any regular trade-party in politics is extremely doubtful: but supposing it existed, ought not the 'captains of the commercial party[5]' to have had some clearer notion of the strength of Sicily, and of the imperative need, when they were presumably in control of affairs at home, of supporting an expedition despatched against the one serious rival of the Athenian maritime power[6]? And

---

[1] Thuc. I, 144. 1—ἢν ἐθέλητε ἀρχὴν μὴ ἐπικτᾶσθαι ἅμα πολεμοῦντες.

[2] Aristoph. *Acharn.* 605-6—Γερητοθεοδώρους Διομειαλαζόνας, τοὺς δ' ἐν Καμαρίνῃ κἀν Γέλᾳ κἀν Καταγέλᾳ (trans. Frere); cf. *Th. M.* p. 48.

[3] *Th. M.* p. 42.   [4] Thuc. I, 36. 2.   [5] *Th. M.* p. 50.

[6] This error of judgement is twice indicated by Thuc. (VI, I. I, II, 65. 11); in the latter place he adds the still worse folly of 'private quarrels for the leadership of the people.' See above, p. 24.

how did the 'secret conclaves[1]' in the Piræus manage to keep their plot—unless they discussed it solely in the Phrygian, Lydian and Syrian tongues—so securely unsuspected?

§ 3

Next we have to consider the 'exclusive concentration of the ancient historians on the motives and characters of men and of states[2].' In the first place, if Isocrates attributed 'the prosperity of Megara to virtuous moderation[3],' this has nothing to do with the mind of Thucydides, who probably knew as well as Socrates that it was due to the manufacture of desirable 'jerseys[4].' But granting that Thucydides fills a large part of his explanatory spaces with those motives which arise from human character, the question remains open, whether he has thereby damaged or improved the truth of his picture. The subject-matter of history is unlike that of logic or metaphysic: its complexion and its whole nature are continually changing, and in different ages demand very different modes of portraiture. It may be useful to strip Thucydides' philosophic position of certain complimentary accretions to which he has no real claim: but in weighing the truthfulness of the impression made by the History as a whole, it is important once more to remember the probable conditions of the society whose life it depicts. We have already noticed his desire to record national characters and representative statesmen[5]. The justice of that choice will appear more plainly, if we consider that life in fifth-century Greece was instinct with romantic and sentimental impulses, which we are able thus to distinguish with special

---

[1] *Th. M.* p. 50.   [2] *Th. M.* p. 65.

[3] Isocr. *De Pace,* 117 ; *Th. M.* pp. 32, 65.

[4] Xenoph. *Mem.* ii, 7. 6—Μεγαρέων δὲ οἱ πλεῖστοι ἀπὸ ἐξωμιδοποιίας διατρέφονται.   [5] See above, pp. 23, 24.

terms because we have learnt to detach our business from their influence, but which guided or obstructed the progress of ancient states in something like the manner revealed by our fuller records of the age of the Italian Renaissance. Hellenic warfare was a light matter com-pared with what it has become in a world whose nations are huge, complex organisations and—as we are told for the purpose of emphasising the dramatic appeal of the History—'whose armoury of slaughter is enriched with siege-gun and ironclad[1].' The aims of educational systems, the themes of plays and orations, the stories of epitaphs and monuments, and the cast of mind reflected in almost every writing of that time, agree in declaring how ready men were to march out from market or study to see how many of their neighbours they could kill; counting chiefly on the satisfaction of compelling the other side to beg for a truce first, or of leaving a trophy on the field of battle. This eager patriotism belonged to the separate character of each civic centre, manifested to us in the difference of local religions, laws, currencies and many other features besides those of their peculiar political constitutions. Isolation of interests appeared early even in their colonial settlements; but when the political difference was so deep as that between democracy and oligarchy, it was everywhere a lively and embittering antagonism. In the middle of the fourth century, when we might suppose that hard experience as well as philo-sophic reason had put some check upon the national disputes, it was possible for Demosthenes to speak to his countrymen in these terms[2]:—'You fight against republics for some private grievance, for a piece of land, or a boundary, or for contentiousness (φιλονεικία) or the leading position (ἡγεμονία); but against oligarchies, for your constitution and liberty. I will venture to say,

---

[1] *Th. M.* p. 79.   [2] Demosth. *Pro Rhod. Libert.* 8 (353 B.C.).

I hold it more desirable that all the Greeks should be waging war under democracies than be friends under oligarchies : for, whereas there is a fair prospect of your making peace, when you should see fit, with peoples that are free, I believe that with such as are ruled by oligarchy not even friendship can be safe.' Nor under the instant menace of the Macedonian power could Athens and Sparta, the chief representatives of political equality and authority, contrive any kind of agreement or union.

When the Peloponnesian War began, the race for ascendancy was being won by the sea-power of Athens, and she was annoyingly eager to show that she enjoyed, along with her strength, the luxuries and amusements of introspective leisure. Sparta, though not herself inclined to expansion, accepted the dignity due to her military prowess in standing at the head of a jealous and nervously apprehensive alliance. It seems likely that a historian who was anxious to keep clear of futile and irrelevant speculations could not do better, in a search for the origin of the war, than sift the numerous pretexts alleged at its outbreak, and make out, among the principal grievances, which accusation or excuse has most value in the market of human feeling. In a world where the clash of pride is readily seconded by the clash of steel, pretexts or grudges have a clear right to the first attention of history ; and too probably, if we are not satisfied with Thucydides' explanations of the war, the fault is either in us, or in the nature of things. Themistocles was so pre-eminently the originator of Athenian expansion that we can hardly be wrong in regarding his personality as one of the main causes of the strife[1]; and in trying to understand this or that important character, we are met not only with the obscurity or complexity of its particular determinants, but with the mist of travesty in which it has been

[1] Cf. above, p. 17.

involved by private or political opposition. For example, so far from taking the scandalous gossip about Pericles' motives to show that 'contemporary Athens believed that Pericles made the war, and was hard put to it to divine his reasons[1],' we should only notice the dissemination of these stories in order to account for the difficulty, confronting Thucydides, Plutarch, and ourselves, in the attempt to divine his reasons with any precision. Plutarch has made a useful statement of the question[2]:—'How it all began, is not easy to decide : but all are agreed in throwing upon Pericles the blame for the fact that the decree was not reversed. It is true that some say his sturdy refusal was made with the best motives, and was the outcome of greatness of spirit allied with insight; whereby he conceived that the demand was an attempt to make him give way, and that concession would be an open confession of weakness.' Others gave the matter a more personal turn, perceiving in his contemptuous attitude towards the Lacedæmonians 'a headstrong and contentious spirit aiming at a display of strength[3]'; and so we pass on to Phidias and Aspasia. In the end, Plutarch finds the variety of traditions so perplexing that he has to conclude[4]:—'These are the causes alleged for his refusal to let the people give way to the Lacedæmonians; but the truth of the matter is obscure.' However, 'as the Lacedæmonians saw that if he could be ruined they would find the Athenians more pliable, they bade them drive out the curse[5].'

'The truth of the matter,' thanks to certain persons who knew it well enough, but whose interest was to conceal it, lies somewhere in Pericles' unique conception

---

[1] *Th. M.* p. 5.　　　　[2] Plut. *Pericl.* xxxi; cf. Thuc. I, 140. 5.
[3] Plut. *Pericl.* xxxii.　　　　[4] *Pericl.* xxxii fin.
[5] Pausan. III, vii, 10 says that the influence of the ephor Sthenelaidas was the chief cause of the war ; cf. Thuc. I, 86.

of both the external and the internal glory of Athens.
The difficulty of determining this is likely to be in
proportion to the difficulties which he himself had to
face. Thucydides has tried to explain how he held
before the people of every class an Athenian ambition
for a strong but generous leadership of Greece, and for
an æsthetic and intellectual refinement at home; how,
to attain these ends, he had to show a stubborn front to
the Peloponnesian alliance, while avoiding in the eyes
of his fellow-citizens the personal . odium of despotic
arrogance; and how 'the curse of the Alcmæonidæ'
was just such a rock as might send his whole endeavour
to pieces[1]. After all this, if we still ask how far Pericles
caused the war, the fault is to be sought less in Thucydides
than in the nature, not merely of all human testimony,
but of all human things.

But in the widest aspect of the quarrel, our judgement
is too apt to belittle those deep-rooted racial antipathies,
as well as the antagonism between progressive and re-
actionary polities. When Thucydides has been careful
to hold before our view the difference of hereditary feeling
between Ionians and Dorians[2], the question whether a
certain pair of nations, at a certain stage in a certain
civilisation, were or were not stirred to war by the
'prejudice and pride of blood' is no whit enlightened
by the argument that 'in fact, two nations do not go to
war on such grounds[3].' We could not listen to such an
argument if we were discussing, for instance, the great
war between Genoa and Pisa from 1277 to 1284 A.D.:
how can it apply to a rather similar struggle in the fifth
century B.C.? Hermocrates may be right in asserting that

---

[1] Thus we may agree that the narrative of Thuc. I, 126. 11 'is very serious
and solemn' (*Th. M.* p. 247), but not more so than the Funeral Oration
(II, 35–46) or the summary of Pericles' career (II, 65).
[2] Cf. Thuc. I, 124. 1 ; VI, 80. 3 ; 82. 2.   [3] *Th. M.* p. 5.

the Athenian designs on Sicily were not the work of racial feeling between Ionians and Dorians[1]: but his words imply that such feeling had long been recognised in the main duel which divided Greece ; and at Camarina, his phrase—'our eternal enemies the Ionians[2]'—is accepted by the Athenian envoy, and used to explain the beginning of the trouble between his city and Sparta[3]. In estimating the pressure caused by the growth of those rival leagues, we must allow full weight to the ties of kinship, language, ancestral custom and other native peculiarities which, even in the prosaic organism of a modern empire, are by no means smothered in the bustle of commercial enterprise.   To these we have seen reason to add the reputation of oligarchy and democracy, which are to be supposed to have had some play among the causes of conflict between communities whose members were so much more intimately concerned with public affairs than the ordinary citizen is now, and where, on one side at least, the freshness of political experiment was one of the chief delights of life.

Furthermore, it is necessary to remember that when we speak of these 'nations' going to war, we are considering bodies of men which are far more analogous to feudal families than to the vast combinations of industrial machinery with individual privacy which we understand by 'nations' to-day.   Accordingly, we must make ample room for ambition and caprice among the causes of an ancient war.   Thucydides' anxiety to disentangle these 'romantic' motives from the more practical is well seen in his account of the forces engaged on either side at the supreme conflict before Syracuse[4]: it may also be observed, in smaller compass, where he explains the quarrel

---

[1] Thuc. IV, 61. 2–3.   [2] Thuc. VI, 80. 3.
[3] Thuc. VI, 82. 2 ; cf. *Th. M.* p. 5.
[4] Thuc. VII, 57–58.

between Corinth and Corcyra[1]. Epidamnus, a Corcyræan colony planted by a founder brought from Corcyra's mother-city Corinth, was constrained by faction-troubles to seek help from one of the two states who could claim to be her parent. Refused by Corcyra, she turned, by order of the Delphic oracle, to Corinth, who promptly and vigorously took her case in hand. The motives of the Corinthians are thus analysed and arranged by Thucydides :—'Considering that the colony belonged to them as much as to the Corcyræans, they undertook its protection from a sense of right (κατὰ τὸ δίκαιον). At the same time, they were moved by hatred of the Corcyræans, for their neglectful treatment of their mother-city.' This rather more genuine motive is then substantiated by instances of the ceremonial slights put upon Corinth by her colony, and by her growing resentment at the financial and military strength of Corcyra, who, worst of all, 'was at times elated by her naval superiority, especially at the thought of the former habitation of her country by the Phæacians, a people renowned for sea-faring.' This piece of romantic sentiment was itself a spur to her nautical efforts : but in the upshot, ' it was with grievances on *all* these scores that the Corinthians gladly sent their aid to Epidamnus.' Feelings are none the less urgent for being various, so long as all work towards one point.

The laborious circumspection of these sentences is typical of the mind which informs the whole History, and which lifted it from the plane of military annals to a subtle presentation of the nervous Hellenic world. Form and substance alike offer mines of precious meaning, could they be worthily explored, to link and illustrate the scattered tokens of one of the most far-reaching movements in the main stream of civilisation. ' The political philosophy of the city-state,' Mr Cornford remarks, as

[1] Thuc. I, 25. 3–26. I.

he turns away from *Thucydides Historicus*[1], 'may be neglected by the modern socialist. The observations upon human nature are less noble than those of an ordinary novelist of to-day.' But shall we allow to Thucydides a nobility of mind, a judicial honesty, and an acuteness of perception, which our experience has at least not taught us to despise; shall we admit that he had commanded both citizens and metics, had directed many operations, and assisted in many debates such as those he has recorded; that for twenty years he was able to stand aloof from the struggles of states and parties, and contemplate the Hellenic world as a whole; and then shall we reject as irrelevant, if not frequently false, the most deliberate and significant lines of his picture? 'After the second invasion of the Peloponnesians, when the Athenians felt the double devastation of their land, and the war and the pestilence together weighing upon them, they began to change their minds, and to find fault with Pericles for having persuaded them to make war, and for being the author of all their sore embarrassments[2].' Failing in their overtures to Sparta, they turned in angry despair on Pericles, who summoned them to a meeting, and addressed them 'with the twofold object of encouraging them and of so diverting their ill-temper as to bring them into a more tractable and unapprehensive state of mind.' When Thucydides is at pains to show us how Pericles worked upon the national imagination of the people, or how his successors pandered to a newly excited taste for rhetoric and disputation, we must not lightly resign the presumption that such management of popular moods had a prominent place in the actual mechanism of Hellenic affairs. But the 'mythistoric' theory raises a suspicion concerning the mind of Thucydides which casts a lurid doubt upon the accuracy of his

[1] *Th. M.* p. 79.   [2] Thuc. II, 59 (430 B.C.).

whole picture. It will now be our duty to examine the main grounds for this suspicion in the body of his narrative.

§ 4

The story of the occupation of Pylos[1] is made out to be defective as history, and is used for revealing how, by an innate tendency of Thucydides' mind, the material has been grouped and distorted to fit a certain mythic pattern. Mr Cornford, in order to describe the impression which the tale makes upon him, has 'brought into prominence a series of suggestions which are anything but conspicuous in the long story as it stands in the text[2]': he has 'cut away the mass in which they are embedded and left them clumsily sticking out, so that no one can miss them.' This explanation is significant: apparently no one, till this new summary was made, had felt that the occupation of Pylos 'was the most casual thing in the world.' Indeed, the carefully connected details of large parts of the narrative may be said to impress everyone rather with the mixture of light-hearted enterprise and undaunted tenacity with which the Athenian soldiers took advantage of a number of favourable accidents. We may admit that Thucydides failed to discover what underlay some of these strokes of luck: but that is a different thing from deliberate or even instinctive design; and taking the story as a whole, we may fairly believe that it reduces rather than strengthens the element of fortune in the popular versions provided by the author's informants. That there were some widely accepted versions which emphasised the bad luck of the Spartans appears from two other passages in his book, where he shows his own impartial detachment from any preconceived theory. The

[1] Thuc. IV, 3–41. [2] *Th. M.* p. 88.

first[1] tells how, after Mantinea, ' by this single action they
cleared themselves of the charge of cowardice, due to
their mishap on the island ; and of general imprudence
and tardiness, under which they then laboured in the eyes
of the Greeks : it was now thought that they owed their
disgrace to fortune, while in resolution they were still the
same.'   Here the word for ' mishap' (ξυμφορά) is used
without any causal colour ; and it is the Greeks, not
Thucydides, who now regard the Spartans as the victims of ill luck.   In the other passage[2], the Spartans
themselves are prompted to the reflection ' that they
were deservedly unlucky, taking to heart their mishap
(ξυμφορά) at Pylos, and any others that had befallen
them.'   Here too Thucydides seems to mark his own
sceptical attitude towards the idea that it was all a piece
of luck.   Yet without these separate hints, the story of
the affair itself is free from many of the collusions or
delusions of Fortune which the new theory espies in
it.   We may call the building of the fort, as told by
Thucydides, a 'piece of mud-larking[3]' or what we please :
but surely he, and the chief of his presumable informants,
Demosthenes, knew what many an English officer in
Spain or India has quickly learnt,—that an idle piece of
mud-larking, sent by Fortune, it may be, or boredom, or
whatever we may care to call the impulse which we
cannot analyse, may be turned into a means of preserving
himself and his men, through the first hazardous hours of
an adventure, right on to a signal success[4].

We come next to the Messenian privateer which
arrives so casually, and proves so conveniently able to
furnish the Athenians with some shields and some heavy-
armed soldiers.   It is to be supposed that such vessels

---

[1] Thuc. V, 75. 3.   [2] Thuc. VII, 18. 2.   [3] *Th. M.* p. 91.
[4] Cf. the combined luck and skill of Themistocles on the ship, Thuc. I,
137. 2.

were no very unfamiliar sight off that stretch of coast, and that they carried not only fighting-men fully armed, but shields for the use of the ship's crew, in case of emergency at sea, or a running fight to the shore from a foray[1]. But even if we ignore this probability, and are left at a loss for a reason why the vessel happened to be there at the moment, is it not making too much of the difficulty to say[2]—'We remember now that in the previous year Demosthenes had been co-operating with these very Messenians in the Ætolian and Acarnanian campaigns,'—when our memory has been strained for about two pages? The 'blanks to be filled by conjecture' are few and slight: they are easily accounted for by supposing that Thucydides was unwilling to fill with his own conjectures the gaps left by the most reliable information. 'The persons who were present at each event,' he has warned us[3], 'did not tell the same tale about the same things, but according as they were swayed towards either side by favour or memory.' Perhaps it is unnecessary to weigh any further, for this part of the History, the charge of 'deliberate distortion[4],' which has somehow pushed aside the recognition of Thucydides' 'austere regard for truth[5].' But it may be well to note that this detailed story of an adventure which became, to Hellenic eyes, a very notable stroke in the main conflict[6], can only be construed into a case of dramatic 'infiguration,' by letting Persuasion strain its early incidents with an infiguration of her own.

---

[1] Cf. Thuc. I, 10. 4, where he shows that the Greek warriors in Homer were rowers (αὐτερέται) as well as warriors, and that their ships were more like privateers (λῃστικώτερον παρεσκευασμένα) than the triremes of his day.

[2] *Th. M.* p. 93.   [3] See above, p. 14.

[4] *Th. M.* p. 95.   [5] *Th. M.* p. 75.

[6] The excitement of Athens is shown by the increase of the fleet at Pylos till it numbered 70 ships—Thuc. IV, 23. 2.

§ 5

Cleon and Alcibiades, two of the most active characters in the progress of the war, naturally offer more scope
for an eloquent exposition of a tragic design. With
regard to Cleon's undertaking to capture or kill the
Spartans on the island within twenty days[1], it is not
easy to see why so 'much ink has been expended on the
phrase *mad as it was*[2].' All that need be noted is that
it is the comment of a military man who had learnt by
bitter experience, as well as by long observation, how
foolish it is to promise, even to oneself, the achievement of
a definite success within a stated number of days. The
cold, shrewd sense of Lucian, exhorting the historian to
be undeterred by the power and vehemence of a popular
orator from recording the truth about his conduct,
seems to hit the mark in the words—'nor shall Cleon
frighten him from saying that this was a mischievous
madman[3].' Thucydides does not say so much : he calls
it 'a madman's promise.' The question, how he can so
describe it, 'at the very moment when he is recording its
fulfilment[4],' finds in his own character a more reasonable
and creditable answer than the suggested inspiration of
Ἐλπὶς μαινομένη, 'the spirit who lured Xerxes to the
sack of Athens[5].'

Passing to the speech of the Spartan envoys on the
men in the island[6], we observe the 'mythistoric' theory
tending again to a 'modernist fallacy.' It dismisses the
theme of moderation in prosperity as 'a most venerable
commonplace'; yet this is only possible because our

---

[1] Thuc. IV, 28 ; *Th. M.* p. 117.

[2] Thuc. IV, 39. 3—καίπερ μανιώδης οὖσα.

[3] Luc. *De Conscr. Hist.* 37—ὡς μὴ εἰπεῖν ὅτι ὀλέθριος καὶ μανικὸς ἄνθρωπος
οὗτος ἦν.

[4] *Th. M.* p. 117.   [5] *Th. M.* p. 172.

[6] Thuc. IV, 17–20.

survey of the literature of the world impresses us *now*
with the triteness of such considerations. But more
important issues are involved in the Mytilenæan debate[1].
' The question of the purpose and true nature of punitive
justice was much in the air at this time[2] '; and though we
may rightly guess that Thucydides' view of the matter,
had he made up his mind, would have followed the
lines of Diodotus' speech, no reason has been offered for
supposing that he has not set out the substance of both
Cleon's and Diodotus' ideas on the question of the
moment. There is, on the face of it, an argumentative
force and connection in Cleon's speech that should forbid
us, as they would surely forbid any intelligent Greek of
that time, to accept him as the minister of Madness,
'intoxicated with ambitious passion[3]' at Sphacteria.
Mr Cornford praises the speech as 'a masterpiece of
characterization[4]'; but as he offers no evidence that its
arguments are other than those which the historian
sincerely judged to have been available on the occasion,
the presumption remains that it is a masterly sketch of
Cleon's actual hold on Athenian politics. Accordingly, it
will be more useful to gather what hints we may, for the
literary history of the time, from this remarkable attack on
the Athenian passion for rhetoric and the practical incom-
petence of the democracy. The forcible acuteness of
the whole speech is aimed at a particular object. Casting
about for the best means of shaming the people into a
strong line of action, the speaker seizes on certain points
in their inclinations and habits which are the signs, not
merely of a weakness in the constitution so proudly
cherished by Pericles, but of a weakness rapidly yielding
to decay. Diodotus argues against the drastic policy of
Cleon, and throws in some poetical eloquence of the sort

---

[1] Thuc. III, 37–48.   [2] *Th. M.* p. 121.
[3] *Th. M.* p. 124.   [4] *Th. M.* p. 114.

which Cleon despises[1]. The voting—and here no one
doubts the accuracy of the picture—is nearly equally
divided. If anything of a Thucydidean doctrine is to be
drawn from this evenly-poised debate, little profit is to be
augured from the postulate that Thucydides has 'chosen to
present[2]' the character of Cleon in a certain tragic light,
while making Diodotus the mouthpiece of his own ideas.
It will be better to expect from the substance and
language of the two speeches, taken together, some
evidence for determining the historian's relation, not
merely to Æschylean tragedy, but to the literary movements of his day.

Correspondences of imagery and phrasing between
passages in the speeches and the Attic drama have long
been recognised, and not a few readers have probably
been tempted by these to feel a tragic scheme in the
History. There are signs that the temptation has come
at length in the guise of Tragic Irony :—' Thucydides
tried to be scientific and hoped to be dull, but he failed[3].'
Yet, as we have seen[4], he was at pains to convince his
readers of the importance of the war, and to suggest that
history need not be dull when stripped of the irrelevant
or obsolete accoutrements of legend. Let us observe
more nearly the vision of Mythistoria. A passage in
Cleon's speech[5] is put forward as ' patently inapplicable
to the revolted island.' His words are—' Where they
thought they saw a chance of success, they set upon us
when we were doing them no wrong' ; and he proceeds
to generalise briefly on the effects of ' exceptional prosperity.' Is this ' simply meaningless' for the occasion, if
we remember the weakness of Athens under the plague

---

[1] Thuc. III, 40. 3—οἱ τέρποντες λόγῳ ῥήτορες ἕξουσι...ἀγῶνα. Cleon seems
to bring us back to Thucydides' own phrases (I, 22. 4)—τὸ μὴ μυθῶδες
ἀτερπέστερον—ἀγώνισμα ἐς τὸ παραχρῆμα ἀκούειν.

[2] *Th. M.* p. 124. [3] *Th. M.* p. 127.

[4] Thuc. I, 22. 4 ; above, pp. 13-14. [5] Thuc. III, 39. 3.

and her crippling expenses? These facts, at least, are
studiously kept before us by Thucydides, first in a note
of his own[1], and then in the words of the Mytilenæan
envoys at Olympia[2]; and we learn besides that the
Mytilenæans made a stubborn fight, without the expected
help from Sparta[3]. Further, the conduct of the new
theory over this point seems to furnish another proof
that it is better to proceed on the plane of rhetorical
'commonplaces,' however tiresome they may sound to us
now, than to set up the skeleton of a connected dramatic
design. For having assumed, as a basis of argument,
that the speech is 'patently inapplicable' to the case in
hand, the theory has to undergo the damaging admission
that the device of tragic irony 'is unskilfully employed,
since dramatic probability is too completely sacrificed';
and the prosecution is accordingly driven to the perilous
excuse that 'after all, Thucydides was only an amateur
tragedian[4].'

§ 6

In truth, any account of Thucydides' literary art
which 'works loose[5]' from the solid frame of the record
he has left must fall to the ground at once. Apart from
his personal statements of method, which we have already
noticed[6], we can instance his anxiety to secure a reasonable
estimate of the Lacedæmonian forces at Mantinea[7]; his
exposure of the disastrous muddle in the popular mind
regarding the character of Alcibiades[8]; his careful analysis
of the different states of mind included under the phrase
—'So a passion for sailing forth (to Sicily) seized hold of
one and all[9]'; and the calm, matter-of-fact tone in which

---

[1] Thuc. III, 3. I.   [2] Thuc. III, 13. 3.   [3] Thuc. III, 5. 2.
[4] Th. M. p. 151.   [5] Th. M. p. 131.
[6] Above, pp. 13–14, 34.   [7] Thuc. v, 68. 2.   [8] VI, 15. 3–4.
[9] VI, 24. 3 ; cf. Th. M. p. 214.

he explains how the Egestæans trapped the sanguine
Athenians with a false display of wealth[1].   These, among
numerous other notes, are gratuitous flaws in a dramatic
scheme which is here to be supposed in the ascent of its
climax ; the only rejoinder can be that Thucydides was a
very amateur tragedian indeed. But admirers of 'Thucydidean caution[2]' cannot leave the matter here.   The chief
duty of the new interpretation has not been performed.
It fails to prove that the conditions and events of the war
did not conform, in the reality of their main features, to a
roughly dramatic shape ; and that we have not to thank
Thucydides for doing the very opposite of what it makes
out that he did,—for reducing the popular conception of
the whole affair, so far as his evidence would safely take
him, to what he regarded as a probable account ; while
preserving a lively picture of the characters and feelings
which produced the largest effect in action.   Just such
a correction we apparently have in his preliminary
sketch of Pausanias[3] : this Mr Cornford 'spurns out of
history' in a footnote to a discussion[4] which seeks to set
Thucydides on the same ' mythic' level with Herodotus ;
to whose type of story, despite this correction, tradition
seems to have reverted.   And in spite of our interest in
this new study of the Tragic Passions[5], its preface and
sequel ought not to persuade us that such figments ruled
the thoughts of Thucydides, if no better device can be
found than that of filling in his careful drawing with
colours from Hesiod, or Theognis, or Æschylus, or Pindar,
or even Plutarch ; the main intentions and efforts of
these writers being exactly those from which Thucydides,
not merely in what he professes, but in continual practice, plainly stands apart.   How far he intended the
Melian Dialogue to point a lesson, we cannot hope to

[1] VI, 46. 3–5.   [2] *Th. M.* p. 82.   [3] Thuc. I, 134.
[4] *Th. M.* p. 166 ; cf. p. 119.   [5] *Th. M.* cc. ix, xiii.

determine, until we have examined its connection with the prevailing rhetorical disputations : here we need only notice another embarrassment of the tragic theory, in the omission of Alcibiades, the author of the Melian massacre, from this decisive scene[1]. But the whole plot of the play is perplexing enough, when, after we have been shown how the popular distrust of Alcibiades was due to a confusion of his private character with his public ability[2], we are to be impressed by the words—καὶ ἔδοξε πλεῖν τὸν 'Αλκι-βιάδην[3]—as finishing off a scene of frenzied ' disregard of omens,' and then, in the event, we are to find the disaster in Sicily an immediate consequence of Nicias' regard for omens. In the artistic realm to which the theory would lift all this part of the History, such obscurity of design, with the encumbrance of the long military narrative, is a strange substitute for the sceptical control of a story which, in less scrupulous hands, and ' with the exaggerations natural to poets[4],' might conceivably have been worked up into comprehensible drama.

'The play is done[5]': we come to the eighth Book, which ' is a mere continuation on the old chronological plan, unfinished, dull, and spiritless. The historian patiently continued his record ; but he seems to grope his way like a man without a clue.' These words give us the inevitable consequence of the view that he ' had traced the "causes" of the Sicilian Expedition from Fortune at Pylos to Nemesis at the quarries of Syracuse.' But let us read the opening words of this unfortunate

---

[1] *Th. M.* p. 186. To unprejudiced eyes, however, Alcibiades is there, in natural proportions. The expedition to Melos is told in almost the same breath with that which Alcibiades had just before conducted to Argos. (v, 84. 1). But the tragic theory meets with a troublesome jolt.

[2] Thuc. VI, 15. 4; *Th. M.* p. 210 : a confusion of the Public and Private Envy distinguished by Bacon (Essay on Envy).

[3] Thuc. VI, 29 fin.; *Th. M.* p. 216.

[4] Thuc. I, 10. 3 ; 21. 1.   [5] *Th. M.* p. 244.

Book[1]. As soon as indubitable news of the disaster
reached the Athenians at home, 'they turned in anger
upon those orators who had borne a part in promoting the
expedition, as if they had not voted it themselves; and
they vented their rage upon the soothsayers and prophets
and all who by any divination had formerly put them in
hopes of gaining Sicily.' Once more our attention is
dispassionately directed to the besetting snares of rhetoric
and superstition: the mind of Thucydides, aloof from the
minds of the people in his book, is determined to keep
Fortune and Nemesis proportionately remote from the
control of his description. That he could feel the stir of
ancient unknown forces behind the passions which swayed
Athenian politics, and had heard the sophists charming
their classes with poetical speculations thereon, is likely
enough: for his purpose, $\dot{\eta}$ $\zeta\dot{\eta}\tau\eta\sigma\iota s$ $\tau\hat{\eta}s$ $\dot{a}\lambda\eta\theta\epsilon\iota as$[2] is the
commanding spirit that will provide him with as much
'drama' as he wants, in the actual bloom and decline
of a brilliant civilisation. Nor, as he proceeds with this
concluding part, can he be said to 'grope his way' so
badly. Some of his best energy and skill is displayed in
describing the malignant or ambitious activity of Alcibiades: the popular mistake as to his public uses must
run to the bitter end. Along with this, we have an impressive record of the vigorous courage of the Athenians
in all quarters of their disordered empire. So far are
we from beholding an Athens which has been lured to
destruction by Luck, that it is the Chians who, in venturing
on revolt because they thought she was now paralysed[3],
'came to grief on one of the incalculable things that turn
up in human affairs; an error of judgement whereby
many others agreed with them in thinking that the power
of Athens would quickly be brought to utter collapse.'

[1] Thuc. VIII, I. I.
[2] I, 20 fin.: 'research of the truth.'
[3] VIII, 24. 5.

But always the Athenians are liable to be carried away by the rhetorical histrionics of Alcibiades[1] : we see him 'bewailing the private misfortune of his exile as guilty of all, and, by talking at great length on public affairs, putting them in good hopes of the future'; 'extravagantly magnifying the extent of his influence with Tissaphernes,' and uttering many 'high bombastic promises'; nay, in the last resort, he would 'realise his bed in cash' to supply them with food. These two chapters show Thucydides near the height of his descriptive power; and it is surely a strange thing, not so much that no one has found in them a sinister lapse from impartiality, nor yet that the 'mythistoric' theory refrains from pointing out a recrudescence of Persuasion and Hope, as that it should be forced to condemn such writing as dull and spiritless[2].

But, indeed, this Book provides some of the ripest and richest fruits of Thucydides' labours, to cast into the scale of true and unbiassed history. There is the well-considered statement[3]—'Possibly it was by some agreement that Agesandridas was hovering about Epidaurus and its neighbourhood; but there is also the probability that he waited there with a view to the present tumult in Athens, hoping to appear on the scene just at the right moment.' There is the description of the desperate terror into which the Athenians were plunged by the loss of Eubœa[4] :—'A panic, greater than any before, came upon them : for neither the disaster in Sicily (though it had seemed heavy at the time) nor any other occurrence had as yet so terrified them.' The first

---

[1] VIII, 81. 2.

[2] Perhaps the reason is that we are awkwardly near to comedy in the amusing portrait of Tissaphernes, who has enough power at his back to hold the balance between Sparta and Athens, and yet is so irresolute that Alcibiades can both 'frighten the Athenians with Tissaphernes and Tissaphernes with the Athenians'—VIII, 82 fin. Cf. above, pp. 19–20.

[3] VIII, 94. 2.   [4] VIII, 96. 1.

of these two passages may serve to show what use the
historian would have made of fuller means for determining
whether Demosthenes had pre-arranged the occupation of
Pylos; while the second suggests that even an amateur
tragedian would have had the sense to stop the narrative
a little sooner than where it came to be broken off.
Finally, we may glance at his wisely worded praise of the
government which succeeded the Four Hundred[1]:—'It
was during the first period of this constitution that the
Athenians clearly had the best government they ever
knew, at least in my time : for there was moderation in
the blending of nobles and commons, and this it was that
first uplifted the city from the sorry condition to which
her affairs had fallen.'   These and many more instances
of vivid description or of diligent observation invest the
eighth Book with a fine and lively character of its own ;
while its main substance shows the author picking out,
with a sureness of vision unsurpassed in any other
part of his work, the strongest and longest threads in a
difficult tangle of events.

§ 7

It has been necessary, for a clear-sighted approach to
the true nature of Thucydides' style, to consider the chief
suspicions which originated and supported the theory of
Thucydides Mythistoricus.   We have had to glance at
many large or dubious matters : ancient commerce and
imperialism ; the 'Piræus party,' together with statistics
of population and enfranchisement of aliens ; the ill repute
of industry, the difficulties of sea-traffic, and other signs of
the immaturity of trade ; and the strange secrecy with
which the commercial plot must have been guarded.
Thence we passed to the alleged pre-occupation of
ancient historians with human motives ; we considered

[1] VIII, 97. 2 (The Five Thousand, 411 B.C.).

how far Thucydides is liable to this charge, and whether it would count seriously against him as an accurate historian. We have weighed the narrow romantic patriotism of Greek citizens, the consequent value of pretexts both to them and to the History, and the apparently successful effort of a defeated opposition to obscure the precise nature of Pericles' policy; and in dealing with these points, we came upon 'modernist fallacies' in the dismissal of racial feeling from the causal account, in the exaggeration of ancient economic development, and in the neglect of the pervading force of rhetoric. On the whole, we have seen reason to find no real strength in the suspicions of the new theory, when they are brought against the unusually solid defences of Thucydides; whose portraits of Cleon and Alcibiades do not seem to have been materially coloured or enhanced for the effects of a dramatic scheme, and whose record of Athenian politics, as exemplified in the Mytilenæan Debate and the Melian Dialogue, rather directs our search to the vogue of rhetorical disputation.

Any fair account of the significance of the History must notice all of its salient features, without prejudice to those which are not immediately interesting or valuable to modern thought. Otherwise proportion must be lost in estimating the general cast of the author's mind, and his particular intention in writing. Further, a theory which shows him subject to a strong mythic obsession is directly and specially damaging to the study of his art, when, scorning the plain traces left on his style by the sophistic movement, it flies up, on a few gusts of poetry blowing here and there, to a dizzy height of tragic design. There are occasional tones in his book which remind us of tragedy: many readers must have wondered how far they are real tones of the time, rescued here from silence; and how far, on the other hand, he was induced by literary fashion to strike them louder than he heard. The mythic theory fills them with a special significance, to find that it has let slip the substance, and grasped the shadow. Still, it has aroused new interest in one of the noblest works of ancient art. Somehow the shadow is a 'thing of beauty and awe[1]'; the book remains 'a possession for ever,' only henceforth it is to be kept on a different shelf. We may be able, however, to conceive of an artistic history which shall be as reliable for the conveyance of truth as a proposition of Euclid. What is the most scientific historian to do, if he sees before him a city prospering, mounting to majesty and power, and then sinking in successive throes of disaster,—all simply, or principally, through what we still describe as fortune and folly? Is he to shut his eyes to the main truth, and wander off into endless speculation on the causes of gold mines and greed, or the dusky psychology of self-confidence and infatuation? The first and last pages of *Thucydides Mythistoricus* seem indeed to assure us that the historian followed the main lines of a real tragedy enacted before his eyes: yet the detection of the 'tragic passions' in the plan of the History has worked from the allegation, brought up at several points, of more or less conscious distortion and suppression of fact[2].

Our diligent Camden[3] has left us an account of the

[1] *Th. M.* p. 250.

[2] The account, for instance, of 'The Luck of Pylos' leaves Thucydides exposed to the true judgement of Casaubon (*Polyb.* Pref. 1609):—'Fallere non minus uidetur qui gesta praeterit sciens, quam ille qui nunquam facta fingit. Mr Cornford can only avert this conclusion by endowing Thucydides with an ardent quasi-religious imagination.

[3] *Hist. of Q. Elizabeth*, Fourth Ed., 1688, Pref.—'I procured all the Helps I possibly could for writing it : Charters and Grants of Kings and great Personages, Letters, Consultations in the Council-Chamber, Embassadours Instructions and Epistles, I carefully turned over and over; the Parliamentary Diaries, Acts and Statutes, I throughly perused, and read over every Edict or Proclamation....I have myself seen and observed many things, and received others from credible Persons that have been before me,

Invincible Armada[1], obtained 'out of the most credible Relations as well of the Spaniards as of our own Countreymen.' Are we to suspect him of ascribing too much influence to 'Queen Elizabeth's prudent Foresight' and 'the credulous Hope of the Spaniards,' and shall we smile at the intrusions of Chance, when the expedition, hardly out of sight of Spain, was 'dispersed by an hideous Tempest,' and at length, after heavy losses in several fights, which cost the English none of their ships 'save only that small one of Cock's,' was 'driven round about all Britain by Scotland, the Orcades and Ireland, grievously tossed, and very much distressed, impaired and mangled by Storms and Wrecks,' to return home, a battered remnant, 'with Shame and Dishonour'? Shall history hold off from Philip's admission that he had suffered for his overweening arrogance, or from the extraordinary good fortune which helped and finished the valiant exploits of the English[2]? In such cases we have no right to assert that the convenient formula—'Fortune plays tricks on the blindness of men'—is one jot prejudicial to veracious history, or veracious history one jot prejudicial to the convenient formula. The conflict that we shall watch for and consider will not be one in which the servant of truth appears constricted by the rules and trappings of mythic drama; it will be the most obvious and measurable part of the issue joined by luminous art with laborious fidelity. In a certain limited sense, the decision will be seen to fall in favour of dramatic effect; but the settlement, if not perfect in formal harmony and smoothness, may yet claim to present the lively lineaments of a genuine history.

men who have been present at the transacting of Matters, and such as have been addicted to the Parties on both Sides in this contrariety of Religion.' Cf. above, p. 14.   [1] *Ib.* Bk. III.

[2] Camden has set forth clearly both the immediate and the more ancient causes of the war, religious and commercial as well as personal.

CHAPTER III

THE MIND OF THE WRITER

§ 1

AFTER this digression, which was necessary, and will be 'not unuseful[1],' we pursue our account of the literary influences that may be assumed or shown to have acted on the youth and manhood of Thucydides. We have already considered the rough basis of epic form lying ready to the hand of anyone who in the fifth century should undertake a description of the Hellenic world. We have guessed at the presence in this particular man, though the historian repressed it, of a genuine feeling for poetry. We have mentioned the prevalent taste for hearing a well-argued case on either side of a political or social question, which favoured the Sophoclean and especially the Euripidean type of drama, and which abandoned Æschylus to the cloudy obscurity that envelopes so many high-souled pioneers. It will now be our business to observe how, and in what sense, the form of Thucydides' History came to bear very striking testimony to the effects of that taste upon the public speech of his time; while we examine, among other notable points, his own endeavour to indicate the effects of language upon affairs. The natural cast of his mind must be briefly stated. It is severe and steady, not easily yielding to emotion; synthetic, logical; extremely sceptical and reserved. He is deeply interested in

[1] Above, p. 17.

Pericles and his conduct of the democracy ; has heard him deliver a fine discourse on the aspirations and prospects of Athens. The orator must have prepared that speech : some assert that he wrote it out beforehand, every word[1]. Such a composition should hold a high place in a vivid history of the time, and will be specially convenient for a record of policies and characteristic states of mind. How will Thucydides set about the task of showing compendiously the whole stir and struggle of the peculiar civic nationalities of fifth-century Greece ?

The Age of Pericles was marked by artistic innovations more wonderful, for extent and variety of advance, than any that the history of the world displays. In poetry alone, the Homeric characters were made to raise new emotions on the stage, so that the art of the rhapsode began to fade before this intenser light. But while Sophocles and Euripides were elaborating, through the means exploited by Phrynichus and Æschylus, a subtle intellectual discourse of the passions, the conscious cultivation of prose-writing had a much cruder substrate to work upon than that provided by Homer for tragedy. Unfortunately we do not possess any considerable examples of Attic prose which can be dated before the visit of Gorgias to Athens in 427 B.C. Our almost total ignorance of what Antiphon was doing in those years of ' carefully obscure life[2] '—from the time of his birth (about 480 B.C.) till he won fame as a speech-writer for the courts (425 B.C.)—forbids any accurate measurement of the credit due to his single share in the formation of Attic prose. The influence of Protagoras, Prodicus and Gorgias may be traced, as we shall see, in his extant writings, and a rough

---

[1] Suidas, s.v. Περικλῆς—ὅστις πρῶτος γραπτὸν λόγον ἐν δικαστηρίῳ εἶπε, τῶν πρὸ αὐτοῦ σχεδιαζόντων. Plato, *Menex.* 236 B, suggests that it was really the work of Aspasia.

[2] Jebb, *Att. Or.* I, p. 7.

notion may be formed of the initiative of his own not
very profound or forcible mind.   It is fairly clear that he
and other speech-writers and pamphleteers were concerning themselves, in the middle of this century, with the
arrangement of topics, the regulation of the dialect, and
the choice of stately or telling words : at least, we have
Plato's testimony, though given with something of a
sneer, that Antiphon was a well-known teacher of rhetoric
in Athens[1].   As in the Age of Elizabeth, material expansion discovered a world of fresh and confident thought,
which in turn created the need for effective expression.
It seems likely that the preference of Antiphon, like that
of Pericles, lay in the direction of a studied dignity,
contrived by the selection of sonorous words and a slow,
emphatic delivery.

But whatever was the state of Attic prose before
427 B.C., the arrival of Gorgias marked a turning-point
in its career of which the importance can hardly be
over-estimated.   For the first time Athenian ears were
made acquainted with the force of antithetic and epigrammatic point in public speech.   If it is hard for us to
understand the enthusiasm of such an intelligent people
for the artificial graces of Gorgias, it is partly because,
having grown weary of many mannerisms, we have come
to distrust any sort of ornament at all ; yet still more,
perhaps, because we enjoy as a natural heritage the more
valuable and enduring results of the innovation.   When
wine, or beer, or whatever potency precedes[2], was first
invented, men drank it eagerly in full draughts, and
worshipped the great dispenser of their ecstasy ; and
although their liquor would hardly tempt us to-day,
humanity must always be interested in the very excess of
their drinking.   It was not so much the poetic imagery

[1] Plato, *Menex.* 236 A.
[2] Cf. J. E. Harrison, *Proleg. Gr. Relig.* pp. 415–425.

of Gorgias' speeches that appealed to the Athenians : they must have long employed, for their practical needs, some sort of prose which had definitely to reject the charms of poetry. But their democratic debates were calling for a new set of tools whose acquisition and use were as yet only faintly conceived. Gorgias was able to show them certain tricks and graces in the disposition of words ; out of vague desires he shaped for them an appetite, and at once they were intoxicated. When he split a thought into two halves, polished each half with a distinctive word, and tied them up again with a jingle, they felt that a great day had dawned for Athens[1]. Everyone who had the least political or literary ambition would experiment in the new contrivance. Thucydides, whose age at this time was about thirty-five, had for the last four or five years been making notes for his book, and perhaps composing some portions in the rough. Antiphon, ten or fifteen years older, might help him to distinguish the faults from the virtues of Gorgias' style : probably the historian practised and selected for himself. At any rate, the style attracted and interested him. It may be supposed that he was already able to write simple narrative, more concisely and weightily than Herodotus : but here was a device which would serve a higher artistic purpose, and enable him to present great sayings, large principles, and the double aspect of each notable dispute, in a compact and memorable form. Some such welcome he must have given to the Sicilian fashion during the three years which intervened before his military command, and the greater part of which he doubtless spent in Athens.

It should be observed that even this broad preliminary statement of the case is different from that provided by

---

[1] Cf. Diod. Sic. XII, 53—τῷ ξενίζοντι τῆς λέξεως ἐξέπληξε τοὺς Ἀθηναίους ὄντας εὐφυεῖς καὶ φιλολόγους.

Mure[1] :—'His rhetorical mannerism reflects the vicious taste of his age, working on his own natural turn for nice distinctions and logical refinements.' The taste of his age, whether vicious or not, was productive no less of nice distinctions and logical refinements than of rhetorical mannerism. The two sides must be kept together, if we are to understand how the sophists had any vogue at all. If we are further to appreciate rightly the more artificial features of the History, we must look for something which its author deliberately imposed, as an intellectual and artistic whole, upon the simple structure of his original scheme. Just as we condemn the vain adorn- ments of this or that rhetorician by reference to the thought or lack of thought behind them, we shall not pass sentence on the art of the speeches and disquisitions in the History, till we have at least tried to determine how much of their form is due, and how much is not due, to the individual mind of Thucydides.

§ 2

The particular cast and eminence of that mind will be made more definite for this purpose, by considering a few further hints which are to be gathered from his management of the History, and especially his treatment of certain topics. At a later stage we shall examine more in detail his most obviously dramatic piece, the Melian Dialogue : here we shall agree with Dionysius[2] and Mr Cornford[3] that the interlude is remarkable both for its length and for the heartless, elaborate language of the Athenian speaker. Dionysius, in complaining[4] that 'it would not be like Athenians speaking to the Greeks, whom they had freed from the Persians, to say

---

[1] Above, p. 4.   [2] Dionys. Hal. *De Thuc.* 37–41.
[3] *Th. M.* pp. 174–187.   [4] *De Thuc.* 39.

that between the weak and the strong the issue rests with violence,' seems to forget that in the event all the manhood of Melos was put to the sword, while the women and children were sold into slavery[1]. It is reasonable to suppose that some declaration was made, about this time, of the attitude which Athens meant to adopt towards the island communities. But Thucydides' way of presenting that attitude is peculiarly forcible. We need not descend to Dionysius' suggestion of 'a grudge against the city which had condemned him,' any more than to the pedantic censures of the grammar which occupy the first part of that criticism[2]. We have had warning of danger in suspecting a continuous tragic design of which the Dialogue might appear to be a part[3]. Yet there is an obvious intention of contrasting the overbearing conduct of the great city, not merely with the inoffensive existence of a little town, but with the oppressor's own approaching disaster in Sicily, the story of which begins immediately after this Melian affair. Dionysius has remarked on the labyrinthine contortions of the Athenian part in the Dialogue, comparing it unfavourably with the language used by Archidamus to the Platæans in the second Book[4]. It is worth while to be reminded of that other conversation, as also of the fact that the Melian Dialogue was admired by ancient amateurs of this kind of composition[5]; for modern critics are apt to lay too much stress on the 'dramatic' appearance of this discussion. But a better sense might have prompted Dionysius to take a more significant illustration from the opening of the Sicilian enterprise, where Thucydides puts in the mouth of Nicias a speech[6] of so simple and

---

[1] Thuc. v, 116. 4 (416 B.C.).   [2] *De Thuc.* 37–38.
[3] Above, p. 61.   [4] Thuc. II, 72–74.
[5] *De Thuc.* 37 init.—ὃν μάλιστα ἐπαινοῦσιν οἱ τοῦ χαρακτῆρος τούτου θαυμασταί.   [6] Thuc. VI, 9–14.

direct a style, that we are forced to feel an intended contrast with the preceding Dialogue.

Now Nicias was a man who, though deplorably subject to common superstition, and mediocre in his personal aims, may be thought to share with Pericles and Brasidas, if not an equal, yet a certain degree of the historian's sympathy. He was not afraid to tell his countrymen some unpalatable home-truths:—'You have come to despise the Spartans,' he said, 'because your defeat of them was so unexpected in the light of your original fears; and so you are grasping at Sicily[1].' Again— 'Remember that success is seldom achieved by desire, most often by forethought; let others be love-sick for what they have not got[2].' To the last he was unlucky, but the universe must answer for that: the worth of his character remains. Obliged to lead an invasion which he had so reasonably condemned; harassed by sore disease and the lack of proper support from Athens; and finding at last no grace in return for his former efforts on behalf of the Spartan prisoners from Sphacteria; he still could draw one of those rare pronouncements from Thucydides:—'a man who least deserved, of all the Greeks in my time, such an utterly hapless lot; since he had pursued the conventional practice of all that is right[3].'

Hence, on a general view, it is fair to conclude that, if the historian purposely inserted the Melian Dialogue

---

[1] VI, 11. 5.   [2] VI, 13. 1.

[3] VII, 86. 5—ἥκιστα δὴ ἄξιος ὢν τῶν γ᾽ ἐπ᾽ ἐμοῦ Ἑλλήνων ἐς τοῦτο δυστυχίας ἀφικέσθαι διὰ τὴν πᾶσαν ἐς ἀρετὴν νενομισμένην ἐπιτήδευσιν. Bury (*Anc. Gr. Historians*, p. 119) interprets (with F. Cauer) 'conventional virtue,' and then presses the phrase to signify malicious irony on the historian's part. He sees irony also in the account of Nicias' aims (V, 16. 2); which, however, include a very laudable sort of patriotism. Are we to take it as ironical, and not merely a remark on the ways of the universe, when we read that the plague was most deadly to those who had any pretensions to virtue—διεφθείροντο, καὶ μάλιστα οἱ ἀρετῆς τι μεταποιούμενοι (II, 51. 5)?

where it stands, he meant us to feel some contempt for the extreme policy professed by Athens towards the typical victim of her ambitions. Here he expresses no opinion of his own : the actual course of events will speak more eloquently than any words that he could write on the perplexing theme of political expediency. But we can perceive that, in his earnest endeavour to give those events their full opportunity, he has invested the Athenian part of the Dialogue with such an elaborate and involved argumentation as betrays his personal feeling on the state of his country's policy. Nicias speaks clear and pointed sense : the treatment of Melos is enveloped in a rhetorical mist which he judged appropriate to the case. Our discussion of that judgement, as a conscious stroke of art, must be taken up elsewhere.

There are one or two other matters, belonging to his general outlook on the world, which should be added here. His independence and scientific caution in extracting a few significant truths from the Homeric legends[1] are, in their masterly combination, an example to modern archæologists and critics. With regard to oracles and omens, it has been remarked that 'his tone about them is not one of mere contempt, as for a foolish popular superstition[2].' Yet it is hard to see anything but contempt in the sarcastic comment on the *varia lectio* (λοιμός —λιμός) in the oracle which the old men recalled at the time of the plague[3]—' people suited their memory to their present troubles ; and I fancy that if another Dorian war ever comes upon them after this one, and a *famine* (λιμός) chances to occur, they will probably recite the other version.' At a momentous point in the operations at Syracuse[4], the weak spot in Nicias' character is noted in the words—'he was rather too much addicted to

---

[1] Thuc. I, 3–12. [2] Forbes, Bk I, Intr. p. xxiv.
[3] Thuc. II, 54. 3. [4] VII, 50. 4.

divination and that sort of thing'; where the phrase καὶ
τῷ τοιούτῳ is made particularly contemptuous by the
preceding sentence; for it was the mass of the soldiers
who were so strongly affected by the eclipse of the moon
that they begged the generals to stay where they were.
Thus Nicias is exposed in the act of clinging to the vulgar
superstition. We remember the rage of the disappointed
people against 'the soothsayers and prophets and all who
by any divination had formerly put them in hopes of
gaining Sicily[1]'; and the confident scorn of the Athenian
speaker to the Melians—'soothsaying and oracles and
all such disastrous inducements of hope[2]';—which, while
appropriate to the more intelligent Athenians of the
time, may be considered rather too violent for the view
of Thucydides himself. The calm, sceptical detachment of that view is well exemplified in his almost
humorous note on the death of Hesiod[3]:—'the precinct
of the Nemean Zeus, in which Hesiod the poet is said to
have been killed by the people of this place, an oracle
having informed him that this would befall him in Nemea.'
He tells us that he remembers how, during the whole
period of the war, he heard the common prediction of its
lasting 'thrice nine years[4]'; and remarks that this is the
only case known to him where a confidence in oracles
was justified by the event. But of far more importance
to him and to us are the possible conquests of rational
foresight across the border of chance. Even an oracle
may show this sort of intelligence, though its meaning is
too likely to be mistaken. There was one which declared[5]
it would be an evil day for Athens when a plot of ground
under the Acropolis, known as the Pelargicon, came to be

[1] Thuc. VIII, I. I—above, p. 62.
[2] Thuc. V, 103. 2—καὶ ὅσα τοιαῦτα μετ᾽ ἐλπίδων λυμαίνεται.
[3] III, 96. I—ἐν ᾧ Ἡσίοδος ὁ ποιητὴς λέγεται ὑπὸ τῶν ταύτῃ ἀποθανεῖν,
χρησθὲν αὐτῷ ἐν Νεμέᾳ τοῦτο παθεῖν.
[4] V, 26. 4.   [5] II, 17. 1-2.

inhabited. The population of Attica, on the advice of
Pericles when the war began, crowded into the city, and
this spot was occupied. It was expected that troubles
would arise in consequence : whereas, if there were
troubles, they were the general distresses of the war ;
and it was to the cause, not the result, of the occupation that the oracle referred. So, again, he praises
Themistocles for his sagacity in conjecturing the future
course of events[1] : Nicias, after the words we have noticed
for their candid truth[2], is made to say that instead of
being elated by their enemies' mishaps, his countrymen
ought to find confidence only through superior force of
design[3] ; and, in his second speech, when they have
voted the expedition, that although good fortune will be
needed as well as good counsel, it is best not to count on
such an uncertainty, but to take what reasonable precautions they can[4]. It is from ignoring the freshness and
strength of this doctrine—for as such it has stepped into
the place of haphazard daring and trust in one's lucky
star—that so much ink has been expended on Cleon's
' mad promise[5].'

§ 3

Connected with this dislike of unreasoned belief and
hasty confidence is the historian's alertness for detecting
and exposing illogical thought in the conduct of public
business. We have noticed the episode of Hippias and
Hipparchus[6] as specially prominent among the digressions : let us see if it will yield some light for the question
of Thucydides' view of Athenian politics, with which we
seemed to be faced in discussing the Melian Dialogue[7].

[1] I, 138. 3.
[2] VI, 11. 5 ; above, p. 74.
[3] VI, 11. 6—χρὴ δὲ μὴ πρὸς τὰς τύχας τῶν ἐναντίων ἐπαίρεσθαι, ἀλλὰ τὰς διανοίας κρατήσαντας θαρσεῖν.
[4] VI, 23. 3.
[5] Above, p. 56.
[6] VI, 53-59 ; above, p. 18.
[7] Above, p. 75.

The transition to this second discussion[1] of the Pisistratidæ from the account of Alcibiades and the mutilation
of the Hermæ has been generally noted as rather
sudden. 'What analogy is there between the case of the
tyrannicides and that of Alcibiades; between the jealousy
felt by the Athenians on account of a breach of religious
ceremonial committed by the two patriots in the cause of
national liberty, and the jealousy inspired by the intrigues
of Alcibiades in the cause of despotism?[2]' The connection in the historian's mind is reduced to this:—
' Harmodius took the opportunity of a religious ceremony
to assert (as vulgarly believed) the liberties of Athens
against her tyrants ; therefore the Athenians have ever
since looked upon all tampering with religious ceremonial
as evidence of plots to establish tyranny...It is difficult to
comprehend how so acute a writer should have been blind
to what must strike every intelligent reader as a palpable
inconsistency[3].' But it is just this inconsistency, *in the
state of the popular mind*, that the nature of the transition
at each end of the episode serves to reveal. Thucydides
has other and more particular mistakes to show : but we
had best review in brief his whole handling of the matter.

The Salaminia had come to fetch Alcibiades : ever
since the expedition started, the people at home had
been in a mood of nervous and credulous suspicion ; for
there was a legend which said that the last oppressions
of the Pisistratid tyranny had been removed, not by
Athenians and Harmodius, but by the Lacedæmonians[4].
The main muddle is thus declared point-blank. To see
why the people thought of the Pisistratidæ at all, we must
recall the story of Harmodius and Aristogiton, noting
some further muddles in the vulgar tradition of that affair ;

[1] Cf. Thuc. I, 20.
[2] Mure, *Lang. and Lit. Ant. Gr.* vol. v, pp. 130 ff.
[3] *Ibid.*   [4] Thuc. VI, 53. 2.

for it can be shown that 'even the Athenians are no
nearer being accurate than other people in their accounts
of their own tyrants or of what actually occurred[1].' They
think that Hipparchus succeeded Pisistratus. They are
wrong : it was Hippias. Their mistake is due to the
fact that it was Hipparchus whom the conspirators
managed to kill. Up to that moment the tyranny had
not been really oppressive or unpopular : but after the
murder—the issue of a private quarrel, aggravated in a
manner not mentioned in the common tradition—the
oppressions of Hippias began ; and these were only
stopped by the Lacedæmonians and the Alcmæonidæ[2].
The people, though aware of this last point, had persisted
in their error, and had come to look upon Hipparchus as
the oppressive tyrant who was removed by the heroic
patriotism of Harmodius and Aristogiton[3]. All this is
stupid enough : but when the affair of the Hermæ arose,
they went about reminding one another that it was a
religious ceremony (of the Great Panathenæa) that gave
the occasion of the attack on the Pisistratidæ, and that
this new profanation must betoken another revolutionary
plot[4]. And so they completely lost their heads. As the
Bastard put it to King John—

> 'I finde the people strangely fantasied,
> Possest with rumors, full of idle dreames,
> Not knowing what they feare, but full of feare.
> And here's a Prophet that I brought with me
> From forth the streets of Pomfret, whom I found
> With many hundreds treading on his heeles :
> To whom he sung in rude harsh sounding rimes,
> That ere the next Ascension day at noone,
> Your Highnes should deliver up your Crowne[5].'

[1] VI, 54. I.
[2] VI, 59. 4.   [3] VI, 55. 4.
[4] VI, 60. I. Cf. the suspicions of an attempt at tyranny on the part of
Alcibiades (VI, 15. 4) which were mentioned to show the popular distrust of
his character.
[5] Shakespeare, *K. John*, IV, ii, 150 ff.

The common fear, arising partly out of the vagueness and the very discrepancies of oral tradition, and partly from the scares and superstitions which are rife in a time of war, became focussed on the thought that Alcibiades, like Pisistratus, might come in upon an unguarded Athens by the help of Sparta, who was even readier to set up a tyranny where there was none, than to pull down one that already existed. Besides, was there not a small force of Lacedæmonians now at the Isthmus, apparently about to act in concert with the Bœotians[1]? Over certain other points in the body of the digression we need not linger. Few will think it enough to utter the mythic formula—'Heavenly Twins and Insulted Sister[2]'—and pass on : no one who cares to observe how the evidence for a correct version of the story has been sought and sifted and arranged[3] will welcome the device of classing Thucydides with Herodotus, Plutarch and other uncritical writers, in order to show that he ought so to be classed[4]. We may perhaps agree that the controversial tone of the discussion suggests that the writer had been subjected to criticism with regard to his earlier treatment of the matter[5]; which, according to this view, must have become known by the separate publication of his first project, the History of the Ten Years' War. But what concerns us now is to note the effectiveness with which some special knowledge of facts about the traditional tyrant-slayers has been employed to expose the inconsistencies of popular thought and their immediate results, —a confused feeling of fright, blundering apprehensions, and indiscriminate arrests[6]. It is the more likely, therefore, that even in the high places of politics Thucydides

---

[1] VI, 61. 2.　　　　　　　[2] *Th. M.* p. 133.
[3] Cf. esp. VI, 54–55.　　　[4] Cf. above, p. 60.
[5] Grundy, *Thuc. and the Hist. of his Age*, p. 426.
[6] VI, 60. 2.

will indicate the faults and failures of that 'enlightenment' of which he is usually considered to have been more a partaker than a spectator.

§ 4

It may be no unprofitable fancy, if we suppose for a moment that Thucydides had remained in Athens during those 'twenty years after the command at Amphipolis[1].' When we remember that Socrates, for the whole of that period[2], was living, thinking and talking in Athens, and when we find him frequenting those private intelligent circles on the fringe of political life in which Thucydides must have been a conspicuous figure, it is worth while to try to calculate our probable loss and gain.   It is to be supposed that the historian would have ranked politically with 'the middle sort of citizens[3],' which would also include Nicias, Theramenes and Socrates.   This neutral party, as the History tells us, suffered doubly in the revolutions of the Greek states, falling a prey in turn to the democrats and to the aristocrats ; and it was represented in Athens by the moderate or old-fashioned democracy professed by Alcibiades[4].   Its principles were broadly those of the democracy contrived by Theramenes in 411 under the name of the 'Five Thousand,' which we have seen commended by Thucydides[5].   It may have been Socrates' rigid adherence to these principles which provoked the extreme democrats to remove him in 399; just as Theramenes had been a victim of the Thirty in 403. Thucydides, when he returned to Athens, would come under the same sort of suspicions : but as to where and how he died, we have no real information.

[1] v, 26. 5.

[2] The order of words in Plato, *Apol.* 28 F, implies that Socrates served at Amphipolis before he fought at Delium (424 B.C.).

[3] III, 82 fin.—τὰ μέσα τῶν πολιτῶν.   [4] VI, 89. 6.

[5] VIII, 97. 2 ; above, p. 64.

Had he never been banished, it is possible that he might have been drawn away from history, and led by moral inquiry into the discussion of matters which make hardly any express appearance in the book which he wrote.   On the other hand, he might have distrusted the Socratic subtleties, and followed rather, with Antiphon, the path of rhetoric and politics.   But it is most likely that he would have pursued his historical researches, and travelled occasionally to obtain the best material for his work.   However, imagine what we may, the effort is not wasted, if it helps to fix our opinion of his intellectual power.   About equal in age with Socrates, and subject, in youth and early manhood, to the same surrounding influences, he possessed a mind of almost equally penetrative force.   Socrates, it is true, has done more solid and extensive service to humanity ; he had rare qualities of character which first prompted him to that service, and then, sustaining his endeavour, gained fuller strength with each recruit of intimacy and conviction.   Thucydides, while gifted with a larger faculty of observation, stood aloof, at least as it befell in the end, from those petty problems of every-day life of whose real greatness it required the genius of Plato to persuade the world.   He was as proud as anyone of the splendid civilisation which attained its bloom in the sway and ease and beauty of Athens ; of this admiration he has made the Funeral Oration an everlasting witness.   Yet Athens, to his eye, was but the consummate centre of the whole Hellenic tapestry.   He could not fasten attention on his native city alone ; and fate forbade him a place in the intricate texture of her interior life.

Both of these men were stirred by the utility of examining the ways of the world as it passed before their eyes; with this difference, however, that while Thucydides relied, for the significance of his report, on the appeal to the best prevailing conceptions of justice, honesty and 'the unwritten laws[1],' Socrates busied himself, in a more limited sphere, with investigating those conceptions themselves.   Both, on this practical plane, felt a sacred hunger for the truth ; yet neither would readily venture on a positive assertion.   The spectacle of life and thought was so absorbing, and besides, so complicated, that the personal utterance of the interpreter seemed like a vain intrusion ; and the authoritative tone is almost as remote in Thucydides' History as in the earlier Dialogues of the disciple of Socrates.

Yet, if the historian makes no pretension to the real secrets of existence, neither is he to be regarded as a humble or diffident thinker in his chosen field of view. His grasp of each series of events, and of the characters and motives which mainly determined these, has a sureness and a strength which must depend on something more than a sharp perception aided by the local detachment of his exile.   There is a peculiar pride of independence and security which makes itself felt, not merely in his few corrective essays and notes, but in the very quality of his reserves and silences on every page. As the war progressed, and particularly as it dragged out its final stages, he came to feel and rely upon the confidence of a unique understanding.   Other judgements, he seems to have assured himself, were ignorant, or vague, or partial, or circumscribed : he alone saw how the whole story hung together, and how it might be presented as a unity, compendious and intelligible to future ages, with all the intermingling of accident and calculation, of thought and action, of persons, words and events.   But nevertheless, even the horses of Alcibiades[2] shall not draw from him an explicit lesson or moral. Here and there he will let fall a sentence of blame or

[1] II, 37. 3.   [2] VI, 12. 2 ; 16. 2.

praise, but chiefly in terms of actual reputation, and seldom risking the claims of his own consideration as a judge. He will simply set down feelings and facts in their proper places, and leave us to judge for ourselves. And lastly, he has a special dislike of many words. His abstract of Hellenic life will contrive to imply much that has to be left untold ; and if his readers, in excited curiosity, are importunate for further explanation, he is determined, like Pericles[1], to give these anxious people the best of his material service, and say no more. If they demand theories, they must make them on their own account : he is not going to join the pitiful company of historians who have a genius for saying things that turn out to be foolish.

[1] II, 21. 3–22. I—ἐκάκιζον ὅτι στρατηγὸς ὢν οὐκ ἐπεξάγοι...Περικλῆς δὲ... πιστεύων ὀρθῶς γιγνώσκειν...τήν τε πόλιν ἐφύλασσε καὶ δι' ἡσυχίας μάλιστα ὅσον ἐδύνατο εἶχεν.

CHAPTER IV

NARRATIVE PROSE

§ I

Iᴛ has been necessary to dwell on the intellect of Thucydides, not for the reason that it happens to be interesting in itself and deserving of a correct appreciation to-day, but because the mind and style of a serious writer are connected with each other like the stem and leaves of a tree. It is useless to criticise a manner of speech without some regard to the shape and foundation of the spirit within. Dr Johnson assured the readers of his Dictionary that he was 'not yet so lost in lexicography, as to forget that *words are the daughters of earth, and that things are the sons of heaven*[1].' If we shall be occupied with the outward shows of artifice, it will be in order to watch the interior struggle, betrayed especially in the style of Thucydides, between thought and expression. In cases of a more thoroughly accomplished skill, the study of style is notoriously delusive: a form perfectly suited to its matter defies, as impossible or absurd, our analytic dissection. In some exquisite feats of writing, the words seem to retire from notice, as it were, at the very moment of bringing us into contact with the informing mind, and with the thought or scene which is in possession there: such was the supreme touch of art that wrought the conclusion of the *Phædo*. A piece like

---

[1] Johnson, *Dict. Eng. Lang*. Pref.

this is not to be anatomised: the thing is a perfect whole, and we can do little more towards marking the perfection, than to say there is hardly any style at all[1]: as lately has been said of a great lyric poet,—'his Muse has become a veritable Echo, whose body has dissolved from about her voice[2]'; while the effect of ordinary words under the impulse of keen thought and feeling is familiar to us in the satire of Swift. But there are also certain elevations of style, where it is largely the sound of the words that lifts and sustains the thought upon heights of noble splendour. In this sort of writing also—for example, in the elaborate imagery of the *Phædrus* and in the persuasive myths of other dialogues—Plato seems to smile at any particular inspection of his technique: just as in some places of Sir Thomas Browne and Jeremy Taylor, and of such truants from traditional strictness as Ruskin and Pater, we can note a cunning device here and there, but cannot take account of the variously conscious searching and selection which went to the fashioning of the whole piece. Its art is too complex, too copious in resource of rhythm and tune and suggestion, to be measured by a neat and rigorous rule. It is rather where a new instrument is wielded by an original mind, and some new modes of thought are met and developed by the practice of a growing skill, that the devices of expression can be clearly observed and described. No doubt there are phrases and sentences, even in the stage of formative effort that we shall illustrate by the style of Thucydides, which for simple nobility can stand among the greatest of their kind: the Funeral Oration, and several passages in the Sicilian Expedition,

[1] Cf. Archer-Hind's note (*Phædo*, 1894, p. 147)—'the sad music of this solemn close.' This critic, above most others in recent times, had an ear for the melody unheard.

[2] Francis Thompson, *Shelley*, 1909, p. 66. The article was written in 1889 but not published till 1908 (*Dublin Review*, July: separately printed, 1909).

will supply some shining examples. But it is our purpose to follow his main endeavour as an artist; and this happens to have aimed at something rather different from the 'simplicity which is a large part of nobility[1].'

This phrase demands particular notice, as it comes at the close of a very remarkable essay in literary art. The chapter on the Troubles in Greece[2] shows a frank ambition for effect, in the deliberate choice and arrangement of its words, implicitly avowed by the author. It is a part of his narrative, and yet it glitters forth in bold relief from the rest; nor can any of it, like the several complexions of the speeches, be attributed to any intention save that of the writer's own direct pronouncement to the reader. The manner of it is vigorous, terse, and for the most part clear. Two or three small corrections have been proposed by the critics: but taking the chapter as a whole, we find no difficulty as to the meaning; while the expression tends to be so uniform that its character is only too easily perceived. The distinctive features will appear most plainly if we set it beside a piece of the more ordinary narrative. A chapter of the first Book offers an instance of straightforward story-telling: the adventures of Themistocles[3], as we have already noticed, seem to bring Thucydides near to the manner of Herodotus :—

κat (ἦν γὰρ ἀγνὼς τοῖς ἐν τῇ νηί) δείσας φράζει τῷ ναυκλήρῳ ὅστις ἐστὶ καὶ δι' ἃ φεύγει, καὶ εἰ μὴ σώσει αὐτόν, ἔφη ἐρεῖν ὅτι χρήμασι πεισθεὶς αὐτὸν ἄγει· τὴν δὲ ἀσφάλειαν εἶναι μηδένα ἐκβῆναι ἐκ τῆς νεὼς μέχρι πλοῦς γένηται· πειθομένῳ δ' αὐτῷ χάριν ἀπομνησθήσεσθαι κατ' ἀξίαν. ὁ δὲ ναύκληρος ποιεῖ τε ταῦτα καὶ ἀποσαλεύσας ἡμέραν καὶ νύκτα ὑπὲρ τοῦ στρατοπέδου ὕστερον ἀφικνεῖται ἐς Ἔφεσον.

1 Thuc. III, 83. 1—τὸ εὔηθες, οὗ τὸ γενναῖον πλεῖστον μετέχει.
2 III, 82.   3 I, 137. 2 ; above, p. 16.

Now let us turn to the Troubles in Greece[1]:—

καὶ τὴν εἰωθυῖαν ἀξίωσιν τῶν ὀνομάτων ἐς τὰ ἔργα ἀντήλλαξαν τῇ δικαιώσει. τόλμα μὲν γὰρ ἀλόγιστος ἀνδρία φιλέταιρος ἐνομίσθη, μέλλησις δὲ προμηθὴς δειλία εὐπρεπής, τὸ δὲ σῶφρον τοῦ ἀνάνδρου πρόσχημα, καὶ τὸ πρὸς ἅπαν ξυνετὸν ἐπὶ πᾶν ἀργόν· τὸ δ᾽ ἐμπλήκτως ὀξὺ ἀνδρὸς μοίρᾳ προσετέθη, ἀσφάλεια δὲ τοῦ ἐπιβουλεύσασθαι ἀποτροπῆς πρόφασις εὔλογος.

The former piece, to be sure, is carefully written, with attention to the rise and fall of the clauses. The parenthesis ἦν γὰρ...νηί is answered by δείσας...φεύγει, and εἰ μὴ...αὐτόν by ἔφη...ἄγει, these two 'periods' or 'compasses' making two limbs of the larger period, from the beginning to ἄγει. The sentence is wound up by a couple of clauses—τὴν δὲ...γένηται, and πειθομένῳ δ᾽... κατ᾽ ἀξίαν—which are roughly poised against each other, and together make some effort at balancing that larger period : but they are loosely tacked on, and the sense of incompleteness is remedied by the length and weightiness of the following sentence—ὁ δὲ...Ἔφεσον. The total effect is of rising steadily, then hesitating, and finally sliding back to the level of inaction. Thus we can observe a definite attempt to arrange the 'running' or 'strung-together' style (λέξις εἰρομένη),—which in its rude beginnings is mere babble,—in some kind of order corresponding to the thought ; though probably the effort is only so far conscious, that it springs from a desire to be brief as well as clear,—to choose a few plain words, and make the most of them.

The second piece is no less intent on brevity, but its method bears witness to an entirely new ambition in prose-writing. The first sentence is not so strikingly different from the ordinary narrative : but already there are

[1] III, 82. 4.

contrasts of thoughts and words (τῶν ὀνομάτων ἐς τὰ ἔργα, ἀξίωσιν—δικαιώσει). After this preparation for the claims of sense upon sound, we enter at once upon a series of examples whose similarity and persistence more than amply illustrate the opening proposition. It might seem enough to say that the author has seized the opportunity of indulging in a little 'fine writing': but what, in fact, has he done? Not only has he split up each limb of each minor period into two opposing halves, and thus reduced the elements of the sentence to nearly the lowest limit of each (τόλμα ἀλόγιστος—ἀνδρία φιλέταιρος),—indeed, but crudely avoiding the phrase τὸ ξυνετὸν ἀργόν,—but in one case he insists on the balance of two halves by a kind of jingle (μέλλησις προμηθής—δειλία εὐπρεπής). So for some length further they move along, two abreast, as it were, in quick procession : some pairs more adorned or interesting than others, but always white and black, white and black. We may glance at them, to laugh and turn away with a shrug: but, on the other hand, they are the work of a man whose attempts to impress his thought upon our minds are likely to be the more interesting for being over-laboured. If he were only a shallow phrase-maker, there would be excuse enough for relegating such artificial experiments to the monkey-house frivolities of a curious scrap-book. Here, in an extreme case selected for contrast, we should see how the same man who can often make words the almost unnoticed servants of his more straight-running thought, is engrossed in the task of drilling them for a peculiar moral effect. He has got a grasp, and is trying the first uses, of that instrument whose compendious force was afterwards developed and recognised as periodic form ; and if his efforts seem awkward in their lack of disguise, it is because he is urged by the unusual importance of some complex ideas to express and communicate them

in their original organic vigour. 'The utmost energy of
the nervous style of Thucydides,' observes a writer[1] whose
own strength of thought and style gives him a special
claim to be heard, 'and the copiousness and expression
of the Greek language, seem to sink under that historian,
when he attempts to describe the disorders which arose
from faction throughout all the Grecian commonwealths.
You would imagine that he still labours with a thought
greater than he can find words to communicate.' This
remark of Hume's rightly points to the stern *labour* of
the struggle in bringing out a particular thought; but
the difficulty comes not so much of *greatness* of thought
and lack of forcible language, as of a sudden endeavour
to make the reader or hearer realise, under a steady
process of clashing and drumming, the unique mental
scene which the author desires to represent. In cold
scholastic phrase, he is applying antithesis to the construction of the period; and he is anxious to enforce his
antitheses with similarities of size and sound[2]. It follows
naturally from the severe economy of such a structure,
that words are occasionally stretched into unusual shades
of meaning, and poetical or uncustomary compounds are
brought into play. Dionysius has filled many pages with
corrections and complaints[3]. But for us at this stage it
will be enough to grasp the main difference between the
two schemes we have just considered, before proceeding
to inquire how Thucydides could have seriously devised
them both. Our best plan will be to look at once for
signs of the period in early Greek prose.

---

[1] Hume, *Of the Populousness of Ancient Nations.*
[2] Dionys. *De Thuc.* 887—παρίσωσις, παρομοίωσις.
[3] *De Thuc.* 883–896.

§ 2

Dionysius begins his criticism of Thucydides' historical
method with the mention of those earlier historians whose
works were extant in his day[1]. The first eight of these
—Eugeon, Deïochus, Eudemus, Democles, Hecatæus,
Acusilaus, Charon and Melesagoras—are placed a good
while previous to the Peloponnesian War. After them,
as flourishing a little before it, and living on till
Thucydides was in his manhood[2], he gives the names
of Hellanicus, Damastes, Xenomedes and Xanthus ; and
adds that there were a number of others. Each of these
dealt with the traditions of some single tribe or city,
either Greek or foreign ; and their aim was to make a
plain story, for general knowledge, out of the ancient
records attached to each place. He tells us incidentally
that their style was, for the most part, clear, ordinary,
simple and concise, keeping close to their matters, and
showing no artistic elaboration[3]. He next mentions
Herodotus, notes the wide range and variety of his field,
and remarks that he made his style complete by adding
the excellences neglected by his predecessors[4]. Some
way further on, the critic prefaces his examination of
Thucydides' style by repeating and amplifying these
statements : he tells now[5] of two very early writers—
Cadmus of Miletus and Aristæus (the Aristeas quoted
by Herodotus[6]) of Proconnesus ; but the works of these
and other ancient chroniclers, he says, are either wholly

---

[1] *De Thuc.* 818–820.

[2] I.e. when he began to compile his notes : *De Thuc.* 818—μέχρι τῆς
Θουκυδίδου παρεκτείναντες ἡλικίας. Cf. Thuc. V, 26. 5—αἰσθανόμενος τῇ
ἡλικίᾳ.

[3] *De Thuc.* 820—λέξιν τὴν σαφῆ καὶ κοινὴν καὶ καθαρὰν καὶ σύντομον καὶ
τοῖς πράγμασι προσφυῆ καὶ μηδεμίαν σκευωρίαν ἐπιφαίνουσαν τεχνικήν.

[4] *De Thuc.* 821—τῇ λέξει προσαπέδωκε τὰς παραλειφθείσας ὑπὸ τῶν πρὸ
αὐτοῦ συγγραφέων ἀρετάς.

[5] *De Thuc.* 864.   [6] Herod. IV, 13.

lost or extant only in fragments of doubtful authenticity. Before turning to Thucydides, he bestows a more specific praise on the narrative manner of Herodotus; nor, as his criticism proceeds on its rather querulous way, does he forget the rhetorical influence of Gorgias and his school[1].

The only one of these historians whom Thucydides has mentioned by name is Hellanicus[2], the Ionian chronologist who lived to record Andocides as an orator of repute[3], and to see the end of the Peloponnesian War[4]. That Thucydides was familiar with the History of Herodotus (the contemporary of Hellanicus) is almost certain: apart from the controversial tone of some of his statements[5], it is hardly credible that he should have missed reading the great story of the Persian Invasions, if not in his exile, at least after his return to Athens[6]. But the same approach to certainty, though greatly to be desired for our purpose, is impossible as regards the other writers. It is safe only to suppose that he probably read, or heard read, a good number of their chronicles, before he made his contemptuous remark on certain prose-writers (λογογράφοι) who sought to be attractive rather than truthful[7]. We need only look at a few translations of their fragments[8] to see how alike they are in an ingenuous addiction to marvels: though it would

---

[1] *De Thuc.* 869.　　　　　　[2] Thuc. I, 97. 2.

[3] Suidas, s.v. Ἀνδοκίδης ; Plut. *Alcib.* xxi ; Müller, Hellan. frag. 78.

[4] Schol. Aristoph. *Ran.* 706 ; Müller, frag. 80.

[5] E.g., Thuc. I, 20—Herod. VI, 57, IX, 53 ; Thuc. II, 97—Herod. V, 3, IV, 46; see further examples in Jebb, 'The Speeches of Thuc.' (*Hellenica*), § 3.

[6] In spite of Plut. *de Herod. Malign.* 862 a, it is quite probable that Herodotus read some part of his History in public at Athens about 445 B.C.; cf. Euseb. *Chron.* II, 339. The recitation at Olympia (Lucian, *Herod.* i) is on several grounds improbable. The story of the young Thucydides being moved to tears by Herodotus reading some of the book to Olorus, may perhaps be regarded as an echo of some real meeting in private.

[7] Thuc. I, 21. 1.　　　　　　[8] Cf. Forbes, Bk I, Intr. pp. xlvi-l.

be wrong to judge their whole work, both historical and literary, on the evidence of a few examples preserved by curiosity-hunters like Athenæus. It is easy to imagine how far we should be from the real Herodotus if his work had survived on the same unhappy terms. As for the tale of Orestheus and his bitch, whether we are to suppose it a quotation made by Hecatæus himself or not, it is such a useful example of the 'strung-together' style, in nearly its purest form, that it will be worth while to glance at the original[1] :—

Ὀρεσθεὺς ὁ Δευκαλίωνος ἦλθεν εἰς Αἰτωλίαν ἐπὶ βασιλέα, καὶ κύων αὐτῷ στέλεχος ἔτεκε. καὶ ὃς ἐκέλευσε αὐτὸν κατορυχθῆναι· καὶ ἐξ αὐτοῦ ἔφυ ἄμπελος πολυστάφυλος. διὸ καὶ τὸν αὐτοῦ παῖδα Φύτιον ἐκάλεσε. τούτου δ' Οἰνεὺς ἐγένετο, κληθεὶς ἀπὸ τῶν ἀμπέλων· οἱ γὰρ παλαιοὶ Ἕλληνες οἴνας ἐκάλουν τὰς ἀμπέλους. Οἰνέως δ' ἐγένετο Αἰτωλός.

The clauses are merely tacked on, as the need of explanation arises ; there is no working up to the etymological point, no aim at producing a distinct impression. The writer's technique, if such he can be said to possess, goes no further than marking off each clause, where he conveniently can, by means of a long final word. Another good instance of this jerky, piecemeal style is provided by a fragment of the mythographer Pherecydes[2], which relates the story of Pelias and Jason :—

ἔθνε ὁ Πελίας τῷ Ποσειδῶνι, καὶ προεῖπε πᾶσι παρεῖναι. οἱ δὲ ἦσαν οἵ τε ἄλλοι πολῖται καὶ ὁ Ἰήσων· ἔτυχε δὲ ἀροτρεύων ἐγγὺς τοῦ Ἀναύρου ποταμοῦ. ἀσάνδαλος δὲ διέβαινε τὸν ποταμόν· διαβὰς δὲ, τὸν μὲν δεξιὸν ὑποδεῖται πόδα, τὸν δὲ ἀριστερὸν ἐπιλήθεται. καὶ ἔρχεται οὕτως ἐπὶ δεῖπνον. ἰδὼν δὲ ὁ Πελίας συμβάλλει τὸ μαντήϊον.

---

[1] Athenæus II, 35 ; Müller, Hecat. frag. 341.
[2] Schol. Pindar, *Pyth.* IV, 133 ; Müller, Pherec. frag. 60.

There is an attempt at impressiveness here in the alliteration of the first sentence ; and a sort of connective balance is obtained by διέβαινε...διαβάς, and τὸν μὲν δεξιόν...τὸν δὲ ἀριστερόν; but the general effect of even so small a piece is patchy and tiresome.

Moving down from the beginning towards the middle of the fifth century we meet, in the chief fragment of Charon of Lampsacus, a distinct advance towards large-ness and freedom ; though there is still no sign of a definite plan. A few sentences will show the larger reach and more varied arrangement of phrase[1] :—

καὶ ἀποδρὰς ἐκ τῆς Καρδίης εἰς τὴν πατρίδα τοὺς Βισάλτας ἔστειλεν ἐπὶ τοὺς Καρδιηνούς, ἀποδειχθεὶς ἡγέμων ὑπὸ τῶν Βισαλτέων. οἱ δὲ Καρδιηνοὶ πάντες τοὺς ἵππους ἐδίδαξαν ἐν τοῖς συμποσίοις ὀρχεῖσθαι ὑπὸ τῶν αὐλῶν. καὶ ἐπὶ τῶν ὀπισθίων ποδῶν ἱστάμενοι τοῖς προσθίοις ὠρχοῦντο ἐξεπιστάμενοι τὰ αὐλήματα. ταῦτα οὖν ἐπιστάμενος Ὄναρις ἐκτήσατο ἐκ τῆς Καρδίης αὐλητρίδα.

Yet the writer has no command of effective order. At the beginning of the story we had been told that the Bisaltians invaded Cardia successfully ; then that the Bi-saltian general Onaris had been at one time enslaved to a Cardian barber; and that in the shop he had heard people talk of an oracle about a Bisaltian invasion. The piece here quoted relates how he escaped to his native country, and led a Bisaltian army against the Cardians : but to understand the tactical device (of making the horses dance to the flute) on which he based his hopes, we have to go back to an ancient custom of the Cardians, glance again at the time of his servitude (to see how he came to know of this custom), and then note the provision he made before invading Cardia. And when the horses behaved as he expected in the battle, we have to be told that the Cardians

---

[1] Athenæus, XII, 19 ; Müller, Charon, frag. 9.

set great store by their cavalry, before we reach the concluding καὶ οὕτως ἐνικήθησαν. One obvious result of this haphazard manner is the constant repetition, for clearness, of the proper names : but this was probably an enjoyment to the writer, who found that he could give his clauses a kind of finish by weighting them at the end, now and again, with these sonorous words[1].

There is a sentence of Thucydides where the same kind of awkwardness appears : possibly we ought to take it as an unrevised note, whose substance has been abstracted from one of the Peloponnesian authorities on which he is relying for the moment[2]. It is rather a costly moment for his style, as this part of the sentence will show :—

Εὐρυσθέως μὲν ἐν τῇ Ἀττικῇ ὑπὸ Ἡρακλειδῶν ἀπο-θανόντος, Ἀτρέως δὲ μητρὸς ἀδελφοῦ ὄντος αὐτῷ καὶ ἐπιτρέψαντος Εὐρυσθέως, ὅτ᾽ ἐστράτευε, Μυκήνας τε καὶ τὴν ἀρχὴν κατὰ τὸ οἰκεῖον Ἀτρεῖ (τυγχάνειν δὲ αὐτὸν φεύγοντα τὸν πατέρα διὰ τὸν Χρυσίππου θάνατον), καὶ ὡς οὐκέτι ἀνεχώρησεν Εὐρυσθεύς, κ.τ.λ.

Dionysius[3] quotes this merely to show the mischief wrought by over-much parenthesis : we shall view it rather as a reminder of the entanglements which the emphatic and compendious narrative of Thucydides was struggling to avoid.

The collected 'fragments' of Hellanicus provide us with a considerable amount of material for estimating the variety and extent of his writings[4] : but very few can be

---

[1] Note also the repetition, in the last two sentences, of ἱστάμενοι—ἐξεπιστάμενοι—ἐπιστάμενος, in which the variation of the compound points to a clumsy design of emphasis.

[2] Thuc. I, 9. 2—οἱ τὰ σαφέστατα Πελοποννησίων μνήμῃ παρὰ τῶν πρότερον δεδεγμένοι.

[3] Dionys. Ep. ad Amm. ii, 15.

[4] For the best classification and discussion, see Kullmer, Jahrb. für Class. Philol. 1902, Suppl. Band, xxvii, pp. 455-696.

regarded as preserving his original manner. From his book on Egypt the following short sentences remain, in a direct quotation of Athenæus[1] :—

πόλις ἐπιποταμίη, Τίνδιον ὄνομα. αὕτη θεῶν ὁμήγυρις, καὶ ἱερὸν μέγα καὶ ἁγνὸν ἐν μέσῃ τῇ πόλει λίθινον καὶ θύρετρα λίθινα. ἔσω τοῦ ἱεροῦ ἄκανθαι πεφύκασι λευκαὶ καὶ μέλαιναι. ἐπ' αὐτῇσι στέφανοι ἐπιβέβληνται ἄνω τῆς ἀκάνθου, τοῦ ἄνθεος καὶ ῥοιῆς ἄνθεος καὶ ἀμπέλου πεπλεγμένοι. καὶ οὗτοι ἀεὶ ἀνθέουσι.

After this and other examples which might be shown of the same sort, it is surprising to find one quotation whose style is built on a really shapely design. The Leyden Scholia on the *Iliad* give us the following passage from the *Trojan History*[2] :—

ὑπὸ τοῦτον τὸν χρόνον ἐν τῇ Ἴδῃ, ὅθεν καὶ ὁ Σκάμανδρος τὸ ῥεῖθρον ὑπερβαλὼν ὑπὸ τοῦ ὀμβρίου ὕδατος τὸ ἔχον κοῖλα χωρία ἐπῆλθεν, τῷ ῥοῒ τούτῳ ὁ Ἀχιλλεὺς ἡγούμενος τοῦ στρατοῦ πρῶτος ἐνέτυχε καὶ δείσας τὸν ῥοῦν, μή τί μιν πημήνῃ, ἐν τῷ πεδίῳ πτελέας πεφυκυίας λαβόμενος, ἐμετεώρισεν ἑαυτόν· οἱ δ' ἄλλοι προϊδόμενοι τὸν ῥοῦν ἐτράποντο, ὅπου ἐδύνατο ἕκαστος, ἄλλος ἄλλῃ, καὶ ἐπὶ τὰ τῶν ὀρῶν ὑπερέχοντα τοῦ πεδίου ἀπέβαινε.

It may be that the scholiast wrote from memory, and unconsciously recast the sentence : on the other hand, Hellanicus may have been able to rise at times from the level of the formless jottings which make up the greater part of his remains[3]. But whether it belongs to Hellanicus or not, it will serve to illustrate the early growth of prose-structure, both in extension and arrangement. The Scamander flows down from Mount Ida, swollen with

---

[1] Athenæus, XV, 679 f.; Müller, Hellan. frag. 150.

[2] Schol. Leid. Hom. *Il.* XXI, 235 ; Müller, Hellan. frag. 132.

[3] There are signs of this in a long sentence quoted from his Attic Records by the scholiast on Eurip. *Orest.* 1648 ; Müller, Hellan. frag. 82.

the rains; overflows its banks; and covers the low-lying ground with water. When he has told us so much, the writer collects it (τῷ ῥοῒ τούτῳ) for Achilles and his exploit; which are also given us in proper order, leading up to the top or turning-point of the period (ἐμετεώρισεν ἑαυτόν). Hence we descend, rather hurriedly, in the account of what the army did. The affair is barely and briefly told, and the structure is therefore all the easier to see; while the *intention* of building for continuous effect is evident, not only from the neat use of participles, but from the insertion of the one phrase (ἄλλος ἄλλῃ) which could almost be spared, yet which serves to stretch out the time of the conclusion. The whole piece may thus be regarded as an attempt, though probably not conscious in every detail, towards a larger and more powerful form than the old patchwork of little clauses; and this design, together with its economy of words, brings it nearer to the normal narrative of Thucydides than to the ample, flowing style of Herodotus.

§ 3

The true period, which attained its full strength in Demosthenes, is here seen in a very elementary stage. So far we have only remarked how the λέξις εἰρομένη began to be arranged for a composite effect; and if we speak of Herodotus as 'an artist in language[1],' we must try to delimit the sense in which this title is to be applied. That ever-fresh curiosity about each new aspect of human life, which we have considered[2] in relation to the moral interest of his discourses, is not accompanied by the rarer intensity of thought and feeling which strains every sinew of language in the endeavour to touch the bleak and often misty summit of truth. In the ordinary run of

---

[1] Murray, *Hist. Gr. Lit.* p. 141. [2] Above, pp. 29-30.

his story we find little more than an easy command of
speech, which is kept 'close to the matters[1]'; it is because
these are clearly seen, and imaginatively shaped into
attractive masses, and not because of any steady grasp on
their meaning and importance, that we are ready to call
him a literary artist. Indeed, without this looseness of
hold, he would lack much of his ingenuous charm. A
notable instance, where he interrupts his fine account of
Thermopylæ with the topic of the inheritance of Darius,
has been well cited against him in a comparison with
Thucydides[2]. His best effects are to be measured, like
those of Boccaccio or Malory, by the chapter rather than
the paragraph : at least a couple of pages would have
to be quoted, if justice should be done to his excellence.
Still, the pleasant unapprehensive air of his writing may
be illustrated by the following sentence[3], whose laxity is
just kept in significant order :—

Πηδασέες μέν νυν χρόνῳ ἐξαιρέθησαν, Λύκιοι δέ, ὡς ἐς
τὸ Ξάνθιον πεδίον ἤλασε ὁ Ἅρπαγος τὸν στρατόν, ἐπεξιόντες
καὶ μαχόμενοι ὀλίγοι πρὸς πολλοὺς ἀρετὰς ἀπεδείκνυντο,
ἐσσωθέντες δὲ καὶ κατειληθέντες ἐς τὸ ἄστυ συνήλισαν ἐς
τὴν ἀκρόπολιν τάς τε γυναῖκας καὶ τὰ τέκνα καὶ τὰ χρήματα
καὶ τοὺς οἰκέτας καὶ ἔπειτα ὑπῆψαν τὴν ἀκρόπολιν πᾶσαν
ταύτην καίεσθαι.

So it is that Herodotus pictures the affair to his mind,
and we cannot but admire the facility with which he
transmits the scene to us. A variety of examples might
be taken to show a greater or a less degree of formal
structure : for the present, it will be enough to note, in
this typical sentence, the use of μέν and δέ, the correspondence of ἐπεξιόντες καὶ μαχόμενοι and ἐσσωθέντες καὶ
κατειληθέντες, and the long final verbs ἐξαιρέθησαν and

---

[1] Above, p. 91.
[2] Croiset, *Notice sur Thuc.* p. 98.   [3] Herod. I, 176.

ἀπεδείκνυντο in the first and third clauses. Herodotus has a few pieces of carefully formal writing, which we shall have to consider in connection with rhetorical style: but the search for influences which may have helped to shape the normal narrative of Thucydides will find more promising ground in his intellectual relationship with Hippocrates.

The severe precision of Thucydides' mind, to which the methods of all former and contemporary chroniclers seemed so unsatisfactory, would find at least one writer whose works it could approve as creditable to the intellectual progress of Greece. The disputes and discussions which have wound themselves about the name of Hippocrates need not detain us here. Two modern experts[1] have probed to the solid core, and have established a certain number of treatises as the genuine works of the physician of Cos who was a contemporary of Socrates and Thucydides. One of these works, the *Prognostic*, which seems to have been among his earliest compositions, begins in this manner[2]:—

τὸν ἰητρὸν δοκέει μοι ἄριστον εἶναι πρόνοιαν ἐπιτηδεύειν· προγιγνώσκων γὰρ καὶ προλέγων παρὰ τοῖσι νοσέουσι τά τε παρεόντα καὶ τὰ προγεγονότα καὶ τὰ μέλλοντα ἔσεσθαι, ὁκόσα τε παραλείπουσιν οἱ ἀσθενέοντες ἐκδιηγεύμενος, πιστεύοιτ' ἂν μᾶλλον γιγνώσκειν τὰ τῶν νοσεόντων πρήγματα, ὥστε τολμᾶν ἐπιτρέπειν τοὺς ἀνθρώπους σφέας ἑωυτοὺς τῷ ἰητρῷ. τὴν δὲ θεραπείην ἄριστα ἂν ποιέοιτο προειδὼς τὰ ἐσόμενα ἐκ τῶν παρεόντων παθημάτων.

One can hardly read even so far without thinking of Thucydides' preface to his account of the plague[3]:—

ἐγὼ δὲ οἷόν τε ἐγίγνετο λέξω, καὶ ἀφ' ὧν ἄν τις σκοπῶν,

[1] Littré, *Œuvres d'Hippocrate*, 1840; Greenhill, *Smith's Dict. Gr. Rom. Biog. Myth.* 1846. [2] Littré, *Œuv. d'Hipp.* II, p. 110.
[3] Thuc. II, 48. 3.

εἴ ποτε καὶ αὖθις ἐπιπέσοι, μάλιστ᾽ ἂν ἔχοι τι προειδὼς μὴ
ἀγνοεῖν, ταῦτα δηλώσω αὐτός τε νοσήσας καὶ αὐτὸς ἰδὼν
ἄλλους πάσχοντας.

Besides the grave confidence in diligent study which
supports the thought of both passages, we should observe
what a serious, persevering intelligence it is that forms
the very framework of each long sentence. In the first
piece, there is a steady rise to the important clause
πιστεύοιτ᾽ ἄν...πρήγματα : but it is also remarkable how
many things are comprised in so small a number of
words. The sphere of προγιγνώσκων and προλέγων is
extended, to make a fuller impression of thoroughness,
to τὰ παρέοντα and τὰ προγεγονότα ; which increases the
scope of the verbs to something like 'seeing and telling
at a glance,' or 'without hearing all that the patient has
to say': while the effect of this little climax consists in
the use of present and past symptoms for predicting the
future course of the malady. Thus, by his choice and
arrangement of words, Hippocrates has filled his small
space with a great deal of meaning. The case is like
that of a heavy man ascending a ladder which is just able
to bear his weight: it bends, but can be trusted not to
break. The sentence of Thucydides, quoted in the first
instance for the similarity of its general outlook and
tone, will serve at the same time as a fair example of his
economy in reaching a point like ταῦτα δηλώσω, and of
a satisfactory descent or return, where he gives his
personal justification. The main support of the close-knit
structure in each passage is the dexterous management
of participles,—a method apparent in every chapter of
the History. We also find in this piece of Hippocrates that pregnant μᾶλλον which has been distinguished
as specially Thucydidean[1]. But although there is this

---

[1] Cobet, *Var. Lect.* p. 291 (1873); Dobree, *Advers. in Thuc.* ed.
Wagner, 1883, I, p. 44 (*e.g.* Thuc. I, 3. 2, VIII, 71. 3).

conciseness and weightiness in Hippocrates, he does not venture on such daring short-cuts as Thucydides,—for instance, when an adverb is made to work with a preposition[1] :—

ὄντα ἀνεξέλεγκτα καὶ τὰ πολλὰ ὑπὸ χρόνου αὐτῶν ἀπίστως ἐπὶ τὸ μυθῶδες ἐκνενικηκότα—

or when he thrusts a negative on to a verbal noun[2] —

τὴν οὐ περιτείχισιν—τὴν οὐκ ἐξουσίαν—τὴν τῶν γεφυρῶν...τότε δι᾽ αὐτὸν οὐ διάλυσιν—

the first of which provoked Dionysius to a sadly confused misquotation[3]; or when he compresses rather too much thought into a note on the Athenian character[4] :—

οἷς τὸ μὴ ἐπιχειρούμενον ἀεὶ ἐλλιπὲς ἦν τῆς δοκήσεώς τι πράξειν.

Thucydides was an Athenian too; and merely by observing his own way of putting it, one might be prompted to say of his literary daring that to it 'a feat left unattempted was so much success resigned.' For in these and similar cases the condensation is due to a desire, not simply of brevity, but of stamping a strange phrase on the reader's memory, even at the risk of not being immediately understood. We shall have to notice some bold attempts of this sort in the speeches, along with the influences to which this ambition is in part to be ascribed. But the narrative of the History, though occasionally contracted—particularly where the tone is personal and self-conscious—into this difficult sententious brevity, achieves on the whole an excellent union of freedom with precision. The wonderful results of such a rare combination appear especially in large pieces of

---

[1] Thuc. I, 21. 1.
[2] Thuc. III, 95. 2; V, 50. 4; I, 137. 4; cf. Eurip. *Hippol.* 196—κοὐκ ἀπόδειξιν τῶν ὑπὸ γαίας.
[3] Dionys. *Ad Amm.* II, 796.   [4] Thuc. IV, 55. 2.

the Sicilian Expedition[1]. Leaving the more elevated and complex passages for a later inspection, we must consider here a rather lengthy sentence, where Thucydides attains one of his best successes in the expansive structural schemes on which he continually spent his most serious and persistent efforts[2]:—

οἱ δ᾽ ἐχώρουν, Συρακόσιοι μὲν περί τε πατρίδος μαχούμενοι καὶ τῆς ἰδίας ἕκαστος τὸ μὲν αὐτίκα σωτηρίας, τὸ δὲ μέλλον ἐλευθερίας, τῶν δ᾽ ἐναντίων Ἀθηναῖοι μὲν περί τε τῆς ἀλλοτρίας οἰκείαν σχεῖν καὶ τὴν οἰκείαν μὴ βλάψαι ἡσσώμενοι, Ἀργεῖοι δὲ καὶ τῶν ξυμμάχων οἱ αὐτόνομοι ξυγκτήσασθαί τε ἐκείνοις ἐφ᾽ ἃ ἦλθον καὶ τὴν ὑπάρχουσαν σφίσι πατρίδα νικήσαντες πάλιν ἐπιδεῖν· τὸ δ᾽ ὑπήκοον τῶν ξυμμάχων μέγιστον μὲν περὶ τῆς αὐτίκα ἀνελπίστου σωτηρίας, ἢν μὴ κρατῶσι, τὸ πρόθυμον εἶχον, ἔπειτα δὲ ἐν παρέργῳ καὶ εἴ τι ἄλλο ξυγκαταστρεψάμενον ῥᾷον αὐτοῖς ὑπακούσεται.

Here is a framework holding in a compact yet regular order several collective states of mind. It makes rather heavy, though not really difficult, reading. But what is the nature of the strain? How is it that this sentence differs from anything that Herodotus ever dreamt of writing? The foremost answer is that neither Herodotus nor any of those earlier chroniclers ever had this kind of thing to say. If we are to rank Thucydides, along with Herodotus, as a tragic historian, let us recognise how widely their methods diverge. It will not suffice to say that Thucydides here prepares the dramatic scene of the first fight at Syracuse with a brief prologue which puts us in possession of the leading motives of the action. Dramatic enough, in fact, the incident was, like many more that were to follow; tragic also their leading features must have appeared, to the contemplation of

1 E.g. VII, 75.   2 Thuc. VI, 69. 3.

Thucydides : but we shall miss the chief intention and value of the History, if we neglect the formal conduct of this laborious sentence. In this one period we are presented first with the patriotic ardour of the Syracusans, and then with the gambling spirit of the Athenians; passing on to the allies, we find the independent primarily bent on a share in the conquest, with a secondary desire of seeing their homes again, while the subject feel that they have everything to lose and perhaps a little to gain. Shall we call this a piece of dramatic imagination ? Granted the object of describing a battle as fought by live human creatures who had their definite aims and feelings, shall we not rather perceive in the bare, explicit manner of this psychological summary almost the best evidence that Greek or any literature could afford us of a cool, scientific analysis ? So far from presenting a group of human puppets in the toils of delusive Hope, and hurried perforce into the clutch of Nemesis, Thucydides seems to ask us to attend for a moment to the distinctive thoughts and emotions which underlay the different sides in the struggle he is about to describe[1]. *Appellez vous cela fureur poëticque*[2] ?

This rigorous 'text-book' manner, which he instinctively chooses in his approach to a crucial point of his narrative, deserves more notice than it has received from our modern bias of interest towards the ornamental parts of his work. Attention has been drawn by at least one modern critic[3] to the fact that the smallest and most usual Thucydidean idioms are the witnesses of a constant strictness of logical thought,—'of such precision in the use of language as it would be difficult to parallel from

---

[1] Cf. the sentence in I, 25-26, noticed above, p. 51.
[2] Rabelais, *Pantagr.* III, 22.
[3] Rutherford, *Thuc. Bk* IV, 'On the Style and Diction of Thuc.,' 1889.

other authors[1].'   So a fair survey of the structure of his
sentences will bring home to us how strongly protected
he is against a fanciful or mythical interpretation of
events ; and we shall agree that when he came to set
down the matters most worthy of record, one of the
plainest and largest points he made was about himself,—
that he was 'not an imaginative writer like Aeschylus[2].'

§ 4

We turn now to a less successful result of Thucydides'
scientific zeal for vivid history,—a long sentence[3] whose
purpose might again be hastily termed dramatic, since its
office is not unlike that of a modern stage-direction at a
change of scene ; but which, on a closer view, will be
found to be more like a cold paraphrase, or a dry, methodical explanation.   Brasidas and Cleon are dead ; the
two great 'pestles of war,' as Aristophanes[4] called them,
are broken.   Two other figures take their places,—
Pleistoanax and Nicias.   The former pair are briefly
labelled with a couple of notes which contrast their public
aims ; and we pass to their successors, who are opposed
to them by the peacefulness of their ambitions, yet
contrasted with each other by the difference of their
private tastes.   This last comparison is more amply
expounded—so as to introduce the new course of affairs—
than that between Brasidas and Cleon ; and although the
author has in both cases availed himself of the ordinary
connections[5], the frame of the sentence is overloaded, and
drags heavily.   He is trying to tell in one breath what
this change in the leadership of the contest meant to
the discerning minds of Greece.   From all the talk and

---

[1] Rutherford, *l.c.* p. xviii.   [2] *Ib.* p. xvi.
[3] Thuc. V, 16. 1.   [4] Aristoph. *Pax*, 269, 282.
[5] E.g. the particles μέν and δέ.

speculation aroused thereby he has abstracted this essence, as most important for us to know: he has determined that it shall be grasped as one organic whole; he has endeavoured to express it accordingly, in compendious shape; and he has not quite succeeded. While our thoughts are made to dwell so earnestly on Pleistoanax and Nicias, the corresponding figures of Brasidas and Cleon seem to fade away. So again, at the end of the next chapter[1], the same arduous ambition, less cautiously pursued, has encumbered the sentence with two parentheses, the former of which is so big and busy with an argument of its own, that it spoils the continuous virtue of the period. It is possible that a skilful recital could carry such systems through, with their main force intact: but they are clumsy; and because they are the work of Thucydides, and fundamentally different from the other kinds of prose-writing which we have so far adduced for comparison with his, we ought to make sure that we are in a good position for observing more narrowly the plan of his contrivance.

It will be well, in the first place, to fix the meaning of the term 'period,' if not absolutely, at any rate for the uses of our discussion. We have already applied the word to the beginnings of orderly form in narrative prose[2]; for in its widest and most literal sense it merely means the rounding or circuit made by the rise and fall of the voice in anything beyond the simplest statement of fact; and this general meaning is fairly well given by the English word 'compass.' If we remember the conditions under which early prose began, the elementary stage of what Aristotle calls 'the period' may be viewed as an arrangement of words in a short sentence or clause,

---

[1] Thuc. V. 17. 2.
[2] Above, pp. 88, 97.

which would lead the reader's voice to rise a little, and
then fall to its first level : we hardly need the authority
of Aristoxenus for this familiar effect in ordinary conversation[1]. But it was the extension of this effect over
a number of clauses, combined for a system of thoughts,
that impelled the writer to range his important words in
prominent places, and to increase their impression by
the suspense of a rise or climax ; also to vary in appropriate degrees the abruptness of his descent to the
normal tone.

It may be guessed that the first transition from
singing to recitation, wherever it took place, was marked
by the construction of the hexameter out of two lines of
a short ballad metre ; and the desire for a still larger
literary form, conveying its own instruction to the voice,
produced the composite whole of the elegiac couplet; or
again, working on other metric bases, that of the lyric
'strophe.' The first efforts to arrange the artless 'bead-
stringing' style of prose (λέξις εἰρομένη) in the groups
which eventually grew to be periods is to be ascribed
to the same sort of impulse. As in the case of verse,
the primary object is to erect a framework that will create
a feeling of *suspense*, and defer the satisfaction of the ear
while the mind is intent on the meaning. Then, as the
writer came to be less dependent on skilful recitation to
help out the emphasis and connection, the completeness
of the period was made to coincide with a completeness
of grammar. For example, in the piece of Thucydides
quoted to illustrate his ordinary narrative[2], the periodic
effect, such as it is, can only be felt if the reader exerts
his intelligence to follow a few slight formal marks in
the light of the obvious meaning of the words. We have

---

[1] Aristoxenus, *Harm.* I, 18—φυσικὸν γὰρ τὸ ἐπιτείνειν καὶ ἀνιέναι ἐν τῷ
διαλέγεσθαι.

[2] Thuc. I, 137. 2 ; above, p. 87.

noticed an approach to a grammatically rounded period in a reputed fragment of Hellanicus[1]. If the story had been concerned with Achilles alone, the period would be complete at ἐμετεώρισεν ἑαυτόν: but the army has been mentioned (ἡγούμενος τοῦ στρατοῦ), and we vaguely expect something of the nature of the last sentence (οἱ δ' ἄλλοι κτλ). The promise is made a little clearer to the *mind* by the insertion of πρῶτος before ἐνέτυχε: but if it had been proposed that the main point (ἐμετεώρισεν ἑαυτόν) should be structurally supported, so as to make room in the scheme for the coming close, and should not be dropped down as if *it* were the close, we should have had Achilles equipped with the regular sound-signal (μέν); and this would have made the period grammatically complete.

Thus it is clear that the ordinary pairs of conjunctions[2] (μέν—δέ, τε—καί) are the simplest means of binding a period together; while relatives, participles and other resources can be used to elaborate the system. Periodic structures may be found where the grammar is, strictly speaking, complete before the period ends or is even half accomplished. In such cases, the sense of expectation which leads us to call the system a period is raised in us either by clearly hinting to our *minds* that something is about to be explained or justified or controverted, or by so arranging the phrases that they suggest to our *ears*, already accustomed to the cadence of a grammatical climax, that the regular sort and amount of sound is to follow. But in whatever degree of distinctness the mental or oral suspense is contrived, it will be convenient to speak of the grammatical as the true or original period, and of the looser systems, derivative therefrom, as *periodic* structures or forms.

[1] Hellan. *frag.* 132; above, p. 96.
[2] The useful effect of τε—καί on an unwieldy mass of material is well shown by the sentence in VII, 50. 3.

A further point to be observed is the essential value
of the period for literary art.   This chiefly consists in
the entertainment of mind and ear together, by causing
curiosity and promising its satisfaction : but, in the result
also, we commonly obtain the secondary advantages of
finding an ampler or more brilliant fulfilment than we
hoped for ; and of having the whole incident packed away,
as it were, with the clear-cut effect of its conclusion, for
the background or basis of a new system of ideas.   Something of this sort, apparently, is what Aristotle, or rather
the uncertain text of his account of this matter, is
attempting to explain.   The close-knit style[1] of the
period, he says, is that which has a beginning and an end
in itself, and a size which can be readily taken in at a
glance[2].   It is agreeable because it is the opposite of
the limitless, and because the listener has the sense of
continually having something, and finding he has got
something definitely done.   It is intelligible too, since it
is easy to remember.   Its conclusion should be made to
depend on the conduct of the thought.   Undue shortness
of periods or of their members will cause the hearer to
stumble, and will thwart his forward progress according to
the measure which the form marks out for itself[3] ; and if
they are too long, they make the sentence lag behind
him, like racers who take too wide a turn at the corner
of the course[4].

At the beginning of the second century B.C. Demetrius
of Phalerum quoted this metaphor[5] to explain the word

[1] Aristot. *Rhet.* III, ix, 1409 a—λέξις κατεστραμμένη, opposed to λ.
εἰρομένη.
[2] λέξιν ἔχουσαν ἀρχὴν καὶ τελευτὴν αὐτὴν καθ᾽ αὑτὴν καὶ μέγεθος εὐσύνοπτον.
[3] 1409 b—ἔτι ὁρμῶν ἐπὶ τὸ πόρρω καὶ (κατὰ Hayduck) τὸ μέτρον οὗ ἔχει ἐν
ἑαυτῷ ὅρον.
[4] τὰ δὲ μακρὰ ἀπολείπεσθαι ποιεῖ, ὥσπερ οἱ ἐξωτέρω ἀποκάμπτοντες τοῦ
τέρματος.
[5] Demetr. Phal. *de Elocut.* 11.

'period,' as picturing the arrangement of an ancient race-course : the goal is obvious along with the starting-place[1]. He repeats a good deal of Aristotle's statement, but adds an image of his own : 'the members of a period are like the stones which support and hold together a vaulted roof, whereas in the disconnected style they are like stones flung casually together and not fitted one to another[2].' For this and much else of his exposition of detail Demetrius may be indebted to his master Theophrastus, who is known to have developed the rhetorical doctrine of Aristotle[3]. The two ideas of a loop made by joining the two ends of a line (περίοδος), and of a solid ball of string which has been wound about itself (κατεστραμμένη), seem to be combined in the phrase of Cicero —'circuitus et quasi orbis uerborum[4]'; while Dionysius alludes chiefly to the compactness when he speaks of 'winding up the thoughts together and producing them in a rounded form[5].' These and similar descriptions, down to the 'melliti uerborum globuli' so contemptible to Petronius[6], will apply of course to schemes which do not coincide with a single grammatical system. But it will be most convenient to view the period as a sentence built up, by means of grammatical devices, and often in several stages, so as to produce a single main impression. It is of no great importance where the chief point is placed, so long as we feel it, in conjunction with its subsidiary points, to be εὐσύνοπτος. The top of the curve may be near to either end, or in the middle,—supported, as it were, on one side only, or on both.

---

[1] συνεμφαίνεται τῇ ἀρχῇ τοῦ δρόμου τὸ τέλος.

[2] de Elocut. 13.

[3] An elaborate reconstruction of Theophrastus' work from Demetrius, Dionysius, Cicero, Quintilian, etc. has been made by A. Mayer, *Theophrasti περὶ λέξεως*, Leipzig, 1910. [4] Cic. de Orat. III, 198.

[5] Dionys. *de Lysia*, 6 --ἡ συστρέφουσα τὰ νοήματα καὶ στρογγύλως ἐκφέρουσα λέξις. [6] Petron. *Satyr.* I.

Now the two long sentences we have noticed in the fifth Book of Thucydides are laboriously compacted periods, and the effort they reveal is interesting for the very clumsiness of its vigour. The former[1] is constructed on the following plan :—

ἐπειδὴ...ἐτεθνήκει Κλέων τε καὶ Βρασίδας, οἵπερ...ἠναντι-
    οῦντο...εἰρήνῃ,   (2½ lines[2])
ὁ μὲν διὰ τὸ εὐτυχεῖν...   (1 line)
ὁ δὲ...διαβάλλων,   (3 lines)
τότε δὴ...Πλειστοάναξ τε...καὶ Νικίας...προυθυμοῦντο,
                                             (4 lines)
    Νικίας μὲν βουλόμενος...   (6 lines)
    Πλειστοάναξ δὲ... διαβαλλόμενος... ὡς...ταῦτα ξυμ-
    βαίνοι.   (4 lines)

If Thucydides had been content to stop at προθυμ-
οῦντο, he would have produced a period of tolerable dimensions ; but he would have had to abandon the main purpose which set him working on such a scheme at all. A fully accomplished writer would feel that the suspense created by ἐπειδή and carried on by μέν and δέ through about six lines and a half, would be comfortably satisfied by τότε δή and its four lines. Thucydides, however, is so anxious to place the two pairs of men together, and to bring out, at one and the same instant, a group of significant contrasts, that he does not sufficiently consider his readers' part in the transaction. He is afraid that if these contrasts are spread over more than a single sentence, they will either lose their aggregate force, or require a much larger expenditure of words to preserve it. He therefore treats the word προυθυμοῦντο as though it needed a supplement, and appends to it a lengthy explanation ; which he tries to excuse by matching Nicias' εὐτυχία with Brasidas'

---

[1] Thuc. V, 16. 1.   [2] Oxford Text, ed. H. Stuart Jones, 1898.

εὐτυχεῖν, and Pleistoanax' διαβαλλόμενος with Cleon's διαβάλλων; and also by echoing the 'chiasmus' of the first part, whereby the persons are described in the opposite order to that in which their names are mentioned. But the effect of the whole may be compared to the case of a man who should break his leg through mere obesity. The period has been given too much to carry all at once, and then has not been given a fair chance : for προυθυμοῦντο does not necessarily lead us to expect any more from that sentence; and yet we soon realise that there is a good deal more to come. The other system we have noticed in the next chapter[1] is more accurately constructed. The two considerations put forward as accounting for the practical result (τότε δὴ...ποιοῦνται τὴν ξύμβασιν) are the intention of the Lacedæmonians and the effort of the delegates ; and although the co-ordination is rather perfunctorily managed (παρασκευή τε ... καὶ ἐπειδὴ...), it is enough to keep the suspense, if awkwardly strained, at least unbroken. But the sentence is sadly overweighted, further on, by a long parenthesis, due to that same desire of synthetic force and verbal economy which appeared in the former example.

§ 5

In thus exploiting the resources of grammar for a definite artistic purpose, Thucydides was clearly fixing, with all the strength and authority of his genius, an entirely new complexion upon historical prose. While adopting, in some parts of his narrative, a simple style which can be classed with that of Ionian ἱστορίη— a recognised manner for describing countries, places, nations and persons,—he passes here and there, even in the region of narrative, to a laboriously complex system.

---

[1] v, 17. 2; above, p. 105.

We have observed the change which seems to come over Ionian prose with the grave, calculated manner of Hippocrates[1]; we compared the sententious brevity of Thucydides; and then examined his heavy periodic method. The three things must be considered together. In Hippocrates the Ionian ease is impressed with a regular formality, which Thucydides enlarged and strengthened for the more philosophic or reflective passages of his description. It is of no great consequence whether we suppose Thucydides to have studied Hippocrates or not: the medical treatises show the same sort of transitions as his, from looseness to system, and thence back again. Our business now is to look for some earlier impress of sententious brevity upon the flowing Ionian language, presuming that there was a separate influence which worked upon Thucydides either directly or through Hippocrates: for both of them appear to be too amply provided with grammatical organisation to be fitly regarded, in this most notable point of structure, as pioneers.

The Ionic dialect, as employed by Herodotus, was in the main a literary convention which he adopted for his geographical and ethnological history. Perhaps he could learn it in his native city, the Dorian Halicarnassus, which must have come under many Ionian influences; at any rate he early contracted a strong sympathy with Ionian democracy, and particularly with that form of it which was developed by the Athenian state. This connection with Athens soon drew him into such a close affection for her political and social ideals, that he came to despise the Asiatic Ionians, as though they had fallen behind in the race for freedom and strength. The origin of this preference has been traced with much probability to a personal contact with Pericles[2]. Whether

---

[1] Above, pp. 99–100.
[2] Bury, *Anc. Gr. Historians*, pp. 62–64.

we are to refer certain appearances of formality in his style to the beginnings of the rhetorical movement in Athens[1], or to a more general impulse of the inventive Ionian *esprit*[2], must remain uncertain : but the decision of this question will become the less important, if we can perceive the seeds of such formality as might connect Herodotus with Athenian sophistry in some utterances of those Ionian philosophers who are known to have left their mark upon Athenian thought.

Turning back to the first half of the sixth century B.C., we catch a glimpse of a didactic prose whose practical intent is just able to renounce the rhythmic spell of poetry. The political, or perhaps the moral[3], force of the metaphor in a saying of the second and greatest of the three Milesian sages, Anaximander, is the more interesting to us, that its imaginative substance is not supported by a metrical form[4]:—

δίδωσι γὰρ [τὰ ὄντα] δίκην καὶ τίσιν ἀλλήλοις τῆς ἀδικίας κατὰ τὴν τοῦ χρόνου τάξιν—

while the method of ordinary verse is hardly set aside in two other phrases[5]—

[τὸ ἄπειρον δοκεῖ] περιέχειν ἅπαντα καὶ πάντα κυβερνᾶν —ἀθάνατον γὰρ καὶ ἀνώλεθρον.

At the beginning of the fifth century we come to a larger scheme of sentence in the oracular pronouncements of Heracleitus, whose passion for putting together the two sides or aspects of a thing led him to balance the size, and even the sound, of his phrases. It is worth while to note, so far as his scanty fragments allow, by what devices the lonely seer of Ephesus sought to fix his opinions in the memory of a bustling world :—

---

[1] Cf. above, p. 30.   [2] Bury, *l.c.* p. 54.
[3] See Cornford, *From Religion to Philosophy* (1912) pp. 19, 147 *al.*
[4] Diels, *Frag. Vorsokr.*[2] i, p. 13.   [5] D. *F.V.*[2] i, p. 14.

κόσμον τόνδε τὸν αὐτὸν ἁπάντων οὔτε τις θεῶν οὔτε
ἀνθρώπων ἐποίησε, ἀλλ᾽ ἦν αἰεὶ καὶ ἔστι καὶ ἔσται πῦρ
ἀείζωον, ἁπτόμενον μέτρα καὶ ἀποσβεννύμενον μέτρα[1].

The insistent vigour of this sentence is mainly the
force of a vivid imagination bent on expressing a great
idea: but the structure relies, more and more as it
proceeds, on the sound-value of the words. In particular,
the repetition of μέτρα may be regarded as a first essay
in an artifice which the rhetoricians afterwards canonised
with the name 'anaphora.' How close Heracleitus brings
us to a calculated formality may be seen by comparing
a more obvious experiment in Herodotus[2] :—

τί δείσαντες; κοίην πλήθεος συστροφήν; κοίην δὲ
χρημάτων δύναμιν; τῶν ἐπιστάμεθα μὲν τὴν μάχην,
ἐπιστάμεθα δὲ τὴν δύναμιν ἐοῦσαν ἀσθενέα· ἔχομεν δὲ
αὐτῶν παῖδας καταστρεψάμενοι, τούτους οἳ ἐν τῇ ἡμετέρῃ
κατοικημένοι Ἴωνές τε καὶ Αἰολέες καὶ Δωριέες καλέονται.

The artificial balance of ἐπιστάμεθα μέν and ἐπιστάμεθα δέ, and the repetition of δύναμιν only to call it
ἀσθενέα, make a sudden contrast with the surrounding
narrative[3]; while the periodic effect procured by the long
sentence which balances the foregoing group of short
clauses seems, like the sentence about the army leaving
Achilles up in the tree[4], to show the way to those larger
schemes which Thucydides built up by stages of antithesis[5]. But if we are here on the borders of regular
rhetoric, it is because the method is wavering between
the choice of devices which will help to set prose in

[1] Bywater, *Heracliti Ephes. Reliquiae*, xx ; D. *F.V.*[2] i, p. 66.
[2] Herod. VII, 9.
[3] Cf. the striking emphasis in Thuc. VII, 24. 2—ἀπέθανον καὶ ἐζωγρήθησαν
πολλοί, καὶ χρήματα πολλὰ τὰ ξύμπαντα ἑάλω· ὥσπερ γὰρ ταμιείῳ χρωμένων τῶν
Ἀθηναίων τοῖς τείχεσι πολλὰ μὲν ἐμπόρων χρήματα καὶ σῖτος ἐνῆν, πολλὰ δὲ καὶ
τῶν τριηράρχων—.
[4] Above, p. 96.   [5] Above, pp. 110–112.

useful order and the retention of old poetic forms from which prose ought to be releasing its eager limbs. Μέν and δέ, of course, like the heralds Talthybius and Idæus[1], had long ago shown their usefulness in epic ; while Idæus himself will serve to illustrate the decisive finality which a repeated word can bestow[2]—

νὺξ δ' ἤδη τελέθει· ἀγαθὸν καὶ νυκτὶ πιθέσθαι,—

even if we had not a suggestion of poetry in the metrical ring of Herodotus' concluding phrase[3]—

Ἴωνές τε καὶ Αἰολέες καὶ Δωριέες καλέονται.

But it appears that both Heracleitus and Herodotus made some more definite advances in the artificial arrangement of words. Of the former there is a saying reported by Plutarch[4]—

πυρὸς ἀνταμείβεται πάντα καὶ πῦρ ἁπάντων, ὥσπερ χρυσοῦ χρήματα καὶ χρημάτων χρυσός—

where the repeated sounds are worked into an epigrammatic system ; while Herodotus, in the next chapter to that just cited, makes Artabanus reply to Mardonius[5] :—

τὸ δὲ αὐτοῖσι ἔνεστι δεινόν, ἐμέ σοι δίκαιόν ἐστι φράζειν.

The effort, though more subtly conducted, is equally obvious, when we consider the slightness of the meaning. Yet, like the more elaborate work of the Persian Debate[6], it is meant to have the solemnity and precision of well-weighed counsel, which happens to be more profound in the oracular utterances of Heracleitus. He, moreover, appears to have thrown out some hints on the mystical virtues of language, which encouraged certain thinkers to build a ' Heracleitean' theory of knowledge upon the

[1] *Il.* VII, 276.   [2] *Ib.* 282.   [3] Above, p. 114.
[4] Bywater, xxii ; D. *F.V.*[2] i, p. 75.
[5] Herod. VII, 10.   [6] *Ib.* III, 80–82.

names whereby things are known[1]. The following fragment, at least, with its serious ' word-play ' on ξὺν νόῳ—
ξυνῷ and perhaps also on πόλις—πολύ, shows that
Heracleitus felt the magical affinity of like-sounding
words which is familiar to us in the 'name-play' of
Aeschylus, and which probably underlay the mediæval
device of rhyme :—

ξὺν νόῳ λέγοντας ἰσχυρίζεσθαι χρὴ τῷ ξυνῷ πάντων,
ὅκωσπερ νόμῳ πόλις καὶ πολὺ ἰσχυροτέρως[2].

Thus, whatever be the exact meaning of the λόγος[3]
which he identified with the common reason, he was a
practical exponent, in his grudging way, of the oral
charm of language.

The calculated force of these and other sentences of
Heracleitus is enough to indicate the origin of the steady
progressions of Hippocrates and the contrast-periods of
Thucydides : but the comparison with Herodotus has
shown how near it brings us to a studied mode of public
argument. The reasonings of Anaxagoras and Democritus will supply further evidence of the cultivation of
periodic form. As the traces of these philosophic models
appear most distinctly in Thucydides' speeches, we shall
turn at once to those portions of his work, and successively
consider the influences of philosophers, sophists and
rhetoricians upon his most remarkable ventures in
formal art.

---

[1] The theory is combated by Plato, *Cratylus*, 435–440. Cf. H. Jackson,
Camb. Prælections, 1906, pp. 1–26 ; Cornford, *Relig. Philos.* p. 192.

[2] Bywater, xci ; D. *F.V.*² i, p. 78.

[3] Cf. Bywater, xcii ; D. *F.V.*² i, p. 62.

CHAPTER V

THE RHETORICAL INVASION

§ 1

In approaching the style of Thucydides' speeches as a specimen of Athenian culture, we must keep steadily in sight the nature of the mind whose sensibilities and severities we have traced in some outstanding features of the History[1]. We must consider that mind not merely in its original quality and strength, but as sharing in the enlightenment of the age. But the search for particular influences, in a case where native vigour is so evident, is likely, if pushed far, to be fruitless and perverse. There is no need to single out Anaxagoras or any individual thinker as the cause of that sceptical tone towards popular beliefs, and that insistent trust in rational policy, which are all that we can fairly point to as the philosophic basis of Thucydides. They are the joint product of many minds at work upon a particular stage in social development, though one or two men may drive the course of thought a good deal faster than the rest. Perhaps we may detect a special connection with Anaxagoras, through Pericles, in that contempt for the illogical proceedings of a professedly intelligent democracy, which we have felt in the account of Alcibiades and the Hermæ[2]. It is clear that Anaxagoras came to Athens and remained there at the instance of Pericles[3], and that

---

[1] Above, pp. 68–84. [2] Above, pp. 78–81.
[3] Burnet, *Early Gr. Phil.* 1908, p. 294.

the period of his residence was from about 462 to
432 B.C.[1] Plato, while arguing in the *Phædrus*[2] for the
institution of a new psychological rhetoric, attributes the
lofty-minded excellence of Pericles' oratory to his converse
with Anaxagoras ; whose sublime speculations on the
opposite principles of mind and mindlessness in Nature
suggested to the statesman an improvement of his
persuasive art.   The connection between the two men is
here strained, it may seem, for the needs of the argument ;
since Plato is unable to show that the philosopher, to
whom the Athenians paid merely the mock-respect of the
nickname Νοῦς, ever deigned to concern himself with
public or even human affairs[3].   Plutarch[4], who enlarges
on the effects of this connection, is probably most reliable
where he states that Pericles learnt thereby ' to despise
all the superstitious fears which the awe-striking signs of
the heavens inspire in those who are ignorant of the
causes of such things and, from having no experience in
them at all, let their apprehensions about the gods throw
them into grievous alarm.'   Thus, although Anaxagoras
took no active part in the life of Athens, it is well to
remember here that he long held an honoured place in
the Periclean circle, where intellectual and artistic aims
were being shaped for the energies of the younger
generation.

   This later group does not supply more than two
minds which are worthy to be compared with that of
Thucydides ; and one of these, since Euripides was his
elder by ten or fifteen years[5], cannot strictly be counted as

---

[1] Burnet, *Early Gr. Phil.* 1908, p. 291.   [2] Plato, *Phædrus*, 270 a.
[3] We may imagine that he was a little surprised at finding himself on his
trial for teaching that the sun was a red-hot stone, but hardly incommoded
by imprisonment.
[4] Plutarch, *Pericl.* 6.
[5] The common tradition fixed Euripides' birth on the day of the battle of
Salamis, in the autumn of 480 B.C. ; the Parian Marble, less adroitly and so
more probably, puts the date at the end of 485.

contemporary. We may presume that he admired the
art of the rationalising poet; though personally he might
disapprove of a life so jealously withdrawn from public
affairs, and so closely devoted to the study of the passions.
But Socrates, the younger friend and most intimate associate of Euripides, is the only person equal in age with
Thucydides who can be set beside him as certainly his
equal in intellectual power[1]. Among eminent minds
whose fame had entered Athens from outside, that of his
younger contemporary Hippocrates[2] might strike him as
more akin to his own than any that he knew: the
physician's wide experience, his carefully reasoned method,
and his attention to the large general causes of disease,
are such as we should have praised in Thucydides himself,
had he written a treatise solely on the great Plague, in its
course from Ethiopia, through Egypt, Libya and Asia
Minor, into Greece[3]. But the mind which devised and
achieved the History was cast in a far larger mould. A
comparison has been drawn between Thucydides and
Democritus[4], with the help of such meagre lights as the
fragments of the latter afford. Out of the splendid array
of sixty treatises on ethical, physical, mathematical,
musical, literary and other more practical subjects, only a
few pages of general precepts now remain. It would seem
that many other works, chiefly of a fabulous or magical
tendency, were passed off under the recommendation of
his posthumous fame[5]. This accretion of spurious
writings, which appears so plainly in the Hippocratean
treatises, was particularly unkind to Democritus; who,
as we have the sound authority of Lucian for believing,
was able to meet such miracles 'with an adamantine under-

[1] See above, pp. 82-3.   [2] Born probably in 460 B.C.
[3] Thuc. II, 48.   [4] Forbes, Bk I, *Intr.* pp. lxv–lxviii.
[5] E.g. on the use of an owl's heart or a frog's tongue for discovering the
infidelities of women, as quoted from Democr. by Pliny, *Hist. Nat.* XXIX, 4,
XXXII, 5: other such marvels are quoted X, 49, XXVIII, 8.

standing, so as to disbelieve them and conjecture what
they were; and if he could not detect the manner of
them, could at any rate fall back on the position that he
had failed to see how the jugglery was done, and that
one way or another the thing was a cheat, and could not
have happened as pretended[1].'

The philosophic theories of Democritus are extremely
interesting, and still offer many problems : it is not our
business to pursue them here.　Suffice it to observe that
this ἀδαμαντίνη γνώμη which Lucian ascribes to him, and
which certainly speaks in many of his genuine fragments,
is a strong point of intellectual kinship between him and
Thucydides[2].　More important to us is the statement of
Diogenes Laertius that he wrote treatises on the rhythms
of verse, the sound-values of words, the style and diction
of Homer, and the uses of verbs and nouns[3].

Further, we find that ancient critics used to compare
his writings to the Dialogues of Plato, for the poetic
qualities of their style : the eager speed of their movement, says Cicero, and the brilliant distinction of their
language, gave them more right to be called poems than
any that the comic poets had to show[4].　Elsewhere we
find Cicero remarking that Democritus was ornamental,
yet never obscure[5]; and Plutarch, that his style had a
marvellous and magnificent power[6].　Turning to what
survives of his writing, we find that the quotations of his
actual words are almost all in the class of his ' moral '

[1] Lucian, *Alexander*, 17: cf. his remark to the bogeys—παύσασθε παίζ-
οντες—*Philopseudes*, 32.　The hasty mistake of Pliny is expressly noted by
Aulus Gellius, *Noct. Att.* X, 12.

[2] His encyclopædic researches might suggest that he combined the
insatiable curiosity of Herodotus with the strict thinking of Thucydides.
There are signs that his inquisitive energies were at times absurdly
squandered.　Cf. the story of his scolding the maid for telling him how the
figs came to taste of honey (Plutarch, *Sympos.* I, x, 2).

[3] Diog. Laert. IX, vii, 48.　　　　[4] Cic. *Orat.* 67.
[5] Cic. *de Orat.* I, 49 ; *de Divin.* II, 133.　　[6] Plut. *Symp.* V, vii, 6.

fragments; and here, though these brief apophthegms can give no idea of the rapidity which must have belonged to his argumentative style, there certainly is no lack of brilliant and stately phrases. But first we should notice how the new interest in men's thoughts and motives at once produces, in the barest amount of material, a simple antithesis :—

ἀγαθὸν οὐ τὸ μὴ ἀδικέειν, ἀλλὰ τὸ μηδὲ ἐθέλειν—

or again :—

ἐχθρὸς οὐχ ὁ ἀδικέων, ἀλλὰ καὶ ὁ βουλόμενος[1].

These are but the raw material of epigrams. More pomp appears in the following :—

χαριστικὸς οὐχ ὁ βλέπων πρὸς τὴν ἀμοιβήν, ἀλλ' ὁ εὖ δρᾶν προῃρημένος.
τὸν οἰόμενον νοῦν ἔχειν ὁ νουθετέων ματαιοπονεῖ.
ἀνοήμονες βιοῦσι οὐ τερπόμενοι βιοτῇ[2].

If we could suppose that the wide diversity of Democritus' speculations, combined with his weighty manner of pronouncement, first drew Thucydides into the serious discussion of politics, we might connect his interest with this plain emphatic sentence :—

πόλις γὰρ εὖ ἀγομένη μεγίστη ὄρθωσίς ἐστι · καὶ ἐν τούτῳ πάντα ἔνι, καὶ τούτου σωζομένου πάντα σώζεται, καὶ τούτου φθειρομένου τὰ πάντα διαφθείρεται[3]—

since, as Mr Forbes remarks, the same sentiment occurs in one of Pericles' speeches; only Thucydides, by opening out the πάντα into the individual and his relation to the community, produces a more vividly impressive argument :—

---

[1] Mullach, *Democr. Frag.* 109, 110; D. *F.V.*[2] i, p. 401, 403.
[2] Mull. 160, 59, 51; D. *F.V.*[2] i, p. 404, 400, 422.
[3] Mull. 212; D. *F.V.*[2] i, p. 429.

καλῶς μὲν γὰρ φερόμενος ἀνὴρ τὸ καθ᾽ ἑαυτὸν διαφθειρ-
ομένης τῆς πατρίδος οὐδὲν ἧσσον ξυναπόλλυται, κακοτυχῶν
δὲ ἐν εὐτυχούσῃ πολλῷ μᾶλλον διασῴζεται[1].

There is a Thucydidean exposure of human weakness,
and encouragement of human strength, in this of
Democritus :—

ἄνθρωποι τύχης εἴδωλον ἐπλάσαντο πρόφασιν ἰδίης
ἀβουλίης. βαιὰ γὰρ φρονήσει τύχη μάχεται, τὰ δὲ πλεῖστα
ἐν βίῳ εὐξύνετος ὀξυδερκίη κατιθύνει[2],—

while that he could indulge in the experimental imagery
which Thucydides has exhibited in some of the eloquence
of his speakers appears from this :—

τύχη μεγαλόδωρος, ἀλλ᾽ ἀβέβαιος, φύσις δὲ αὐτάρκης·

which proceeds with a pregnant brevity very near to that
of the History :—

διόπερ νικᾷ τῷ ἥσσονι καὶ βεβαίῳ τὸ μεῖζον τῆς
ἐλπίδος[3].

A more homely picture of Fortune is ushered in with the
rather excessive sound of—

τράπεζαν πολυτελέα μὲν τύχη παρατίθησιν, αὐταρκέα δὲ
σωφροσύνη[4].

In this other and larger scheme we almost hear the voice
of a Thucydidean speaker :—

τὰ μὲν καλὰ χρήματα τοῖς πόνοις ἡ μάθησις ἐξεργάζεται,
τὰ δ᾽ αἰσχρὰ ἄνευ πόνων αὐτόματα καρποῦται[5].

Without lingering too long over the fine incisive phrases
of this sadly ruined and neglected writer, we may notice
the broad humanity and excellent common-sense of the
following :—

---

[1] Thuc. II, 60. 3.　　　　[2] Mull. 14 ; D. F.V.² i, p. 407.
[3] Mull. 15 ; D. F.V.², i, p. 417 : cf. Thuc. IV, 55. 2, quoted above, p. 101.
[4] Mull. 36 ; D. F.V.² i, p. 423.　　　[5] Mull. 236 ; D. F.V.² i, p. 418.

βίος ἀνεόρταστος μακρὴ ὁδὸς ἀπανδόκευτος.

ἀνδρὶ σοφῷ πᾶσα γῆ βατή· ψυχῆς γὰρ ἀγαθῆς πατρὶς ὁ ξύμπας κόσμος.

ἔνιοι θνητῆς φύσεως διάλυσιν οὐκ εἰδότες ἄνθρωποι, συνειδήσει δὲ τῆς ἐν τῷ βίῳ κακοπραγμοσύνης, τὸν τῆς βιοτῆς χρόνον ἐν ταραχαῖς καὶ φόβοις ταλαιπωρέουσι, ψεύδεα περὶ τοῦ μετὰ τὴν τελευτὴν μυθοπλαστέοντες χρόνου[1].

That this sceptical attitude towards popular beliefs included a distrust of sophistic erudition, is clear from five words, with which we may leave Democritus engaged yet not entangled in the multifarious enlightenment of his time :—

πολλοὶ πολυμαθέες νοῦν οὐκ ἔχουσιν[2].

§ 2

It will be useful, after viewing these advances achieved, through figurative speech, in the art of formal writing, and before we pass on to the more professional elaboration derived from Sicily, to take a glance at the background of merely thoughtful style in Athens which is to be connected chiefly with the influence of Anaxagoras. There was a Cretan philosopher, generally known as Diogenes of Apollonia, who seems, like Anaxagoras his teacher, to have come near suffering death for his opinions[3], and of whose treatise *On the Nature of Things* we possess eight fragments. Though a Dorian by birth, he writes in the conventional Ionic dialect[4]; and he insists on his point in the old repetitive manner :—

---

[1] Mull. 32, 225, 119; D. *F.V.*[2] i, p. 426, 429, 438.

[2] Mull. 140; D. *F.V.*[2] i, p. 401 (emphatic assonance in ordinary words). Another form of this saying is added in the collections—πολυνοίην, οὐ πολυμαθίην ἀσκέειν χρή. A more wide-spread tradition ascribes a similar phrase. to Heracleitus—πολυμαθίη νόον ἔχειν οὐ διδάσκει,—see Bywater, xvi, n.

[3] Diog. Laert. IX, ix, 1.   [4] Above, p. 112.

αὐτὸ γάρ μοι τοῦτο [ὁ ἀὴρ] θεὸς δοκεῖ εἶναι καὶ ἐπὶ πᾶν
ἀφῖχθαι καὶ πάντα διατιθέναι καὶ ἐν παντὶ ἐνεῖναι[1]—

but yet, a few lines further on, he makes this careful and
effective division :—

καὶ πάντων τῶν ζῴων δὲ ἡ ψυχὴ τὸ αὐτό ἐστιν, ἀὴρ
θερμότερος μὲν τοῦ ἔξω ἐν ᾧ ἐσμεν, τοῦ μέντοι παρὰ τῷ
ἡλίῳ πολλὸν ψυχρότερος.

Further, in the longest of these pieces, which gives a
minute account of the veins, we come to a good instance
of the orderly progression and conclusion which result
from a succinct, equable treatment of the single and
double parts of the body :—

αἱ δ᾽ εἰς τὴν κεφαλὴν τείνουσαι διὰ τῶν σφαγῶν φαίνονται
ἐν τῷ αὐχένι μεγάλαι· ἀφ᾽ ἑκατέρας δ᾽ αὐτῶν, ᾗ τελευτᾷ,
σχίζονται εἰς τὴν κεφαλὴν πολλαί, αἱ μὲν ἐκ τῶν δεξιῶν εἰς
τὰ ἀριστερά, αἱ δ᾽ ἐκ τῶν ἀριστερῶν εἰς τὰ δεξιά· τελευτῶσι
δὲ παρὰ τὸ οὖς ἑκάτεραι[2].

This power of setting things out, so that a number
of details can be surveyed in one compendious system, we
have already seen at work in a passage of Hippocrates[3].
It is important to remember that Ionian science, with its
eager pursuit of a single principle throughout the
complex phenomena of nature, was thus steadily forging
in the rough that instrument which we shall presently
observe being whetted and polished for the passionate
fields of civic debate. At the same time, the cautious
empirical method of Hippocrates continually reveals his
Dorian nature beneath the Ionian enterprise of his
language ; his foremost concern is with the accurate
observation of detail, and the various causes to which

---

[1] Mull. *Frag. Diog. Apoll.* 6 ; D. *F.V.*[2] i, p. 335.
[2] Mull. 8 ; D. *F.V.*[2] i, p. 338.
[3] Above, p. 99.

certain classes of established facts may be referred[1]. Hence, his application to this new and important work, whereby the care of human ailments began to shake off the bonds of priestcraft and common quackery[2], kept him very properly apart from the study of elegant expression. If he is confident of the usefulness and success of his teaching, he does not indulge in anything more than that amount of ornament which will serve to impress his views upon the minds of his disciples. He makes a deliberate choice of sonorous words, but his sentences do not strive after any formal pattern :—

ὅκου δ᾽ ἐστὶν ἡ χώρη ψιλή τε καὶ ἀνώχυρος καὶ τρηχείη, καὶ ὑπὸ τοῦ χειμῶνος πιεζομένη, καὶ ὑπὸ τοῦ ἡλίου κεκαυμένη, ἐνταῦθα σκληρούς τε καὶ ἰσχνοὺς καὶ διηρθρωμένους καὶ ἐντόνους καὶ δασέας ἂν ἴδοις·...τά τε ἤθεα καὶ τὰς ὀργὰς αὐθάδεας καὶ ἰδιογνώμονας...εὑρήσεις[3].

The effect of this habit is apt at times to become too ponderous:—

τὴν δ᾽ αὔξησιν καὶ ἡμερότητα παρέχει πλεῖστον ἁπάντων, ὁκόταν μηδὲν ᾖ ἐπικρατέον βιαίως, ἀλλὰ παντὸς ἰσομοιρίη δυναστεύῃ[4].

Sometimes he attempts a simple sort of balance in the disposal of these great words :—

εἰσὶ γὰρ φύσιες, αἱ μὲν ὄρεσιν ἐοικυῖαι δενδρώδεσί τε καὶ ἐφύδροισιν, αἱ δὲ λεπτοῖσί τε καὶ ἀνύδροισιν, αἱ δὲ λειμακεστέροισί τε καὶ ἑλώδεσιν, αἱ δὲ πεδίῳ τε καὶ ψιλῇ καὶ ξηρῇ γῇ[5].

Here he seems to make up for the lack of size in the

---

[1] Thus a large part of his undoubted writings consists of material very similar to that of a modern doctor's 'case-books'—*Epidem.* i, iii ; *De Rat. Vict. Acut.*

[2] Cf., for example, the arguments against the divine origin of impotence among the Scythians—*De Aëre*, 22.

[3] *De Aëre, ad fin.*   [4] *Ib.* 12.   [5] *Ib.* 13.

closing words by their continuance of the same long
vowel-sound[1]. Similar efforts appear from time to time
in the more discursive parts of his genuine writings;
but it is only in some of the contemporary or later
treatises included in the collection that we can find a
steady artistic aim.

§ 3

The chief originator of the new culture in Athens
was Protagoras of Abdera[2], who was born about 480 B.C.,
and was thus, like Euripides and Gorgias, some years
older than Thucydides and Socrates. It is unlikely,
therefore, that there is any truth in the statement of
Diogenes Laertius and others[3] that he was a disciple
of the still younger Democritus. There is no need to
look behind his views for the direct influence of any
other mind than his own. The philosophers had fallen
from their first estate of oracular authority: as their
number increased, they were found to be not merely
differing and disputing among themselves, but to be
explaining their own or their masters' doctrines more and

[1] Cf. the last quotation from Democritus, above, p. 123.
[2] Hecatæus and Democritus were also natives of this prosperous and
important city in the S.W. corner of Thrace, which by Cicero's time had
acquired a reputation for the *madness* of its inhabitants (Cic. *ad Att.* IV, 17;
VII, 7; *De Nat. Deor.* I, 120). This earlier tradition belongs to Hippocrates'
account (*Epidem.* iii, *passim*) of the fever *with delirium* to which the
Abderites were subject, and to the story in Lucian (*De Hist. Conscr.*, init.) of
their midsummer-madness, when the acting of Archelaus in Euripides'
Andromeda had so impressed them, that they went about reciting and
performing pieces of the play till the coldness of winter cured them. This
infection of light-headedness has nothing to do with the *stupidity* which
was later ascribed to them for some reason that does not appear (Juvenal, X, 50;
Martial, X, 25. 4). These two traditions are perplexingly confused and treated
as one in the commentaries of Tyrrell on Cicero's Letters, and of Mayor on
Juvenal. The various legends have been collected by K. F. Hermann,
Gesamm. Abhandl. 1849, pp. 90-111.
[3] Diog. Laert. IX, viii, 2; Philostr. *Vit. Soph.* I, x, 1; Euseb. *Præp.
Evang.* XIV, iii, 7.

more upon the level of common reason; which on its part also had been rapidly advancing with the sudden expansion of civic life. Accordingly, by the middle of the fifth century, it would appear to even the most eagerly enquiring minds of Athens that, as all these different theories could not be true, so the peculiarities of this one or that must, in some degree at least, be referable to the particular bent or outlook of its author's mind. The personal element in each philosophy could now be made an excuse for discrediting the whole; especially where, as in the case of Anaxagoras, the person was obviously out of touch with the course of public business. ' Man,' said Protagoras, ' is the measure of all things, of what is, that it is, and of what is not, that it is not[1].' Many years afterwards, Plato[2] found that his philosophy could best attack this position by refuting the Heracleitean theory of universal flux, from which it might be supposed to have sprung; and even before he turns to this latter task, there are hints that he is making the dignity of Protagoras support a much more elaborate doctrine than this person ever actually held[3]. The real teaching of the sophist was the outcome of a philosophic situation, which he was able to sum up because he had some part in it himself, and to build upon because he understood the needs of his day. For he was learned in many things. He was well enough versed in logic to state and maintain with force the position from which he started[4]; and he had definite, if not very profound, ideas on ethics and politics[5]. But his main interest was in literature, and especially in argumentative speech, on which he lectured with a view to excellence in debate and writing. He was the first teacher in Athens who took regular fees

---

[1] Sextus, *Adv. Math.* VII, 60.   [2] In the *Theætetus.*
[3] *Theæt.* 152 c, 172 b.   [4] In the treatise (now lost) *On Truth.*
[5] Diog. Laert. IX, viii, 6; Plato, *Protag. passim.*

for this kind of work ; and he continued it in that and other cities of Greece and Sicily for about forty years[1]. At what time he wrote his treatise *On the Gods* is uncertain ; we only know that its opening words were these :—'Concerning the gods, I have no means of knowing either that they exist, or that they do not exist, or of what sort is their form : so many things prevent me from knowing,—as their obscurity, and the shortness of human life' ; and that this dictum was brought up against him in 411 B.C., when the Four Hundred succeeded in getting him banished[2].

The attentive portraiture of Plato[3] has granted us the rare fortune of realising the personality of the First Professor. In putting him to the test of the Socratic method, Plato clearly intends him to appear as the leader and chief exponent of practical reason ; and, though at first we are allowed to smile at the figure he makes in his own and his disciples' eyes[4], the earnest tone and inconclusive result of the discussion show that his position seemed far from unimportant to Plato. We gather from this Dialogue that he was ready for the interchange of short argument, as well as for lengthy discourse[5]: yet that, although he was accustomed to 'contests of words[6],' he was unwilling, at any rate in the presence of Socrates, to be cross-examined at a moment's warning. He protests that his business is not, in substance, anything new: he has only systematised the teaching covertly instilled by poets, mystics, physical trainers and musicians[7]. Merely technical instruction in the arts he leaves to Hippias and others[8]: his own strong point is a sort of

---

[1] From about 450 to 411 B.C. ; Diog. Laert. IX, viii, 1, 7.
[2] *Ib.* 5. 3.   [3] Plato, *Protagoras*.
[4] E.g. the news of his arrival, *Protag.* 310 b; his disciples following him up and down the portico, as though under the charm of Orpheus' voice, 315 a.
[5] 335 b.   [6] 335 a.   [7] 316 d, e.
[8] 318 e.

stately declamation upon moral subjects; and his conversation betrays a tendency to run into rather lengthy speeches. Nevertheless, if this dialogue be read with an unbiassed attention, it is clear that, at the time when it was written, Plato saw a good deal to respect and honour in his ability, so far as it went. Even the high-soaring *Republic* can mention him and his disciple Prodicus as holding far better claims to the gratitude of Greece than her old educators, Homer and Hesiod[1]. Indeed, it would not be too fanciful to infer from the dignity and authority of his manner—a little heightened, of course, for the contrast with Socrates, yet in the main historical—that he had contrived to invest himself with something of that old infallibility which was the customary distinction of the popular sage. If it is true to say that sophistic culture came in to supplant philosophy, it is equally clear that the movement was started by a philosopher, who saw that there was a great practical good to be done[2]; nor could he have done it so well, or at all, had he not promptly discerned the embarrassments of speculative thought, and grasped the opportunity which awaited its coolly reasoned method among the affairs and ambitions of public life.

One striking feature of his lectures, apparently, was that they recommended and illustrated a correct use of words[3]. We have noticed a special branch of this interest, which sprang from Heracleitus[4]: but, considering the careful choice of expression in Democritus and Hippocrates[5], and the natural result of a study of the poets, we may fairly ascribe this kind of work to his

---

[1] Plato, *Respubl.* X, 600 c, d.

[2] So, in our time, Henry Sidgwick gave some of his best energies to organising the education of women. Protagoras, while inventing education, had to make himself Professor of it.

[3] Plato, *Phædrus*, 267 c—ὀρθοέπεια. [4] Above, pp. 115–6.

[5] Above, pp. 121–3, 125–6.

own enterprise, at a moment when men, though aware of some of the powers of language, were uncertain how they could best be applied to an increasing variety of matters.

We have no accurate means of judging to what extent the linguistic part of his craft affected the style of his own discourses. In the *Protagoras* he delivers a ' show-piece ' (ἐπίδειξις) of some length. There is no sign that it is meant to be a parody ; Plato may simply be exerting his own versatility to show how fine a Protagorean myth can be. One modern editor supposes that the speech is probably taken from one of the sophist's actual works : perhaps it is safer to conclude that 'it is carefully modelled on his way of writing[1]'; without forgetting, however, that if it contains 'rare and often poetic rhythms, words, constructions and turns of expression[2],' these are things which often find their way into genuine Platonic myths. Yet at one or two places in this speech they certainly seem to strike a special note of characterisation[3] :—

νέμων δὲ τοῖς μὲν ἰσχὺν ἄνευ τάχους προσῆπτεν, τοὺς δ' ἀσθενεστέρους τάχει ἐκόσμει· τοὺς δὲ ὥπλιζε, τοῖς δ' ἄοπλον διδοὺς φύσιν ἄλλην τιν' αὐτοῖς ἐμηχανᾶτο δύναμιν εἰς σωτηρίαν. ἃ μὲν γὰρ αὐτῶν σμικρότητι ἤμπισχεν, πτηνὸν φυγὴν ἢ κατάγειον οἴκησιν ἔνεμεν · ἃ δὲ ηὖξε μεγέθει, τῷδε αὐτῷ αὐτὰ ἔσῳζεν· καὶ τἆλλα οὕτως ἐπανισῶν ἔνεμεν. ταῦτα δὲ ἐμηχανᾶτο εὐλάβειαν ἔχων μή τι γένος ἀϊστωθείη.

· The short balanced clauses and poetic diction[4] suggest that the myth is meant to be recognised as Protagorean ; though, taking the whole speech[5] together,

---

[1] Adam, *Protag.* (1905) p. 108. [2] *Ib.* p. 110. [3] Plato, *Protag.* 320 e.
[4] Notice also the rhythm in ἐμηχανᾶτο δύναμιν εἰς σωτηρίαν.
[5] *Ib.* 320 d–328 c.

we shall not err in supposing that the mannerism appearing in this and some other passages is subdued rather than heightened from its original strength. There is just so much attempt at imitation as will allow us to catch, here and there, the tones of the lecturer's voice. The *Theætetus*, however, seems to confront us with the actual Protagoras, so much more sharply do his habits of thought and speech stand out from the rest of the dialogue. It is probable that Plato's maturer view of him has led to a little exaggeration; but the point of such imitations as the following must be that they are substantially true to life[1] :—

τὸν δὲ λόγον αὖ μὴ τῷ ῥήματί μου δίωκε, ἀλλ᾽ ὧδε ἔτι σαφέστερον μάθε τί λέγω. οἷον γὰρ ἐν τοῖς πρόσθεν ἐλέγετο ἀναμνήσθητι, ὅτι τῷ μὲν ἀσθενοῦντι πικρὰ φαίνεται ἃ ἐσθίει καὶ ἔστι, τῷ δὲ ὑγιαίνοντι τἀναντία ἔστι καὶ φαίνεται· σοφώτερον μὲν οὖν τούτων οὐδέτερον δεῖ ποιῆσαι· οὐδὲ γὰρ δυνατόν· οὐδὲ κατηγορητέον ὡς ὁ μὲν κάμνων ἀμαθὴς ὅτι τοιαῦτα δοξάζει, ὁ δὲ ὑγιαίνων σοφὸς ὅτι ἀλλοῖα· μεταβλητέον δ᾽ ἐπὶ θάτερα· ἀμείνων γὰρ ἡ ἑτέρα ἕξις.

The methodical use of οὐδέ and γάρ to pick up and enlarge on a foregoing clause, the dogmatic repetition of words (φαίνεται—ἔστι, ἔστι—φαίνεται) and the carefully measured balance of the phrases, seem to revive the actual delivery of the famous teacher. The same short-winded style prevails throughout the mimic defence of him supplied by Socrates[2]; who tells us at the end that if Protagoras had been alive, he would have maintained his doctrines on a much grander scale[3]. It is admitted, however, to be a gallant attempt[4]. Further, we may hazard

[1] *Theæt.* 166 e. [2] *Ib.* 166 a–168 c.
[3] *Ib.* 168 c—εἰ δ᾽ αὐτὸς ἔζη, μεγαλειότερον ἂν τοῖς αὐτοῦ ἐβοήθησεν.
[4] *Ib.*—πάνυ νεανικῶς τῷ ἀνδρὶ βεβοήθηκας.

a guess that the imitation here is not solely a matter of style. Plato's aim is to expose once more, but in a stronger light, the sophist's aversion to the Socratic method; and this he contrives by making Socrates extemporise a Protagorean homily on the dangers which philosophy incurs by an unscrupulous conduct of cross-examination. The humour of this homily, addressed in fancy to Socrates himself, depends not merely on the well-known professional manner, but probably also on the re-appearance of a favourite illustration. It is possible, at least, that the instance of the sick man and the healthy man, with the ensuing comparison of the doctor and the sophist, and of their respective remedies, had come to be a byword like the μαιευτική of Socrates. But, although it is tempting to see this significance in the passage, there is nothing in the tradition to connect Protagoras with the discussion of medicine. We only hear that, like Thucydides, he was at Athens during the plague (430–429 B.C.), and praised the heroic fortitude of Pericles under the loss of his two sons. A fragment of what appears to have been a eulogy of the statesman, written by Protagoras in the Ionic dialect, has been preserved; the first half of the piece is as follows[1]:—

τῶν γὰρ υἱέων νεηνιῶν ὄντων καὶ καλῶν, ἐν ὀκτὼ δὲ ταῖς πάσῃσι ἡμέρῃσι ἀποθανόντων νηπενθέως ἀνέτλη · εὐδίης γὰρ εἴχετο, ἐξ ἧς πολλὸν ὤνητο κατὰ πᾶσαν ἡμέρην εἰς εὐποτμίην καὶ ἀνωδυνίην καὶ τὴν ἐν τοῖς πολλοῖσι δόξαν.

Here the grandeur of single words, and the repetition of simpler ones (πάσῃσι ἡμέρῃσι—πᾶσαν ἡμέρην : πολλὸν—πολλοῖσι), accord pretty closely with the manner portrayed by Plato. This manner is the direct descendant of that terse solemnity which we have observed

[1] [Plutarch] Cons. ad. Apoll. xxxiii, 118 e ; D. F.V.[2] i. p. 540.

in Heracleitus and Herodotus[1].   It is feeling its way, as we have seen[2], towards a scheme of word-echoes more attractive than mere 'anaphora,' but yet, so far as our evidence shows, it either will not or cannot descend to patterns of complex elegance.   The frequent short speeches in Herodotus maintain on the whole this reserved and almost abrupt simplicity ; though here and there we meet with obvious attempts at artifice.   Thus Crœsus, when Cyrus asks him how he came to invade Persia, replies[3] :—

ὦ βασιλεῦ, ἐγὼ ταῦτα ἔπρηξα τῇ σῇ μὲν εὐδαιμονίῃ, τῇ ἐμεωυτοῦ δὲ κακοδαιμονίῃ· αἴτιος δὲ τούτων ἐγένετο ὁ Ἑλλήνων θεὸς ἐπαείρας ἐμὲ στρατεύεσθαι· οὐδεὶς γὰρ οὕτω ἀνόητός ἐστι ὅστις πόλεμον πρὸ εἰρήνης αἱρέεται· ἐν μὲν γὰρ τῇ οἱ παῖδες τοὺς πατέρας θάπτουσι, ἐν δὲ τῷ οἱ πατέρες τοὺς παῖδας.

It is not our business here to distinguish the various degrees of formality in the numerous speeches and conversations of Herodotus' History.   Such a study would be well worth while, since it is in this part of his work that he appears, contrary to the usual opinion of his style, to have made a deliberate effort towards that art of characteristic intonation, which we have just surveyed in the easy accomplishment of Plato.   Perhaps our purpose will be sufficiently served, if we look into the composition of that particularly formal debate of Otanes, Megabyzus and Darius, which we adduced for a brief comparison with the speech-writing of Thucydides[4].

Like all the speeches in Herodotus, and like the most sententious parts of Protagoras' discourses, this debate

---

[1] Above, pp. 113–116: cf. what was said of the professor taking the place of the popular sage, p. 129.
[2] Above, p. 131 (*Theæt.* 166 e).   [3] Herod. I, 87.
[4] Above, p. 30 (Herod. III, 80–82).

on the three forms of government is designed to make a special impression on the ear by means of short, weighty clauses, many of which contain less than ten words, and some only five or six. In a few places these members are made to concert an epigrammatic effect. First we have a moral study[1], fresh, it might seem, from Solon or Theognis :—

ἐγγίγνεται μὲν γάρ οἱ ὕβρις ὑπὸ τῶν παρεόντων ἀγαθῶν, φθόνος δὲ ἀρχῆθεν ἐμφύεται ἀνθρώπῳ. δύο δ᾽ ἔχων ταῦτα ἔχει πᾶσαν κακότητα· τὰ μὲν γὰρ ὕβρι κεκορημένος ἔρδει πολλὰ καὶ ἀτάσθαλα, τὰ δὲ φθόνῳ.

A little further on in this same speech of Otanes there is some obvious manœuvring of words :—

ἀναρμοστότατον δὲ πάντων· ἤν τε γὰρ αὐτὸν μετρίως θωμάζῃς, ἄχθεται ὅτι οὐ κάρτα θεραπεύεται, ἤν τε θεραπεύῃ τις κάρτα, ἄχθεται ἅτε θωπί.

Here the artificial repetitions of ordinary verbs are outdone by the concluding assonance of θωπί with θωμάζῃς. The case for democracy ends thus :—

τίθεμαι ὦν γνώμην μετέντας ἡμέας μουναρχίην τὸ πλῆθος ἀέξειν· ἐν γὰρ τῷ πολλῷ ἔνι τὰ πάντα.

In the speeches of Megabyzus and Darius there is nothing quite so elegant : but the latter, arguing for monarchy against oligarchy, builds an insistent climax of repetition[2] :—

αὐτὸς γὰρ ἕκαστος βουλόμενος κορυφαῖος εἶναι γνώμῃσί τε νικᾶν ἐς ἔχθεα μεγάλα ἀλλήλοισι ἀπικνέονται, ἐξ ὧν στάσιες ἐγγίγνονται, ἐκ δὲ τῶν στασίων φόνος, ἐκ δὲ τοῦ φόνου ἀπέβη ἐς μουναρχίην, καὶ ἐν τούτῳ διέδεξε ὅσῳ ἐστὶ τοῦτο ἄριστον.

There is no good reason for ascribing the composition of the debate to anyone but Herodotus : yet it clearly

---

[1] Herod. III, 80.　　　　[2] Ib. 82.

shows the influence of that elementary practice in pointed phrasing which is best illustrated by the manner of Protagoras as it appears in the *Theætetus*, and which most probably caught the historian's attention either at Athens or at Thurii.

The lasting value of this stately method, which, so far as we can see, was adapted by Protagoras from the lofty pronouncements of Heracleitus, has earned very inadequate—indeed hardly any—recognition. When once it is set before us as a distinct manner of speech, we can perceive how Plato's own style owes some of its noblest effects to a judicious use of such abrupt formality. That he had felt its power in his youth is clear, for example, from what is said of Diotima's manner in the *Symposium*[1]:—'She went on thus, like the professors in their glory, "I would have you know, Socrates...".' And so, in the myth which dismisses the *Republic* with a halo of supernatural splendour, the mysterious ministrant of the Fates, as he is about to fling the lots of life to the assembled souls of men, delivers his message thus[2]:—

Ἀνάγκης θυγατρὸς κόρης Λαχέσεως λόγος· ψυχαὶ ἐφήμεροι, ἀρχὴ ἄλλης περιόδου θνητοῦ γένους θανατηφόρου. οὐχ ὑμᾶς δαίμων λήξεται, ἀλλ᾽ ὑμεῖς δαίμονα αἱρήσεσθε. πρῶτος δ᾽ ὁ λαχὼν πρῶτος αἱρείσθω βίον, ᾧ συνέσται ἐξ ἀνάγκης· ἀρετὴ δ᾽ ἀδέσποτον· ἣν τιμῶν καὶ ἀτιμάζων πλέον καὶ ἔλαττον αὐτῆς ἕκαστος ἕξει. αἰτία ἑλομένου· θεὸς ἀναίτιος.

It is very true, as Proclus remarks, that the words here are 'like shafts loaded with mind and with lofty intent[3],' especially when contrasted with the exuberant flow of the myth-narrative[4]: but the passage acquires a larger interest, when we can say where Plato learnt such

---

[1] Plato, *Sympos.* 208 c.   [2] *Respubl.* X, 617 d.
[3] Proclus, *In Rempubl.* ii, 269 (quoted in Adam's note *ad loc.*).
[4] E.g. *Respubl.* X, 618 b-c.

repetitions as δαίμων—δαίμονα, λήξεται—λαχών, αἱρήσεσθε—αἱρείσθω. And there is another solemn utterance,
where perhaps he reaches his sublimest height of mythic
vision ; it opens thus [1] :—

θεοὶ θεῶν, ὧν ἐγὼ δημιουργὸς πατήρ τε ἔργων, δι᾽
ἐμοῦ γενόμενα ἄλυτα ἐμοῦ γε μὴ ἐθέλοντος· τὸ μὲν οὖν δὴ
δεθὲν πᾶν λυτόν, τό γε μὴν καλῶς ἁρμοσθὲν καὶ ἔχον εὖ
λύειν ἐθέλειν κακοῦ.

But we must return to the progress of this and other
methods in their experimental stages.

§ 4

Perhaps the most striking evidences of early rhetorical
influence are to be seen in those treatises in the Hippocratean collection which, while certainly not belonging to
the great doctor himself, are probably to be placed among
his pupils and friends in the middle of the fifth century[2].
The literary qualities of these works have received from
students of Hellenic civilisation even less notice than
their intellectual and moral worth[3]. Merely to appraise
and range them in order of external accomplishment
would be a useful and interesting task ; but this, even in

---

[1] *Tim.* 41 a.

[2] Greenhill (*Dict. Gr. Rom. Biog. Myth. s.n. Hippocrates*) makes these
17 or 18 in all, without counting 11 more which were '*perhaps* written by
Hippocrates.'

[3] Thus a few pages of one are quoted by Diels (*De Victu*, D. *F.V.*[2] i,
pp. 81–85) for its obvious connection with Heracleitus; Gomperz attempts
to prove that another is by Protagoras (*De Arte; Die Apologie der Heilkunst*[2],
1910); and only a passing glance is given to a third and fourth by Blass, in
his study of ancient rhetoric (*De Prisca Medicina, De Ventis*; *Att. Bered.*
1887, I, pp. 89–90). The best history of the art of prose-writing quotes once
from the piece appearing in Diels (Norden, *Ant. Kunstprosa*, 1898, p. 21),
and notices the tendency to poetic rhythm in the *De Ventis* (*ib.* p. 44).
Attention had been drawn to the style of these pieces by J. Ilberg, *Studia
Pseudippocratea*, 1883. Taylor, *Varia Socratica*, 1912, has pointed out their
importance for the history of sophistry.

summary, would lead us too far afield. We must be
content, as in the case of the authentic writings[1], to
select only a few examples ; taking advantage of the
general similarity of subject-matter for the purpose of
observing in brief the steady progress of formality. This
done, we shall turn to the personal history of Sicilian
rhetoric.

The treatise *On Ancient Medicine* is intended to
support Hippocrates' method of empirical observation
against the *a priori* theories of certain doctors ;
who, under the influence of the Eleatic philosophy,
attributed all sorts of disease to a single universal
cause. It is a sincere and able piece of writing, in which
the ample yet orderly scheme of the sentences is well
suited to a confident command of the subject. The
medical art began, the writer declares, when men first
noticed that sickness required a different diet and mode
of life from those of health[2] :—

τὴν γὰρ ἀρχὴν οὔτ' ἂν εὑρέθη ἡ τέχνη ἡ ἰατρική, οὔτ'
ἂν ἐζητήθη (οὐδὲν γὰρ αὐτῆς ἔδει), εἰ τοῖσι κάμνουσι τῶν
ἀνθρώπων τὰ αὐτὰ διαιτωμένοισί τε καὶ προσφερομένοισι,
ἅπερ οἱ ὑγιαίνοντες ἐσθίουσί τε καὶ πίνουσι καὶ τἄλλα
διαιτέονται, ξυνέφερε, καὶ εἰ μὴ ἦν ἕτερα τουτέων βελτίω.

Not only is the argument presented in a single
and almost completely self-connecting system, but the
rhyming pairs of verb-forms are plainly meant to regulate
its motion. Yet there is no attempt at ornament for its
own sake : the author is preoccupied with the importance
of his theme. He passes to the art of cookery, and
compares its elimination of the unsuitable with that
devised by medicine[3] :—

ὁ μέν, ὅσων μὴ ἠδύνατο ἡ φύσις ἡ ἀνθρωπίνη ἐπί-
κρατέειν ὑγιαίνουσα ἐμπιπτόντων, διὰ ἀγριότητά τε καὶ

[1] Above, pp. 99, 125.   [2] *De Prisca Medic.* 3.   [3] *Ib.* 7.

ἀκρησίην, ὁ δέ, ὅσων ἡ διάθεσις ἐν οἵῃ ἂν ἑκάστοτε ἕκαστος
τύχῃ διακείμενος μὴ ἦν δυνατὸς ἐπικρατέειν, ταῦτα ἐζήτησε
ἀφελεῖν.

In such industrious arrangements as these we ought
to recognise the pattern of those anxiously laboured
comparisons in Thucydides[1]. But we must also note
how simple effects of sound, such as began to be heard
in Heracleitus and Herodotus[2], are gaining an entrance
here. The two short treatises *On the Nature of Man*
and *On the Regime for Health* are written from the same
scientific standpoint, the former especially tracing the errors
of some theorists to the doctrine of Melissus[3]. It is not
unlikely that their author was Polybus, the son-in-law of
Hippocrates, since we find here another account of the
views which Aristotle quotes and ascribes to him[4].
There is little to remark in the style, beyond what we
have seen in the master himself[5]. But the vigorous
writer *On the Sacred Disease*, while following out the
denial of divine intervention which we saw in Hippocrates[6], shows a more adventurous eloquence. His long
prefatory chapter is an indignant refutation of the view
that epilepsy is a specially god-sent affliction : it sternly
exposes the magical tricks by which that belief is
maintained for the advantage of charlatans[7] :—

καὶ τὰ μὲν τῶν καθαρμῶν γῇ κρύπτουσι, τὰ δὲ ἐς
θάλασσαν ἐμβάλλουσι, τὰ δὲ ἐς τὰ οὔρεα ἀποφέρουσι, ὅπη
μηδεὶς ἅψεται μηδὲ ἐπιβήσεται· τὰ δ' ἐχρῆν ἐς τὰ ἱερὰ
φέροντας τῷ θεῷ ἀποδοῦναι, εἰ δὴ θεός γέ ἐστι αἴτιος. οὐ
μέντοι ἔγωγε ἀξιῶ ὑπὸ θεοῦ ἀνθρώπου σῶμα μιαίνεσθαι, τὸ

---

[1] Above, p. 110-1.   [2] Above, pp. 115-6.
[3] *De Nat. Hom.* 1 ; cf. Plato, *Phædrus*, 270, and Thompson's note.
[4] *Ib.* 11 ; Aristot. *Hist. Anim.* III, 3. 512 b.
[5] Galen, in his commentary on the *De Nat. Hom.*, tells us that Polybus
adhered closely to the teaching of Hippocrates. See a note on the passage
of Aristotle by D. W. Thompson, in his translation of the *Hist. Anim.* (1910).
[6] Above, p. 125, n. 2.   [7] *De Morbo Sacro.* 1 ad fin.

ἐπικηρότατον ὑπὸ τοῦ ἁγνοτάτου· ἀλλὰ κἢν τυγχάνῃ ὑπὸ
ἑτέρου μεμιασμένον ἤ τι πεπονθός, ἐθέλοι ἂν ὑπὸ τοῦ θεοῦ
καθαίρεσθαι καὶ ἁγνίζεσθαι μᾶλλον ἢ μιαίνεσθαι.

The writer of this, whether he is Hippocrates or one
of his colleagues, appears to have had some lessons from
Protagoras.   So again, in declaring that heredity plays
its part in this as in other diseases, he developes an
insistent emphasis [1] :—

ἄρχεται δὲ ὥσπερ καὶ τἄλλα νουσήματα κατὰ γένος· εἰ
γὰρ ἐκ φλεγματώδεος φλεγματώδης· καὶ ἐκ χολώδεος
χολώδης γίνεται, καὶ ἐκ φθινώδεος φθινώδης καὶ ἐκ
σπληνώδεος σπληνώδης, τί κωλύει ὅτῳ πατὴρ καὶ μήτηρ
εἶχετο, τούτῳ τῷ νουσήματι καὶ τῶν ἐκγόνων ἔχεσθαί τινα;
ὡς ὁ γόνος ἔρχεται πάντοθεν τοῦ σώματος, ἀπό τε τῶν
ὑγιηρῶν ὑγιηρός, ἀπό τε τῶν νοσερῶν νοσερός.

Another treatise *On Regime* is a lengthy exposition,
in four parts, of the discovery that health depends on an
equipoise between nutrition and exercise.   The first part
is occupied with showing that, as the human body, like
everything else, is composed of fire and water and also
undergoes perpetual change, so its processes are to be
discerned at large, since they are everywhere reflected,
in the various arts of man.   The Heracleitean basis of the
work is obvious [2] ; and both here, and throughout the
succeeding three books, which provide the details of a
corrective regime, we seem to possess such a piece of
a priori reasoning as the writer *On Ancient Medicine*
condemns [3].   But more interesting to us is the conduct
of the style.   At first it aims merely at a regular, steady
balance [4] :—

[1] *De Morbo Sacro,* 2.
[2] Cf. the doctor Eryximachus' discussion of a saying of Heracleitus in
Plato, *Sympos.* 187 a.
[3] Above, p. 137.   [4] *De Victu,* 2.

φημὶ δὲ δεῖν τὸν μέλλοντα ὀρθῶς ξυγγράφειν περὶ διαίτης ἀνθρωπίνης πρῶτον μὲν παντὸς φύσιν ἀνθρώπου γνῶναι καὶ διαγνῶναι· γνῶναι μὲν ἀπὸ τίνων συνέστηκεν ἐξ ἀρχῆς, διαγνῶναι δὲ ὑπὸ τίνων μερῶν κεκράτηται—

but, as the author approaches the philosophy of the matter, he shortens his stride[1]:—

φάος Ζηνί, σκότος Ἀιδη, φάος Ἀιδη, σκότος Ζηνί· φοιτᾷ κεῖνα ὧδε καὶ τάδε κεῖσε, πᾶσαν ὥρην, πᾶσαν χώρην, δια-πρησσόμενα κεῖνά τε τὰ τῶνδε, τάδε τ᾽ αὖ τὰ κείνων—

and soon he is almost giddy with the dance[2]:—

πρίουσιν ἄνθρωποι ξύλον· ὁ μὲν ἕλκει, ὁ δὲ ὠθεῖ, τὸ δὲ αὐτὸ τοῦτο ποιοῦσι· μεῖον δὲ ποιοῦντες πλέον ποιοῦσι. τοιοῦτον φύσις ἀνθρώπου· τὸ μὲν ὠθεῖ, τὸ δὲ ἕλκει· τὸ μὲν δίδωσι, τὸ δὲ λαμβάνει· καὶ τῷ μὲν δίδωσι, τοσούτῳ πλέον, τοῦ δὲ λαμβάνει, τοσούτῳ μεῖον.

The same kind of excitement continues for several chapters. When he comes to deal with the particular vicissitudes of the human body, he is sober and steady again; though here and there he seems to be only just refraining from the verbal game. We could hardly have a livelier illustration of the seductive arena prepared by Ionian philosophy for these first students of formal prose. The effect as we read is like that of witnessing what at first appears to be a dangerous seizure, but soon is understood to be the passing flutter of a harmless enthusiasm. It is clearly a genuine transport, and as such it is worthy to be classed and compared with the sharp clatter of those coupled phrases in Thucydides' sketch of the troubles in Greece[3].

Before we enquire into the immediate cause of such behaviour, we must notice a few more examples of literary

---

[1] De Victu, 5; D. F.V.[2] i, p. 80. [2] Ib. 6; D. F.V.[2] i, p. 81.
[3] Above, pp. 88–91.

craft in these 'iatrosophists.' We find in a short essay
On the Winds another case of philosophical theory
applied to the explanation of disease.   Here it is Anaxi-
menes' doctrine—that the underlying substance of everything is air[1]—which is made to unlock all the secrets of
human health and infirmity.   But the discussion is less a
matter of detailed argument than of adroitly persuasive
suggestion : the writer relies chiefly on the charm of his
elegant phrases ; and he pleasantly declares that, if he
were to deal with every sort of ailment, his discourse
would be longer, but not a whit truer or more convincing.
His particular skill is not in medicine, but in antithesis,
which he is learning to use in a variety of ways.   He
can arrange it in one clause, and illumine it with a poetic
figure, as when he says of the doctor[2] :—

ἐπ' ἀλλοτρίῃσι ξυμφορῇσι ἰδίας καρποῦται λύπας—

or work it out till the sound is forced to conspire with the
sense[3] :—

αὖθις αὖ δίψαν ἔπαυσε πόσις· πάλιν αὖ πλησμονὴν
ἰῆται κένωσις, κένωσιν δὲ πλησμονή· πόνον δὲ ἀπονίη,
ἀπονίην δὲ πόνος—

so that when he tells us that all this is merely *en passant*
to his main business [4], there is little chance of illusion as to
what that business is.   For immediately he is enforcing
a contrast with word-play[5] :—

τῶν δὲ δὴ νούσων ἁπασέων ὁ μὲν τρόπος ὁ αὐτός, ὁ δὲ
τόπος διαφέρει—

and soon, when unable to provide an antithesis, he
contrives a jingle[6] :—

---

[1] Burnet, *E.G.P.*[2] p. 77.
[2] *De Ventis*, 1 ; cf. the use of καρποῦται by Democr., above, p. 122.
[3] *Ibid.*
[4] *Ibid.*—τὰ μὲν οὖν ἐν παρέργῳ τοῦ λόγου τοῦ μέλλοντος εἴρηται.
[5] *Ib.* 2.   [6] *Ib.* 3.

ἄνεμος γάρ ἐστιν ἠέρος ῥεῦμα καὶ χεῦμα—

besides the childish assonance and alliteration of the statement [1]—

τὰ γὰρ σώματα τῶν τε ἀνθρώπων καὶ τῶν ἄλλων ζώων ὑπὸ τρισσέων τροφῶν τρέφεται· ἔστι δὲ τῇσι τροφῇσι ταύτῃσι ταῦτα τὰ οὐνόματα, σῖτα, ποτά, πνεύματα.

The combined effect of these examples is of course unfair to the general quality of the author's style : it is only as supplying clear evidence of the professional study of prose-form, and of the lines which that study was pursuing, that they are rightly important.

Some ingenious learning has been employed to urge that the treatise *On the Art* is the composition of Protagoras [2]. It is a defence of the physician's art, manifestly written by a man of letters who is not a regular physician, in reply to an attack made by some other sophist. The writer has got hold of just enough technical information to serve his purpose of showing that medicine is a real and effectual art in most cases which are not plainly desperate : but the discussion as a whole has the air of a literary exercise. So far there is room for supposing its author to be Protagoras. In some points, indeed, it corresponds with Plato's parody, as in this passage [3]:—

τῶν μὲν οὖν τοιούτων πάντων ἐν πᾶσι τὰς ἀκεσίας ἀναμαρτήτους δεῖ εἶναι, οὐχ ὡς ῥηιδίας, ἀλλ' ὅτι ἐξεύρηνται· ἐξεύρηνταί γε μὴν οὐ τοῖσι βουληθεῖσιν, ἀλλὰ τούτων τοῖσι δυνηθεῖσι· δύνανται δὲ οἷσι τά τε τῆς παιδείης μὴ ἐκποδὼν τά τε τῆς φύσιος μὴ ταλαίπωρα.

Yet there are also some much more elaborate devices :

[1] *Ib.*—Ilberg, *Stud. Pseudippocr.*, has collected further instances.
[2] Gomperz, *Die Apol. der Heilkunst*, 1890 (2nd ed. 1910).
[3] *De Arte*, 9.

words are not merely repeated, but repeated for the purpose of a jingling epigram [1] :—

οἶμαι δὲ ἔγωγε καὶ τὰ ὀνόματα αὐτὰς διὰ τὰ εἴδεα λαβεῖν· ἄλογον γὰρ ἀπὸ τῶν ὀνομάτων ἡγεῖσθαι τὰ εἴδεα βλαστάνειν καὶ ἀδύνατον. τὰ μὲν γὰρ ὀνόματα νομοθετ-ήματά ἐστι, τὰ δὲ εἴδεα οὐ νομοθετήματα, ἀλλὰ βλαστήματα φύσιος [2].

The steady connection by assonance and rhyme (ὀνόματα—νομοθετήματα—βλαστήματα) is obviously deliberate, as if to illustrate, in the act of asserting, the helpful properties of words [3]. Glancing for a moment at the rhetorical parts of Thucydides, we find very similar devices here and there. We have this rhyme in the letter of Nicias [4]—

οἰόμενοι χρηματιεῖσθαι μᾶλλον ἢ μαχεῖσθαι—

or a verb re-compounded, as in Hermocrates' speech [5]—

οὐ Λεοντίνους βούλεσθαι κατοικίσαι, ἀλλ' ἡμᾶς μᾶλλον ἐξοικίσαι.

As a rule, the historian makes his speakers more inclined to this sort of distinction between words partly the same or etymologically connected, than between those whose sound alone is similar. Pericles matches φιλοσοφοῦμεν and φιλοκαλοῦμεν [6], φρονήματι and κατα-φρονήματι [7]. But we find one artificial sentence of Hermocrates [8] :—

εὐπρεπῶς ἄδικοι ἐλθόντες, εὐλόγως ἄπρακτοι ἀπίασιν—

---

[1] *Ib.* 2.

[2] Littré's translation—'Les noms sont des conventions que la nature impose, mais les réalités sont non des conventions qu'elle impose, mais des *productions* qu'elle enfante'—might be improved by putting *inventions* for *productions*. The German version of Gomperz effaces all the elegance.

[3] Cf. above, p. 116.   [4] Thuc. VII, 13. 2.

[5] VI, 76. 2.   [6] II, 40. I.   [7] II, 62. 3.   [8] IV, 61 fin.

which may be compared, for its alliteration, with a
contrivance in the *De Arte*[1] :—

ἀγνοεῖ ἄγνοιαν ἁρμόζουσαν μανίῃ μᾶλλον ἢ ἀμαθίῃ.

To show how intemperately this nameless writer
has yielded to the fashion of sonorous repetitions and
amplifications, we may take the following passage[2] :—

οὐ γὰρ δὴ ὀφθαλμοῖσί γε ἰδόντι τούτων τῶν εἰρημένων
οὐδενὶ οὐδὲν ἔστι εἰδέναι · διὸ καὶ ἄδηλα ἐμοί τε ὠνόμασται
καὶ τῇ τέχνῃ κέκριται εἶναι. οὐ μὴν ὅτι ἄδηλα κεκράτηκε,
ἀλλ᾽ ᾗ δυνατὸν κεκράτηται· δυνατὸν δ᾽ ἕως αἵ τε τῶν
νοσεόντων φύσιες τὸ σκεφθῆναι παρέχουσιν αἵ τε τῶν
ἐρευνησόντων ἐς τὴν ἔρευναν πεφύκασι · μετὰ πλέονος μὲν
γὰρ πόνου καὶ οὐ μετ᾽ ἐλάσσονος χρόνου—

So he runs on, with his giddy delight in mere empty
word-patterns, of which there is no hint even in the
mockery of the *Theætetus*. If Protagoras is the author
of this treatise, we must conclude that he was far more
trivial in his writing than in his conversation or his
lectures ; and, although there is much in these verbal
repetitions, as also in some of the thought, to indicate
his influence[3]—we remember too that suggestion of a
medical theory in the Platonic imitation[4],—it seems most
probable that we have here the work of some literary
pupil, who has cultivated a greater variety of graces than
the stately style of his first instructor ever reached or
sought.

§ 5

This disciple may perhaps have been Prodicus, whose
'minute pedantry[5]' could draw from Plato little more

---

[1] *De Arte*, 8.   [2] *Ib.* 11.   [3] Cf. Gomperz, *l.c.*, pp. 22 foll. ; 180.
[4] Plato, *Theæt.* 166 e ; above, pp. 132-3.
[5] Thompson, on Plato, *Phædr.* 267 b : for a reference to a medical work
of Prodicus, see Galen, *De Virt. Phys.* II, 9 ; D. *F.V.*[2] i, p. 571. Diels
(*F.V.*[3] II, p. 292) seems to ascribe the *De Arte* to Antiphon the Sophist.

than a mild contempt. Yet Aristophanes[1] seems to commend his 'learning and discernment'; and Plato himself testifies to the universal respect he enjoyed. He was competent, like Gorgias and Hippias, to instruct the youth in any city that he chose to visit[2]. 'Our good friend Prodicus,' says Socrates, 'had a great success, both publicly and privately[3]'; and in fact it appears that Socrates once attended his lectures[4]. These frequently dealt with ethical subjects, but their chief aim was to fix the precise meanings of words. The amusing picture of him in the *Protagoras* shows him industriously distinguishing between ἀμφισβητεῖν and ἐρίζειν, κοινός and ἴσος, εὐδοκιμεῖν and ἐπαινεῖσθαι, εὐφραίνεσθαι and ἥδεσθαι, in a series of nicely balanced clauses[5] :—

ἀμφισβητοῦσι μὲν γὰρ καὶ δι' εὔνοιαν οἱ φίλοι τοῖς φίλοις, ἐρίζουσιν δὲ οἱ διάφοροί τε καὶ ἐχθροὶ ἀλλήλοις—

and so on. Further, we have Xenophon's quotation—from uncertain memory—of his moral fable, *The Choice of Heracles*. Here the speeches of Ἀρετή and Κακία consist chiefly of full-sounding phrases strung in a regular succession ; Virtue proclaims herself thus[6] :—

ἀγαπητὴ μὲν συνεργὸς τεχνίταις, πιστὴ δὲ φύλαξ οἴκων δεσπόταις, εὐμενὴς δὲ παραστάτις οἰκέταις, ἀγαθὴ δὲ συλλήπτρια τῶν ἐν εἰρήνῃ πόνων, βεβαία δὲ τῶν ἐν πολέμῳ σύμμαχος ἔργων—

where the metaphors suggest the influence of tragedy, and remind us of the poetical patch in the Athenian speech to the Melians[7] :—

ἐλπὶς δέ, κινδύνῳ παραμύθιον οὖσα, τοὺς μὲν ἀπὸ περιουσίας χρωμένους αὐτῇ, κἂν βλάψῃ, οὐ καθεῖλε, κτλ.

[1] Aristoph. *Nub.* 361.　　[2] Plato, *Apol.* 19 e.
[3] *Hipp. Maj.* 282 b—ὁ ἡμέτερος ἑταῖρος.
[4] *Meno*, 96 d ; *Cratyl.* 384 b.　　[5] *Protag.* 337 b; cf. *Charmid.* 163 d.
[6] Xenophon, *Mem.* II, i, 32; who remarks (34) that the style of the original was even more ornate than that of his version.
[7] Thuc. V, 103. 1.

It is worth notice that in the one jingling sentence of the fable we seem to hear the voice of Prodicus himself, when Virtue tells Vice that 'praise of oneself is the sweetest sound of all to hear[1]':—

ἀθάνατος δὲ οὖσα ἐκ θεῶν μὲν ἀπέρριψαι, ὑπὸ δὲ ἀνθρώπων ἀγαθῶν ἀτιμάζῃ· τοῦ δὲ πάντων ἡδίστου ἀκούσματος, ἐπαίνου σεαυτῆς, ἀνήκοος εἶ, καὶ τοῦ πάντων ἡδίστου θεάματος ἀθέατος· οὐδὲν γὰρ πώποτε σεαυτῆς ἔργον καλὸν τεθέασαι.

This habit of repeating a word in slightly different forms, which we have just seen developing, for the sake of mere sound, in the medical treatises, is probably to be connected with the work of Gorgias; and particularly so when these echoes are combined with poetic imagery.

Hippias, whom Plato repeatedly associates with Prodicus, was a man whose widely useful achievements in the advancement of learning cannot now ensure him more than a titular fame. His mind appears to have been a little too abundantly furnished to allow of the ready movement of his wits[2]: but history must always remember, and Thucydides must have respected, the first compiler and publisher of a table of Olympian victors. He used to lecture on a prodigious variety of subjects; but, like Prodicus, he made a speciality of moral discourses, whose language was offered as a model of elegance and propriety[3]. The mimicry of the *Protagoras*, however, seems to reveal a more interesting accomplishment in the structure of his sentences. In this dialogue, the setting and conduct of the two short speeches delivered by Prodicus and Hippias have something of the air of an epic debate: we find them turning

---

[1] Xenophon, *l.c.* 31.

[2] Xenophon, *Mem.* IV, iv, 6; Plato, *Gorg.* 490 e, and Thompson's note.

[3] Plato, *Hipp. Maj.* 286 a—ἔστι γάρ μοι περὶ αὐτῶν [ἐπιτηδευμάτων καλῶν] παγκάλως λόγος συγκείμενος, καὶ ἄλλως εὖ διακείμενος καὶ τοῖς ὀνόμασι.

a very ordinary appeal or argument into a means of
exhibiting 'salient points in their public reputation¹.'
Thus, when Prodicus has given his little display of verbal
precision, Hippias takes up his parable and says² :—

ὦ ἄνδρες οἱ παρόντες, ἡγοῦμαι ἐγὼ ὑμᾶς συγγενεῖς τε
καὶ οἰκείους καὶ πολίτας ἅπαντας εἶναι,—φύσει, οὐ νόμῳ·
τὸ γὰρ ὅμοιον τῷ ὁμοίῳ φύσει συγγενές ἐστιν, ὁ δὲ νόμος,
τύραννος ὢν τῶν ἀνθρώπων, πολλὰ παρὰ τὴν φύσιν
βιάζεται.

We remark the topic of φύσις and νόμος—one of the
popular fruits of Ionian philosophy—and the short,
balanced clauses in which it is treated ; but the sentence
continues thus :—

ἡμᾶς οὖν αἰσχρὸν τὴν μὲν φύσιν τῶν πραγμάτων
εἰδέναι, σοφωτάτους δὲ ὄντας τῶν Ἑλλήνων, καὶ κατ᾽ αὐτὸ
τοῦτο νῦν συνεληλυθότας τῆς τε Ἑλλάδος εἰς αὐτὸ τὸ
πρυτανεῖον τῆς σοφίας καὶ αὐτῆς τῆς πόλεως εἰς τὸν
μέγιστον καὶ ὀλβιώτατον οἶκον τόνδε, μηδὲν τούτου τοῦ
ἀξιώματος ἄξιον ἀποφήνασθαι, ἀλλ᾽ ὥσπερ τοὺς φαυλο-
τάτους τῶν ἀνθρώπων διαφέρεσθαι ἀλλήλοις.

The largeness of the periodic scheme makes a sudden
contrast with the method of Prodicus; which Hippias
seems to follow for a moment, and then to abandon for
his own extensive and imaginative manner. His tendency to vivid homely metaphor, such as we found in
Democritus, has fuller scope further on in a still more
lengthy sentence, in which occur these words³ :—

ἀλλ᾽ ἐφεῖναι καὶ χαλάσαι τὰς ἡνίας τοῖς λόγοις, ἵνα
μεγαλοπρεπέστεροι καὶ εὐσχημονέστεροι ἡμῖν φαίνωνται,
μήτ᾽ αὖ Πρωταγόραν πάντα κάλων ἐκτείναντα, οὐρίᾳ
ἐφέντα, φεύγειν εἰς τὸ πέλαγος τῶν λόγων ἀποκρύψαντα γῆν,
ἀλλὰ μέσον τι ἀμφοτέρους τεμεῖν.

¹ Jebb, *Hellenica* 'The Speeches of Thuc.', § 4; see above, p. 29.
² Plato, *Protag.* 337 c   ³ *Ib.* 338 a.

The sentiment about Athens in the former of these passages, and the sonorous flow of both, are very suggestive of what the oratory of Pericles may have been when Thucydides heard it, as distinguished from the quintessence of it which the History conveys to us now. The elaborate metaphor, for instance, in the latter piece is admirably managed : but Pericles' and Thucydides' own taste was doubtless for leaving such sallies to the professional shows and contests of the day[1].

Of the more business-like style of Hippias we have possibly a specimen in a fragment of prose discovered at El-Hibeh. The writer argues against a theory of musical rhythms such as that propounded by Plato in the *Republic*[2]; and although his vocabulary is quite simple, his sentences are carefully composed of short and evenly-weighted clauses[3] :—

λέγοντες γὰρ ὅτι ἁρμονικοί εἰσι καὶ προχειρισάμενοι ᾠδάς τινας ταύτας συγκρίνουσιν τῶν μὲν ὡς ἔτυχεν κατηγορ

οῦντες, τὰς δὲ εἰκῇ ἐγκωμιάζοντες· καὶ λέγουσι μὲν ὡς οὐ δεῖ αὐτοὺς οὔτε ψάλτας οὔτε ᾠδοὺς θεωρεῖν· περὶ μὲν γὰρ ταῦτα ἑτέροις φασὶν παραχωρεῖν, αὐτῶν δὲ ἴδιον εἶναι τὸ θεωρητικὸν μέρος· φαίνονται δὲ περὶ μὲν ταῦτα ὧν ἑτέροις παραχωροῦσιν οὐ μετρίως ἐσπουδακότες, ἐν οἷς δέ φασιν ἰσχύειν ἐν τούτοις σχεδιάζοντες.

Thucydides has just this sort of balance, contrived by two long final participles :—

τῶν μὲν πείρᾳ αἰσθομένων, τῶν δὲ ἀκοῇ νομισάντων[4]—
τῶν σωμάτων τὴν πόλιν οὐκ ἀλλοτριοῦντες, ἀλλ' ἐς τὴν συγγένειαν οἰκειοῦντες[5]—

[1] Cf. Thuc. I, 22 fin.; Bunyan, *Pilg. Prog.* II (Greatheart)—'I make bold to talk thus Metaphorically, for the ripening of the Wits of young Readers.'
[2] *Respubl.* III, 398–400.
[3] Grenfell and Hunt, *Hibeh Papyr.* 1905, I, p. 47 ; cf. Plato, *Hipp. Min.* 368 d.
[4] Thuc. IV, 81. 2 (sketch of Brasidas).
[5] III, 65 fin. (speech of Thebans).

and there is one sentence of this fragment which may be considered to stand half-way between *The Choice of Heracles* and the Troubles in Greece :—

εἰς τοῦτο δὲ ἔρχονται τόλμης ὥστε ὅλον τὸν βίον κατα-
τρίβειν ἐν ταῖς χορδαῖς, ψάλλοντες μὲν πολὺ χεῖρον τῶν
ψαλτῶν, ᾄδοντες δὲ τῶν ᾠδῶν, συγκρίνοντες δὲ τοῦ τυχόντος
ῥήτορος,—πάντα πάντων χεῖρον ποιοῦντες.

One more piece in the Hippocratean collection may help us to fix our conception of the stately figurative style which Pericles encouraged in public speech, and which Thucydides admired and studied in both its early and its middle stages of elaboration. There is a little piece called *The Law*, consisting of four short paragraphs, which asserts the necessity of a distinctive qualification or 'degree' for the genuine doctors who travel in the course of their practice from city to city. After speaking of their long and careful training, the writer thus describes their work and the faults of their fraudulent rivals[1] :—

ταῦτα ὧν χρὴ ἐς τὴν ἰητρικὴν τέχνην ἐσενεγκαμένους,
καὶ ἀτρεκέως αὐτῆς γνῶσιν λαβόντας, οὕτως ἀνὰ τὰς πόλιας
φοιτεῦντας, μὴ λόγῳ μοῦνον, ἀλλὰ καὶ ἔργῳ ἰητροὺς νομίζ-
εσθαι· ἡ δὲ ἀπειρίη, κακὸς θησαυρὸς καὶ κακὸν κειμήλιον
τοῖσι ἔχουσι αὐτήν, καὶ ὄναρ καὶ ὕπαρ, εὐθυμίης τε καὶ
εὐφροσύνης ἄμοιρος, δειλίης τε καὶ θρασύτητος τιθήνη.

§ 6

For full light on all these artifices, we must turn to the rise of rhetoric, as the specific art of persuasion, in Sicily. The actual beginnings will not detain us long, for we have no sure knowledge of them. Aristotle mentions a handbook written by a certain Corax, which

---

[1] *Lex*, 4.

gave exemplary cases of probability for the use of litigants[1]. Tisias and Gorgias are classed together in the *Phædrus* as literary artists who perverted the truth by seductive pleading[2]; though by his choice of the words διὰ ῥώμην λόγου Plato seems to point at the result more than the intention. Tisias, from whatever part of Sicily he originally came, at any rate accompanied Gorgias on his Leontine embassy to Athens in 427 B.C.; and he was teaching the young Isocrates in Athens a few years later[3]. Gorgias, according to a fairly persistent tradition, was a pupil of Empedocles[4].

The effect of the ambassador's rhetoric on the Athenians we have already noticed[5]. But this same passage of the *Phædrus* contains a phrase which recalls a curious expression used by Thucydides in his own person, and which throws some light on the mood of the more intelligent public in its sudden bout of 'Gorgiasm.' The Platonic Socrates describes this new literary fashion as giving novelties an antique ring, and antiquities a novel ring[6]. Thus a part at least of Gorgias' mission was to preach μὴ τὰ ἀρχαῖα λέγειν ἀρχαίως. The familiar thoughts of every day must be clothed in fresh distinction; and it was by the alien air of his speech, as Diodorus says, that the people were excited[7]. Now Thucydides, in describing the last distracted appeals which Nicias made to his officers before the battle in the harbour of Syracuse, seems to contrast his manner with the full-dress elegance of a studied harangue. 'He

---

[1] Aristotle, *Rhet.* II, 1402 a. [2] Plato, *Phædr.* 267 a.

[3] Dionysius, *Isocr.* I.

[4] Diog. Laert. VIII, ii, 58; Aristot. *Soph. El.* 33, 183 b, 31. Diels (*Berl. Sitzungsber.* 1884, pp. 343 foll.) has traced some interesting connections between the philosopher of Acragas and the rhetorician of Leontini.

[5] Above, pp. 70–1.

[6] Plato, *Phædr.* 267 a—καινά τε ἀρχαίως τά τ' ἐναντία καινῶς. Cf. Isocr. *Paneg.* 8.

[7] Diod. Sic. XII, 53; above, p. 71 n.

reminded them of their country, its peculiar freedom, and the personal liberty it allowed to all without restraint in their daily life; and he used other words appropriate to a critical situation.   For at such times a man is unreserved, and cares not if his expressions sound old-fashioned; but shouts aloud the phrases—which, with little change, are made to serve for all occasions—about wives and children and ancestral gods, believing they must be useful in the trepidation of the moment[1].'

If the occasion had not been such as to reduce Nicias to platitudes, what might we have fairly expected to hear?   Some variations, presumably, on the theme which is suggested only to be abandoned in the flurry of a supreme effort—

πατρίδος τε τῆς ἐλευθερωτάτης ὑπομιμνήσκω καὶ τῆς ἐν αὐτῇ ἀνεπιτάκτου πᾶσιν ἐς τὴν δίαιταν ἐξουσίας—

such, in fact, as we have met before in Pericles' words[2]:—

ἐλευθέρως δὲ τά τε πρὸς τὸ κοινὸν πολιτεύομεν καὶ ἐς τὴν πρὸς ἀλλήλους τῶν καθ᾽ ἡμέραν ἐπιτηδευμάτων ὑποψίαν, οὐ δι᾽ ὀργῆς τὸν πέλας, εἰ καθ᾽ ἡδονήν τι δρᾷ, ἔχοντες, οὐδὲ ἀζημίους μέν, λυπηρὰς δὲ τῇ ὄψει ἀχθηδόνας προστιθέμενοι. ἀνεπαχθῶς δὲ τὰ ἴδια προσομιλοῦντες τὰ δημόσια διὰ δέος μάλιστα οὐ παρανομοῦμεν, κτλ.

The great aim, therefore, is not only to find new things to say (like Hippias[3]), and to give them a recognised dignity of expression, but to disguise common-places in an exquisite dress.   Henceforth it is equally disgraceful for a public speaker to be told that he has merely blurted out some new ideas, and that he has

---

[1] Thuc. VII, 69. 2—ὅσα...οὐ πρὸς τὸ δοκεῖν ἀρχαιολογεῖν φυλαξάμενοι εἴποιεν ἄν, καὶ ὑπὲρ ἁπάντων παραπλήσια...προφερόμενα.

[2] Thuc. II, 37. 2.

[3] Cf. Xenoph. *Mem.* IV, iv, 6—(Σωκ.) οὐ μόνον ἀεὶ τὰ αὐτὰ λέγω, ἀλλὰ καὶ περὶ τῶν αὐτῶν. σὺ δ᾽ ἴσως διὰ τὸ πολυμαθὴς εἶναι περὶ τῶν αὐτῶν οὐδέποτε τὰ αὐτὰ λέγεις. ἀμέλει, ἔφη (Ἱππ.), πειρῶμαι καινόν τι λέγειν ἀεί.

merely repeated old ones. But how did this fashion begin ?

If we look at the one considerable fragment remaining from the genuine compositions of Gorgias, we find him busily exploiting the uses of antithesis for momentary decoration, and taking little account of periodic system. He produces something like a string of twin-shaped beads on a slender thread of apposition[1]:—

μαρτύρια δὲ τούτων τρόπαια ἐστήσαντο τῶν πολεμίων, Διὸς μὲν ἀγάλματα, ἑαυτῶν δὲ ἀναθήματα, οὐκ ἄπειροι οὔτε ἐμφύτου ἄρεος, οὔτε νομίμων ἐρώτων οὔτε ἐνοπλίου ἔριδος, οὔτε φιλοκάλου εἰρήνης—

So far the thread is kept quite strong by means of οὔτε : but we pass on to this appendage :—

σεμνοὶ μὲν πρὸς τοὺς θεοὺς τῷ δικαίῳ, ὅσιοι δὲ πρὸς τοὺς τοκέας τῇ θεραπείᾳ, δίκαιοι μὲν πρὸς τοὺς ἀστοὺς τῷ ἴσῳ, εὐσεβεῖς δὲ πρὸς τοὺς φίλους τῇ πίστει·—

and although there is no reason appearing why the affair should ever come to a close, it ends at last in this richly knotted tassel :—

τοιγαροῦν αὐτῶν ἀποθανόντων ὁ πόθος οὐ συναπέθανεν, ἀλλ᾽ ἀθάνατος οὐκ ἐν ἀθανάτοις σώμασι ζῇ οὐ ζώντων[2].

The Athenians have been called barbarians, because they had no printed books, and because the speeches of Demosthenes had little effect on their actions[3]. If we cannot agree with Dr Johnson, we need not run to the other extreme, and regard them as hot-headed fools. In the first place, the intellect of Gorgias was a good deal more than ordinarily acute and active. There is

[1] D. F.V.[2] i, p. 557: it is a piece of his Funeral Oration on Athenian warriors.
[2] Cf. Fuller, *Holy War*, I, 17—'Famine, which is the worst of tyrants, and murdereth men in state, whilst they die in not dying.'
[3] Boswell, *Life of Johnson*, an. 1772.

clear evidence that for about the first half of his life,
which was nearly conterminous with the fifth century,
he was seriously engaged in physical speculations on
lines suggested by Empedocles[1]; and that then, influenced by the dialectic of Zeno, he developed a logical
disbelief in the first assumptions of philosophy. His
plain, thorough-going mode of argument is preserved
for us in almost its original form by a sceptic of the third
century A.D. In the following sentence he is busy with
the puzzle of being and existence[2] :—

εἰ γὰρ τὸ μὴ ὂν ἔστιν, ἔσται τε ἅμα καὶ οὐκ ἔσται·
ᾗ μὲν γὰρ οὐκ ὂν νοεῖται, οὐκ ἔσται, ᾗ δὲ ἔστι μὴ ὄν, πάλιν
ἔσται· παντελῶς δὲ ἄτοπον τὸ εἶναί τι ἅμα καὶ μὴ εἶναι·
οὐκ ἄρα ἔστι τὸ μὴ ὄν.

Euclid could do no better. But Gorgias seems to have
lost interest in these high disputes, and to have applied
all the energies of his riper years to the art of rhetoric.
The antithetical structure of the composition which he
now developed was directly the outcome of the logical
alternatives which his philosophic writing had so neatly
exposed. At the same time it is probable that his lively
mind had long ago perceived in the poetic style of
Empedocles and others an outline of an art which only
awaited the call of a popular need. As he might have
put it, if poetry could be useful as well as entertaining,
he was going to make an entertainment of the uses of
prose. So he leads philosophy and poetry into the
market-place, to work and smile and, above all, be sold.

He was already well on in years when he secured his
fame as a master of witty speech-making; but it was in
a spirit of youthful enjoyment that he sought and found
success. He had the happy gift of seizing and turning

[1] Plato, *Meno*, 76 c; Theophrastus, *De Igne*, 73; D. *F.V.*[2] i, pp. 555–6.
[2] Sextus, *Adv. Math.* VII, 65 foll.; D. *F.V.*[2] i, p. 552.

to account the material from which proverbs, epigrams and other self-supporting, self-recording sentences are made: it is a gift which brings a bright individual glory, but draws its honours together with it to the grave, and wins no place in the general list of human virtues. We have seen its shy attempts in some phrases of Democritus[1], Protagoras[2] and Herodotus[3]; and have then watched its cheerful incursions upon the domain of bodily disease[4]. The confident spirit of the latter kind of work, as though it throve every moment on applause, is to be attributed, for good or ill, to the influence of Gorgias. The teachers and politicians of Greece, and especially of Athens, were discovering the difference between flatness and point in their daily speech; and here came one who understood their business enough to enliven it with metaphorical light and the chime of verbal figures. They were familiar with the effects of such things in the poetry of the *Ajax* and *Antigone*, the *Medea* and *Hippolytus*: they were now to learn how to make prose an equally impressive and memorable art, in writing as well as speaking. Their first lessons, of course, had been drawn from the stately deliverances of Pericles and Protagoras: but ideas come only—and that by stern labour—to the few, and the Olympian manner was not to be bought. Take, however, a commonplace or a truism, and try dividing it into a variety of contrasted terms: you may make it worth hearing; and new thoughts, or new shades of the old thought, will probably turn up as you go along :—

ἐκέκτηντο ἔνθεον μὲν τὴν ἀρετήν, ἀνθρώπινον δὲ τὸ θνητόν[5]—

τὰ χρήματα ἐκτᾶτο μὲν ὡς χρῷτο, ἐχρῆτο δὲ ὡς τιμῷτο[6]—

---

[1] Above, p. 121. [2] pp. 131-2. [3] p. 134. [4] pp. 137-144.
[5] D. *F.V.*[2] i, p. 557. [6] *Ib.* p. 561.

for indeed that other saying, of which Aristotle approved, holds good of much besides lawsuits—'Abolish your adversary's zeal with laughter and his laughter with zeal[1]'; discretion, at any rate, was but young in Athens when the Peloponnesian War began. We may scoff at these tricks, as a mere buzzing of words ; but behind them is a power which might turn the laugh against us, and so they would have their sting. 'Words are the counters of wise men, and the money of fools,' says Thomas Hobbes[2]: the very strength of the epigram shows to what use these counters may be put. Literature may begin as a game ; it grows earnest, and we call it an art.

This saying of Hobbes has metaphor as well as antithesis. Gorgias described vultures as 'living tombs[3],' and Xerxes as ' the Zeus of the Persians ' ; but he could also, after calling a state of affairs 'sallow and bloodless[4],' proceed to the antithetical imagery of—

$$\sigma\grave{\upsilon} \,\delta\grave{\epsilon}\, \tau\alpha\hat{\upsilon}\tau\alpha \,\alpha\grave{\iota}\sigma\chi\rho\hat{\omega}\varsigma \,\mu\grave{\epsilon}\nu \,\check{\epsilon}\sigma\pi\epsilon\iota\rho\alpha\varsigma, \,\kappa\alpha\kappa\hat{\omega}\varsigma \,\delta\grave{\epsilon}\, \grave{\epsilon}\theta\acute{\epsilon}\rho\iota\sigma\alpha\varsigma—$$

an epigram which Aristotle can hardly persuade us to condemn[5]. It is, further, not improbable that Gorgias

---

[1] Aristot. *Rhet.* III, 18. 1419 b—δεῖν ἔφη Γοργίας τὴν μὲν σπουδὴν διαφθείρειν τῶν ἐναντίων γέλωτι, τὸν δὲ γέλωτα σπουδῇ, ὀρθῶς λέγων.

[2] *Cit.* Whately, *Rhet.* III, iii, 14.

[3] So Jeremy Taylor (*Holy Dying*, v, 8) speaks of ' sepulchral dogs.'

[4] His brother Herodicus was a doctor. Plato (*Gorg.* 456 b) makes him tell how he would often visit the sick in company with the doctors, and when the patients refused to obey medical orders, he would induce them to obey 'by the mere art of rhetoric.' The reading ἄναιμα is preferable to ἔναιμα for the context of Aristotle: see however A. Mayer, *Theophrasti περὶ λέξεως*, p. 149, where the phrase is combined with Demetrius, *De Elocut.* 116.

[5] Aristot. *Rhet.* III, 3. 1406 b; D. *F.V.²* i, p. 560. Empedocles (D. *F.V.²* i, p. 189) had called the sea 'the sweat of earth,' and Chœrilus, the early tragedian, had said that rocks and streams were 'the bones and veins of earth,' to the disgust of the ancient critics (Haigh, *Trag. Dram. Gr.* p. 40). Englishmen of the present day are apt to resent a picturesque phrase when applied to ordinary things, at least by anyone below the status of Poet Laureate : see A. E. Taylor, *Varia Socrat.* 1st Ser. p. 148, for Tennyson's complaint that some neglect of his comfort in the country had 'awaked a dormant cold.' For real extravagance, see Pepys, *Diary* an. 1666, Sept. 9th

was amused at his success with the Athenians; while they were amused at their new discovery, including him. He adopted something of a theatrical pose, and his brilliance made it an imperious fashion; for we may fairly apply to his own case what he said of the tragic actor and his art,—that here 'the deceiver is more honest than he who deceives not, and the deceived more shrewd than he who is not deceived[1].' If he added to the gaiety of nations, we have partly to thank his own intention[2]: like Rabelais and Heine he died—or was fitly supposed to have died—with a characteristic jest on his lips[3]. But his exploits in antithesis had an effect on the structure of Greek prose which would have contented his best ambitions, if by any chance he could have foreseen its value. Lesser men indeed, as he might have said, spun webs on the pattern of Arachne, which caught nothing, and were quickly blown away. Some of these egregious imitations have been swept up for our inspection; and if anyone would see how many pages can be filled with mere style, when the pen is released from all purpose of saying anything in particular, let him try to peruse the *Encomium of Helen*. This piece, which a late tradition has given to Gorgias, is a compact summary of the alliterations, assonances and antithetical chimes which belong properly enough to the Sicilian rhetoric, and which forced themselves, to a certain extent, upon the most serious writers of the fifth century. At the same time, it utterly lacks the grandeur—even the rather inflated grandeur—of the *Epitaphius*. The ignorance of

---

—'but methinks, a bad, poor sermon, though proper for the time; nor eloquent, in saying at this time that the City is reduced from a large folio to a decimo-tertio.'

[1] Plutarch, *De Glor. Athen.* 5, p. 348 c; D. *F.V.*[2] i, p. 561.

[2] Cf. his remark to the swallow, Aristot. *l.c.*

[3] Ælian, *Var. Hist.* II, 35—ἤδη με ὁ ὕπνος ἄρχεται παρακατατίθεσθαι τἀδελφῷ.

those who ascribed such trifles to Gorgias is sufficiently
exposed by the fact that they similarly classed the
Apology for Palamedes; a tiresome piece of argument in
short balanced clauses, which attempt only a monotonous
repetition of ordinary words[1].   Over these futilities we
need not pause.   It is 'the sober follies of the wise and
great' that are really instructive.   These leave their
impress on literature, for evil or for good, and not seldom
for both at once.

'There can be no comparison,' said Thompson[2],
'between the sparkling ingenuity of the Sicilian rhetorician and the vivid and penetrating intellect of the
historian'; but the fact remains that Thucydides grasped
the importance of Gorgias' artifices for the progress of
literary art.   The chief benefit resulting to us now is the
establishment of balance in the constitution of a sentence;
though our properly tempered use of epigram has only
been evolved by a continual warfare between brilliancy
and common-sense.   Antithesis was bound to lead from
a small to a large periodic form, when practice in the
craft was able to answer the calls of fuller thought; and
from Gorgias came the impulse needed for the early

---

[1] Other good reasons for regarding these pieces as spurious are given by
Thompson, *The Gorgias of Plato* (1871), p. 177.   Blass appended them to
his text of Antiphon (1892), and declared in his Preface:—'Gorgiae utraque
mihi genuina videtur, quoque saepius relego, eo firmius id apud me iudicium
stat.'   The position is a strong one; for most critics have surely shrunk
from imperilling their judgement by the experiment of reading these works
many times over.   Yet their genuineness is maintained by another eminent
scholar (cf. Diels, *F.V.*[2] i, p. 558).   Considering Plato's tone towards Gorgias,
and the character of the undisputed fragments, it seems best to suppose that
the *Helen* was written by some witless zealot in 'Gorgiasm,' and the
Palamedes by some student who was practising the rhetorical question and
a kind of Protagorean 'anaphora.'   His skill is comparable with that of
Herodotus in the sentence quoted above, p. 115 (Herod. VII, 10).   Such
studies as these remind us usefully of the professional, lecture-room side of
the new rhetoric: but they cannot compete in interest with the seriously
practical manifestoes of the medical colleges.

[2] *Gorgias of Plato*, Append. p. 177.

stages of the process. We have seen already, in his
Funeral Oration, that he himself was more concerned
with each separate point than with the suspense which
he was thus too carelessly prolonging. He gives us an
epigrammatic period—

    οὗτοι γὰρ ἐκέκτηντο ἔνθεον μὲν τὴν ἀρετήν, ἀνθρώπινον
δὲ τὸ θνητόν—

but he tacks on to it a lengthy series of participial and
adjectival antitheses which is at least twice as heavy as
any such appendage ought to be. We may wonder at
such a feverish delight in contrasts of thought and word ;
but only if we forget that the so-called practical culture
of the early sophists was largely occupied with subjects
which are chiefly pursued in the unpractical departments of
our Universities. Protagoras, Hippias and Gorgias were
'sophists' in the sense of persons who applied careful,
discriminating thought to the confused beginnings of
sciences and arts. When once these fields of mental,
political, legal, medical, musical and other theory were
opened up for discourse, an intelligent and leisured public
could not but feel the imperative need, and not merely
an easy scope, for accurate distinctions and precise
language. Of this many-sided awakening we should
regard Gorgias as the most lively advocate and the most
significant witness. Even as late as Plato, it was worth
while to emphasise the difference between word and
deed, and to obtain a special point from the man who
'would not seem, but be, most excellent[1].' But Thucydides was observing the whole Hellenic scene, noting
the relation between profession and practice in the chief
political centres, and testing the reputation of this or that
person by the evidence of his real aims or worth. The
pursuit of this practical or civic psychology led him, as

[1] Plato, *Respubl.* II, 361 b, c,—working, in sophistic manner, from Æschylus'
ἄριστος, by way of ἀγαθός, to δίκαιος.

we saw, into the comprehensive schemes of his contrast-
periods[1] : but it was in composing the speeches that he
felt most at liberty to employ the short self-important
antithesis of Gorgiasm.   Here, in varying degrees which
we must attempt to mark and understand, he glances
aside with the time 'to new-found methods and to
compounds strange[2]' ; and we shall expect that, as he
displays in some cases what he considers to be the right
admixture of ornament with wise exhortation, so he will
allow us to hear in others 'the rattling tongue of saucy
and audacious eloquence[3].'   His care in selection will
be felt at once, if we read a sentence of Pericles' Funeral
Oration[4] after what we have seen of Gorgias' treatment
of the same theme[5] :—

καὶ ἐν αὐτῷ τῷ ἀμύνεσθαι καὶ παθεῖν μᾶλλον ἡγησάμενοι
ἢ τὸ ἐνδόντας σῴζεσθαι, τὸ μὲν αἰσχρὸν τοῦ λόγου ἔφυγον,
τὸ δ' ἔργον τῷ σώματι ὑπέμειναν, καὶ δι' ἐλαχίστου καιροῦ
τύχης ἅμα ἀκμῇ τῆς δόξης μᾶλλον ἢ τοῦ δέους ἀπηλ-
λάγησαν.

Nevertheless, the faults and dangers of the method
are only too evident.   In spite of the ingenuity which
has contrived such a noble rhythm, a suspicion arises, as
we listen, that the thought is being pulled about and
tattered in the process.   We have just had the opposition
of ἐλπίς and ἔργον ; while as for that μᾶλλον ἢ τοῦ δέους,
we call it *cheville*, and hope we have learnt better ways.
We cannot deny, however, the combined effect of
antithesis and sonorous diction in what we have heard
but a short while before[6] :—

καὶ οὐδὲν προσδεόμενοι οὔτε Ὁμήρου ἐπαινέτου οὔτε
ὅστις ἔπεσι μὲν τὰ αὐτίκα τέρψει, τῶν δ' ἔργων τὴν ὑπόνοιαν

---

[1] Thuc. III, 82, V, 16.   [2] Shakespeare, *Sonnet* 76.
[3] *Mids. Night's Dream*, V, i, 109.   [4] Thuc. II, 42 fin.
[5] Above, p. 152.   [6] II, 41. 4.

ἡ ἀλήθεια βλάψει, ἀλλὰ πᾶσαν μὲν θάλασσαν καὶ γῆν
ἐσβατὸν τῇ ἡμετέρᾳ τόλμῃ καταναγκάσαντες γενέσθαι,
πανταχοῦ δὲ μνημεῖα κακῶν τε κἀγαθῶν ἀίδια ξυγκατοικίσαντες.

Throughout the speech there runs that united strength
of formal balance and resonant phrase which, though
probably unknown in such intensity to the hearers of the
real Pericles, has been the glory and terror of our
countrymen on the lips of a Pitt.

The contrast of word and deed, which is said to
occur 'some eighteen times[1]' in this Funeral Oration, is
apt to weary us with the dull weight of a commonplace.
But the distinction meant a great deal to people who
were eagerly exploring the unknown realm of political
rhetoric. Words were discovered, on this closer approach,
to be even more wonderful beings than primitive thought
had vaguely conceived. A short acquaintance with their
habits and faculties could enable one to conjure up tears
or laughter in a crowd of fellow-citizens, or incite them
to policies and wars. So, when prose-writing had become
a definite art, we find Plato describing the written word
as a phantom which continues in a sort the life of the
animate creature begotten by speech[2]. Before Gorgias
came, it is likely that the Athenians were in no little awe

---

[1] Jebb, *Hellenica*, 'On the Speeches of Thuc.'

[2] Plato, *Phædr.* 276 a—τὸν τοῦ εἰδότος λόγον λέγεις ζῶντα καὶ ἔμψυχον, οὗ ὁ
γεγραμμένος εἴδωλον ἄν τι λέγοιτο δικαίως. Cf. 275 d, e. The attitude of the
early sophists towards the power of words had perhaps a little of the pride of
the oriental sage: cf. the following passage from Mardrus' translation of the
Arabian Nights, vol. XIII, p. 228 (Night 846)—'Les lettres forment les mots,
et les mots composent les oraisons; et ce ne sont que les esprits représentés
par les lettres et assemblés dans les oraisons écrites sur les talismans qui
font ces prodiges qui étonnent les hommes ordinaires, mais ne troublent
point les sages, qui n'ignorent point la puissance des mots et savent que les
mots gouvernent toujours le monde, et que les paroles écrites ou proférées
pourront renverser les rois et ruiner leurs empires.' In Greece this feeling
started from Heracleitus.

of the great compelling words which Homer and Pindar
and Æschylus had sounded in their ears ; something, in
fact, of that fear, though not so morally moved, with
which Plato afterwards shrank from the power of both
poetry and music[1]. But Gorgias put into his audiences a
light-hearted courage. As they began to handle their
new bright weapon familiarly, it dazzled them a little, and
they were in danger of supposing that the only important
work in the world was to try how many things it would
cut. Slight Euphuists, as we have seen, were happy to
mince the vapour of their own breath. A serious mind,
however, would be struck with the advantage suddenly
won for prose-style, when it was groping for effective
form, by these alien tricks of assonance and balanced
rhythm ; so the question arose, whether these cross-
patterns of sound and sense would fit on to the plain
serviceable stuff without spoiling its various worth.

Antiphon and Thucydides, in different measure,
decided that they would, and that the change, if judiciously
made, would be a positive help to intelligence and art. It
was not a poverty, but a superfluity of ideas that induced
this decision. In our day, we can see how a middling
and perhaps even an excellent poet is frequently helped
to success by the guidance of rhyme : the sustained
vigour and speed required for good blank verse are the
rare gifts of a great master. There is the same practical
difficulty in passing from verse to prose : in the absence
of a regular metre, the form has to be broken and
moulded afresh—within the limits, as prose-writers
eventually learnt, of a large regularity—according to the
need of each successive thought. Thucydides had a
great many things to say, but was not going to say them
anyhow : on every hand the new rhetoric was enlivening
the tones of political and ethical disputation ; and in

---

[1] *Respubl.* III, 398–9.

preparing his brief record of a wide and passionate
conflict, he selected from the methods of contemporary
debate the means of marshalling and connecting what he
judged to be the prominent features of the whole affair.
He could not be alive to the manifold progress of his
time without finding his thoughts occupied with comparisons and distinctions.   But in order to set them out
as such, he required a comprehensive yet close-knit form
of expression : the luminous imagery and neatly poised
clauses of Gorgias were just the instruments he wanted
for the compact economy of the building.   So he went
earnestly to work, yet with some glow of experimental
daring: for it may be said that in antithesis and metaphor
he found his only recreations.

At the same time, it is clear that he had his misgivings.
The tragic pomp of Gorgias was largely composed of
reminiscence or imitation of poetry.   It is probable that
the substance and style of performances in the theatre
were often the themes of his declamation.   We have
noticed what he said of tragedy[1]: our scanty fragments
of him also show that he called the *Seven against Thebes*
a play ' brimful of Ares ' ; and perhaps he might illustrate
at length from such dramas his doctrine that ' being is
obscure, if it have no seeming, and seeming is strengthless if it have no being[2].'   That the style of his discourses
was often ' very much in the manner of a dithyramb[3],'
we can easily believe.   But this gay splendour of phrase,
so ready to run into the florid and meretricious, finds
little countenance in the choice of Thucydides.   Metaphors like that of Alcibiades—

στορέσωμεν τὸ φρόνημα τῶν Πελοποννησίων[4]—

or of Pericles—

κηπίον καὶ ἐγκαλλώπισμα πλούτου[5]—

[1] Above, p. 156.   [2] D. F.V.[2] i, p. 561.   [3] Dionys. Hal. *De Lys.* 3.
[4] Thuc. VI, 18. 4.   [5] II, 62. 3.

occur so rarely that they seem to be really the property
of the persons who utter them.   We have noted how,
at the outset of his work, Thucydides must have stopped
his ears against the sirens of epic and legendary poetry[1];
we have also seen reason to reject the view that his mind
could admit a mythic theory of life[2].   Let us now
consider if the Mytilenæan debate will afford any further
hint of his attitude towards the new fashion of tragic
pomp in public speech.

§ 7

We have already observed the character of Cleon's
arguments in connection with his alleged frenzy[3]: it
remains now to observe the total effect of his vigorous
attack on the orators and their charming phrases[4], together with the gist of Diodotus' reply.   It is remarkable
that both speakers, though in direct opposition, make a
point of decrying rhetorical tricks.   Cleon, appealing to
the lust of vengeance—thinly disguised as the eternal
fitness of things—rallies the people on their suscepti-
bility to the sound of fine words.   Diodotus, talking
plain sense on the question of good policy, finds that
he has to defend the use of speech as a vehicle of
argument; and asserts that the confused distrust of
public orations is tending to deter wise men from
offering their advice[5].   'Things have come to such a
pass,' he declares, 'that good counsel given from straightforward motives is no whit more exempt from suspicion
than bad; so that not only must he who would promote
the most dangerous policy employ deceit to seduce the
commons, but he who brings the better advice must
likewise win belief by lying[6].'   Once more Thucydides is

---

[1] Above, pp. 26–8.   [2] pp. 53–67.   [3] pp. 57–58.
[4] Thuc. III, 40. 3—οἱ τέρποντες λόγῳ ῥήτορες.
[5] III, 42.   [6] III, 43. 2.

suggesting, in terms of the best contemporary opinion, the perils to which a sharp-witted but thoughtless democracy is exposed.

So much for the two speeches taken together : but, if we look at the individual manner of each performance, a further curious point will be seen to emerge. Not only is the sort of imaginative rhetoric, to which Cleon directs his attack, illustrated to some extent by a passage in Diodotus' reply ; but Cleon, just before and even in the act of accusing the people of yielding to sophistic enchantments[1], partially exemplifies, in the even beat of his own phrases, the declamatory skill which Diodotus blames for bringing politics into the contempt of sensible men.   Here are some of Cleon's antitheses :—

εἰώθατε θεαταὶ μὲν τῶν λόγων γίγνεσθαι, ἀκροαταὶ δὲ τῶν ἔργων—

οὐ τὸ δρασθὲν πιστότερον ὄψει λαβόντες ἢ τὸ ἀκουσθέν—

δοῦλοι ὄντες τῶν αἰεὶ ἀτόπων, ὑπερόπται δὲ τῶν εἰωθό-των—

which lead up to this insistent drumming on a repeated syllable :—

ὀξέως δέ τι λέγοντας προεπαινέσαι, καὶ προαισθέσθαι τε πρόθυμοι εἶναι τὰ λεγόμενα καὶ προνοῆσαι βραδεῖς τὰ ἐξ αὐτῶν ἀποβησόμενα.

One other remark must be noticed in this lengthy climax of condemnation : he tells the people they are 'adepts at allowing the novelty of a word to deceive them, and refusing to follow the guidance of one that has been tried and approved[2].' Our conclusion is that the epigrammatic vigour of Cleon's tirade was such as

---

[1] III, 38 fin.—ἀκοῆς ἡδονῇ ἡσσώμενοι καὶ σοφιστῶν θεαταῖς ἐοικότες καθημένοις.

[2] III, 38. 5—μετὰ καινότητος μὲν λόγου ἀπατᾶσθαι ἄριστοι, μετὰ δεδοκιμασμένου δὲ μὴ ξυνέπεσθαι ἐθέλειν.

could seem permissible and fitting for a politician who, however passionate and unscrupulous, was at the moment disclaiming the aid of sophistic art. Thucydides has obviously designed this large sentence to convey some sense of the demagogue's vehement eloquence[1]; and we must expect that the concentrated force of the portraiture has required some heightening of the details: but this hint of language that has been 'tried and approved' (δεδοκιμασμένου) sticks in our minds, and we are prompted to regard the style of this sentence as nearly representing the amount of Thucydides' own appropriations, for his immediate purpose, from the devices of Protagoras and Gorgias.

We pass on to hear Diodotus upholding the credit of oratory. It is fair to assume that his one imaginative passage is so controlled as to give no handle, but rather, by dint of its manifest worth, a repulse to the charges of Cleon. Hence, although we cannot claim that the grave judicial tone of the whole speech betrays the historian's own feeling on the question, we can conclude that the image connecting Hope and Desire and Fortune would be accepted by serious-minded persons as happily conceived and suitably expressed. The most striking sentence runs as follows[2]:—

ἥ τε ἐλπὶς καὶ ὁ ἔρως ἐπὶ παντί, ὁ μὲν ἡγούμενος, ἡ δ' ἐφεπομένη, καὶ ὁ μὲν τὴν ἐπιβουλὴν ἐκφροντίζων, ἡ δὲ τὴν εὐπορίαν τῆς τύχης ὑποτιθεῖσα πλεῖστα βλάπτουσι, καὶ ὄντα ἀφανῆ κρείσσω ἐστὶ τῶν ὁρωμένων δεινῶν.

This was probably written many years after Gorgias' first visit to Athens (427 B.C.); the debate itself took place in the year of that visit. Thucydides may be supposed to have heard the speeches on this occasion,

[1] Cf. above, p. 57.
[2] III, 45, 5; the passage and its context are translated in Cornford, *Th. M.* p. 122.

when a 'monstrous resolution[1],' involving the destruction
of a whole community, was being reconsidered at the
last moment. It is possible too that Gorgiasm had
already found its way into public speeches. But in any
case, when he came to work up his material into an
adequate presentation of the scene, there was one
dominant note which he wished to be clearly heard. He
had been impressed with the fact that the Athenians were
already losing their sense of political reality, and in their
hunger for artistic display were growing impatient of
sincerity and plain truth. Thus the sentence just quoted,
and the descriptions, in the context, of the effects of
Poverty and Licence and of the wiles of Fortune, can be
justly viewed as conveying what Thucydides would call
a serious and useful contribution to political thought.
At the same time, whatever value we attach to this
contribution now, and even supposing it to have been made
by Thucydides rather than Diodotus, we are bound first
of all to read it as a brief incident of a typical debate ;
and secondly, if we propose to speculate on the attitude
of mind which it may reveal, we must take as our surest
guide the general literary method to which it certainly
conforms. The balanced regularity of its structure
belongs, as we have seen, to sophistic, and particularly
Sicilian, rhetoric ; which, in this respect at least, was now
refunding many times more than it ever owed to tragic
poetry : but just as Thucydides applied the formal
suggestions of Protagoras and Hippias for the cold
divisions of what we have termed his practical psychology,
so the more imaginative or picturesque colouring of
Gorgias has tinged, here and there, the livelier complexion of individual pleading.

To make sure that the antithesis of word and
deed, which has re-appeared in Cleon's speech, was to

---

[1] Thuc. III, 36. 4—ὠμὸν τὸ βούλευμα καὶ μέγα.

Thucydides' view of Athenian policy a deadly earnest
fact, staring him in the face through no golden haze of
fashionable glamour, nor any grey mist of supernatural
influence, let us look beyond these speeches to his own
brief words[1] :—' These very opposite judgements were
expressed';—and what then?—'the Athenians came, *after
all*, to a contest of opinion[2].' They had decided on a step
of grave moment to their reputation[3]; had yielded to
a revulsion of feeling; had been swayed back by Cleon,
and the other way again by Diodotus: but the simple
issue had to come at last, and—momentous as it was—
it found them about equally divided. 'After that,' we
may fancy Thucydides remarking, ' how are we to expect
anything like a clear consistent policy from the Ecclesia?
Why, it is becoming a mere debating society!' And
after sixteen years of ill-management at home and abroad,
when the democracy has been turned out into the cold
and has to shift for itself at Samos, how does it stand as
regards speech and action? ' Having thus debated in
Assembly together and encouraged one another, they
set about making their preparations for war *with equal
energy*[4].' Times have changed indeed.

This contrast of speech and action appears in all the
great writers of Greece, from Homer to Demosthenes.
If we consider for a moment its use in Æschylus, we
observe that it occurs rather rarely, by comparison with
a certain mystical emphasis on *words* or *names* alone[5],
and on the duty of speaking rightly, or cautiously, or not

[1] III, 49. 1.
[2] ἦλθον ἐς ἀγῶνα ὅμως (so all MSS.: ὁμοίως Bredow) τῆς δόξης.
[3] Cf. Bury, *Hist. Gr.* p. 415—'The action of Mitylene was in truth an
indictment of the whole fabric of the Athenian empire as unjust and
undesirable.'
[4] VIII, 77—τοιαῦτα ἐν ἀλλήλοις ἐκκλησιάσαντες καὶ παραθαρσύναντες σφᾶς
αὐτοὺς καὶ τὰ τοῦ πολέμου παρεσκευάζοντο οὐδὲν ἧσσον.
[5] Especially in such phrases as λέγειν τὰ καίρια, *Suppl.* 446; *Sept.* 1, 619;
Cho. 582; *Prom. Ign.* fr.

at all. The prominence of this point seems to show
that Æschylus, and the main body of his first audiences,
were wont to regard words with that intense but indefinite awe whose conversion to a more familiar attitude
we have remarked as one of the initial labours of Sicilian
rhetoric[1]. It is also, of course, very natural that such
emphasis should be frequent in a form of drama which
relied so much less on action than on speech. Accordingly, among the half-dozen cases or so[2] where the two
functions are coupled together, there are some at least
where the doing seems to be overshadowed by the
superior force of the saying, and comes in, on sufferance,
as a rather insignificant adjunct. Perhaps it is owing to
the interested testimony of literature as a whole that
speech has retained some of that advantage throughout
the story we are able now to tell of Greek civilisation.
But in attempting to understand the extraordinary
persistence of the contrast in the Thucydidean speakers,
we must base our private judgement on two important
considerations. The first is that Thucydides was the only
writer of that century who undertook to show the Hellenic
spirit rejoicing the more in distinct and forcible utterance,
the more it expanded into civic and national activity.
He was himself a man of action who turned his brain and
hand to writing ; and while vividly impressed by the
pace at which democracy was driving its course, he felt
the freshness of a personal discovery in his realisation of
the practical force of oratory. Hence his close attention
to the forms of the new rhetoric. This brings us to our
second point. To carry out the work which he finally

---

[1] Above, pp. 160–1.

[2] *Suppl.* 515—σὺ καὶ λέγων εὔφραινε καὶ πράσσων φρένα: *Pers.* 174—μήτ᾽
ἔπος μήτ᾽ ἔργον: *Prom.* 338—ἔργῳ κοὐ λόγῳ τεκμαίρομαι: 659—δρῶντ᾽ ἢ
λέγοντα δαίμοσιν πράσσειν φίλα: *Agam.* 1648—δοκεῖς τάδ᾽ ἔρδειν καὶ λέγειν:
Eum. 899—ἔξεστι γάρ μοι μὴ λέγειν ἃ μὴ τελῶ. Perhaps a few more could be
added.

designed, he borrowed some of these forms as tools : but his use of them betrays at times the awkwardness of a slightly too eager, though perfectly serious, amateur. At the call of each occasion where he felt the strength of men's thoughts and words behind their deeds, or the conflict of motives in leading individuals and groups, he sharpened his few sophistic instruments, and was doubt-less pleased to find what striking effects they could produce : or (if we in our turn should borrow an image from Euripides) we need only watch his various opera-tions with a little care, to be able to espy him arranging the remedies of Oblivion, in syllables made ready for the lettered craft of men[1]. For it is just because he, like Palamedes, left plenty more to be achieved by later enterprise, that we can detect the traces of his struggle ; and thus, remembering its sincerity and worth, find a peculiar interest in his most ungainly efforts.

§ 8

For in balancing the shape of his clauses he was not always certain to balance the meaning too.   One obvious instance of *cheville* has come before us[2], and a few more could be quoted.   Yet these are as nothing compared to the unnatural postures into which the Attic language is thrown, while striving to execute the impatient orders of his thought.   Severe and self-contained, his mind appears to have practised an expression of its favourite discoveries rather by some kind of internal colloquy than by familiar intercourse with other minds[3].   The first sophists, while eager for a certain elevation above the

---

[1] Eurip. *Palamedes*, fr. 2—τὰ τῆς γε λήθης φάρμακ' ὀρθώσας...συλλαβάς τε θεὶς ἐξεῦρον ἀνθρώποισι γράμματ' εἰδέναι.   [2] Above, p. 159.

[3] Cf. the style of our acute modern observer, George Meredith : Carlyle, from whom he learnt much of his literary method, was always in touch with the public.

average tone[1], were kept by their profession within easy grasp of the average intelligence. But in Thucydides, if we can see that some of the tools are borrowed, the workmanship is almost entirely independent ; and continually, for these rhetorical experiments, he forces the few lessons he has learnt into tasks of which they are hardly capable. The wealth of his ideas is not always to be brought within the compass of his stiff and limited art. Thus understood, the character of his writing, as of his whole book, is sternly opposed to the method of any sophist.

It may be further suggested that, as he pressed on to the upper levels of his work, he conceived some notion of clothing his ideas in a little of the strangeness with which they first arose in his mind. For if we look at the strenuous course of a sentence which belongs to our class of strict psychological summaries,—though it has been used as evidence of a mythical design[2],—the awkward changes of grammatical construction within the hard-worked antithetical scheme are best accounted for, when observed in their correspondence with the fresh attitude or strength of each occurring thought :—

καὶ ἔρως ἐνέπεσε τοῖς πᾶσιν ὁμοίως ἐκπλεῦσαι, τοῖς μὲν γὰρ πρεσβυτέροις ὡς ἢ καταστρεψομένοις ἐφ᾿ ἃ ἔπλεον ἢ οὐδὲν ἂν σφαλεῖσαν μεγάλην δύναμιν, τοῖς δ᾿ ἐν τῇ ἡλικίᾳ τῆς τε ἀπούσης πόθῳ ὄψεως καὶ θεωρίας, καὶ εὐέλπιδες ὄντες σωθήσεσθαι, ὁ δὲ πολὺς ὅμιλος καὶ στρατιώτης ἔν τε τῷ παρόντι ἀργύριον οἴσειν καὶ προσκτήσεσθαι δύναμιν ὅθεν ἀίδιον μισθοφορὰν ὑπάρξειν.

The prefatory flash of ἔρως is quickly succeeded by the laborious fervour of analysis. Several instances

---

[1] For Protagoras, see above, p. 129 : for Gorgias and his pomp of phrase, cf. Dionys. Hal. *De Imitat.* ix—Γοργίας μὲν τὴν ποιητικὴν ἑρμηνείαν μετήνεγκεν εἰς λόγους πολιτικούς, οὐκ ἀξιῶν ὅμοιον τὸν ῥήτορα τοῖς ἰδιώταις εἶναι.

[2] Thuc. VI, 24. 3 ; Cornford, *Th. M.* p. 214.

might be given from the speeches, where the same
anxiety for the life of his ideas has made him unscrupulous towards the sophistic vehicle ; the following must
suffice[1] :—

καὶ γὰρ ὅτε ἐδρῶμεν, ἐπ᾽ ὠφελίᾳ ἐκινδυνεύετο, ἧς τοῦ
μὲν ἔργου μέρος μετέσχετε, τοῦ δὲ λόγου μὴ παντός, εἴ
τι ὠφελεῖ, στερισκώμεθα.

Sometimes, too, an apparent case of *cheville* can pass
with the excuse that compression, and not expansion,
was the cause. In the example censured by one eminent
critic[2]—

ἔτι δὲ τοῖς μὲν σώμασιν ἀλλοτριωτάτοις ὑπὲρ τῆς πόλεως
χρῶνται, τῇ δὲ γνώμῃ οἰκειοτάτῃ ἐς τὸ πράσσειν τι ὑπὲρ
αὐτῆς—

the οἰκειοτάτῃ of the latter half is not really otiose. A
modern orator might thus extol the warriors of Japan—
' Dying, they yield up life and limb to the interests of
their country ; living, they devote to her welfare the best
energies of their minds : and while, in the hour of death,
there is nothing that they will less willingly claim than
the possession of their persons, at every moment of their
lives their most jealous care is for those intellectual
powers.'
The object is to display a combination of intellectual
pride and moral humility, which are wholly and equally
devoted to the service of the state. Thucydides has
attempted, not quite successfully, to squeeze all this into
one short sentence. In the result, his pregnant adjective
is in danger of missing the attention which its meaning
requires. He has taken over a machine which was made
for stretching out thought in an alluring display, and has
used it for folding and packing. If we would see how a

[1] I, 73. 2 ; see more exx. in Blass. *Att. Bered.*[2] pp. 215-6.
[2] Croiset, *Hist. Lit. Gr.* IV, p. 162 ; Thuc. I, 70. 6.

more ornamental artist employed this same machine on the same kind of material, we can turn to Agathon's speech in Plato's *Symposium*[1]:—

οὗτος δὲ ἡμᾶς ἀλλοτριότητος μὲν κενοῖ, οἰκειότητος δὲ πληροῖ, τὰς τοιάσδε συνόδους μετ' ἀλλήλων πάσας τιθεὶς συνιέναι, ἐν ἑορταῖς, ἐν χοροῖς, ἐν θυσίαις γιγνόμενος ἡγεμών· πρᾳότητα μὲν πορίζων, ἀγριότητα δ' ἐξορίζων· φιλόδωρος εὐμενείας, ἄδωρος δυσμενείας·—

and so on, through many more lines, to the end of this *gorgeous* peroration[2]. In fact, the beginning and end of Agathon's speech might serve as a brief conspectus of the various devices which we have seen pushing their way into the literature of the medical colleges.

Another useful comparison with the antitheses of the History may be drawn from the eulogy of Athens which Socrates delivers in the *Menexenus*. Commentators of Pericles' Funeral Oration in Thucydides have referred the student to ' Plato's parody '; yet if we examine the later speech[3], we cannot help feeling that, if this is a parody, its author must be a little overrated as a wit and a man of letters. Socrates professes to have learnt the piece from Aspasia, who made it up partly off-hand, and partly out of ' fragments left over from the funeral speech that she once composed for the use of Pericles[4].' Menexenus,

---

[1] Plato, *Sympos.* 197 d.

[2] The Gorgiastic touch—the smile that has become a mere grimace—is fitly acknowledged, when Socrates does it the mock-honour of a pun (the Gorgon's head, 198 c). The affectations of Agathon were less delicately handled by Aristophanes (*Thesm.* 29 foll.) at the time when the democracy was showing such energy at Samos (411 B.C.: see above, p. 167). The comedian had already (414 B.C.), in his brilliant satire on Athenian flightiness, jeered at the 'tongue-fill-belly' Gorgias (*Aves*, 1701). Plato (*Protag.* 315 d) speaks of Agathon as a pupil also of Prodicus.

[3] The speech in the *Menexenus* seems to mention events as late as the ' King's Peace' of 386 B.C. It was in the year before this that Plato returned to Athens from Syracuse, about the age of forty.

[4] *Menex.* 236 b.

a youth afterwards admitted to the intimacy of the *Phædo*[1], desires the recital of such a speech, 'whether it be the work of Aspasia or of anyone else soever.' Then Socrates, deprecating the scornful laughter of his friend, if such diversions should seem unsuited to his time of life, begins the performance thus :—

ἔργῳ μὲν ἡμῖν οἵδε ἔχουσι τὰ προσήκοντα σφίσιν αὐτοῖς, ὧν τυχόντες πορεύονται τὴν εἱμαρμένην πορείαν, προπεμφθέντες κοινῇ μὲν ὑπὸ τῆς πόλεως, ἰδίᾳ δὲ ὑπὸ τῶν οἰκείων· λόγῳ δὲ δὴ τὸν λειπόμενον κόσμον ὅ τε νόμος προστάττει ἀποδοῦναι τοῖς ἀνδράσι καὶ χρή. ἔργων γὰρ εὖ πραχθέντων λόγῳ καλῶς ῥηθέντι μνήμη καὶ κόσμος τοῖς πράξασι γίγνεται παρὰ τῶν ἀκουσάντων· δεῖ δὴ τοιούτου τινὸς λόγου—

and immediately adds on to these antithetical arrangements (of ἔργον—λόγος, κοινῇ—ἰδίᾳ, and πράττειν—λέγειν —ἀκούειν) two couples of neatly matched verbs (ἐπαινέσεται—παραινέσεται, παρακελευόμενος—παραμυθούμενος).

The prominence given here, in the beginning of the first two sentences, to the favourite contrast of the Thucydidean Funeral Oration is certainly striking : but could anything be more unlike Thucydides' handling of the method than these ample, explanatory clauses ? The dull flatness of—ἔργων εὖ πραχθέντων λόγῳ καλῶς ῥηθέντι, made duller still by—τοῖς πράξασι παρὰ τῶν ἀκουσάντων, the commonplace inflation of—πορεύονται τὴν εἱμαρμένην πορείαν, and the lameness of—δεῖ δὴ τοιούτου τινὸς λόγου,—are things for which Thucydides could feel nothing but contempt. And as the speech proceeds, it loses even the superficial solemnity with which it began. In the course of a tedious review of the origin and exploits of the Athenians, we come upon these empty Sicilian jingles—

---

[1] *Phædo*, 59 b.

οὐ γὰρ γῆ γυναῖκα μεμίμηται κυήσει καὶ γεννήσει, ἀλλὰ γυνὴ γῆν[1]—

παντὸς πᾶσαν πάντως προθυμίαν πειρᾶσθε ἔχειν[2]—

πᾶσαν πάντων παρὰ πάντα τὸν χρόνον ἐπιμέλειαν ποιουμένη[3]—

and, as though to distinguish the speech yet more sharply from the manner of Thucydides, one or two of Pericles' topics are treated thus[4] :—

ἐγκρατὲς δὲ τῆς πόλεως τὰ πολλὰ τὸ πλῆθος, τὰς δὲ ἀρχὰς δίδωσι καὶ κράτος τοῖς ἀεὶ δόξασιν ἀρίστοις εἶναι, καὶ οὔτε ἀσθενείᾳ οὔτε πενίᾳ οὔτ' ἀγνωσίᾳ πατέρων ἀπελήλαται οὐδεὶς οὐδὲ τοῖς ἐναντίοις τετίμηται, ὥσπερ ἐν ἄλλαις πόλεσιν, ἀλλὰ εἰς ὅρος, ὁ δόξας σοφὸς ἢ ἀγαθὸς εἶναι κρατεῖ καὶ ἄρχει.

Observing ἀρχάς and κράτος,—οὐδὲ τοῖς ἐναντίοις τετίμηται, ὥσπερ ἐν ἄλλαις πόλεσιν,—κρατεῖ καὶ ἄρχει, let us listen to Pericles[5] :—

μέτεστι δὲ κατὰ μὲν τοὺς νόμους πρὸς τὰ ἴδια διάφορα πᾶσι τὸ ἴσον, κατὰ δὲ τὴν ἀξίωσιν, ὡς ἕκαστος ἔν τῳ εὐδοκιμεῖ, οὐκ ἀπὸ μέρους τὸ πλέον ἐς τὰ κοινὰ ἢ ἀπ' ἀρετῆς προτιμᾶται, οὐδ' αὖ κατὰ πενίαν, ἔχων γέ τι ἀγαθὸν δρᾶσαι τὴν πόλιν, ἀξιώματος ἀφανείᾳ κεκώλυται—

or, after glancing at his words on Homer and the poets, let us note the verbosity of the following[6] :—

ὅ τε χρόνος βραχὺς ἀξίως διηγήσασθαι, ποιηταί τε αὐτῶν ἤδη ἱκανῶς τὴν ἀρετὴν ἐν μουσικῇ ὑμνήσαντες εἰς πάντας μεμηνύκασιν.

It is no part of our purpose to discuss the intention of the *Menexenus*, except in so far as we are able to consider its alleged connection with Thucydides, and to use it for a striking contrast with his style. But it will not be out of place to remember, in connection with the

[1] 238 a.   [2] 247 a.   [3] 249 c.   [4] 238 d.   [5] Thuc. II, 37.   [6] *Menex.* 239 b.

vogue of rhetoric, that Plato has here given some of his mature ability to the composition of a lengthy Epitaphius, such as those which were afterwards attributed to Lysias and Demosthenes ; and that the sophistic devices at its beginning and end were perhaps inserted, as the flattering version of Athenian history was designed, to catch the judges' votes in a public competition[1].

We have noticed, in our account of the Protagorean manner, some traces of its influence at two of the most impressive points in all Plato's writings[2]. So here, however scornful be the smile which the Socratic dialogues present to Gorgias and his followers, it is fair that Plato should be made to acknowledge some debt to their experiments in the sound-effects of words. A hundred places of ardent persuasion or description might be cited to show his subtle improvements on their artifices. We will take only a single instance, which has been chosen because it suggests that the irresistible artist is confidently risking the exposure, in almost its early naked form, of the rhetorical craft on which he has more covertly relied elsewhere[3] :—

---

[1] Cf. 234 b—νῦν μέντοι ἀφικόμην πρὸς τὸ βουλευτήριον πυθόμενος ὅτι ἡ βουλὴ μέλλει αἱρεῖσθαι ὅστις ἐρεῖ ἐπὶ τοῖς ἀποθανοῦσιν· ταφὰς γὰρ οἶσθ᾽ ὅτι μέλλουσι ποιεῖν. The conversation in which the speech is set has all the masterly ease of Plato's best manner, and may well be a later addition, to introduce and laughingly apologise for the speech among his collected works: cf. 235 c—ἀεὶ σὺ προσπαίζεις, ὦ Σ., τοὺς ῥήτορας. The pretence of Aspasia's authorship would be part of the joke: M. is a little incredulous of this at the outset (236 c—εἴτε Ἀσπασίας βούλει λέγειν εἴτε ὁτουοῦν); but at the end he says more plainly (249 e)—χάριν ἔχω τούτου τοῦ λόγου ἐκείνῃ ἢ ἐκείνῳ ὅστις σοι ὁ εἰπών ἐστιν αὐτόν. The ἐκεῖνος, whose gender is thus emphasised, can be none other than Plato himself. A phrase of the speech is twice cited by Aristotle, Rhet. I, 1367 b; III, 1415 b. The latest editor of the Menex. (J. A. Shawyer, Oxford, 1906) gives a useful summary of the opposing arguments of Stallbaum and Grote ; Wendland (Hermes XXV) discusses its connection with the sophists of the 4th century: but no satisfactory explanation has been given of the dialogue as a whole.

[2] Above, pp. 135–6.

[3] Leges, IV, 713 c—probably his latest work.

ἀλλὰ μιμεῖσθαι δεῖν ἡμᾶς οἴεται πάσῃ μηχανῇ τὸν ἐπὶ
τοῦ Κρόνου λεγόμενον βίον, καὶ ὅσον ἐν ἡμῖν ἀθανασίας
ἔνεστι, τούτῳ πειθομένους δημοσίᾳ καὶ ἰδίᾳ τάς τ' οἰκήσεις
καὶ τὰς πόλεις διοικεῖν, τὴν τοῦ νοῦ διανομὴν ἐπονομάζοντας
νόμον.

The cross-lines of sense in δημοσίᾳ—ἰδίᾳ, οἰκήσεις—
πόλεις are due to an early device of the poets ; but the
daring persuasive assonance of the final phrase is
perilously near the diversions of the *De Arte*[1].

§ 9

These and the like gallantries of Gorgiasm, when they
appear in Thucydides, have a cramped or clumsy motion,
as though suddenly caught in a grim emergency.   It
is curious to see something of the same effect in the
earliest piece of Attic prose preserved to us—the
Constitution of Athens, which used to be included among
the works of Xenophon.   The effect of sophistry here is
the more interesting for the fact that the unknown author
is quite obviously of the sort that would stand proudly
aloof from the sophistic movement.   His brief but
trenchant discourse is informed with a sarcastic mixture
of prejudice and perception : he is a conservative who,
writing in the earlier part of the Peloponnesian War[2],
sees that the advance of democracy is inevitable and,
after reasoning out the successful methods of his
opponents, congratulates them with a dry, superior smile.
This peculiar state of mind is reflected in the style of the
treatise—at once voluble and stately, heedless of effect,

---

[1] Above, p. 143.

[2] Kirchhoff, *Berl. Sitzungsber.* 1878, argues well for the year 424 B.C. :
Müller-Strübing (*Staat der Ath.* 1880) brings it down to the Sicilian Expedition (415 B.C.).   Since the present pages were written, a full discussion
of the problems connected with the tract has appeared (E. Kalinka, *Die Ps.-
Xen. 'Αθ. Πολ.* 1913): it does not conflict with any views put forward here.

and yet often impressive. For the writer has not escaped
the influence of Protagoras,—perhaps one might add,
though his denial would be loud, of Prodicus :—

πολλὰ μὲν περὶ τοῦ πολέμου, πολλὰ δὲ περὶ πόρου
χρημάτων, πολλὰ δὲ περὶ νόμων θέσεως[1]—

and so on, with πολλὰ δέ twice more, of the business of
the Boule. The repetition is more elaborate in this—

ἀνάγκη τοίνυν, ἐὰν μὴ ὀλίγα ποιῶνται δικαστήρια, ὀλίγοι
ἐν ἑκάστῳ ἔσονται τῷ δικαστηρίῳ[2]—

and still more in this noisy affair—

ἐν ταῖς χορηγίαις αὖ καὶ γυμνασιαρχίαις καὶ τριηρ-
αρχίαις γιγνώσκουσιν ὅτι χορηγοῦσι μὲν οἱ πλούσιοι,
χορηγεῖται δὲ ὁ δῆμος, καὶ γυμνασιαρχοῦσι μὲν καὶ
τριηραρχοῦσιν οἱ πλούσιοι, ὁ δὲ δῆμος τριηραρχεῖται καὶ
γυμνασιαρχεῖται[3].

Here the insistence becomes antithetical, and so builds
a crude periodic form. Another example will show more
clearly the difference from the compressed style of the
History :—

ὅστις δὲ μὴ ὢν τοῦ δήμου εἵλετο ἐν δημοκρατουμένῃ πόλει
οἰκεῖν μᾶλλον ἢ ἐν ὀλιγαρχουμένῃ ἀδικεῖν παρεσκευάσατο,
καὶ ἔγνω ὅτι μᾶλλον οἷόν τε διαλαθεῖν κακῷ ὄντι ἐν δημοκρατουμένῃ πόλει μᾶλλον ἢ ἐν ὀλιγαρχουμένῃ[4].

This remarkable tract has been described as representing the practical Athenian style of writing, before
literature was affected by Gorgias and the orators[5]; and
another authority tells us that it has 'no declamation'
about it[6]. Such expressions are somewhat misleading.
For in these passages—to which others could be added
—there is a clear intention of formality, within such

[1] *Ath. Resp.* III, 2.   [2] III, 7.   [3] I, 13.
[4] II, 20.   [5] Murray, *Anc. Gr. Lit.* p. 167.
[6] Croiset, *Hist. Gr. Lit.* IV, p. 349.

narrow limits as we have illustrated from the vigorous essay *On the Sacred Disease*[1]. In fact, there is almost a Sicilian jingle in the conclusion of the second sentence quoted above :—

ὥστε καὶ διασκευάσασθαι ῥᾴδιον ἔσται πρὸς ὀλίγους δικαστὰς καὶ συνδεκάσαι, πολὺ ἧττον δὲ δικαίως δικάζειν.

This intelligent critic—whose whole manner is perhaps to be best explained by supposing that he wrote with the heat of a political wrangle still upon him—leads us naturally to another member of the oligarchical party. The orator Antiphon was probably more than fifty years old when Gorgias came to Athens, but he seems to have been only just coming to the front as a professional speech-writer for the law-courts. He must have acted for some time as a sort of consulting barrister to litigants and, besides practising as a rhetorician[2], have begun to interest himself in the scheme which lifted him to a brief political eminence in 411 B.C. His part in the Revolution of the Four Hundred is described by Thucydides[3] in one of his rare expressions of personal feeling; though it is carefully given us in terms of the general opinion. It was Antiphon, he says, who contrived the whole affair; a man of the highest capacity, though suspected by the people on account of his approved dialectical skill in points of law; when the Four Hundred got into difficulties, ' he is agreed to have met the accusation of having been a prime mover in this same business with the ablest defence ever made by any man, up to my time, on trial for his life.' Cleon, in the threadbare mantle of Pericles, had contrived to maintain the democracy in such strength, that it was not till almost two years after the Sicilian disaster that Antiphon, now

---

[1] Above, pp. 138–9.
[2] Plato, *Menex.* 236 a.   [3] Thuc. VIII, 68. 1–2.

nearly seventy, could begin to realise his patiently
ripened schemes. After a few months of unsubstantial
power, he found that the skill which had often justified
others could not avail to save himself.

His literary importance is to be placed in the years
immediately following the visit of Gorgias. He belonged
originally to the stately school of rhetoric which we have
attributed to Protagoras and Pericles; it is interesting to
observe how he faced and came through the blaze of the
Sicilian fashion. The tradition that Thucydides was at
one time his pupil, whether invented by ancient critics or
founded on fact, is not difficult to believe. At any rate,
we can be certain of friendship and some literary
sympathy between the two men, merely from the climax
of the account just noticed in the History. Thus it is
reasonable to imagine that they discussed the extent of
their own submission to the vogue of Gorgiasm. On
comparing their writings, we can gather that they agreed
not only in matters of dialect and vocabulary, but in the
regular use of antithesis for the balanced organisation of
points in a debate. It is possible that Antiphon had
studied under Tisias, and had learnt from him the
selection and arrangement of topics: these powers, with
a steady care for symmetry in his sentences, form the
structure of his mature style. The regularity appears in
the opening words of the poisoning case *Against the
Stepmother* :—

νέος μὲν καὶ ἄπειρος δικῶν ἔγωγε ἔτι, δεινῶς δὲ καὶ
ἀπόρως ἔχει μοι περὶ τοῦ πράγματος, ὦ ἄνδρες· τοῦτο μέν,
εἰ ἐπισκήψαντος τοῦ πατρὸς ἐπεξελθεῖν τοῖς αὐτοῦ φονεῦσι
μὴ ἐπέξειμι· τοῦτο δέ, εἰ ἐπεξιόντι ἀναγκαίως ἔχει οἷς
ἥκιστα ἐχρῆν ἐν διαφορᾷ καταστῆναι, ἀδελφοῖς ὁμοπατρίοις
καὶ μητρὶ ἀδελφῶν.

The devices by which this fairly ample system is held

together (νέος μὲν καὶ ἄπειρος—δεινῶς δὲ καὶ ἀπόρως: ἀπόρως ἔχει—ἀναγκαίως ἔχει: τοῦτο μέν—τοῦτο δέ: ἐπεξελθεῖν—ἐπέξειμι—ἐπεξιόντι) are more than sufficient, but neither are they obtrusive. A little further on in the same speech, we find some play made with compounds and rhymes, on a par with some expressions of Thucydidean speakers[1] :—

ἐξ ἐπιβουλῆς καὶ προβουλῆς[2]—
εἶναι φάσκουσα αὐτῆς μὲν τοῦτο εὕρημα, ἐκείνης δ᾽ ὑπηρέτημα[3]—

and the forked tongue of epigram is just visible at one or two points, as here :—

ἄλλως τε καὶ τοῦ μὲν ἐκ προβουλῆς ἀκουσίως ἀποθανόντος, τῆς δὲ ἑκουσίως ἐκ προνοίας ἀποκτεινάσης[4].

A barrister's speech does not afford much scope for continuous ornament; and accordingly, these instances are enough to prove a careful attention paid to the methods of Gorgias, even though none of his poetic imagery appears. The speeches of Antiphon, in their formal quality throughout, suggest that with him, as with Thucydides, an argument or exposition is conceived to have its highest effect, if it is conducted in a series of separately emergent points, rather than by the gradually compelling process of deduction. At this stage of public speech, persuasion depends more on the number of hits that can be scored in a given time, than on the cumulative force of ingenious reasoning or description. Both writers, then, are seen applying the plain mechanism of antithesis to the substance of their work ; though Antiphon, having only ordinary, every-day matters to express, does not seek to enhance his method with any peculiar lights and shades.

The most striking part of the resemblance lies in

[1] Above, p. 143.   [2] Antiphon, *Or.* i, 3.   [3] *Ib.* 15.   [4] *Ib.* 5.

their common pursuit of the 'word-and-deed' contrast. Antiphon does not often dwell on it with reiterations in the same sentence : but the exordium of one speech indulges in it to a degree unexampled in the rest of his extant works. The following passage[1] will serve besides to show how much more regularly planned are the periods of Antiphon than those of Thucydides :—

τοσοῦτον δὲ προέχων ἐν τοῖς <u>λόγοις</u> ἡμῶν, ἔτι δὲ ἐν οἷς <u>ἔπρασσε</u> πολλαπλάσια τούτων, οὗτος μὲν οὐχ ὁσίως δεῖται ὑμῶν συχνῶς τὴν ἀπολογίαν ἀποδέχεσθαι αὐτοῦ· ἐγὼ δὲ <u>δράσας</u> μὲν οὐδὲν κακόν, <u>παθὼν</u> δὲ ἄθλια καὶ δεινά, καὶ νῦν ἔτι δεινότερα τούτων <u>ἔργῳ</u> καὶ οὐ <u>λόγῳ</u>, εἰς τὸν ὑμέτερον ἔλεον καταπεφευγὼς δέομαι ὑμῶν, ὦ ἄνδρες ἀνοσίων <u>ἔργων</u> τιμωροί, ὁσίων δὲ διαγνώμονες, μὴ <u>ἔργα</u> φανερὰ ὑπὸ πονηρᾶς <u>λόγων</u> ἀκριβείας πεισθέντας, ψευδῆ τὴν <u>ἀλήθειαν</u> τῶν <u>πραχθέντων</u> ἡγήσασθαι· ἡ μὲν γὰρ πιστότερον ἢ ἀληθέστερον σύγκειται, ἡ δ᾽ ἀδολώτερον καὶ ἀδυνατώτερον λεχθήσεται.

This unusually long sentence becomes more and more closely woven with antithesis, the further it proceeds. The warning of λόγοις—ἔπρασσε in the first clause is followed by two plain oppositions of word and deed, which are diversified with other contrasts arising out of them ; and the structure is crowned with two couples of neat comparatives. The ambition here is the same as we have seen in Thucydides[2],—to display a large contrast in terms of the lesser ones which are its organic members : but the risks of the method are almost as obvious. The connection of two or three antitheses may make a satisfactory period. Increase, however, their number and, even if there is little variation of thought, all the sinews of grammar will not avail · to

---

[1] Antiphon, *Tetral.* II, iii, 3.   [2] Above, pp. 102, 104, 110.

produce a useful creature. The main point is too apt to be obscured by the crowd of subsidiary, yet equally prominent, points. Antiphon, of course, was more comfortably placed for such attempts. His central contrast was before the eyes of his audience, as the subject of the whole discussion : what he has undertaken is to expose this contrast in a particular light, with the aid of as many details as he can effectually produce in a short space of time. In spite of this, and although the case is essentially simple, we feel in this sentence that the organism is defeating itself, as it were, by an excess of faculties.

It is, however, an exception from his ordinary habit. A fair sample of his writing, taken from the more elaborately planned oration *On the Murder of Herodes*[1], shows a downright abruptness of manner which reminds us of Alcibiades at Sparta :—

κατὰ γὰρ τοὺς νόμους ὠμόσατε δικάσειν· ἐγὼ δὲ καθ᾽ οὓς μὲν ἀπήχθην, οὐκ ἔνοχός εἰμι τοῖς νόμοις· ὧν δ᾽ ἔχω τὴν αἰτίαν, ἀγών μοι νόμιμος ὑπολείπεται· εἰ δὲ δύο ἐξ ἑνὸς ἀγῶνος γεγένησθον, οὐκ ἐγὼ αἴτιος, ἀλλ᾽ οἱ κατήγοροι.

The wit, or at least the ingenuity, of Alcibiades runs on just the same lines[2] :—

φυγάς τε γάρ εἰμι τῆς τῶν ἐξελασάντων πονηρίας, καὶ οὐ τῆς ὑμετέρας, ἢν πείθησθέ μοι, ὠφελίας· καὶ πολεμιώτεροι οὐχ οἱ τοὺς πολεμίους που βλάψαντες ὑμεῖς ἢ οἱ τοὺς φίλους ἀναγκάσαντες πολεμίους γενέσθαι. τό τε φιλόπολι οὐκ ἐν ᾧ ἀδικοῦμαι ἔχω, ἀλλ᾽ ἐν ᾧ ἀσφαλῶς ἐπολιτεύθην—

though this has a tune and a splendour which are far beyond the anxious pleading of Antiphon. Indeed, if we compare the two speeches, and note how Alcibiades can resume the larger, but no less effective, type of sentence which he has used two chapters before, we are compelled

---

[1] Antiphon, *Or.* v, 85.　　　　　　　[2] Thuc. VI, 92. 3.

by the copious wealth of thought, and the command of
sharp and flexible language, to set Thucydides' genius
immeasurably above the mere talent of Antiphon. For
in the historian's field of vision was a vast company of
persons, movements and events which, as he sorted them
out for the proper significance of his record, acquired
light and life from each other by opposition or combination.
That he could as easily surpass Antiphon in brilliance as
he could Gorgias in power, was due in either case to his
quick sense of human values, controlled by his keen
unwavering insight into facts. It is the double activity
of this sense and this insight which explains the too
laborious regulation of the too fervent course of his larger
rhetorical periods, and also the forging of strange impressive phrases in the smaller. For he varies his
compass as freely in the speeches as in the reflective
passages of his narrative. The abruptness of Alcibiades[1],
soon changing back to lengthy explanation; the heavy
symmetry of the Thebans[2]; the plain emphasis of
Nicias[3]; the long sonorous phrases of Hermocrates[4],
answered by the incisive tones of Athenagoras[5]; and
other distinctive features, in almost every piece, can help
to indicate each speaker's mood upon each momentous
occasion.

§ 10

To pursue the discussion of these variations among
delicate shades of thought and feeling would take us
beyond the objective scope of the present study. Our
account of the beginnings of formal prose in Greece has
tried to eschew mere personal impressions and fancies,

---

[1] In two places (VI, 90. 1; 91. 1) he ends a short sentence with a
peremptory and disdainful μάθετε ἤδη.   [2] III, 65.

[3] VI, 9-14.   [4] VI, 34 (esp. § 5).

[5] VI, 38. 5—τί καὶ βούλεσθε, ὦ νεώτεροι; πότερον ἄρχειν ἤδη; ἀλλ' οὐκ ἔννομον.

though at the risk of being charged with a mean and
piece-meal pedantry.   This is a crime of which Englishmen are justly shy.   They are apt, however, to give it
too wide a berth, preferring, as in other affairs, to be
excellent or execrable without wanting to reason either
why or how.   For it is a heedlessness which has its
disadvantages: they are too likely to remain insensible
to the refinements of a noble artist, as well as to the
rusticities of a scribbling dunce.   And indeed, if we have
dwelt so long on the matter-of-fact 'summers and
winters' of Thucydides' style, it is because we cannot
approach any true conception of his literary worth except
from this substantial, though admittedly arid, basis.
Classical Greek Prose, of which Plato and Demosthenes
are the complete masters, emerged in the first place from
Ionian travellers' tales and Ionian poetry : an impress of
form can be traced to Ionian philosophy ; but one of the
chief impelling and controlling forces which set it on the
way of its various development was the mind of Thucydides.   Had the sophistic movement never arisen, he
would still have accomplished much in the placing of.
words, and in widening the capacities of vocabulary and
grammatical machinery.   Larger resources, however,
were placed at his disposal; and the most important of his
innovations was that frank, often crude, use of antithesis
which, under the different conditions produced by his
work, aimed always at balancing the weight of sound in
the sentence.

Its use belongs, in general, to his philosophic, contemplative and discursive moods ; and there is no small
interest in watching and trying to account for its
appearances among the less regulated portions of the
History.   For, broadly speaking, Thucydides has a
conscious command of two quite separate methods—the
simple and the complex : he finds each of these useful in

its own province, but especially where a sudden change from one to the other accentuates the change of mood. Everyone must feel the impressive dignity of the first words that Pericles utters in the book[1] :—

τῆς μὲν γνώμης, ὦ 'Αθηναῖοι, αἰεὶ τῆς αὐτῆς ἔχομαι, μὴ εἴκειν Πελοποννησίοις, καίπερ εἰδὼς τοὺς ἀνθρώπους οὐ τῇ αὐτῇ ὀργῇ ἀναπειθομένους τε πολεμεῖν καὶ ἐν τῷ ἔργῳ πράσσοντας, πρὸς δὲ τὰς ξυμφορὰς καὶ τὰς γνώμας τρεπομένους—

though few, perhaps, have even looked for the cause. Its effect, as prepared by the historian, is far greater than what we should expect from meeting its old-fashioned thought and manner on a modern page. Not merely does it express the simple strength of an un-swerving determination ; not merely does it suggest all the previous occasions on which the speaker had put forward his plans for the dominion of Athens, and had quelled the murmurs of sceptical objectors ; but, first and foremost, it induces a sense of calm, comprehensive reflection, philosophically seated above, yet practically guiding, the opinions and passions of the crowd[2]. How is it that these words inspire so complete a conviction ? By little else than their formal opposition to the loosely-strung sentences which lead us up to them. The Funeral Oration provides a still clearer instance of the same design. The plain directness of the account of the burial ceremony[3] provides, as it were, a simple prelude for the full grave harmonies to which the politician's utterance is tuned. So throughout the book we can feel the simul-taneous change of mood and style : a piece of reported

---

[1] Thuc. I, 140. I.

[2] Cf. Plato, *Phædrus*, 270 a—τὸ ὑψηλόνουν καὶ πάντη τελεσιουργόν...ὃ καὶ Περικλῆς πρὸς τῷ εὐφυὴς εἶναι ἐκτήσατο—(referred to above, p. 118).

[3] Thuc. II, 34.

186   CLIO ENTHRONED

speech will bring on alliteration and deliberate equipoise,
as here[1]—

ὅπως ξυμμαχία τε αὐτοῖς παραγένηται καὶ τὸν πρὸς
Ἀθηναίους πόλεμον βεβαιότερον πείθωσι ποιεῖσθαι ἐκ τοῦ
προφανοῦς ὑπὲρ σφῶν τοὺς Λακεδαιμονίους, ἵνα ἢ ἀπὸ τῆς
Σικελίας ἀπαγάγωσιν αὐτοὺς ἢ πρὸς τὸ ἐν Σικελίᾳ στράτευμα
ἧσσον ὠφελίαν ἄλλην ἐπιπέμπωσιν—

or in Gylippus' encouragement of his troops[2]—

καὶ διανοεῖσθαι οὕτως ἐκέλευεν αὐτοὺς ὡς τῇ μὲν
παρασκευῇ οὐκ ἔλασσον ἔξοντας, τῇ δὲ γνώμῃ οὐκ ἀνεκτὸν
ἐσόμενον, εἰ μὴ ἀξιώσουσι Πελοποννήσιοί τε ὄντες καὶ
Δωριῆς Ἰώνων κτλ.—

The author's policy is more obvious in his laboured
passages, as in the study of faction-strife, from which
this enquiry into his formal experiments began[3] : but
no less certainly is the sophistic influence to be traced
in large tracts of his narrative. With the decisive
weight of his genius, he pronounced against shapelessness,
commonplace diction and lack of point in Greek prose.
We may choose to believe, on the word of Lucian, that
Demosthenes copied out the History eight times[4]; or
our admiration of both writers may be contented with a
less solid link between them[5] : but the fact remains that
the representative sayings and arguments of the Peloponnesian War, which were soon to have currency among
literary students like Isocrates, have been coined with
this stamp[6]. The influence of the complex antithetical

[1] VI, 73. 2; cf. 72. 4.   [2] VII, 5. 3-4.   [3] III, 82; above pp. 87-90.
[4] Lucian, Adv. Indoct. 102.   [5] Cf. Dionys. De Thuc. 944.
[6] The interesting but delicate task of tracing the Sicilian influence in the
sober style of Lysias, 'the most graceful and most versatile interpreter of
ordinary Athenian life' (Jebb), cannot be attempted here. For his use of
antithesis, and his place in the rhetorical tradition, see Jebb, Att. Or. ,
pp. 158-198.

period is clearly seen in the reasonings of both Plato and Demosthenes. From these, particularly the latter, it passed into Cicero, from whom again, since the Renaissance, it has been constantly employed in European prose. Thus in Thucydides, while the speeches were the glittering fruits in which his art had its highest satisfaction, his narrative could not but be frequently affected by this new method of cultivation, and so could leave, as a more useful and durable gift, the close-grained timber of the stem. Many examples might be cited of this profitable regulation: we will only glance here at the following neat summary of the situation after an obstinate contest[1] :—

ἀποπλευσάντων δὲ τῶν Ἀθηναίων ἐς τὴν Ναύπακτον οἱ Κορίνθιοι εὐθὺς τροπαῖον ἔστησαν ὡς νικῶντες, ὅτι πλείους τῶν ἐναντίων ναῦς ἄπλους ἐποίησαν, καὶ νομίσαντες δι' αὐτὸ οὐχ ἡσσᾶσθαι δι' ὅπερ οὐδ' οἱ ἕτεροι νικᾶν· οἵ τε γὰρ Κορίνθιοι ἡγήσαντο κρατεῖν, εἰ μὴ πολὺ ἐκρατοῦντο, οἵ τ' Ἀθηναῖοι ἐνόμιζον ἡσσᾶσθαι, εἰ μὴ πολὺ ἐνίκων.

Just as we are liable to underrate the considerations of martial pride to which the substance of this sentence bears witness, so it is not easy for us to realise the value of the decision which gave this form to rational discourse. In this light, it is no exaggeration to regard Thucydides as the settled breeze from Zeus, which a fine Homeric simile describes as sweeping in—a little roughly, perhaps—upon the lesser wandering airs, and setting all the uneasily stirring waves in one definite direction[2]. We have had our Euphuists, whose influence can be traced in such different writers as Raleigh, Donne and Hooker: but we can point to no single figure that stands in such a

[1] Thuc. VII, 34. 7.
[2] *Iliad*, XIV, 16—ὡς δ' ὅτε πορφύρῃ πέλαγος μέγα κύματι κωφῷ | ὀσσόμενον λιγέων ἀνέμων λαιψηρὰ κέλευθα | αὔτως, οὐδ' ἄρα τε προκυλίνδεται οὐδετέρωσε, | πρίν τινα κεκριμένον καταβήμεναι ἐκ Διὸς οὖρον.

commanding position, no case of a choice so momentous, as the history of Greek prose must associate with the style of Thucydides.   Perhaps our best parallel would be an imaginary one.   Suppose the literature in our possession to have been limited by destiny or disaster to a very few prose fictions—for example, *Robinson Crusoe*, *Humphrey Clinker*, and *Lavengro*,—one or two plays of Shakespeare and Dryden, and the lyrics of Shelley. Suppose that we had been much attracted by a preacher who was making a success with some epigrams on vice and virtue, life and death, interspersed with reminiscences of our two or three poets; and suppose that a book appeared which, among many obscure and ugly sayings, contained the following sentence[1] :—

'Now, as long as they did no palpable wrong about them, Nataly could argue her case in her conscience— deep down and out of hearing, where women under *scourge* of the *laws* they have not helped decree may and do *deliver* their *minds*.   She stood in that subter- ranean recess for *Nature* against the *Institutions of Man*: a woman little adapted for the post of rebel ; but to this, by the agency of circumstances, it had come ; she who was designed by *nature* to be an *ornament* of those *Institutions opposed* them ; and when thinking of the *rights* and the *conduct* of the decrepit *Legitimate*— virulent in a *heathen* vindictiveness declaring itself *holy* —she had *Nature's logic, Nature's voice* for self-defence.'

This is a sentence whose shape and context alike suggest how Thucydides might have turned aside to ponder on Antigone : in our supposed condition of English literature, it would astonish not merely by its mode of thought, but far more by its overbearing strength of expression ; which would reveal itself, to careful study,

---

[1] Meredith, *One of Our Conquerors*, xi; for the topic of φύσις and νόμος, see above, p. 147.

as a system of antitheses and alliterations, closely woven on a periodic frame.   Some of us would soon be busily imitating ; the majority would be dissuaded by the advice and example of critics who are established because they are easily read : but all would have to agree that something great had been achieved, and the influence would act insensibly upon one or two writers of progressive genius.   It is in some such peculiar distinction that Thucydides should be conceived as standing apart, and yet claiming respect, from subsequent prose-writers : not as providing a good model; rather as having brought into human use some half-hidden or unwieldy forces,—as having made, in fact, an *invention*.

CHAPTER VI

THE MELIAN DIALOGUE

§ 1

STILL trusting in the sincerity of the 'vivid and penetrating intellect[1]' which produced the History of the War, we have to meet one last billow of Mythistoria— the debate of the Melians with the Athenians[2] which immediately precedes the Sicilian Expedition. One strong point of the mythic theory was that it seemed to furnish a clear, simple answer to the puzzle presented to intelligent readers by the fine-spun arguments and laboured language of the Dialogue. We have seen however, that whereas that theory needed all, and more than all, the support it might obtain in this quarter, it was not at ease over the momentary withdrawal of Alcibiades from the proceedings[3]. We have further seen reason, in the contrast offered by the ensuing speech of Nicias, to expect that some attention to the sophistic movement would throw light on the historian's aim in composing the Dialogue, and also, perhaps, on his estimate of the modern tendency in public discussion[4]. That the rapid growth of rhetorical debate had stirred a serious concern in him as well as in others, has been noticed in our review of the affair of Mytilene[5].

The waverings and disputes of eminent critics, from the time of Dionysius to the present day, are evident

---

[1] Above, p. 157.   [2] Thuc. v, 85–113.   [3] Above, p. 61.
[4] pp. 73–5.   [5] pp. 163–7.

enough in the ponderous mass of comment which has gathered about the Dialogue. Much of this, like the mythic theory itself, has built too hastily on the 'dramatic' arrangement of the speeches on either side[1]. The case of one high authority in literature and history will perhaps excuse us for adding a little more to what has been written on the subject, and also for leaving some part of it (as is only too likely) unexplained. Professor Bury was formerly inclined to take the Dialogue as evidence of a comprehensive dramatic scheme. 'The conquest of Melos,' he wrote, 'is remarkable...for the unprovoked oppression of Athens, without any passable pretext. By the curious device of an imaginary colloquy ...Thucydides has brought the episode into dramatic relief' :...he 'has merely used the dialogue to emphasize the overbearing spirit of the Athenians, flown with insolence, on the eve of an enterprise which was destined to bring signal retribution and humble their city in the dust.'... 'The check of Athens rounded the theme of the younger, as the check of Persia had rounded the theme of the elder, historian; and although Nemesis, who moves openly in the pages of Herodotus, is kept carefully in the background by Thucydides, we are conscious of her influence[2].' But more recently the same critic has taken a different view:—'That such a conference was held, there cannot be a reasonable doubt'... 'The attitude of the Athenians on this occasion is exactly the same as that of Diodotus in arguing for leniency towards Mytilene. Both alike are ruthlessly realistic; both alike refuse to consider any reason but reason of state'...'The discussion in the Melian council-chamber before the siege has nothing to do with the rigorous treatment of the people after the capture of the city.'...

[1] Cf. p. 73.
[2] Bury, *Hist. Gr.* 1900, p. 463.

' It has been supposed by various critics that he introduced a cynical dialogue for the purpose of holding
up to obloquy the conduct of Athens, and even of
making it appear an ill-omened prelude to the disastrous
expedition against Sicily.   The theory will not, in my
opinion, bear examination.'   Thucydides' object, accordingly, is ' to examine and reveal political actions from an
exclusively political point of view[1].'

There can be no doubt that this later judgement is
nearer to the truth : for the whole study in which it
occurs, though perhaps too ready to see an ironical
meaning in the description of Nicias[2], takes a wide,
impartial survey of the evidence supplied by other
political discussions in the History.   To rely on
Thucydides' sympathy with Nicias or Diodotus or even
Pericles, would too probably be to lean on a bruised
reed : still less shall we argue a dramatic tendency from
this particular effect of a historical detachment, which for
the moment seems to make human characters move and
speak as on a tragic stage.   For the Dialogue is dramatic
only in the sense that it shows, in quoted conversation, a
contrast of opposing doctrines and a trial of wits in the
interchange of reason.   Its *academic* nature is plainly
suggested by the historian.   The Athenians have just
been waging war on their old ally Perdiccas, who had
begun to withdraw from their friendship[3].   Alcibiades
has seized some three hundred Argives, suspected of
Lacedæmonian intrigue[4] : this is followed at once by an
Athenian descent upon Melos—a Lacedæmonian colony
which desires to be neutral ; but before the invaders
proceed to actual hostilities, a consultation of representatives is arranged.   The Melians will not allow the
Athenians to speak before the people at large : whereupon

[1] *Anc. Gr. Historians*, 1909, pp. 138–140.
[2] *Ib.* p. 119; above, p. 74 n. 3.   [3] Thuc. v, 83. 4.   [4] v, 84. 1.

they are taunted with fears of seductive oratory, and are mockingly offered the advantage of interrupting and replying to whatever they dislike in the Athenian proposals. It is as though Protagoras were kindly invited to the sort of contest in which he had too good reason to fear defeat[1]. The Melians complain that this is all very well; but the Athenians are there as open enemies, whose professions of fairness are empty. The complaint is dismissed as a mere flight of fancy : the idea is to convince the Melians, if possible, by reason instead of force. The islanders reply that they were simply regarding the probabilities of their situation. However, they consent to the arrangement.

To disbelieve this introduction, and hold that no such conference actually occurred, would be virtually consigning the substance of the History, and the whole aim of its author, to the sphere of deliberate romance. Dionysius, on the false ground that Thucydides, after his banishment, 'spent *in Thrace* all the remaining years of the war,' questions the accuracy and propriety of the Dialogue, as a report of a colloquy which he allows to have taken place. Mr Cornford, tacitly endorsing this position, answers the queries of Dionysius with the theory that Thucydides, out of touch with the facts of the affair, worked it up to provide one of the chief scenes in his tragedy of *The Downfall of Athens*[2]. But there is no reason for doubting that a conference on the meaning of this unprovoked invasion was really held; that Thucydides obtained information of at least its outlines from one or more of the Athenian delegates; and that it did consist of an intellectual contest on the new topic of reason of state, which was marked by a frank avowal

---

[1] Cf. above, p. 128.

[2] See the whole passage of Dionysius (*De Thuc.* 918) translated and discussed in *Th. M.* pp. 179 foll.

from the Athenians of their 'might-is-right' policy. We
may grant that 'the circumstance that no public was
present gave the author the artistic pretext for candour[1]':
on the other hand, the Athenian intentions could not have
been at all obscure or new in the sight of Greece; since
we read that, ten years before, a strong expedition under
Nicias had attempted to reduce the Melians, 'who were
islanders, and yet were unwilling to be subject to Athens,
or even to enter her confederacy.' The island was
ravaged; but the invaders failed to subdue the city, and
soon went off to further marauding elsewhere[2]. On the
later occasion, moreover, the Athenians were ready for
just as public an interchange of views as we find between
the Platæan envoys and Archidamus[3], or in the Mytilenæan debate[4]: the substance of their words must have
been passed about the cities of Greece, both before and
after the conference, in the various colours of popular
scandal. Shall we regard the Dialogue as largely
fictitious, merely because this *was* a critical moment in
the career of Athens, and her policy *was* being formulated
in terms which ignored, in a startling degree, the claims
of social justice?

§ 2

'You must make the best of circumstances,' say the
Athenians, 'and take counsel, on the facts before your
eyes, for the preservation of your state[5].' The pretence
that the parties will be equally free in the proposed
contest of reason is thus frankly abandoned: the Melians
clearly distinguish the nature of the debate:—'This
conference is after all on the question of our preservation,
so let the discussion proceed, if you like, in the manner you
suggest[6].' Nothing is more likely than that the Athenians

---

[1] Bury, *Anc. Gr. Historians*, p. 140.   [2] Thuc. III, 91. 2; 426 B.C.
[3] II, 71-4.   [4] III, 37-48.   [5] V, 87.   [6] 88.

really meant to convince the Melians of sin by a regular eristic debate, thus cheaply gaining a good πρόφασις for the action on which they had long decided. We know that such considerations often took a foremost place, from the evidence of many quarrels among Greek cities[1], and obviously enough from Sparta's attempt, after the allies had decided on war, to put Athens in the wrong by means of a malicious embassy aimed at the authority of Pericles[2]. It is impossible to determine exactly how much artistic colouring has entered into the historian's emphatic summary of the affair: only we must bear in mind that the Athenians had the might and used it as right; and further, that they were more than willing to discuss this question at the very stage which, in modern warfare, is not the prelude but the sequel to a rupture of negotiations. Still, the proportion of the Dialogue to the scale of the History shows that the emphasis was specially designed; and although the arguments on either side may well have been the same as those presented here, we ought certainly to look for some particular purpose in the 'contorted tropes and incoherencies' of which Dionysius complains, when he contrasts these speeches with those of Archidamus and the Plataeans[3].

As for the arguments, it is plain that the Athenians have really very little to say: 'it is a question of expediency, not of equity'; and yet the Melians are given time to express the hopes they repose in the justice of their cause, in fortune, in heaven, and in Sparta, simply in order that the Athenians may scout them, one by one, as unpractical and absurd. But in so doing, the latter reveal themselves in the unmistakable character of

---

[1] See above, pp. 46–8.

[2] I, 126: cf. the Spartan calculations on a technical offence of Athens, VII, 18. 2.

[3] Dionys. *De Thuc.* 920; *Th. M.* p. 180.

the strong to whom the weak must yield[1]. 'Even
thus,' say the Melians, 'it may go hard with you one
day': the answer given to this must have seemed as
unconvincing to Thucydides as it does to us:—'We
have no fears about our own fall, because the Lacedæmonians, if victorious, are not to be dreaded as
conquerors[2]'; it is merely a controversial refinement to
add that Athens is more afraid of her revolted subjects[3].
When the Melians protest that they are neutral and
friendly, and hence are no cause for fear, the Athenians
can only rejoin that the best way to assert strength is
aggressive hostility[4]. The only safety for Athens lies in
subduing every one, friend and foe alike; especially Melos,
for islanders are particularly helpless when once reduced
by a strong sea-power. The Melians point to the evil
consequences that must be expected from a reputation
for unprovoked violence. Here the Athenians make
another twist: people on the mainland, not fearing
invasion, will be slow to take precautions; it is the
independent islands that are dangerous[5]. When the
Melians announce that they prefer to fight and trust to
luck, the answer in brief is this:—'You are like the fools
who are guided by divination; as for the gods on whom
you rely, we can claim their favour just as much. We
follow the common beliefs, and yet find the pattern of
our policy in the god's morality. Expediency is also
the motto of the Spartans: you cannot count on their
willingness to help you, still less on their power[6].'

The picture, in fact, is of a giant who is going to use
his strength like a giant, but, before acting, talks loudly
of the value of reason; then shows, in spite of much

---

[1] Thuc. v. 89—δυνατὰ δὲ οἱ προύχοντες πράσσουσι καὶ οἱ ἀσθενεῖς ξυγχωρ-
οῦσιν.   [2] 91.

[3] Grundy (*Thuc. and Hist. of his Age*, p. 503) takes this sentence as
evidence of a tragic design.   [4] 97.   [5] 99.   [6] 105.

heavy ingenuity, that his reasoning is neither very sound nor very clear; and lastly, crushes with a small part of his strength a slight and harmless creature. This latter holds out bravely for a while, owing to the giant's over-confidence and miscalculation[1]: in the end, it is starved into surrender and destroyed[2]. We pass on to watch how the great power fares in a larger but quite feasible undertaking at Syracuse. As the long story unfolds itself, the determination of the people at home is first shaken by a superstitious scare[3], and then crumbles into sheer bad management[4]: success in Sicily—from various causes, but partly owing to the continuance of Nicias in command—gives place to failure[5]. After the terribly vivid picture of the last retreat, when the soldiers have to abandon their sick and wounded comrades, we are shown the grim reversal of their fortunes, not as a moral retribution, but simply as a pathetic exasperation of their pain:—'Whereas they had come to enslave others, they departed now with fear of meeting with that fate themselves: instead of prayers and pæans, such as accompanied their sailing forth, they were starting back with ejaculations of the opposite import[6].'

§ 3

If we are impelled to ask what Thucydides regarded as the chief cause of this grievous though by no means crippling disaster, and if we are to look for the answer in the tenour and form of this Dialogue, we shall remember

[1] 115.

[2] The impression made on sensible men by this ruthless proceeding is shown by the proverbial phrase 'Melian Starvation' in Aristoph. *Aves* 186 (413 B.C.; cf. Zenobius, iv, 94; Diogenianus, vi, 14): but something of the sort must have been expected, after the massacre at Scione in 421 B.C. (Thuc. V, 32. 1).

[3] VI, 53.   [4] VI, 61; VII, 16.   [5] VII, 50.   [6] VII, 75. 7.

that the Eighth Book has already proved to be an awkward
obstacle in the path of the mythic theory; while it supplied,
on the contrary, some striking hints that the historian was
inclined to lay the blame on the gradual degeneration of
Athenian politics, after the death of Pericles, into an
orators' game. Not the least of these hints was his praise
of the government of the Four Hundred, with the old-
fashioned Antiphon at its head[1]. The same point has
emerged from our survey of the Mytilenæan debate[2]. If
we also recall the triumphant vogue of sophistic disputation, we may be able to see how the Dialogue fits into
the History, and perhaps to make a fair inference, from
this peculiarly treated piece of his canvas, concerning
the author's main attitude of mind.

'Protagoras,' we are informed, 'was the first person
to set up contests of speech.... It was he who begot
the present ubiquitous tribe of wranglers[3].' At any
rate, the Athenians, from Socrates onwards and down-
wards, improved eagerly on what he and Prodicus had
taught them. The contest of the two Reasons, which
Aristophanes added to his *Clouds*, is announced with the
remark that it will show young Pheidippides how to
confute all pleas of justice[4]. The Unjust Reason relies
for its victory on 'the devising of new maxims[5]': it maintains that there is no such thing as Right[6]: it will take
the very words out of its adversary's mouth, and turn
them into 'a withering volley of new-fangled phrases and

---

[1] Above, pp. 62-4.   [2] pp. 163-4.

[3] Diog. Laert. IX, viii, 52—πρῶτος...λόγων ἀγῶνας ἔθετο...καὶ τὸ νῦν
ἐπιπόλαζον γένος τῶν ἐριστικῶν ἐγέννησεν. We find here also that he was
originally a porter, and that he invented the porter's knot. Perhaps this was
a magnanimous repayment for what his former mates had taught him in the
art of dispute.

[4] Aristoph. *Nub.* 888—πρὸς πάντα τὰ δίκαι' ἀντιλέγειν δυνήσεται.

[5] *Ib.* 896—γνώμας καινὰς ἐξευρίσκων.

[6] *Ib.* 902—οὐ γὰρ εἶναι πάνυ φημὶ δίκην.

conceits[1].' ' Now for good and all,' sing the Chorus, in
words which might announce our Dialogue, 'the hard
trial of wit is here set loose, and makes a fine debate for
our friends to hear[2].' When the Unjust Reason gets a
hearing, he boasts that his accomplishment is ' worth more
than ten thousand crowns '—namely, the art of ' choosing
the worser arguments, and yet winning the case[3].'
Finally, as though to remind us of what the Athenian
delegate said about the gods' morality, the following advice
is proffered to the young lecher who may be caught in
the act:—'Tell her good man that you've done no wrong;
then refer him to Zeus, and show how even He was a
victim of love and women ; surely you, a mortal, are not
to be asked to surpass the powers of Heaven[4]!' The
godless rhetor is represented as beating conventional
morality with the old stick of anthropomorphic theology ;
which he himself, or his more philosophic brethren,
had flung down in the dust. The young man, of
course, makes rapid progress in this pleasant craft: in
the sequel, he not only beats his father, but is able to
demonstrate the duty of beating one's father and one's
mother too[5]; for now 'fine-drawn maxims, discourses
and reflections' are his only company[6]. It is a brave
new world.

The topics of might and right, expediency and
equity, and primitive justice, came forward in the schools
of the early sophists to fill the gap left by the discredit of

---

[1] *Ib.* 943—κᾆτ' ἐκ τούτων ὧν ἂν λέξῃ ῥηματίοισιν καινοῖς αὐτὸν καὶ διανοίαις
κατατοξεύσω.

[2] *Ib.* 955—νῦν γὰρ ἅπας ἐνθάδε κίνδυνος ἀνεῖται σοφίας, ἧς πέρι τοῖς ἐμοῖς
φίλοις ἔστιν ἀγὼν μέγιστος.

[3] *Ib.* 1042—αἱρούμενον τοὺς ἥττονας λόγους ἔπειτα νικᾶν.

[4] *Ib.* 1080—εἶτ' εἰς τὸν Δί' ἐπανενεγκεῖν κτλ. Cf. 904—πῶς δῆτα δίκης οὔσης
ὁ Ζεὺς οὐκ ἀπόλωλεν τὸν πατέρ' αὐτοῦ δήσας;

[5] *Ib.* 1400 foll.

[6] *Ib.* 1404—γνώμαις δὲ λεπταῖς καὶ λόγοις ξύνειμι καὶ μερίμναις.

religion : hence the length and elaboration of the Melian Dialogue must be taken to indicate some private interest, on Thucydides' part, in working out a theme such as Plato assigned to Callicles[1] and Thrasymachus[2]. Which side he would himself prefer to take in the simple nucleus of the controversy, must remain uncertain ; for all that we can tell of him, he was wise enough not to settle down on either. What stands out here, as in the arguments of Diodotus on the side of clemency[3], is that Thucydides has felt, and has communicated to us, the importunate claims of political expediency. Here, he might say— as Hippocrates would of a strange climate or disease—is a force which demands our best investigations, and whose assaults on the common rights of humanity[4] will supply our intelligence with all it needs of solemn awe. He knows how vain is the Melians' faith in 'the fortune from heaven[5]'; but their cause has its deep importance too. Thus here, as elsewhere, appeal and counter-argument must have their share in a reliable and lively record of his age[6].

§ 4

The meaning of the deliberate care which he bestowed on the Dialogue as a whole, and particularly on some parts of it, must now be considered. We have

---

[1] Plato, *Gorg.* 482.

[2] *Resp.* II, 367.

[3] Thuc. III, 44. 47.

[4] Cf. the 'unwritten laws' which hold over us 'an acknowledged shame' (II, 37. 3).

[5] v, 104.

[6] Grundy however (*Thuc. and Hist. of his Age*, p. 436) regards the historical pretensions of the Dialogue as 'too farcical' to allow us 'to suppose that Thucydides could have been guilty of representing such a thing to have taken place.' It is 'a sketch which he never intended to see the light in the form in which it is extant.'

observed how the Athenians seem to confess their case
almost as openly as the Duchess of Malfi[1]—

> 'As a tyrant doubles with his words,
> And fearfully equivocates, so we
> Are forced to express our violent passions
> In riddles and in dreams, and leave the path
> Of simple virtue, which was never made
> To seem the thing it is not.'

Nevertheless, we must not too freely accept Dionysius' complaint of 'contorted tropes and incoherencies.'
In the first place, the passage against which he thus
protests—the imaginative picture of Hope and Danger—
is not in *substance* so elaborate as the similar piece which
Diodotus seemed to utter in all propriety and sincerity[2].
But in *form* it is different. Instead of the short, even
gait of those sentences about Hope, Desire and Fortune,
where each step was sharp and clear, we now have rather
less meaning conveyed in a lengthy involved manner[3] :—

ἐλπὶς δὲ κινδύνῳ παραμύθιον οὖσα τοὺς μὲν ἀπὸ περιουσίας
χρωμένους αὐτῇ, κἂν βλάψῃ, οὐ καθεῖλε, τοῖς δὲ ἐς ἅπαν τὸ
ὑπάρχον ἀναρριπτοῦσι (δάπανος γὰρ φύσει) ἅμα τε
γιγνώσκεται σφαλέντων καὶ ἐν ὅτῳ ἔτι φυλάξεταί τις αὐτὴν
γνωρισθεῖσαν οὐκ ἐλλείπει.

It is difficult not to conclude from this comparison
that Thucydides felt he was composing the Dialogue in a
style which was not only appropriate to the occasion, but
far different in quality and effect from the manner of
Pericles, Protagoras and Antiphon. The Athenians
here, with their 'abundant resources,' are enlivening
their own hopes as well as discrediting those of the
Melians. Just so does Alcibiades, 'talking at great
length on public affairs, put the Assembly in good hopes
of the future'; and on the other hand, by setting the

---

1 Webster, *Duch. Malfi* I, i.
2 Above, pp. 165-6.   3 Thuc. V, 103. 1.

enemy at odds with Tissaphernes, 'strip them of the hopes on which they counted.' If Thucydides had thought fit, he could have given us a specimen of this wily ingenuity: he only goes on to describe the 'high-sounding bombast[1]' of Alcibiades' promises to the army. Such a remark as this should raise hopes in us also, when we try to attach a meaning to the particular complexion of this or that speech; while we have met with too many warnings to let ourselves be foolishly deceived. Another sentence in the Dialogue[2] will make a striking contrast with the plain simplicity of the Platæans and Archidamus, or of Nicias :—

πολλοῖς γὰρ προορωμένοις ἔτι ἐς οἷα φέρονται τὸ αἰσχρὸν καλούμενον ὀνόματος ἐπαγωγοῦ δυνάμει ἐπεσπάσατο, ἡσσηθεῖσι τοῦ ῥήματος, ἔργῳ ξυμφοραῖς ἀνηκέστοις ἑκόντας περιπεσεῖν καὶ αἰσχύνην αἰσχίω μετὰ ἀνοίας ἢ τύχῃ προσλαβεῖν.

The verbose pretentiousness of this complication is declared almost before we attempt to extract the little thought it conceals: still more, when we take it with the whole of the sententious last chapter in which it occurs. Indeed it is only a windy expansion of what has immediately gone before :—

οὐ γὰρ δὴ ἐπί γε τὴν ἐν τοῖς αἰσχροῖς καὶ προὔπτοις κινδύνοις πλεῖστα διαφθείρουσαν ἀνθρώπους αἰσχύνην τρέψεσθε.

Very similar ideas are developed, at what may seem to us now an excessive length, by the Corinthians at the second congress of Sparta[3]; but their style is both direct and economical of words.

This question is a delicate one, and must ultimately depend on the impression gained by an intelligent reader

---

[1] VIII, 81. 3—ὑπισχνεῖτο δ' οὖν τάδε μέγιστα ἐπικομπῶν (above, p. 63).
[2] V, 111. 3.   [3] I, 120. 3–5.

from several large portions of the History within a short
space of time. Here we must be content to suggest that
Thucydides would have us regard the Dialogue as
academic, not in the sense of aiming at truth or useful
instruction, but of turning aside from an affair already
settled to hedge it about with moral surprises and intellectual
riddles. For, as the Thebans have urged elsewhere, it
it is when acts are in the wrong that speeches of high-
wrought phrase are used to veil them[1]. It is quite with
the air of the Unjust Reason, or of his pupil Pheidippides,
that the Athenians dismiss the last declaration of the
Melians[2]:—' We are struck by the fact that, after saying
you would consult for your safety, in all this conversation
you have mentioned nothing which could give men confidence for believing they might be saved.'

§ 5

This kind of disputation was a luxuriant growth from
the sophistry of Prodicus, Hippias and their disciples.
It was a rhetoric of ingenious complication, such as both
parties in the Mytilenæan debate were careful to eschew,
and Thucydides—even more than Aristophanes—must
have despised. We know that he admired the style of
Antiphon, which we connect with the simple dignity of
Protagoras and the neat, stiff elegance of Gorgias[3]; also
that he has remarked with contempt on some wordy
bombast of Alcibiades. There is justice enough in
Dionysius' complaint, when he protests against the
admiration of those who delighted in this sort of composition[4]. These persons were obviously the supporters
of the late eristic sophistry, as such; not, as Mr Cornford
seems to argue, the patient spectators of the difficult

---

[1] III, 67. 6.   [2] V, 111. 2.
[3] Above, p. 179.   [4] p. 73 n. 5.

drama which he has revealed[1]. We need take no further
notice of Dionysius' suggestion of 'a personal grudge'
which the historian nursed against the city that condemned
him, than to describe it, like the other argument drawn
from his exile[2], as the hasty expedient of a mind too
narrow for the spirit of philosophic history. Neither
can the mythic theory avoid the charge of having unfairly
restricted its view. Its general neglect of the popular
sophistry is nowhere more misleading than in its interpretation of this Dialogue. For the present we shall
only notice a slight though significant point. Just as
the academic character of the discussion begins to be
fully displayed by the overbearing tone and obscurely
pompous expansiveness of the Athenian speakers, the
dramatic conception of their performance 'will follow this
horrible conversation no further[3].' Yet the most natural
explanation, on all the available facts, of this empty
verbiage is, firstly, that there was a great deal of empty
verbiage going on in Athens at this time ; and secondly,
that all Greece was aware that for this grim business it
had been employed to dress up the nakedness of a
foregone conclusion.

If we pry further into the personal tastes of the
historian, we are brought up against a wall of darkness—
that veil of impartiality which had a great share in making
him worthy of our investigation. Thus it is not safe to
build much upon even those deliberate complexities of
speech that appear in the Dialogue, when we have watched
his serious experiments in several manners of writing.
One important point, however, has yet to be discussed,
on which we can be more securely positive. We have
seen how that imaginative passage in Diodotus' speech
belongs quite naturally to the lines of a typical debate on

---

[1] *Th. M.* p. 181.   [2] Above, p. 193.
[3] *Th. M.* p. 179.

a momentous public question : argument is reinforced by a sincerely conceived, though carefully restrained, poetic image.   More extravagant flights would be liable to the fierce censure of Cleon.   So at Melos the Athenians, after abjuring the seduction of fine speech, are forced at length by the difficulty of sustaining their case on bare logic to take refuge in an imaginative study of human motives.   Such studies are to be connected with the myths which Plato developed from the essays of Protagoras and Prodicus for the succour of his dialectic.   In Thucydides' view, they were integral parts of sophistic debate.   That we should find close parallels in the poetry of drama[1] is not surprising, when we remember how much that drama, as conducted by Sophocles and Euripides, owed to the topics and argumentative inventions of sophistry.   We have been told to remark the subtle notes of tragic irony in the Athenian speaker's words : ' the "dim mist of unconsciousness" has stolen down upon him ; he is smitten with madness—blind[2].' The view we must rather take of the matter is that Thucydides, in setting out the character of the conference, knew that the best chance for the Athenians, in maintaining their pretence of an open mind, was to adopt an air of learned profundity.   If there is a sound of irony in their words, it is because things turned out so.   The historian must have seen in the passion for unpractical talk the main and most sinister contrast of word and deed[3].   Not now is Athens content, like Pericles, to pursue a well-weighed policy in silence[4].

If we turn to the evidence of Thucydides' own words, we find him applying this same philosophy of the delusions of hope to the rebellious subjects of Athens[5] :—' They

---

[1] Cf. *Th. M.* pp. 184–7.   [2] *Th. M.* p. 185.
[3] See above, pp. 166–7.   [4] p. 84.
[5] Thuc. IV, 108. 4 ; cf. VIII, 24. 5 (above p. 62).

even supposed there was no danger, being as deeply deceived in their estimate of the Athenian power as it afterwards approved itself on trial; preferring to judge by their vague wishes instead of a safe foresight; for such is the fashion of men, to entrust what they desire to inconsiderate hope, and by an arbitrary reckoning to fling aside what they feel is unwelcome.' This philosophy, in so far as Thucydides has a philosophy at all, is always perceptive, sceptical, critical: only from the lips of his orators can we glean anything like a constructive theory. The manner in which he has expressed himself here is strongly redolent of the early sophists; but its parsimonious stretching and straining of words appear to bring us face to face with his own peculiar energy:—

καὶ γὰρ καὶ ἄδεια ἐφαίνετο αὐτοῖς, ἐψευσμένοις μὲν τῆς Ἀθηναίων δυνάμεως ἐπὶ τοσοῦτον ὅση ὕστερον διεφάνη, τὸ δὲ πλέον βουλήσει κρίνοντες ἀσαφεῖ ἢ προνοίᾳ ἀσφαλεῖ[1], εἰωθότες οἱ ἄνθρωποι οὗ μὲν ἐπιθυμοῦσιν ἐλπίδι ἀπερισκέπτῳ διδόναι, ὃ δὲ μὴ προσίενται λογισμῷ αὐτοκράτορι διωθεῖσθαι.

As before[2], we shall not fail to draw from the structure of Thucydides' style a reminder of that hard intellectual force which sets him above even the best lecturers and phrase-makers of his time. Proceeding on this solid and auspicious ground, we must now try to attain a clearer estimate of his occasional experiments in 'poetic' or imaginative speech.

---

[1] Cf. Gorgias' saying, D.F.V². i, p. 561—τὸ μὲν εἶναι ἀφανὲς μὴ τυχὸν τοῦ δοκεῖν, τὸ δὲ δοκεῖν ἀσθενὲς μὴ τυχὸν τοῦ εἶναι (transl. above, p. 162).

[2] Above, pp. 169–170.

CHAPTER VII

PERSONIFICATION

§ 1

F EW of us at the present day, if asked for a short account of personification, are likely to start from the position of the Lady in *Comus* :—

> 'A thousand fantasies
> Begin to throng into my memory
> Of calling shapes, and beckning shadows dire,
> And airy tongues, that syllable mens names
> On Sands, and Shoars, and desert Wildernesses[1]':

for we have grown as matter-of-fact and prudent as Launcelot Gobbo, when he says :—

' The young gentleman according to fates and destinies, and such odde sayings, the sisters three, and such branches of learning, is indeede deceased, or as you would say, gone to heaven[2].'

Perhaps the phrase of some faded drawing-room song, such as—' Hope told a flatt'ring tale,'—will dimly cross our minds. If the tune is present too, we may find that the word ' Hope' is allowed such a mere perfunctory *flick* of a note, that we feel certain that nobody was ever expected to care who told the ' flatt'ring tale ' ; but that the listener was only to understand, with a delicate vagueness, that it must be a regrettable case of amatory delusion. With more emphasis and conviction, in a time

---

[1] Milton, *Comus*, 205.   [2] Shakespeare, *Merch. Ven.* II, ii.

nearer to that of *Comus*, they festively sang—'Begone, dull Care!' Nor, when we turn back to Sir Walter Raleigh, who came to view life as something more than a brilliant sport, can we feel sure that it is only an idle fashion which uplifts this famous apostrophe :—

'O eloquent, just and mightie Death! whom none could advise, thou hast perswaded ; what none hath dared, thou hast done ; and whom all the world hath flattered, thou only hast cast out of the world and despised [1].'

Indeed, it will only take a little reflection to revive in our minds a hundred instances, not merely from the poetry, but from the prose of the last three centuries, that could show the varying degrees of reality assumed or enforced by this method (as grammarians have named it) of Prosopopœia. For the present we may call it the device of picturing the passions and fortunes of men, or the forces and forms of the sensible world, as figures looming in some sort of human shape and strength and quality. It may perhaps be thought that this affair is quite simple and familiar ; and that the allegation of a tragic theory of life in Thucydides, which has claimed support from his employment of Hope, Desire, and Fortune, is sufficiently answered by protesting that he ' could borrow the personified abstractions of tragedy for purposes of expression, without meaning to suggest anything occult[2].' The history of literary art, however, may have an interest in knowing by what promptings, without and within, he was moved to borrow these ready-made figures ; what purposes he intended them to serve; and what exactly we shall let them suggest to us.

We know that the Greeks had shrines and altars in honour of many gods, among whom were powers in some degree corresponding to our social feelings, our private

---

[1] Raleigh, *Hist. of the World*, ad fin.
[2] Bury, *Anc. Gr. Historians*, p. 130.

aspirations, delights and despairs. They worshipped Shame and Shamelessness, Peace and Strife[1] : Plutarch says that at Sparta ' Fear, Death, Laughter, and all other things that may affect one had shrines[2]' ; Scopas supplied Megara with a statue of Desire[3] ; at Olympia, the Moment or Nick of Time (καιρός) had its altar[4] ; and a fourth-century orator could appeal to the popular sense of the divinity of Rumour[5]. This habit of conceiving and honouring as a personal power almost anything abstract or intangible if only felt at the same time to be highly important, reappears in the grave constructors of the Roman State : the qualities which they chose for worship are noted for a wholly domestic or civic utility. But in Greek poetry we find evidence of an almost boundless licence in the creation of these imaginary persons. The works of Æschylus are especially remarkable for a metaphorical splendour which is largely drawn from this resource ; and the modern commentators of his plays have to be ever maintaining their explanations by reference to his strange but notorious propensity for personification. Perhaps some examples of his taste in this respect are stranger, and less notorious, than they have realised.

Let us consider one or two pictures in the *Agamemnon*. The prayer of Calchas to Artemis, as reported by the Chorus, has these words of appeal against the slaughter of Iphigenia :—' Press not forward a second sacrifice, unlawful, uneatable, an inbred craftsman of quarrels, without awe of a husband[6].' Here the sacrifice, after the descriptions 'unlawful, uneatable,' is shaped in the character of a workman, bred up in the clan, and

---

[1] Pausan. III, 20. 10; Suidas s.v. θεός; Plutarch, *Cimon*. 13; Hesiod, *Op.* 11. Cf. Herod. VIII, 111. [2] Plutarch, *Cleom.* 9. [3] Pausan. i, 43. 6.
[4] *Ib.* V, 14. 9. [5] Æschin. *Contra Timarch.* 57–8.
[6] Æsch. *Agam.* 158 foll.—θυσίαν ἄνομον, ἄδαιτον, νεικέων τέκτονα σύμφυτον, οὐ δεισήνορα.

producing discord therein; and further, as 'having no
awe of husbands,' because he tempts Clytæmnestra to
see no value in the life of her lord Agamemnon.   At the
close of the same play, Ægisthus retorts upon the
protests of the Chorus in these terms[1]:—' Him who
obeys not his master I will yoke in a heavy yoke, with
no high feeding, I warrant you, like a horse running in
the trace.   Yea, Hunger, housemate unfriendly to Spite,
shall stay to see him tamed.'   At first Ægisthus himself
is the ' master '; then his vassal is pictured as a horse;
and finally the horse is given two rival and mutually
exclusive masters—Hunger and Spite[2].   Another place
in this drama shows a strange connection of personified
powers.   Clytæmnestra, triumphantly justifying her
deed, makes this tremendous boast :—' By the accom-
plished Right ($\Delta i\kappa\eta$) of my child, by Doom ("$A\tau\eta$) and
Retribution ('$E\rho\iota\nu\upsilon\varsigma$), to whom I slew this man a victim,
Hope walks not for me in the halls of Fear, so long as
Ægisthus kindle fire upon my hearth, loyal to me as
ever[3].'   Here are five quasi-human personages, of whom
the first three—Right, Doom and Retribution—are
notoriously vast and awful ; while the scene of the abode
of Fear, with Hope avoiding it and all who enter its door,
makes up by dramatic movement for the less imposing
grandeur of the figures.   After all this, it is not our fault
if we feel that Ægisthus, attached to Clytæmnestra's
hearth, is in danger of seeming a little dim and insignificant.   Then in the *Choephori*, among numerous
images, such as that of travellers winning their due
reward (of refreshment) from the long Road of their
journey[4], and a Physician-Hope[5], or perhaps a Curse[6],

[1] *Ib.* 1641 foll.
[2] ἀλλ' ὁ δυσφιλὴς κότῳ λιμὸς ξύνοικος μαλθακόν σφ' ἐπόψεται.
[3] *Ib.* 1435—οὔ μοι φόβου μέλαθρον ἐλπὶς ἐμπατεῖ.   [4] *Choeph.* 711.
[5] *Ib.* 697 (so Headlam, *Plays of Æsch.* 1900, p. 251).
[6] Verrall, *Choeph.* ad loc.

registered as present in a household, we meet with a vision of Fear about to behave like David before the Ark. The vengeance has been accomplished, and Orestes, in the few lucid moments before his wits are distracted by the oncoming Retributions or Furies, declares :—'Close at my heart Fear is ready to sing, yea, and dance a fling to the piping of Spite[1].' This is the sense of the text, before it is altered by modern editors; whose sense of poetic fitness[2], or design of making the poet repeat an image that he has used elsewhere[3], or mere relish of editing, has made them discontented with the sole tradition. One more of these perilous inventions, in a chorus of the same play, tells how ' Requital (Ποινά) came at last with heavy due of penalty upon the sons of Priam ; and so hath she come to the house of Agamemnon, as a lion twofold, and twofold War (Ἄρης): "to the uttermost!" cried the exile, rightly sped by god-sent admonition from the Pythian shrine[4].' The figure of Requital is expanded into a double monster—since Ægisthus and Clytæmnestra must be slain, and Orestes and Pylades are there to do it; then she is a double War-god ; and, in the end, she gives place to the *single* exile Orestes. Here perhaps the anticlimax, or overshadowing of the hero by the shapes conjured up to introduce him, was vaguely felt by the poet ; who seems to bulk out 'the exile' with a ponderous, but not very novel or striking, description[5].

---

[1] *Choeph.* 1025—πρὸς δὲ καρδίᾳ φόβος ᾄδειν ἕτοιμος ἠδ᾽ ὑπορχεῖσθαι κότῳ. (ἡ δ᾽...κρότῳ Abresch, Headlam ; ἡ δ᾽ Conington, Verrall).

[2] Verrall, ad loc., wrongly says that the effect of the text is 'to make fear both player and dancer.'

[3] Headlam (ad loc. and *Class. Rev.* 1902, p. 436) relies on *Choeph.* 167—ὀρχεῖται δὲ καρδία φόβῳ.

[4] *Choeph.* 935 foll.

[5] *Ib.* 941—πυθοχρήσταις (πυθόχρηστος Butler) θεόθεν εὖ φραδαῖσιν ὡρμημένος.

§ 2

The early history of these vividly-imagined passions and forces is largely a matter of conjecture. We may try to see in the *orenda* of the North American Iroquois an elementary form of the invading dæmon which suddenly filled the primitive Greek with panic or desire, drove him this way and that, and left him exhausted and adoring[1]. But since the notion of *orenda* seeks to explain cause and effect without reference to personality—very much as most of us crudely conceive of an electric 'current'—the processes of anthropomorphism are not made any clearer, except by contrast. And further, granting, as everyone must, that these passions appear with strong personal features in the earlier Greek poetry, and play a large part, where most we should expect it, in the dramatic fictions of Æschylus and Sophocles, we must not prejudge the whole question of their appearance in Greek literature by naming them 'Tragic Passions,' as though they had no life, serious or trivial, off the stage[2]. And in particular, when Thucydides is shown to be more religious than Herodotus because his rationalism is less flippant[3]; when his natural inclination to a tragic theory of life is argued merely by the statement that 'his father bore a Thracian name, and came probably of that hard-drinking and fighting stock which worshipped Ares and the northern Dionysus[4]'; we seem to have gained a better understanding of but one phrase in the History—the remark on certain prose-writers which met us at the outset of our search[5].

---

[1] Cornford, *Th. M.* pp. 228–9.
[2] *Th. M.* pp. 221–243 (Ch. xiii—'The Tragic Passions').
[3] *Ib.* p. 239.   [4] *Ib.* p. 241.
[5] Above, p. 14—ὡς λογογράφοι ξυνέθεσαν ἐπὶ τὸ προσαγωγότερον τῇ ἀκροάσει ἢ ἀληθέστερον.

The comparison of vase-paintings with poetic tradition has enabled us to watch the various attitudes of the early Greek mind towards the most mysterious forces of human and external nature[1]. But already—at any rate, before the pictorial record was possible—they have attained the general outlines of baneful sprites. These are usually winged creatures with human heads ; but they differ widely in the combination of other animal features. Generally speaking, they stood for the things which men had most to fear, and could least control. But as we pass on, through Harpy, Gorgon, Siren, Sphinx and Erinys, to the beggarly Old Age who is about to be crushed by Heracles' club, it is apparent that they are being continually drawn into similarity and communion with mankind by the imaginative suggestions of poetry. 'There is nothing that so speedily blurs and effaces the real origin of things as this insistent Greek habit of impersonation[2]'. Out of the confused welter of terrified belief, the poets contrive to select and solidify a certain number of these figures, good as well as evil, whose doings can be intelligibly told, and placed in some relation to the conduct of man. Of course this effort, like that of the sculptors, followed the bent of general opinion ; but its appeal must have rested on the superior brilliance and consecution of the ideas which it placed upon the market. Such qualities were most readily added by investing these ghostly influences with ever more of the higher human attributes.

When sculpture grew to its full height, it was able to meet and support this craving for correlation by dint of its peculiar vividness. Its first maturity in the sixth century maintains just so much of remoteness and reserve as must draw the worshipper to come and wonder often,

---

[1] See the evidence collected by J. E. Harrison, *Proleg. Gr. Rel.*[2] pp. 163–217.　　　[2] *Ib.* p. 215.

with a freshly active mind, before the same abiding image
of his dearest hope or desire.   This visual stimulus was
not available till the close of the ' Mycenæan Age.'
Plastic art had made many fine but small realistic essays
in embossing the cups of wealthy princes : it did not rise
to the task of interpreting the feelings of a *people*, till men
threw off the name and character of vassals, and artificers
began to build and carve, not so much for a chieftain's
glory, as in honour of ideas which were struggling to the
surface of the popular experience and estimate of life.
The god, whether he is merely an old divinity made
more distinct, or a newly personified quality or force, is
now to be the central figure in a house of his own.
There, to emphasise his commerce with mankind, will be
ranged other figures of athlete and maiden, who on their
part will suggest, by some more than human dignity or
grace, how the worshipper is exalted by the divinity to
whom he yields his free devotion.

This is but an obvious, familiar instance of the
artifice we are considering.   The poetic impulse, however,
which is far more deeply concerned in the matter, had
long been at work on the primitive conceptions of the
channels through which our life is invaded by the unseen
and the unknown.   Already in Homer we find even
Sleep endowed with vigorous activities for the service of
Hera, who promises to grant him one of the Graces for
his bride, if he will go and seal the eyes of Zeus ;
and although he cannot quite accomplish this—for Zeus
must first desire to sleep—we are told that, after Hera
had arranged for the necessary condition, the immortal
Father lay at last on Gargarus, ' by Sleep and Endear-
ment subdued[1].'   ' Then Sleep the o'erwhelming arose,
and went swiftly to the ships of the Achæans, bearing the
tidings to Poseidon ; and standing at his side, addressed

[1] *Iliad*, XIV, 353.

to him wingèd words.' When we turn to Æschylus, the remarkable fervour with which he conjures up these personal figures has to be explained by a peculiar aim of revealing human actions as the visible eddies of a mighty stream, which has many currents wandering many ways, though we cannot discern them, as it sweeps over the inequalities of its bed. Inject the colour of humanising imagination into the transparent waters, and the curving or spiral iridiscence will entertain us with the belief that neither the force of gravity, nor the projecting rocks, are wholly responsible for the swirls and bubbles on the surface. Even those strange intermediate powers may seem, as we gaze, to grow intelligible and lovely. The dark avenging Furies, baulked of the blood which, despite the bland prescription of Apollo, they still persist in demanding, relent at last and issue forth into the open light of day. In a single scene, the lingering monster in them dies, and they stand out in the recognisable form and nature of humane, if more than human, ladies.

The whole dramatic interest of the later plays of Æschylus depends on a special application of a theological method which seems to arise from the earliest instincts of his race. The beginnings of steady thought in Greece had aimed at establishing some communion of feeling between men and the forces of nature, by supposing some personal attributes in everything that is not oneself, and particularly in those unaccountable things which gain an entrance into the house of one's mind, and either light it up or fling all within it topsy-turvy. But Æschylus attempted a far greater and more systematic conquest. Everything that troubles us, he thought, may in some degree be controlled, and many of our sorest puzzles be practically solved, if we can somehow discover our right relation to these mysterious forces. They do not lack a certain vague personality ;

this has long been assumed, and variously described, by popular fancy : but in his view they are at once so much greater and so much more real than human beings, that even if we can grasp only an inkling of the rules, or some slight smattering of an etiquette which will bring them within reach of our groping sense, a great step will have been made, and our life will be thereby advanced in ease and dignity and purpose. This, at any rate, was his noble hope. His imaginative construction and sonorous language go far towards consigning to definite provinces those whirling energies of the world which seem so momentous to our affairs, and yet can so cunningly elude our grasp. The almost oppressive zeal with which he thus peoples his stage for a religious vision of life is to blame for what are commonly called his condensed or tangled metaphors. If we remember how he is apt even to smother the human interest under a fantastic canopy of vaticination, we shall explain this by the fact that he attaches a predominant reality to the mythic persons whom he has summoned and equipped for his tragic schemes.

§ 3

The phrases of the early prose-writers of Greece confront us with the delicate question—how far the primitive instinct, or their own beliefs, or some calculated illusion, should be understood in the lively personalities of their occasional imagery. Anaximander, as we saw, spoke poetically of all things 'making reparation and satisfaction to one another for the injustice done[1].' Heracleitus declared that 'fire in its advance will judge and convict all things[2]'; in another saying of his, three personal powers are set in separate ranks :—'the Sun will not overstep his measures ; if he does, the Erinyes,

---

[1] Above, p. 113 : Burnet, *E.G.P.*[2] p. 54.   [2] Burnet, p. 149.

the handmaids of Justice, will find him out[1].' He too is
largely a poet, and personifies on his own account :—
'Time is a child playing draughts[2].' Yet 'Hybris, or
Wantonness, needs putting out, even more than a house
on fire[3]'; and we note that he protests against the
worship of *material* images[4].

Meanwhile Xenophanes, the satirical poet, had been
openly attacking the accepted theology. 'Mortals deem
that the gods are begotten like themselves, and have
clothes like theirs, and voice and form[5]'; 'she that they
call Iris is a cloud likewise, purple, scarlet and green to
behold[6].' In Democritus we seem to meet the first
regular treatment of mythic figures for a merely momentary, artistic impression. 'Fortune,' he said, 'is bountiful
but unsteady'; this might have been taken to imply
some wide theory of her personal influence, had not
another saying been preserved :—'Men fashioned an
image of Fortune as an excuse for their own imprudence.
Fortune is but little hostile to Sagacity[7].' Again, 'the
table she spreads for us is sumptuous, but Temperance
proffers one sufficient for our needs[8].' Clearly we have
now passed into the region of practical phrase-making. A
more extensive picture, for an equally practical effect, is
soon produced by Prodicus[9]. So the writer of *The Law*
enforces his careful reasoning with metaphors which
advance, in the scale of their comparisons, from inanimate
objects to a familiar human character :—'Inexperience,
an evil *hoard* and an evil *treasure* to those who have her,
asleep or waking; no *portion* has she in heartiness and
gaiety, *nurse* alike of cowardice and hardihood[10].' In
fact, the sophists were bringing in allegory to enliven the
matter-of-fact substance of their prose : only instead of
inventing new persons, they took over the mythical

---

[1] *Ibid.*   [2] *Ib.* p. 153..   [3] *Ib.* p. 154.   [4] *Ib.* p. 155.   [5] *Ib.* p. 131.
[6] *Ib.* p. 133.   [7] Above, p. 122.   [8] *Ibid.*   [9] p. 145.   [10] p. 149.

creatures of poetry. Their art consisted in new logical combinations of these figures; and while antithesis helped them to impress the ear, they could make stealthy snatches of appeal to the relics of primitive thought. As Plato learnt from their example, a story of this sort will do much to clinch the loose ends of an argument.

Perhaps the chief stimulus to this device arose from the reflection that one could not be sure whether one's fancy might not strike upon, and stir to temporary life, the half-buried bones of ancestral belief. For this reason alone it must be useless to assert that 'allegory is an artificial business from the first, and foredoomed to failure[1].' Giant Despair may seem to-day a personi-fication 'which can only impose upon a child': but Bunyan's Pilgrim progressed through a dozen editions in the first ten years, not to mention the almost innumerable others which succeeded these: several of the earlier have been nearly thumbed out of existence. And indeed, if an 'artificial business' must fail in the end, we see many graces of life which take a long while coming to their doom. The first systematic and appropriate use of this artifice helped the rhetorical reasoning of Euripides to oust the dramatic dæmonology of Aeschylus. Even Aristophanes, as we saw, in the act of holding the method up to ridicule in his dialogue of the two Reasons, takes advantage of its form for contrasting the old age with the new.

The constructive, argumentative side of these fictions had been exploited by Protagoras, and the strong poetic colouring was supplied by Gorgias. An early application of their serious moralising power has met us in the speech of Otanes[2], who tells at length how Wantonness is begotten by Prosperity, but Envy is a creature congenital with man. Darius, in his turn, dwells similarly on Base-

[1] *Th. M.* p. 230.　　　[2] Above, p. 134.

ness and Liberty[1]; and we have glanced at the elaborate characterisation of Love in Agathon's eulogy[2]. In view, then, of these meagre selections from a vast body of like experiments, and considering the cool psychological analysis which is such a strong feature of Thucydides' History[3], we must beware of construing his employment of mythical figures into a continuous tragic theory of human life. In the case of Herodotus, there is more ground for such an interpretation : but even so, it would be prudent to confine the influence of mythical ideas to the separate occasions on which the corresponding language may seem to be used. Such a reading of Thucydides can only, as we found when Fortune and Hope were forced to preside over the story of Pylos[4], arise from and lead to a neglect of his main principles. To enlarge the scope of his art, he tried his hand at several new devices. One of these, antithesis, he used for providing glimpses of dramatic contrast—dramatic more in our modern than in the Æschylean sense—which display the leading characters of the time in their opposite stations on the scene of Greek politics. Having chosen to make some of them speak, he brings in another piece of contemporary art, and shows the passions of men moving about in the approved or—as the word is sometimes used—the 'classical' manner.

§ 4

When we come to weigh the amount of reality attached by his thought to Poverty and Licence, Wantonness and Pride, Hope, Desire and Fortune, as they appear in Diodotus' little apologue, or again, to the Hope and Desire we have found in his own statements, we shall still keep in mind, besides his peculiar insight,

---

[1] Herod. III, 82.   [2] Above, p. 172.
[3] Above, p. 103.   [4] Above, pp. 53-5.

the pursuits and diversions of sophistic enlightenment. Democritus said that ' the hopes of the right-minded are accessible, but those of the unintelligent are impotent[1].' Socrates, if we are to trust Stobæus[2], said that ' neither a woman without a man nor a good hope without toil brings forth anything useful.' It seems likely that when Thucydides speaks of entrusting what one desires to inconsiderate hope, he is *personifying* in just the same manner. Socrates, we know, believed himself to be guided by a ' spiritual sign.' One of his favourite disciples, the Pythagorean and mystical Simmias, is represented as telling of him that ' he considered it a vain boast when people claimed to be visually acquainted with any divine person; whereas to those who asserted they had heard a voice of such an one, he was all attention, earnestly enquiring into the matter[3].' The words of the dæmons, we are told, can only resound in the ears of such as keep an unruffled temperament, and their soul in tranquillity. These are they whom we call holy and spiritual men ; and in time they may be so perfected, that after death their souls will become dæmons in their turn[4]. The common sort of men are beyond the reach of this guidance. Like swimmers far out at sea, they can be espied, but not assisted, by the spirits on the shore ; who, however, will ' run to those who are near, and wading in to meet them, will succour them with hand and voice together, and so save them alive[5].' Such was the belief of the pious : it was a

---

[1] D. *F. V.*[2] i. p. 400.

[2] Stob. *Flor.* cx, 20: cf. Plato, *Sympos.* 210 C—D (τίκτειν λόγους κ.τ.λ.).

[3] Plut. *De Genio Socr.* 588 C. The indictment of Socrates (Plato, *Apol.* 26 b) shows that he was commonly supposed to have commerce with 'strange spirits.'

[4] Cf. Eurip. *Alc.* 1003—αὗτα ποτὲ προὔθαν' ἀνδρός, νῦν δ' ἐστὶ μάκαιρα δαίμων. Also Lucian, *De Morte Peregr.* 36.

[5] *Ib.* 593 foll. Something of this intermediary function of the dæmons or spirits appears in Socrates' account of the instruction he had from

gracious refinement of the ancient ghost-lore. Yet, even
to Socrates and most of his friends, the poetic figures (as
they had become in their time) of Hope, Desire and the
rest, could have but little life. Still less of it, we may be
sure, can they have had in the view of Thucydides, who
would be content to be classed, in this respect, with ' the
common sort of men'; or rather might declare, with
Endymion :—

> 'No, never more
> Shall airy voices cheat me to the shore
> Of tangled wonder, breathless and aghast[1].'

It was an age of free experiment in thought and
speech. Protagoras could hold Pericles disputing all day
long, with regard to a wound accidentally received by an
athlete, whether the javelin, or the man who threw it,
rather than the clerks of the course, should in strict
reason be held guilty of the hurt[2]. Every kind of
resource was drawn upon for turning up new points of
view, and new modes of dressing up the old. In either of
these aims, which were followed at first from the mere
itch of disputing, the fancy that bestows life on things,
and personality on concepts, is fruitful of impressive
schemes and phrases. So Strepsiades learns to be afraid
that his mattock will prove a traitor to his hopes[3].
When the fashion of eulogy comes in, we hear of declam-
ations in honour of ' humble-bees and salt and such like

Diotima (Plato, *Sympos.* 202 E)—'The spiritual altogether stands between
divine and immortal,...interpreting and transporting human things to the
gods, and divine things to men ; entreaties and sacrifices from below, and
ordinances and requitals from above : standing midway, it makes each to
supplement the other, so that the whole is combined in one.' On the other
hand Orestes (Eurip. *Iph. Taur.* 570 foll.) bitterly complains that spirits
commonly called 'wise' are 'all as deceptive as our wingèd dreams,' and
that there is ' great confusion 'twixt divine and mortal ways.'

[1] Keats, *Endym.* iv, 653.   [2] Plut. *Pericl.* 36 (quoting Stesimbrotus).
[3] Aristoph. *Nub.* 1500.

things[1]'; for on these subjects 'one can always find plenty to say.' Plain Xenophon too has been so far influenced by Prodicus and his tribe, that the characters in the *Cyropædia*, instead of being live people, are the shallow personifications of virtues and vices. In his last comedy Aristophanes hits on the device of displaying the successful effort of blind old Wealth to gain his sight and become divine, by undergoing the famous treatment in Asclepius' temple[2]. Poverty also appears, 'like a Fury from a tragic play, with a lunatic and tragic sort of look[3].' It is a literary game, which by the end of the fifth century was widely accepted as a serious aid to thought, and was expanding along with the popular intelligence into more elaborate creations.

So much for the vogue of this artifice, whose attractions were sometimes followed rather at the expense than in the furtherance of direct observation, genuine feeling, and clear thought. Thucydides, however, borrowed from the sophists a few mechanic aids for his project of depicting the political passions which had arisen in the forefront of the Hellenic scene. His ambition throughout was to provide a compendious synopsis of motives, characters and policies, and hence, in the actual grapple of composition, to seize hold of large amorphous quantities and qualities, and reduce them to significant order. The loose variety of important matters had to be collected in neat classes, which must then be handled as separate entities. The mere management of his language, as we shall presently see, tended to sketch these entities with hardened outlines of the vague personality which had appeared in every primitive interpretation of the world.

---

[1] Isocr. *Hel.* 210 B: cf. Plato, *Sympos.* 177 B, where the very turn of the phrase seems intended as a mockery of the fashion—ἐν ᾧ ἐνῆσαν ἅλες ἔπαινον θαυμάσιον ἔχοντες.

[2] Aristoph. *Plut.* 403 foll. ; 727 foll. (388 B.C.).   [3] *Ib.* 423-4.

For instance, Poverty, Hope, Desire, and the others already mentioned, are by no means the only impersonations in . Diodotus' speech. An earlier passage runs thus [1] :—' I consider that the two things most opposed to Good Counsel are Haste and Anger, whereas the one is wont to accompany Thoughtlessness, and the other Ill-breeding and Scanty Judgement. And whosoever insists that Words are not the teachers of Deeds, is either unintelligent, or has some private ends.' The very phrases 'most opposed' ($\dot{\epsilon}\nu\alpha\nu\tau\iota\dot{\omega}\tau\alpha\tau\alpha$), 'wont to accompany' ($\phi\iota\lambda\epsilon\hat{\iota}$ $\gamma\dot{\iota}\gamma\nu\epsilon\sigma\theta\alpha\iota$ $\mu\epsilon\tau\dot{\alpha}$), and 'teachers' ($\delta\iota\delta\dot{\alpha}\sigma\kappa\alpha\lambda\omicron\iota$) insensibly conspire to raise the illusion or conviction that the speaker—a person dealing with ideas which are recognisable by their personal habits—instead of falling himself or drawing others into a dreamy trance, is wide awake, and *knows what he is talking about.*

Indeed the whole passage, extending for some way further, is a compact assemblage of representative ghosts, whose faces are the brief abstracts of all those worlds of things which cannot be recorded. In the same manner Pericles, though he might publicly revere, when he thought fit, the power of Opportunity ($\kappa\alpha\iota\rho\delta$s) at Olympia, tells the people, in a purely practical spirit, that 'the Opportunities of war wait for no man [2].' So for a moment he will make Truth—though she had no special cult—a greater person than Homer, and go on to exalt Athenian daring to the glory of a conquering invader [3]. In this spirit too can Thucydides say of Archidamus that the delay which occurred at the Isthmus, his dilatoriness in the rest of his march, and especially the halt at Œnoe, *traduced* him [4]. A hundred other cases of a similar,

---

[1] Thuc. III, 42. 1.
[2] Thuc. I, 142. 1—$\tau\omicron\hat{\upsilon}$ $\delta\dot{\epsilon}$ $\pi\omicron\lambda\dot{\epsilon}\mu\omicron\upsilon$ $\omicron\dot{\iota}$ $\kappa\alpha\iota\rho\omicron\dot{\iota}$ $\omicron\dot{\upsilon}$ $\mu\epsilon\nu\epsilon\tau\omicron\dot{\iota}$. There was a proverb —$\mu\epsilon\nu\epsilon\tau\omicron\dot{\iota}$ $\theta\epsilon\omicron\dot{\iota}$, $\omicron\dot{\upsilon}\kappa$ $\dot{\alpha}\pi\alpha\tau\eta\lambda\omicron\dot{\iota}$ (Aristoph. *Aves* 1620, Schol.).
[3] II, 41. 4 ; above, p. 160.   [4] II, 18. 3.

though varying, intensity could easily be collected. The habit which they reveal, and which Thucydides contracted and followed to some curious excesses, came into the prose of Greece, as into that of other regions, from the weighty utterances of early sages and bards. Homer, Pindar and Æschylus developed this method into imaginative theories of life : the sophists, and with them Sophocles and Euripides, into moral or psychological fables. This latter fashion, while tracing for some way the personal relations of political principles, transferred the method from the school of Prodicus to the discussion of public business ; and it accordingly finds a place in the Mitylenæan and Melian debates. Democritus applied this art of figurative speech to the object of attracting and compelling thought in certain useful directions : Thucydides, while packing into the History almost more matter than it could hold[1], was anxious to stamp his phrases, and those of his speakers, upon the minds of all posterity. It is of the essence of his style that these effects should be produced in separate compartments ; for all time, indeed, but primarily for the moment. In this sense only can his vivid phrasing be regarded as dramatic ; and this view of it, added to what we have detected in the laborious straining of his constructions, will correctly account for such strokes as that 'prefatory flash' of Desire[2]. Here also is the explanation of the occasional oddity or obscurity of his metaphors : for it is a stately, concise reasoning, not at all the mystical zeal of Æschylus, that has tied his vivid figures at times into awkward knots. Two examples from the comparatively simple speeches of the Platæans and Hermocrates will serve to remind us how this tendency will tax both our intelligence and our command of equivalent language :—

'For if you assess justice by your immediate advantage,

---

[1] Above, p. 171.   [2] Above, p. 170.

together with their hostility, you will prove yourselves
to be no true judges of right, and only waiters on profit[1].'

The abstractions, as we have just noticed in *The Law*[2]
and in Diodotus' speech[3], seem to gather personality as
the sentence proceeds. In the following case, the
strangeness comes from forcing the personality of the
passion to do duty for the men who are subject to it :—

'Vengeance gets no just claim to success from
suffering injustice[4].'

Particularly in this vivid treatment of mental affec-
tions and powers, it is remarkable how Thucydidean
rhetoric has energised the simple contrivance of the
sophists. We find Gorgias, in his Funeral Oration[5],
procuring a little variety for the long, even procession
of his clauses by glancing away from actual persons
(θεράποντες μὲν τῶν ἀδίκως δυστυχούντων, κολασταὶ δὲ
τῶν ἀδίκως εὐτυχούντων) to a couple of general terms
(αὐθάδεις πρὸς τὸ συμφέρον, εὐόργητοι πρὸς τὸ πρέπον),
and thence to a couple which belong to mental life (τῷ
φρονίμῳ τῆς γνώμης παύοντες τὸ ἄφρον). After this he
returns to actual persons (ὑβρισταὶ εἰς τοὺς ὑβριστάς,
κόσμιοι εἰς τοὺς κοσμίους κτλ.). When at length he concludes with *actual things* (δεινοὶ ἐν τοῖς δεινοῖς), we must
feel that, although the sound has been varied, the tests by
which the warriors have been successively tried are, *all of
them*, conceived in some sort as persons. Antiphon has
one example of a mental state described in this manner

---

[1] Thuc. III, 56. 3—εἰ γὰρ τῷ αὐτίκα χρησίμῳ ὑμῶν τε καὶ ἐκείνων πολεμίῳ τὸ
δίκαιον λήψεσθε, τοῦ μὲν ὀρθοῦ φανεῖσθε οὐκ ἀληθεῖς κριταὶ ὄντες, τὸ δὲ ξυμφέρον
μᾶλλον θεραπεύοντες. (Hude excises πολεμίῳ: Krüger suggests πολεμίως.)
Cf. I, 36. 1.

[2] Above, p. 217.   [3] p. 223.

[4] Thuc. IV, 62. 4—τιμωρία γὰρ οὐκ εὐτυχεῖ δικαίως, ὅτι καὶ ἀδικεῖται. Cf. a
like result of the same economy in Lucan, IX, 404—'laetius est quotiens
magno sibi constat honestum.'

[5] D. *F.V.*[2] i, p. 557. With this συμφέρον cf. the ξυμφέρον in Thuc.,
above, n. 1.

(τὸ θυμούμενον τῆς γνώμης¹), but here he employs the more active means of a participle; and one other, virtually of the same sort, where the participles stand out boldly as personal agents (κρεῖσσον δὲ...τὸ ὑμέτερον δυνάμενον ἐμὲ δικαίως σῴζειν ἢ τὸ τῶν ἐχθρῶν βουλόμενον ἀδίκως με ἀπολλύναι²). Thucydides has adopted this method, but has enlarged and intensified it with peculiar force. Gylippus at Syracuse, after urging his troops to grapple fiercely with 'this obvious Disorder of the foe, and a Fortune that has betrayed herself in their extreme hostility,' declares that in such a situation it is right ' to satiate the raging vigour of the mind³.' Brasidas also can speak of resolution as 'that in the mind which has not been forcibly vanquished, but has in itself some counter-argument⁴.' The personality of this spirit is momentarily reduced by its capacity of being 'dulled' or 'blunted' (ἀμβλύνεσθαι); but soon, after some ordinary portraiture of Knowledge, Skill and Fear, we come to a stand-up fight between expansive adjectives, and between conditioned verbs—all *psychological* figures⁵. Thucydides himself, in his narrative, has twice used participles to the same effect, though without openly insisting on the personality; it is to be noted that in the one case he is analysing the substance of a message from Sparta to Athens⁶, and in the other is introducing a speech of Pericles⁷. Without looking further than this very speech, we find more varieties of

---

¹ Antiphon, *Tetr.* I, iii, 3.   ² *De Herod. Cæd.* 73.

³ Thuc. VII, 68. 1—πρὸς οὖν ἀταξίαν τε τοιαύτην καὶ τύχην ἀνδρῶν ἑαυτὴν παραδεδωκυῖαν πολεμιωτάτων ὀργῇ προσμείξωμεν...ἀποπλῆσαι τῆς γνώμης τὸ θυμούμενον—the phrase of Antiphon above.

⁴ II, 87. 3—τῆς γνώμης τὸ μὴ κατὰ κράτος νικηθέν, ἔχον δέ τινα ἐν αὐτῷ ἀντιλογίαν.

⁵ *Ib.* § 5—πρὸς μὲν οὖν τὸ ἐμπειρότερον αὐτῶν τὸ τολμηρότερον ἀντιτάξασθε, πρὸς δὲ τὸ διὰ τὴν ἧσσαν δεδιέναι τὸ ἀπαράσκευοι τότε τυχεῖν.

⁶ I, 90. 2—τὸ μὲν βουλόμενον καὶ ὕποπτον τῆς γνώμης οὐ δηλοῦντες.

⁷ II, 59. 3—ἀπαγαγὼν τὸ ὀργιζόμενον τῆς γνώμης πρὸς τὸ ἠπιώτερον καὶ ἀδεέστερον καταστῆσαι.

the same practice[1]. Modern commentators and translators, eager for logical connection and anxious for their mother-tongue, have neglected the real character of these con-structions, and often, in straightening out those of the more complex sort, have made them appear more awkwardly perverse than they really are. Still, the fresh importance of the idea to the historian has here also, while claiming distinction, endangered lucidity[2].

§ 5

If we ask how it was possible in fifth-century prose, and to such a remarkable extent in that of the sober-minded Thucydides, to treat almost any general term as a person ; and moreover why, in the highest class of these, the salient mental states are figured in striking types of live human beings, we must first refer to a principle which underlies the constitution of all Indo-European speech. Perhaps this will appear most plainly if we contrast it with the linguistic habit of a different people. A short acquaintance with the elements of the Japanese language discovers in it a very common ab-sence—astonishing to our ways of thought—of the suggestion of an agent behind any occurrence in ordinary life[3]. Sentences, for the most part, have no subjects: they express 'a coming-to-be with reference to some person,' who is often not mentioned at all, or whose sex and number are not distinguished. The notion of ' I ' is indicated by a word meaning 'selfishness'; but usually ' I feel poorly' is given as ' Bodily state is bad,' and even the faint shadow of personal feeling in our 'Good-

---

[1] II, 63. I—τῆς πόλεως...τῷ τιμωμένῳ...βοηθεῖν : 3—τὸ γὰρ ἄπραγμον οὐ σῴζεται μὴ μετὰ τοῦ δραστηρίου τεταγμένον. The personality sinks to a mere state when it is a case of weak or neglected action : v, 9. 6—ἐν τῷ ἀνειμένῳ αὐτῶν τῆς γνώμης : cf. II, 61. 2 ; III, 10. 1 ; I, 142. 8.   [2] Cf. above, pp. 170–1.

[3] See Chamberlain, *Handbook of Colloquial Japanese*[3], 1898 ; MacCulle y *Introductory Course in Japanese*, 1896.

evening!' vanishes in 'As for this night!'   Hardly ever
does any inanimate thing appear as subject, and there is
no personification of any sort in daily parlance[1].   If we
tried to restrict our language to what we call 'interjec-
tions' and 'impersonal' phrases—such as 'Horror!' 'it
is raining,' 'it seems fitting'—we should soon find ourselves hopelessly outclassed by this habitual indifference
to causal connection.   In Thucydides, on the contrary,
our minds are perplexed by a tendency to invest with the
higher degrees of personality a large number of things
and qualities which the long, laborious education of our
thought has persuaded us to regard as impersonal.
It may be worth while to consider how much of this
tendency came from the bare substance of the language
that he had to use, how much from sophistic fashion, and
how much from his own invention in the pursuit of
peculiar effects.

The regular pagan worship of the souls or spirits of
natural objects has been, until quite recently, explained
by the doctrine of 'animism'; which represented primitive man as having assumed 'the animation of all nature,
rising at its highest pitch to personification.'   This belief
was 'bound up with that primitive mental state where
man recognises in every detail of his world the operation
of personal life and will[2].'   But as the evidence from
savage modes of thought increases, and is submitted to
the severer inspection which it obviously requires, we
find reason to suspect that, long before the arrival of
anthropomorphism, or any conscious ascription of human
life and will to inanimate things, the first beginnings of

[1] Hence, after translating a Japanese poem which makes Old Age come
walking up the street, Chamberlain (*Japanese Poetry*, 1911, p. 102) remarks
that we have here 'an instance, rare in Japanese literature, of that direct
impersonation of an abstract idea which is so strongly marked a characteristic
of Western thoughts and modes of expression.'

[2] Tylor, *Primitive Culture*[3], I, p. 285.

thought in every part of the world had roughly marked out the ground on which these religious and artistic edifices, when once conceived and desired, could in certain regions be erected.   Such, at least, is the general suggestion which arises from one of the latest applications of modern psychology to the problem of the belief in souls[1].   Not least among the evidence is that of language.   For we have to conceive of primitive man as passing from the rudest condition of savagery,— where in act, though not in thought, he could distinguish between things animate and inanimate, but could not reflect upon or classify his sensations,—to a point at which he developed, among other activities, the use of speech.   It seems probable that his first attempts at linguistic system were made as soon as the effect of sensation could be regarded as a definite whole—at first including, then slowly excluding, the central ' self' : to hold this body of experience apart for inspection and comparison would be one of the earliest efforts of articulate thought.   Here would be produced a feeble embryo, as it were, of the grammatical period : the ' holophrase,' of which examples are quoted from America[2], shows a rather secondary stage, where we can see that, as the structure became loaded with more and more meaning, it would necessarily burst at length into separate grammatical structures.   These must afterwards be re-combined by art—for instance, in the manner facilitated by antithesis—to satisfy the inherent but suddenly stirred craving for a comprehensive description of groups.

As soon as the effects of things were felt to be different from the perceiving self, language must have been occupied with expressing the relations apparent

[1] See Crawley, *The Idea of the Soul*, 1909, whose particular thesis is to trace this idea to the memory-image.
[2] *Ib.* p. 48.

between several entities, of which the self was the most
important.   Since the mind had visual images of the
external objects with which it was dealing, and could also
feel the existence of the subject, it was the business of
language merely to fix and communicate the relations[1].
Almost immediately, however, the need of indicating
things which were not present to the minds of other
people must have brought the use of substantive terms ;
and it was at this juncture that the thing to be named had
to find a footing within reach of the self, by acquiring some
of the definiteness of a self-contained personality.   The
manner in which this rough personalisation takes place is
obscure.   Psychological opinion seems to refer it un-
certainly to the action either of language upon thought,
or of thought upon language[2].   For our purpose, it is
enough to note that not even the simplest sort of grammatical structure seems to be obtainable, until the things
correlated are made as distinct or nearly as distinct to
the mind as the feeling of 'self.'   There is no necessary
ascription, so far, of human life to the objects : they are
only parcelled off from the whole self-centred complex.
But supposing this to have been done and expressed, the
grammatical group will certainly give scope for an un-
conscious dignifying of this or that object with a personality, animal or human, of its own.   The process at the
earlier stage has been vaguely expounded as 'play'—a
realisation of surplus energy, which shifts the 'I' to the
different personality of 'it' or 'that,' and so on with the
other selected objects in turn[3].   This activity is no doubt
to be distinguished from deliberate, artistic anthropomorphism : but it is hard to understand how the
difference can be other[4] than one of degree, in proportion
to the growth of consciousness.   The former process
obviously opens the way to the latter.   But more

[1] *Ib.* p. 33.   [2] *Ib.* pp. 43, 294; 54, 241.   [3] *Ib.* p. 37.   [4] *Ib.* p. 44.

obscurity meets us at this point. We are told that this primitive 'play' is 'absolutely serious,' although the child (or savage) 'does not believe in the reality of the illusion it creates[1].' The ordinary self-illusion, whatever it precisely is, in the child's pretending to be a cake or a doll, may help us a little to see how the mind could begin its experiments in personalisation : to compare it with 'fetishism, shamanism, mimetic and sympathetic magic[2]' seems to land us all at once in the domain of settled belief; which, if similar in kind, is presumably a long way onward from the primary impulse whence the practice took its rise. As to the nature and conditions of this impulse, and also the mode of its action upon the elements of language, much yet remains to be discovered.

But whether we are able or not to understand this primitive game, in which neither life nor will is ascribed to the other persons in the sentence[3], we may agree that the personality which seems to be distributed, in the beginning of grammar, over all material things need have but a vague and unsteady form. We shall accordingly distinguish it from the deliberate fictions of art, whereby 'the artist instinctively goes back to the ancient mould and fills it with indiscriminate life[4]' : at the same time, we note the likelihood that the *mould* is there already, and that this vivifying aim is *instinctive*. Yet long before this artistic ambition could arise, and indeed, very near the first stage of connected speech, it is probable that the names or symbols employed in statements about the several parts of a complex whole tended, in their turn, to come before the mind as independent beings[5]. It may be guessed that the 'three hundred and thirty million gods' of the Hindu theology, and its 'equally vast host of spirits[6],' are largely the outcome of the mere delight

[1] *Ib.* p. 292.   [2] *Ibid.*   [3] *Ib.* p. 44.
[4] *Ibid.*   [5] *Ib.* p. 191.   [6] *Ib.* p. 140.

of inventing new names, and of attaching to each a variously fancied personality. The same sort of pretence is easy enough when the isolation of an abstract idea is assisted or sanctioned by an entitling word. The 'soul' of it—no less dangerous in the view of primitive thought than the souls of ordinary persons—is thus *embodied*, or imprisoned, in a familiar fixity. At a later stage, when such souls are regarded as adorable or friendly, artistic imagination seeks to embody them in ampler guise, so that this stronger actuality may retain the fleeting presence within ready grasp of the community.

The upshot for our question seems to be that, whereas the grammar of some primitive peoples left the rudimentary persons in that hazy insignificance which is suggested by the habits of Japanese speech, the Indo-Europeans were continually defining and enlivening them with additional touches of humanising fancy. The predilection of the Greek language for active verb-constructions attests the exertions of this impulse, from the moment when predication showed the opportunity in its first dim personalisations. For, as here, so further on in the progress, the influence of grammar may well have been, though not paramount, yet real and important. If we suppose that, by some cause or other, the Greek mind was originally disposed to consider the happenings of the world primarily as they appeared in or upon particular objects; and then, while observing the differences of these and giving them separate names, to connect a number of them with some single event which brought them into notice, we can see how a simple economy of verbs would lead to a rough-and-ready ascription of human attributes to all the objects as they stood before the mind. Thus in the sixth century Simonides, the first composer of a national Greek lyric, has learnt how art may thrive merely by emphasising and enlarging the scope of a popular expression. Danaë, afloat with her child on a dark and stormy sea, bids her little one sleep, 'and may the sea sleep, and sleep the immense harm[1].' More striking and progressive imagery is obtained, as in Homer, by developing the activities of the old popular sleep-spirit amidst those of gods and men[2]. So from above and below, the gods of natural or social energy, the Fates and Fortune (those 'unpretentious dæmones of birth[3]'), great emotions and qualities, and any object of importance to human persons either generally or at a special place or moment—all these are continually being brought to the levelling bar of predication, and there treated as the presiding imagination may direct. For although it is an exaggeration to call the Indo-European sentence 'a little drama in which the subject is always astir[4],' the dramatist found in the settled habit of speech a strong hint for extending the fictions of his art.

§ 6

Towards the last quarter of the fifth century both philosophy and religion were doing little more in Athens than serving the experiments of literary skill. There was argument, but chiefly on the subject of man in the midst of his worldly affairs. As for the gods, they had their statues and shows; yet even these were becoming more and more a matter of glory to the men who produced them. The average citizen could laugh heartily at the trick of addressing Poseidon or Dionysus as he

---

[1] Simonides, *Lament of Danaë*, 15—κέλομαι εὗδε βρέφος, εὑδέτω δὲ πόντος, εὑδέτω δ' ἄμετρον κακόν.

[2] Above, p. 214.   [3] Farnell, *Cults of Gr. States*, V, p. 447.

[4] Bréal, *Essai de Sémantique*, 1904, p. 86—'Les langues indo-européennes présentent la phrase sous la forme d'un petit drame où le sujet est toujours agissant.'

would any fellow in the market-place[1]. The anthropomorphism of this busy, successful people had turned awe
into admiration, as it made beauty a common amusement.
The rhetoricians, as we ventured to guess, did not forego
the hope that their personifications might arouse some
little tremor in the old, disused strings of superstition.
It is far more certain that they never sought, like Bunyan,
to awaken even the ghost of any cognate belief. Their
practice is rather to be compared with that of De Lorris,
whose *Roman de la Rose*, made known to our literature
by Chaucer, displays a multitude of passions and powers
ingeniously modelled on the human types to which they
severally belong, and alive with casual suggestion for
even the least saint-loving and fiend-fearing part of the
public. The nearest approach to the supernatural in the
principles of sophistic style was a vivid sense of the
unaccountable power of words. Yet here too we have
seen that the business of art was to humanise or domesti-
cate these potencies, and drill them for daily service, for
battle, or for dance[2]. The artist develops into a new
æsthetic charm what of old was blindly rehearsed as
mythic belief, whether at the first appearance of name-
creatures, or in the regular rites of magic. But while
poetry is ever striving to float away from practical
accuracy, and plies its wings of rhythm and tune towards
the far primæval haunts of the human mind, the prose of
public speech must apply its formal attractions rather to
the office of encouraging and exalting the discourse of
reason.

Thus when Thucydides draws attention, in that chapter
on the Troubles in Greece, to the arbitrary alterations
made in the accepted usages of names[3], he proceeds

---

[1] Aristoph. *Aves*, 1638—ὦ δαιμόνι' ἀνθρώπων Πόσειδον, ποῖ φέρει; cf.
Ran. 1160, 1472.
[2] Above, pp. 160–1 ; 167–8.   [3] Quoted on p. 88.

immediately to illustrate and explain the phenomenon—significant to the observer of rhetoric—with a laboriously scientific thoroughness. Sophocles, in treating the same sort of point, merely states the fact, and calls up the old fabulous lore for his dramatic impression[1]. What he thought of this lore himself, it is happily not our duty here to determine: the beliefs of accomplished artists are slippery things to handle. But to subject the mind of Thucydides to any such theory can hardly be more reasonable than to take these words in Euripides—'that man is best who has faith in hopes always[2]'—as evidence that either the poet or Amphitryon was tinged with the doctrine of Saint Paul.

As to the 'insistent habit of impersonation' which strikes us at every turn in Greek poetry, we have traced it back to a specially vigorous desire for a clear conception of individual things, which seemed to overcome and absorb the more general primitive study of their conditions and relations; where these required emphasis, they also would be individualised in the mind of the Greek with increasing traits of personality. Here we noticed the psychologists' theory of child-like 'play.' Perhaps it is more useful simply to remember the ancient and wide-spread love of acting a part, and fancying others in one's own place: from the latter pretence, at any rate, the beast-fable most probably arose[3]; and variations or

---

[1] Soph. *Antig.* 622—τὸ κακὸν δοκεῖν ποτ᾽ ἐσθλὸν τῷδ᾽ ἔμμεν ὅτῳ φρένας θεὸς ἄγει πρὸς ἄταν. Perhaps the use of ἔμμεν, an epic form not found elsewhere in tragedy, gives part of the ancient flavour. Jebb ad loc. quotes a more explicit statement of the same notion from Theognis 403.

[2] Eurip. *Herc. Fur.* 101—οὗτος δ᾽ ἀνὴρ ἄριστος ὅστις ἐλπίσι πέποιθεν ἀεί.

[3] Cf. Fitzgerald, *Polonius*, Pref. :—'We are fantastic, histrionic creatures; having so much of the fool, loving a mixture of the lie, loving to get our fellow-creatures into our scrapes and make them play our parts.' Aristotle, *Poet.* 4, derives all poetry from a natural love of imitating, and love of imitations. See the interesting notes of Margoliouth, 1911, ad loc. for views of primitive imitation from the æsthetic writings of Hirn, Wallaschek, Lipps

developments of this game can be recognised in the earliest discernible effort of each form of European art. That the habit of impersonation, when skilfully refined, is one of the main supports of poetry as we know it, is obvious enough : but it may be useful to have in mind the considered judgement of a modern expert[1] :—

'What is a Poet ? To whom does he address himself ? And what language is to be expected from him ?— He is a man speaking to men...a man pleased with his own passions and volitions, and who rejoices more than other men in the spirit of life that is in him ; delighting to contemplate similar volitions and passions as manifested in the goings-on of the Universe, and habitually impelled to create them where he does not find them. To these qualities he has added a disposition to be affected more than other men by absent things as if they were present ; an ability of conjuring in himself passions, which are indeed far from being the same as those produced by real events, yet (especially in those parts of the general sympathy which are pleasing and delightful) do more nearly resemble the passions produced by real events, than anything which, from the motions of their own minds merely, other men are accustomed to feel in themselves:— whence, and from practice, he has acquired a greater readiness and power in expressing what he thinks and feels, and especially those thoughts and feelings which, by his own choice, or from the structure of his own mind, arise in him without immediate external excitement.'

This account of the matter is by no means as complete as the ideal critic, or Wordsworth himself, might possibly

and Groos. The first of these says (*Origins of Art*, p. 77)--' By unconsciously and imperfectly copying in our own body the conduct of a man, we may learn to understand him.' Personalising might seem to begin when one should be led by force of habit to use the same method for understanding the conduct of other things.

[1] Wordsworth, *Lyrical Ballads*, 1800, Pref.

make it: but it will serve to show, in the first place, how important to our poetry is the sense of personal character 'in the goings-on of the Universe,' and the habit of creating it where it does not sufficiently appear. The statement then attempts to explain the workings of poetic imagination in terms which suggest some further results of the histrionic impulse. We are not concerned here with the particular questions on which they touch : but it should be observed that they apply in a considerable degree to the more poetical discourses of Protagoras, Gorgias and Prodicus, and quite closely to the myths of Plato. Sophistic eloquence, of course, aspired and contrived to flourish substantially on the treatment of passions which *are* 'produced by real events,' and on the ready expression of *common* thoughts and feelings. This practical side of the art was gladly accepted, for serious exposition, by Antiphon and Thucydides : the historian, in particular, obtained from it the proportions and colours of his psychological pictures. This lesson learnt, he proceeded, of his own force and for his own ends, to energise with a personal activity almost any concept that might claim the chief interest of the moment. In this linguistic feat of dramatisation he was more of a poet than the sophists. 'By his own choice,' and 'by the structure of his own mind,' these notions were *begotten* in him (if we may join Socrates[1] to Wordsworth) 'without immediate external excitement.' But the very freedom of his policy here is a proof that he stood even further off than his teachers from any mythical doctrine of life. For, while he avoids, with hardly one exception[2], those subjects 'which are pleasing and delightful,' and steadily points to the dangers of abstract disputation, as well as to the uses of good judgement in a haphazard world, the glowing intensity of his writing has produced

---

[1] Above, p. 220.   [2] pp. 27–8.

a swarm of lively figures which the allegation of a dramatic scheme in his work must leave clamouring importunate, as it were, outside the stage-door.

Mythical speculations on the highest class of passions find their proper place in his record of what was said in those critical years. Had he so narrowed his mind as to accept one of these theories himself, we should have had to deepen and dignify it in proportion to his general eminence above the sophistic plane. The few select figures which seem, at first sight, to conduct his speakers upon the tragic stage, are precisely those which were fast becoming the commonplace drudges of Prosopopœia : it was chiefly their economical effect which induced him to give them their company of helpers. His imaginative zeal in working out the detail of this method was of high importance to European prose ; not so much for the value of any particular impersonations—though the ardour of his reasoning invested his creatures with far more luculence and strength than our eighteenth-century poets could bestow on theirs[1]—as for the authority of his example in a fertile province of literary art. It may be granted that ' with the development of Greek thought and art in the fifth century B.C. there seems to have come somehow a hardening of Greek life ; the one overwhelming interest of the City absorbing passion and emotion, as the interest of logic and metaphysics absorbed history and poetry ' : but it is too much to assert, though we make the obvious exception of Euripides, that 'the age of Thucydides and Antipho is not one in which the emotions have a chance[2].' We do not indeed claim for the historian that unifying grasp of all human feelings

---

[1] Cf. Collins, *The Passions*—'Brown Exercise rejoiced to hear, and Sport leapt up, and seized his Beechen Spear,' etc.

[2] Mackail, *Sel. Epigr. Gr. Anth.* 1906, Intr. p. 34 : cf. the words of Jebb quoted above, p. 25.

whose effort is the essence of religion. He is deaf and blind to the 'calling shapes, and beckning shadows dire' with which some of our noblest poetry is peopled. He does not indulge in so much as the half-belief which is continually at play, for instance, in the writings of one of the chief masters of Milton—Jeremy Taylor[1]; whose poetic imagery had arisen as a new inspiration from the Authorised Version of the Hebrew Scriptures[2]. What we recognise in Thucydides is the glow of excitement that belongs to the executive struggle of the artist, and also, perhaps, to the æsthetic satisfaction with which a mathematician might survey, at the moment of its completion, an impassively laboured theorem or curve. In this light the vivid personal feeling impressed upon or hovering over every page of the History is no fanciful paradox. Just as we can regard his periodic structures as a reversion, in mere practical method, to the primitive holophrase, so the strenuous energy of his nouns and participles can be viewed as a business-like revival of that ancient device, whereby vocal communication, to acquire an air of first-hand familiarity, endowed every general notion with the individual behaviour of a representative ghost[3].

[1] Cf. *Twenty-seven Sermons*, 1654, xx: 'And when the minute is gone, so is the pleasure too, and leaves no footstep but the impression of a sigh, and dwells nowhere but in the same house where you shall find yesterday, that is, in forgetfulness and annihilation ; unless its only child, sorrow, shall marry, and breed more of its kind, and so continue its memory and name to eternal ages.'

[2] The fervour of the impersonations in the Psalms of David is well expressed by Sidney (*Defence of Poesie*) who, in arguing for their *poetic* quality, asks—'For what else is the awaking his musicall instruments, the often and free changing of Persons, his notable *Prosopopoeias*, when hee maketh you as it were see God comming in his majestie, his telling of the beasts joyfulnesse, and hilles leaping, but a heavenly Poesie, wherein almost hee shewed himselfe a passionate lover of that unspeakable and everlasting beautie, to bee seene by the eyes of the minde, onely cleared by faith?'

[3] Above, pp. 222-3.

CHAPTER VIII

INTONATION

§ 1

OUR inspection of the poetic patterns which Thucydides applied to the substance of his monumental prose has made it abundantly clear that, while claiming that 'his appeals are to the head rather than the heart,' we must deny that they are 'scarcely ever to the fancy or imagination[1].' We had to notice a similar, though more obvious, misunderstanding of his biographical sketches in our first glance at the general character of the History[2]. We shall now try to make our conception of the beginnings of prose-form more complete, by considering some deliberate appeals to the ear at certain points in the History. In selecting and discussing these devices, we shall keep as much as possible within the pale of objective criticism[3], and shall be content if a small amount of unquestionable evidence provides a plain starting-point for wider and more speculative study. Even so, it may seem that we are spending too much time upon curious trifles. But if, as before, we can use a comparison with other writers to show the superior weight and dignity of Thucydides, and to throw some fresh light on his literary genius, the time thus spent can hardly be wasted.

In watching the cultivation of formality among the writers of early Greek prose, we have already noted a few of its fruits on the upper branches of the History.

---

[1] Above, p. 4.   [2] p. 17.   [3] Cf. pp. 183-4.

With some verbal repetitions in Heracleitus and Herodotus we compared the insistence on πολλοί, πολλά in
Thucydides' account of the capture of Athenian forts on
Plemmyrium[1]. The same manner appeared in a fragment
of Protagoras[2]. The light gallantries of the *De Arte*
have helped to distinguish, by contrast, the solemn
resonance of Hermocrates[3]; and we have heard Cleon
vigorously drumming on the same initial syllable of
different verbs[4]. We passed on, through various sophistic experiments in assonance, alliteration, and measured
compass of phrase, to notice the careful adaptation to
character and mood displayed by Thucydides in various
speeches and descriptions[5]. To these sound-effects of
his writing we shall now add a few more from the narrative, with the view of showing his conscious aim at
appropriate intonation, and of observing his artistic
method a little more closely.

An intentional heaviness and grimness is manifest in
the words which tell how Pausanias was starved to death
in the temple[6] :—

καὶ ἐς οἴκημα οὐ μέγα ὃ ἦν τοῦ ἱεροῦ ἐσελθών, ἵνα μὴ
ὑπαίθριος ταλαιπωροίη, ἡσύχαζεν. οἱ δὲ τὸ παραυτίκα μὲν
ὑστέρησαν τῇ διώξει, μετὰ δὲ τοῦτο τοῦ τε οἰκήματος τὸν
ὄροφον ἀφεῖλον καὶ τὰς θύρας ἔνδον ὄντα τηρήσαντες αὐτὸν
καὶ ἀπολαβόντες ἔσω ἀπῳκοδόμησαν, προσκαθεζόμενοί τε
ἐξεπολιόρκησαν λιμῷ.

Here the ponderous manner, which we found just
realising its opportunities in Hippocrates[7], has been
organised and controlled for an admirable effect : we
notice, as the crisis approaches, the steady use of o and ω,
and the closing long syllables when it arrives[8]. The

[1] p. 114. [2] p. 132.
[3] pp. 143–4 : cf. p. 186. [4] p. 164. [5] pp. 182–7.
[6] Thuc. I, 134. 2. [7] Above, p. 125.
[8] A reference to Jowett's version will show the sort of language into which

L. 16

word ταλαιπωροίη may serve to recall the remark[1]
which introduces Thucydides' statement of his historical
method :—

οὕτως ἀταλαίπωρος τοῖς πολλοῖς ἡ ζήτησις τῆς ἀληθείας—

where the long syllables are obviously designed for a
sense of personal gravity.

The continued miseries of war and plague induce the
same heavy sound[2] :—

τοιούτῳ μὲν πάθει οἱ Ἀθηναῖοι περιπεσόντες ἐπιέζοντο,
ἀνθρώπων τ᾽ ἔνδον θνησκόντων καὶ γῆς ἔξω δῃουμένης.

The long, oppressive train of 'spondees' is varied,
just at the end, with an 'iambus.' An equally calculated
effect, at a more exciting moment, appears in the story of
the siege of Platæa[3], where the bustle of heaping up
faggots is conveyed in something like the latter half of an
epic line ; but the firing of the wood with sulphur and
pitch is given the tone of fatal grimness which we have
heard elsewhere :—

ταχὺ δὲ πλήρους γενομένου διὰ πολυχειρίαν ἐπιπαρένησαν
καὶ τῆς ἄλλης πόλεως ὅσον ἐδύναντο ἀπὸ τοῦ μετεώρου
πλεῖστον ἐπισχεῖν, ἐμβαλόντες δὲ πῦρ ξὺν θείῳ καὶ πίσσῃ
ἦψαν τὴν ὕλην.

So, when he tells how simplicity, which is so large a
part of nobility, was 'derided to annihilation,' he drives
the point home with the 'trochaic' beat of two sonorous
verbs[4] :—

these resonant verbs—rolling in, as it were, on top of one another—ought
not to be translated.
[1] Thuc. I, 20 fin. Cf. above, p. 62. It looks as if the phrase may have
struck Aristophanes : cf. Fr. 250 (Danaïd.)—οὕτως αὐτοῖς ἀταλαιπώρως ἡ
ποίησις διέκειτο. The other uses of the word near that time are in Hippocrates, Aër. 280 ; Acut. 389.   [2] II, 54. I.   [3] II, 77. 3.
[4] III, 83. I : cf. the same effect in Plato (Phædr. 245 a)—ἡ ποίησις ὑπὸ τῆς
τῶν μαινομένων ἡ τοῦ σωφρονοῦντος ἠφανίσθη. Dionys. (De Comp. Verb. 18)
notices the stately rhythms of the Funeral Oration ; esp. Thuc. II, 35.

καὶ τὸ εὔηθες, οὗ τὸ γενναῖον πλεῖστον μετέχει, καταγελασθὲν ἠφανίσθη.

It is hardly necessary to give further examples in illustration of this deliberate, though spasmodic, attention to rhythm : but it may be useful to consider a few carefully wrought passages in the Sicilian Expedition. The analysis of Nicias' state of mind (at a council of war) shows a striking variety of rhythms at the ends of the clauses [1] :—

ἐλπίδος τι ἔτι παρεῖχε πονηρότερα τῶν σφετέρων ἔσεσθαι, ἢν καρτερῶσι προσκαθήμενοι· χρημάτων γὰρ ἀπορίᾳ αὐτοὺς ἐκτρυχώσειν, ἄλλως τε καὶ ἐπὶ πλέον ἤδη ταῖς ὑπαρχούσαις ναυσὶ θαλασσοκρατούντων.

It is plain here that the contrasts of iambus, spondee and dactyl are meant to correspond with the contrasts of the successive thoughts. A still clearer case occurs in that thrilling description of the retreat[2], where the movements of a fight in a narrow pass are marked by alternations of rhythm [3] :—

εἰ μὲν ἐπίοιεν οἱ Ἀθηναῖοι, ὑπεχώρουν, εἰ δ' ἀναχωροῖεν, ἐπέκειντο.

On the whole, of course, it is with a more broadly and loosely flowing resonance that Thucydides has dignified the finest parts of this special narrative. We need only turn to a passage in which he reaches, perhaps, his most tremendous splendour, to see how the verbal echoes are due, not so much to a minute selection, as to suggestions arising in the internal ear under the excitement of the contemplated scene. We have already noticed the feelings of the Athenian soldiers, as they turned away

[1] VII, 48. 2.
[2] Cf. above, p. 2.
[3] VII, 79. 5 : cf. III, 97. 3—ὅτε μὲν ἐπίοι...στρατόπεδον, ὑπεχώρουν, ἀναχωροῦσι δὲ ἐπέκειντο : VIII, 33. 4—ἐς τὴν Μίλητον ἐκομίσθη, ὥσπερ διενοεῖτο.

from their camp and the sight of their dead and wounded
comrades[1] : but the full horror of the situation does not
possess our minds, till we listen to the language of
Thucydides :—

πρὸς γὰρ ἀντιβολίαν καὶ ὀλοφυρμὸν τραπόμενοι ἐς
ἀπορίαν καθίστασαν, ἄγειν τε σφᾶς ἀξιοῦντες καὶ ἕνα
ἕκαστον ἐπιβοώμενοι, εἴ τινά πού τις ἴδοι ἢ ἑταίρων ἢ
οἰκείων, τῶν τε ξυσκήνων ἤδη ἀπιόντων ἐκκρεμαννύμενοι καὶ
ἐπακολουθοῦντες ὅσον δύναιντο, εἴ τῳ δὲ προλίποι ἡ ῥώμη
καὶ τὸ σῶμα, οὐκ ἄνευ ὀλίγων ἐπιθειασμῶν καὶ οἰμωγῆς
ἀπολειπόμενοι—

The dismal sweep of these phrases, which at the same
time are controlled by the main balance of the periodic
scheme, show the magnificent results of sophistic enterprise in a mind of keen sensibility and unrelenting grasp.
So when we come to the 'play' of these compounds, and
the long syllables that follow—

κατήφειά τέ τις ἅμα καὶ κατάμεμψις σφῶν αὐτῶν
πολλὴ ἦν—

we are reminded less of some Euphuistic jingle than of
the ominous harping of Carlyle :—

'There is work for the hangman ; work for the
hammerman, *not* in building[2].'

So again, in the account of the final carnage at the
river Assinarus, the alliteration seems a natural accompaniment of the disturbance[3] :—

ἐς τὰ ἐπὶ θάτερά τε τοῦ ποταμοῦ παραστάντες οἱ
Συρακόσιοι...ἔβαλλον ἄνωθεν τοὺς Ἀθηναίους, πίνοντάς τε
τοὺς πολλοὺς ἀσμένους καὶ ἐν κοίλῳ ὄντι τῷ ποταμῷ ἐν
σφίσιν αὐτοῖς ταρασσομένους...καὶ τὸ ὕδωρ...ἐπίνετό τε
ὁμοῦ τῷ πηλῷ ᾑματωμένον καὶ περιμάχητον ἦν τοῖς πολλοῖς.

Besides the continual alliteration of words beginning

[1] VII, 75; above, p. 197.
[2] Carlyle, *French Rev.* v, 3.
[3] Thuc. VII, 84. 4–5.

with π, there is the striking repetition of τοὺς πολλούς, slightly altered, in the emphatic place at the end: the descriptive intention of these words ought to be rendered by our phrases—'in the mass'—'in a mass,' so as to display the press of the whole multitude struggling to get the same thing at once[1].

§ 2

The use of these emphatic repetitions can be traced, as we found, to the Ionian sages, and past them to epic poetry[2]; the metre of which was also found lingering at the close of some similar formal emphasis in Herodotus[3]. The examples of formal resonance and rhythm which we have just remarked in Thucydides suggest that, although he only sought these poetic aids at casual moments of intensity, they require our notice here, as a part of the general policy which utilised antithesis and personification. The occasional jingles of his rhetorical clauses have been often, if rather vaguely, attributed to 'Gorgiasm': it is no less clear that the neat regularity with which Gorgias often made his clauses rhyme must also have brought metrical echoes into prose. This latter intrusion of poetry cannot be ignored, when we consider such effects as—

Διὸς μὲν ἀγάλματα, ἑαυτῶν δὲ ἀναθήματα[4]—

ἐκτᾶτο μὲν ὡς χρῷτο, ἐχρῆτο δὲ ὡς τιμῷτο[5]—

---

[1] 'Longinus' (De Subl. 38. 3), though he quotes this passage as an instance of a hyperbole which comes of such a vehemence of feeling as not to seem a hyperbole at all, neglects the full force of the expression by transposing thus :—καὶ τοῖς πολλοῖς ἔτι ἦν περιμάχητον. His insertion of ἔτι seems to show that he felt the importance of τοῖς πολλοῖς; and περιμάχητον is the kind of word with which Thuc. commonly ends a sentence. Unfortunately, the effect of his mistake on the latest translator of The Sublime (Prickard, 1906, p. 69) is that τοῖς πολλοῖς is neglected altogether :—'even fighting to have it'—where περιμάχητον itself is cheated of its proper effect in sound. The peculiar turn of the phrase in Thuc. seems to have impressed the memory of Lucian (De Conscr. Hist. 51)—καὶ ὡς ἐδίψων καὶ οἷον τὸ ὕδωρ ἔπινον καὶ ὡς ἐφονεύοντο πίνοντες οἱ πολλοί.

[2] Above, pp. 113-5. [3] pp. 114-5. [4] p. 152. [5] p. 154.

and there can be little doubt that, if we possessed much
more of Gorgias' writings, we should find there some
experiments of the sort which we have observed in
Thucydides[1]. It is recorded of Isocrates that ' up to his
last years he went on sticking together antitheses and
evenly measured and like-sounding clauses, smoothing
down his periods, as one might say, with chisel and file,
and arranging their rhythm[2].' But the aim of making
metre the chief formal support of prose was started by
Thrasymachus of Chalcedon ; who seems to have largely
determined the rhythmic method of Isocrates, and thus
to have opened up a field of experiment hardly less
important than the work of Gorgias to European literature[3]. The main development of metrical structure
in prose does not concern us here : we have only to note
some sporadic signs of Thucydides' interest in the matter
among the more studied language of his book.

The aim of Thrasymachus is remarkable for having
diverged from the commonest poetry with his use of
'pæons' ($-\smile\smile\smile$ and $\smile\smile\smile-$). In what manner he
arranged his effect is not clear. In Thucydides, how-
ever, we shall draw attention to a habit of ending off
sentences and clauses with a more or less pronounced
'heroic' cadence (e.g. $---\smile\smile-\smile$). Considering the
nature of his mind and work, his use of such a device
cannot be expected to be more than fitful ; and at the
stage of formal construction in which we have placed him,
it is not surprising that he should allow the mould of epic

---

[1] Cf. Cicero, *Orat.* 167—' Gorgias, cuius in oratione plerumque efficit
numerum ipsa concinnitas.'

[2] Plutarch, *De Glor. Ath.* 8—ἀντίθετα καὶ πάρισα καὶ ὁμοιόπτωτα κολλῶν
καὶ συντιθεὶς μόνον οὐ κολαπτῆρσι καὶ ξυστῆρσι τὰς περιόδους ἀπολεαίνων καὶ
ῥυθμίζων ἐγήρασε.

[3] A useful collection of the evidence (with bibliography) has been made by
A. C. Clark, *Fontes Prosæ Numerosæ*, 1909 : see also his *Cursus in Mediæval
and Vulgar Latin*, 1910, and his account of Zielinski's discovery of the
scheme of Cicero's *clausulæ*, *Class. Rev.*, 1905, pp. 164 foll.

verse to give a stately finish to his more calculated phrases. How conscious was this choice, we shall probably be unable to decide. What we can do is to observe the most persistent echoes or chimes, and recall what has been said of the influence of Homer[1]. The popularity of the rhapsodes down to the latter part of the fourth century shows that the common knowledge of the epics was acquired, not by the eye, but by the ear. Signs of this fact, as of the variations introduced through forgetfulness or vanity by the reciter, appear in the 'misquotations' that we find not only in Thucydides[2], but in Plato and Aristotle. Large portions of the poems were learnt by heart at school: during the rest of his life, the Athenian relied on this memory, aided by public recitals; and in the course of composition, even a writer who possessed a copy of Homer would regard it as useful rather for reading aloud some less familiar episode, than for verifying a quotation which occurred to his mind. Books were rare; and though learned or leisured men like Sophocles, Euripides[3] and Thucydides must have collected a certain number, the habit of hearing both prose and verse delivered with a practised elocution would continue the appeal to the ear even when they were reading in silence by themselves. Thus in distinguishing his ambition from that of his predecessors Thucydides remarks, as we saw, that his *hearers* will find his avoidance of the fabulous a failure in delight[4]: he does not, however, seek the applause which is won by a contemporary recital, but looks rather to perpetuation on the shelves of the learned. Even so, with him as with

---

[1] Above, pp. 25–8.

[2] Thuc. III, 104 (on the Festival at Delos; above, pp. 27–8).

[3] Euripides and Aristotle are mentioned by Athenæus (I, 3 a) as possessors of books; cf. Tatian, *Or. contra Græcos* 143 b.

[4] I, 22. 4—ἐς μὲν ἀκρόασιν κτλ. (above, p. 14).

Isocrates[1], the verb 'to read' (ἀναγιγνώσκειν) still suggests the notion of 'listeners' (ἀκροαταί). So we find that Socrates' acquaintance with the writings of Anaxagoras was oral[2]. Hence the effect of rhythm, like that of antithetical balance, could never have been missed by fifth-century 'readers,' as our practice so commonly misses it to-day. It is only when an accomplished delivery reveals to us an unsuspected birthright of sound in some well-known discourse or poem, that we can realise the inadvertence of our ways. To the Greek, a metrical cadence was, at the very least, an integral part of the expression.

Thucydides' handling of formal prose might be summarily described as an attempt to bring the attractive and frankly poetic graces of Gorgias to terms with the sententious brevity and gravity of the early philosophers. But there were other famous thinkers besides Heracleitus, Anaxagoras and Democritus; there were sages who sought an impressive utterance through the use of a conventional metre. Xenophanes had written not only in hexameters, but in elegiac and iambic verse; and his attacks on the theology of Homer had been widely spread by discussion. The metaphysical hexameters of Parmenides would be heard in a narrower circle. Empedocles wrote in the same metre: we have noticed his traditional connection with Sicilian rhetoric[3]. Thus, while the drama was presenting its pleas and arguments in the simpler iambic measure, the hexameter continued to resound the thoughts of eminent minds upon ultimate questions. The language also of proverbs and oracles on the most ordinary affairs ran readily in this convenient channel. One of the first difficulties, therefore, which faced the designers of a larger, though still regular,

---

[1] Isocr. *Panath.* 84; 86; 233.   [2] Plato, *Phædo* 97 b.
[3] Above, p. 150.

scheme for prose, was to keep the step of the sentence out of time with the music of popular verse.

In general, it seems that Thucydides, in his efforts towards formal dignity, resolved to stop his ears against the beat of heroic verse. But he was unable to avoid it altogether. Not only do we find phrases like these—

(I, 74. 2) ἡμῖν κατὰ γῆν οὐδεὶς ἐβοήθει—

(I, 133) καὶ τἆλλ' ἀποφαίνοντος καθ' ἕκαστον—

(II, 77. 3) ἀπὸ τοῦ μετεώρου πλεῖστον ἐπισχεῖν—

at the end of a clause, but in one place a speech is finished off with at least a recognisable cadence :—

(IV, 92 fin.) ἀνανταγώνιστοι ἀπ' αὐτῶν οὐκ ἀπίασιν—

and we find several other ends of clauses and sentences which are very near falling into the full shape of the measure :—

(I, 13. 1) πρότερον δὲ | ἦσαν ἐπὶ ῥητοῖς γέρασι πατρικαὶ βασιλεῖαι—

(I, 72. 1) ὡς οὐ ταχέως αὐτοῖς βουλευτέον εἴη—

(II, 49. 5) φλυκταίναις μικραῖς καὶ ἕλκεσιν ἐξηνθηκός—

(II, 95. 2) τὸν ἐπὶ Θρᾴκης Χαλκιδικὸν πόλεμον καταλύσειν—

(III, 70. 3) λέγοντες Ἀθηναίοις τὴν Κέρκυραν καταδουλοῦν—

(IV, 47. 2) καὶ τοὺς τεχνησαμένους ἀδεέστερον ἐγχειρῆσαι—

(IV, 57. 4) τοὺς ἐν τῇ νήσῳ Λακεδαιμονίους καταδῆσαι—

(IV, 92. 1) τεῖχος ἐνοικοδομησάμενοι μέλλουσι φθείρειν—

(IV, 103. 2) ἐν τῇ Ἀμφιπόλει πλὴν τῶν προδιδόντων—

(IV, 107. 2) τὸν ποταμὸν πολλοῖς πλοίοις ἄφνω καταπλεύσας—

(VI, 92. 5) τήν τε οὖσαν καὶ τὴν μέλλουσαν δύναμιν καθέλητε—

They are not elegant specimens of verse, but they
conform, with very slight deficiencies, to the heroic
system.   Taken merely by themselves, they would seem
to be casual lapses such as are to be found in almost any
writer, even the most careful.   But when we notice how
many of these occur in direct or reported speech ; that
several run out into verbs compounded with the same
preposition (κατα-) ; that one of these cases (IV, 107. 2)
is followed after a short space by a double or chiming
cadence of the same sort—

(IV, 108 fin.) τοὺς ἐκ τῆς νήσου κομίσασθαι | καὶ τὸν
πόλεμον καταλῦσαι—

and that these are the words in which Thucydides dismisses his analysis of the Spartan motives ; these cumulative hints appear to call for a thorough investigation, in
order that we may be able to judge whether they are due
to a conscious choice, or at least to an instinctive habit.

We shall begin with two chapters of narrative
(I, 23–4).   In the former of these, the first sentence ends
with ταχεῖαν τὴν κρίσιν ἔσχεν, and the third with διὰ τὸ
στασιάζειν.   The clauses of the fourth have these
endings—ἄπιστα κατέστη—αὐτοὶ ἐπέσχον—μνημονευόμενα
ξυνέβησαν.   The sixth sentence ends with τοῖς Ἕλλησι
κατέστη.   Immediately after these effects of final verbs, we
get what is almost a chime, but on a different basis—

(I, 23. 6) τὴν μὲν γὰρ ἀληθεστάτην πρόφασιν, ἀφανε-
στάτην δὲ λόγῳ—

in a passage of careful explanation : we pass, in the next
two clauses, to a 'pæonic' chime—

ἀναγκάσαι ἐς τὸ πολεμεῖν...αἵδ' ἦσαν ἑκατέρων—

while the next, and last, clause of the paragraph winds
up with ἐς τὸν πόλεμον κατέστησαν (‒ ◡ ‒ ‒ ◡)[1].

[1] A fairly common ending in Demosthenes, and the first of the three
favoured by Cicero (Clark, *Fontes Pr. Numer.* p. 6).

In the second of these two chapters, the second sentence ends with a near approach to a complete hexameter—

(I, 24. 2) τὸν παλαιὸν νόμον ἐκ τῆς μητροπόλεως κατακληθείς—

and, at the close of this paragraph, we have three sentences winding up, in as many lines, with these words—

(I, 24. 7) τῶν βαρβάρων πόλεμον καταλῦσαι—ἐς τὸ Ἡραιον ἐδέοντο—ἀλλ' ἀπράκτους ἀπέπεμψαν—

where the heroic cadence seems to reassert itself, after a slight modification in the direction of the πόλεμον κατέστησαν above (‑ᴗ‑‑‑‑). Of these two chapters or paragraphs, the first makes a bridge—by some general remarks on the cause of the war—between the introductory sketch of early Greece and the account of the rise of the quarrel; the second, in starting this account, describes the unsuccessful appeal of the Epidamnian envoys at Corcyra. A few pages further on, we find the Corcyræan envoys speaking at Athens, and are struck by the following clause-chime—

(I, 36. 2–3) τό τε ἐνθένδε πρὸς τἀκεῖ παραπέμψαι, καὶ ἐς τἆλλα ξυμφορώτατόν ἐστιν. βραχυτάτῳ δ' ἂν κεφαλαίῳ, τοῖς τε ξύμπασι καὶ καθ' ἕκαστον—

which runs out, with the next phrase, into a trochaic cadence—

τῷδ' ἂν μὴ προέσθαι ἡμᾶς μάθοιτε.

The Corinthians' speech in opposition shows some more, but not so remarkable, examples :—

(I, 38. 1) διὰ παντὸς καὶ νῦν πολεμοῦσι...πάσχειν ἐκπεμφθεῖεν.

The next sentence ends similarly—καὶ τὰ εἰκότα θαυμάζεσθαι ; a little further on we find βιάσασθαι τὴν τούτων μετριότητα : but it is only after some space, in which one or two chimes of different type appear—

(I, 39. 3) νῦν μεταδώσετε...τὸ ἴσον ἕξετε—

(I, 40 fin.) τιμωρήσετε...ἡμῖν πρόσεισι...ἡμῖν θήσετε—

(cf. the reassertion in I, 24. 7 above)

and one marked heroic cadence—

(I, 41. 1) ὥστε βλάπτειν οὐδ᾽ αὖ φίλοι ὥστ᾽ ἐπιχρῆσθαι—

that we meet with another heroic chime—

(I, 42. 4) χάρις καιρὸν ἔχουσα...ξυμμαχίαν μεγάλην διδόασι.

A careful search throughout the History provides no ground for suspecting that Thucydides attempted any elaborate metrical scheme, such as may be attributed to Isocrates[1]. In large portions of the book there is no more sign of a recurrent scheme of feet than in the main substance of Herodotus. It is only because these occasional chimes—most markedly in the heroic cadence—are the sole indications of a care or inclination for rhythmic as distinct from assonant balance in Thucydides, that they deserve some further attention.

Aristotle, in the chapter of the *Rhetoric*[2] which treats of prose-rhythm, makes no mention of Thucydides : he gives the first place to Thrasymachus and his use of the pæon. It is curious, however, that when he passes to the subject of the 'strung-together' and 'compact' styles he quotes as an example of the former—which he further describes as the 'antique'—this version of Herodotus' opening sentence—

Ἡροδότου Θουρίου ἥδ᾽ ἱστορίης ἀπόδειξις—

where it looks as if his notion of an old-fashioned style

---

[1] Blass, *Rhythm. Attisch. Kunstprosa*, 1901.　　[2] Aristotle, *Rhet.* III, 8.

were giving an epic turn to a phrase which our tradition
gives thus :—

Ἡροδότου Ἀλικαρνησσῆος ἱστορίης ἀπόδεξις ἥδε.

It may be that the difference in the place-title points
to an Attic version which commemorated the citizenship
bestowed on the author by an Athenian colony : but the
rearrangement of the last three words is probably due to
Aristotle. Demetrius[1], quoting the same sentence as a
'single-membered' or simple period, gives these three
words in the order of our texts : but his other instance of
a short scheme 'rounded at the end' shows something
like a dactylic instead of a trochaic cadence :—

ἡ γὰρ σαφὴς φράσις πολὺ φῶς παρέχεται ταῖς τῶν
ἀκουόντων διανοίαις.

The first mention of rhythm in Thucydides is made
by Cicero[2], who observes that if Herodotus, Thucydides
and other writers of that early time succeeded in producing, here and there, a good rhythmical effect, it was
not through the choice of any special metre, but an
accidental result of their disposition of words. Cicero
also follows the lead of Aristotle[3] in condemning a fixed
metrical scheme for prose, as distinct from the desirable
sense of something like metre on a large scale, which we
understand by the word 'rhythm.' Dionysius[4] mentions
rhythm to the same purpose, in remarking on what we
call the 'swing' or 'roll' of some phrases in the Funeral
Oration. But in opposition to these views there is a
remark of Demetrius on one of Thucydides' phrases
about the plague :—' In the elevated style, the members
should begin with a "procatarctic" and end with a

---

[1] Demetr. *De Eloc.* 17: cf. 44.
[2] Cicero, *Orat.* 228 (probably following Theophrastus : cf. Mayer,
Theophr. περὶ λέξ. p. 35).
[3] Aristotle, *Rhet.* III, 8—δεῖ μήτε ἔμμετρον εἶναι μήτε ἄρρυθμον κτλ.
[4] Dionys. *De Comp. Verb.* 113-4.

"catalectic" pæon, as in this passage of Thucydides—
ἤρξατο δὲ τὸ κακὸν ἐξ Αἰθιοπίας[1].' That is to say, the
phrase begins with $-\cup\cup\cup$, and ends with $\cup\cup\cup-$. In our
text of Thucydides we find—ἤρξατο δὲ τὸ μὲν πρῶτον, ὡς
λέγεται, ἐξ Αἰθιοπίας τῆς ὑπὲρ Αἰγύπτου[2]. Perhaps the last
three words are an interpolation : but it is more likely
that the critic has misquoted, just as Lucian has misquoted the rest of the sentence[3]. Still, the remark is
partly justified[4]; and although there is little persistent
use of pæonic endings such as we have seen above[5], it
will be found that there are a good many combinations
of heroic close with the scheme $-\cup\cup\cup-\stackrel{\smile}{-}$, in the manner
we have noticed a little later[6]. This cadence, like the
heroic, is based on a regular habit of ending with
four-syllable verbs like ἐδέοντο, ὑπεχώρουν, καταλῦσαι
and ἀπέπεμψαν. Some other remarks of this critic are of
interest to us here : 'all of us certainly remember in a
special degree, and are stirred by, the words that come
first and those that come last...The majesty of Thucydides is almost entirely due to the long values in his
rhythm';—which reminds us of the spondaic weightiness
which we have quoted as apparently deliberate[7]. A long
syllable before one of these habitual verbs will give the
minimum of the heroic cadence, while a short one
(e.g. I, 69. 5—μᾶλλον ἐπιόντας) gives a cadence which,
following Demetrius, we may conveniently call 'pæonic.'
The result is that we get a large number of 'Pherecratean' endings, like the close of the 'Glyconic' stanza[8],

---

[1] Demetr. De Eloc. 39 ; Roberts (Demetr. on Style, 1902, p. 64) inclines
to place this treatise in the first century A.D.
[2] Thuc. II, 48. 1.   [3] Lucian, De Conscr. Hist. 15 (omitting Libya).
[4] Cf. I, 35 fin.—ὅστις ἐχυρώτατος, τοῦτον φίλον ἔχειν : 58. 2—ἕως ἂν ὁ πρὸς
Ἀθηναίους πόλεμος ᾖ.   [5] I, 23. 6 ; above p. 250.
[6] Demetr. De Eloc. 41 quotes the phrase—τῶν μὲν περὶ τὰ μηδενὸς ἄξια
φιλοσοφούντων--as 'pæonic.'
[7] Above, pp. 241-2.   [8] E.g. Soph. Oed. Col. 706--χἀ γλαυκῶπις Ἀθάνα.

interspersed with a fair number of endings like the metre of the song about Melanion in the *Lysistrata*[1]. Sometimes the former cadence, which we shall call 'heroic,' shows the trochee instead of the spondee before the penultimate dactyl :—

(I, 62. 5) ἀντικαθίσταντο καὶ αὐτοί, καὶ οὐ πολὺ ὕστερον ξυνέμισγον—

but when we consider all the instances, and especially such cases as the latter of the following two in Sthenelaidas' speech—

(I, 86. 1) ζημίας ἄξιοί εἰσιν, ὅτι ἀντ᾿ ἀγαθῶν κακοὶ γεγένηνται—

we seem justified in regarding this trochee as a break or check in an otherwise too obvious heroic cadence. We also find that this same speech is wound up thus :—

(I, 86 fin.) τοὺς ξυμμάχους καταπροδιδῶμεν, ἀλλὰ... ἐπίωμεν ἐπὶ τοὺς ἀδικοῦντας.

The heroic *clausula* or finish of a period has been shown to be rare in Cicero[2]: Quintilian speaks of it as inadmissible in prose[3]. On this question Greek and Roman tastes were at variance, owing largely to the different constitutions of the two languages. 'Longinus,' in an obscure and defective passage[4], seems to commend a sentence of Demosthenes for its dependence on two separate dactyls, and to remark that the heroic metre is, by virtue of these feet, 'the finest metre we know.' This is not a pronouncement in favour of the heroic *clausula*, but simply a recognition of the value of dactyls for prose. Nevertheless, a glance at any of Demosthenes'

[1] Aristoph. *Lysistr.* 789—κᾆτ᾿ ἐλαγοθήρει | πλεξάμενος ἄρκυς, | καὶ κύνα τιν᾿ εἶχεν.
[2] Wüst, *De Claus. Rhet. Cic.* 1881 ; cf. Clark, *Class. Rev.* 1905 pp. 164 foll.
[3] Quintil. *Inst. Or.* IX, 4. 102.
[4] Longin. *De Subl.* 39 : cf. Verrall, *Class. Rev.* 1905, p. 254.

speeches will find him not averse, in his various use of metre, to endings like these—

(*De Cor.* 270) εἶναι περίεστιν—δῆμος καταρᾶται—

(*Mid.* 574) εἰς χρείαν καὶ ἀγῶν' ἀφίκηται.

There is no *Clauselgesetz* to which the general practice of Thucydides can be reduced. We are only concerned with noticing how, in the course of his formal experiments, he found the ready-made cadence of the hexameter useful for producing a sense of completeness and point in his phrases. The effect is perhaps most obvious where he concludes a piece of speech or explanation or discussion in this manner. In the following example—

(I, 101 fin.) ὡμολόγησαν 'Αθηναίοις τεῖχός τε καθελόντες καὶ ναῦς παραδόντες,...καὶ τὸ λοιπὸν φέρειν, τήν τε ἤπειρον καὶ τὸ μέταλλον ἀφέντες.—

the suggestion of a hexameter in the first phrase (ὡμολόγησαν...καθελόντες) seems to finish the clause with another phrase (καὶ ναῦς παραδόντες) which would have made the measure complete, had it stood in the place of the preceding three words : the next clause ends like an iambic line, but the hexameter reasserts itself in the *clausula*. The same suspense and satisfaction[1] are to be felt, though in a lesser degree, at another ending of a paragraph :—

(I, 111 fin.) ἐστράτευσαν καὶ ἐπολιόρκουν, οὐ μέντοι εἷλόν γε, ἀλλ' ἀπεχώρησαν ἐπ' οἴκου.

We may add, in this connection, the winding-up formula of ὃν Θουκυδίδης ξυνέγραψεν, which has the last two feet of the measure, and which closes a paragraph in nine places; in four of these it is preceded by the ending χειμὼν ἐτελεύτα[2].

---

[1] Cf. above, p. 108.

[2] II, 70 ; 103 ; III, 88 ; 116 ; VIII, 60 ; IV, 51 ; VI, 63 ; VII, 18 ; VIII, 6 : the last four are of the double sort.

§ 3

Without attending to a multitude of smaller metrical curiosities, we shall now pass in review the passages in each Book which display the strongest signs of a systematic appeal to the ear through this heroic intonation and similar devices which may call for notice. We proceed in continuation from the passages already quoted from the Corcyræan and Corinthian speeches[1] and from the terms arranged between the Thasians and Athenians[2] :—

(I, 124. 2) τάδε ἄριστα λέγεσθαι,...τὸ αὐτίκα δεινόν,... αὐτοῦ διὰ πλείονος εἰρήνης ἐπιθυμήσαντες· ἐκ πολέμου μὲν γὰρ εἰρήνη μᾶλλον βεβαιοῦται.

(Corinthians' speech, which closes shortly after with these endings—ἐπελθόντες,...τὸ λοιπὸν οἰκῶμεν...ἐλευθερώσωμεν.)

(I, 144 fin.) ἐς τάδε προήγαγον αὐτά· ὧν οὐ χρὴ λείπεσθαι,...μὴ ἐλάσσω παραδοῦναι.

(End of Pericles' speech.)

This Book also offers more evidence of the way in which four-syllable verbs of the kind already noticed[3] will make the rhythm of the endings waver between pæonic and heroic :—

(I, 50. 2) θαλάσσης ἐπεχουσῶν,...ξυνέμειξαν ἀλλήλοις, ...διάγνωσιν ἐποιοῦντο ὁποῖοι ἐκράτουν ἢ ἐκρατοῦντο·... αὐτῆς γεγένηται....Κορίνθιοι ἐς τὴν γῆν,...τοὺς νεκροὺς τοὺς σφετέρους ἐτράποντο,——

Pericles' speech has two pieces of Protagorean alliteration :—

(I, 140. 2) εἰρημένον γὰρ δίκας μὲν τῶν διαφορῶν

[1] Above, pp. 251-2. [2] I, 101 fin. : above, p. 256.
[3] pp. 250, 254.

ἀλλήλοις διδόναι καὶ δέχεσθαι, ἔχειν δὲ ἑκατέρους ἃ ἔχομεν, οὔτε αὐτοὶ δίκας πω ᾔτησαν οὔτε ἡμῶν διδόντων δέχονται—

(I, 141. 1) τὴν γὰρ αὐτὴν δύναται δούλωσιν ἥ τε μεγίστη καὶ ἐλαχίστη δικαίωσις ἀπὸ τῶν ὁμοίων πρὸ δίκης τοῖς πέλας ἐπιτασσομένη—

in both of which an impressive sound-effect seems to be sought at the cost of brevity. This speech has also a marked iambic chime:—

(I, 142. 7) αὐτοῖς προσγενήσεται....Μηδικῶν ἐξείργασθέ πω·...γεωργοὶ καὶ οὐ θαλάσσιοι.

So too has Archidamus' speech:—

(I, 84. 4) τύχας οὐ λόγῳ διαιρετάς....δεῖ τὰς ἐλπίδας,... ἀσφαλῶς προνοουμένων....ἀναγκαιοτάτοις παιδεύεται.

(II, 15. 2) Θησεὺς ἐβασίλευσε,...(2½ lines[1]) ἐς τὴν νῦν πόλιν οὖσαν,...ἀποδείξας καὶ πρυτανεῖον, ξυνῴκισε πάντας,—

(II, 45. 1) ὁρῶ μέγαν τὸν ἀγῶνα (τὸν γὰρ οὐκ ὄντα ἅπας εἴωθεν ἐπαινεῖν)

which is followed immediately by a trochaic chime:—

ἀρετῆς οὐχ ὁμοῖοι, ἀλλ' ὀλίγῳ χείρους κριθεῖτε.
(Funeral Oration.)

(II, 52 fin.) οἱ μὲν ἐπιθέντες τὸν ἑαυτῶν νεκρὸν ὑφῆπτον, οἱ δὲ...ὃν φέροιεν ἀπῇσαν.
(End of paragraph on the plague.)

(II, 64. 1) ἐθελησάντων ὑμῶν ὑπακούειν,...ἡ νόσος ἥδε, πρᾶγμα, μόνον δὴ τῶν πάντων...γεγενημένων.
(The epic swing of Pericles' quite ordinary words is stopped at the end of the sentence.)

(II, 65. 11) ἐξ ὧν ἄλλα τε πολλά,...ἀρχὴν ἐχούσῃ,...ἐς

---

[1] Oxford text, ed. Stuart Jones, 1898.

Σικελίαν πλοῦς,...πρὸς οὓς ἐπῇσαν,...τοῖς οἰχομένοις ἐπιγιγνώσκοντες,—

(After two trochaic endings, and one pæonic, we seem to return to the heroic.)

(II, 66. 2) καὶ ἐπειδὴ οὐ ξυνεχώρουν, ἀπέπλευσαν ἐπ᾿ οἴκου.

(End of paragraph.)

(II, 89. 3) ἡμῶν μᾶλλον νῦν περιέσται, εἴπερ καὶ τούτοις ἐν ἐκείνῳ, ἐπεὶ εὐψυχίᾳ γε οὐδὲν προφέρουσι,...θρασύτεροί ἐσμεν.

(Phormio's speech ;—three heroic and one pæonic.)

(II, 95. 2) αὐτὸς ὡμολογήκει, ὅτε τὴν ξυμμαχίαν ἐποιεῖτο, τὸν ἐπὶ Θρᾴκης Χαλκιδικὸν πόλεμον καταλύσειν.

(Sitalces' promise. A little before, on the same subject, the emphasis has become pæonic :—τοὺς ἐπὶ Θρᾴκης,...τὴν μὲν βουλόμενος ἀναπρᾶξαι, τὴν δὲ αὐτὸς ἀποδοῦναι.)

The speeches of this Book also show some notable iambic endings. The most persistent series are :—

(II, 37. 2) ἐπιτηδευμάτων ὑποψίαν, οὐ δι᾿ ὀργῆς τὸν πέλας, εἰ καθ᾿ ἡδονήν τι δρᾷ, ἔχοντες—(Pericles).

(II, 40. 2) μετέχοντα οὐκ ἀπράγμονα, ἀλλ᾿ ἀχρεῖον νομίζομεν,...τὰ πράγματα,...βλάβην ἡγούμενοι—(Pericles).

We add one verb-chime of unusual pattern :—

(II, 6 fin.) φρουροὺς ἐγκατέλιπον,...παισὶν ἐξεκόμισαν.

(End of paragraph.)

(III, 21. 2) διανενεμημένα ᾠκοδόμητο,...ἐπάλξεις ἔχον ἀμφοτέρωθεν.

(The blockading wall at Platæa. In the next few lines are also μὴ εἶναι παρὰ πύργον—ἐπάλξεις ἀπέλειπον—τὴν φυλακὴν ἐποιοῦντο.)

(III, 24. 3) γεγενημένων εἰδότες οὐδέν,...ὡς οὐδεὶς περίεστι, κήρυκα ἐκπέμψαντες.

(III, 38. 4) τὰ δὲ πεπραγμένα ἤδη,...λαβόντες ἢ τὸ ἀκουσθέν,...καλῶς ἐπιτιμησάντων·...ἀπατᾶσθαι ἄριστοι.

(Cleon's speech. A few lines later comes the alliterative emphasis noticed elsewhere [1].)

(III, 45. 4) τόδε γε οὐδὲν ἐπίσχει,...τὴν τόλμαν παρέχουσα,...καὶ φρονήματι—

(Diodotus' little apologue. Further on, at short intervals, we find ὁ ἔρως ἐπὶ παντί—τῆς τύχης ὑποτιθεῖσα —ξυμβάλλεται ἐς τὸ ἐπαίρειν.)

(III, 46. 6) σφόδρα κολάζειν,...σφόδρα φυλάσσειν καὶ ...ἐπίνοιαν τούτου ἴωσι,...αἰτίαν ἐπιφέρειν.

(End of paragraph in Diodotus' speech: three suggestions of heroic ending, finished off with a simple pæon.)

(III, 95. 3) Λοκροὶ ξύμμαχοι ἦσαν,...ἐς τὴν μεσόγειαν.

The Platæans' speech shows a tendency to iambic and trochaic endings, as though these belonged to a straightforward simplicity :—

(III, 53. 2) ἂν φέρεσθαι,...ἡμαρτήκαμεν. (§ 4) ὠφελούμεθ᾿ ἄν·...λελέξεται,—

(III, 54. 4) δύναμιν μετέσχομεν. (Fin.) ἐς ἐπικουρίαν· ...ἀμνημονεῖν.

(End of paragraph.)

(III, 55. 3) εἰκὸς ἦν προθύμως. (Fin.) τοῖς ξυμμάχοις, ...εἴ τι μὴ καλῶς ἐδρᾶτο,...ὀρθῶς ἔχοντα.

(End of paragraph.)

(III, 56. 4) ὁ βάρβαρος, (§ 5) νῦν ἁμαρτίας...τὴν τότε προθυμίαν.

---

[1] Above, p. 164.

(III, 58. 5) σκέψασθέ τε· (3 lines later) ποιήσετε,...
(2 lines) καταλείψετε;...δουλώσετε,—

(III, 59. 3) προσήλθομεν (καὶ δίκαιον, εἰ μὴ πείθομεν,...
αὐτοὺς ἑλέσθαι).

So the Thebans end a paragraph with this trochaic
chime :—

(III, 61 fin.) ἡμᾶς ἔβλαπτον, ἀνθ' ὧν καὶ ἀντέπασχον.

(IV, 12 ad fin.) ἐπ' Ἀθηναίους ἀποβαίνειν·...πεζὰ κρατί-
στοις,—

(IV, 16 ad fin.) ἂν παραλάβωσιν....τούτοις ἐγένοντο,...
οὖσαι περὶ ἑξήκοντα,...πρέσβεις ἀπεστάλησαν.

(The heroic cadence seems to grow out of the pæonic,
but the sentence is wound up with the trochaic.)

(IV, 47 fin.) παρατεταγμένων,...ἴδοι ἐχθρὸν ἑαυτοῦ·...
σχολαίτερον προϊόντας.

(IV, 74. 3) μηδὲν μνησικακήσειν,...πόλει τὰ ἄριστα,...
ἐν ταῖς ἀρχαῖς ἐγένοντο—

(The first two cadences belong to the reported terms
of an oath.)

(*Ibid.*) ψῆφον φανερὰν διενεγκεῖν,—(fin.) ἐκ στάσεως
μετάστασις ξυνέμεινεν.

(End of paragraph: the last words are carefully
arranged for an epigram.)

(IV, 97. 3) ἐνόντων ἀπέχεσθαι,...τειχίσαντας ἐνοικεῖν.

(Reported speech of a herald, which also shows, at
short intervals, χέρνιβι χρῆσθαι,...καὶ τὸν Ἀπόλλω,...τὰ
σφέτερα αὐτῶν.)

(IV, 110. 2) καὶ ὡς ᾔσθοντο παρόντα,...(2 lines)
ταχθέντων οὐ κατέδεισαν ἐσελθεῖν.

(IV, 118 fin.) ὅσα ἂν δίκαια λέγητε,...οἱ ξύμμαχοι....
τέλος ἔχοντες ἰόντων,...ἡμᾶς κελεύετε· αἱ δὲ σπονδαὶ
ἐνιαυτὸν ἔσονται.

(End of paragraph. These truce-terms show an alternation of heroic and iambic endings.)

(v, 26. 2) οὐκ ὀρθῶς δικαιώσει·...ὡς διῄρηται ἀθρείτω, ...(2 lines) ἃ ξυνέθεντο,...(2 lines) ἁμαρτήματα ἐγένοντο... δεχήμερον ἦγον.

(v, 26. 5) εἴσομαι·...'Αμφίπολιν στρατηγίαν,...ἀμφοτέροις τοῖς πράγμασι,...διὰ τὴν φυγήν,—

(Thucydides' simple allusion to his banishment brings on the iambic cadence. The paragraph ends 2½ lines later with ἐξηγήσομαι.)

(v, 35. 6) αὐτοὶ τοὺς ἀπὸ Θρᾴκης,...τὸ χωρίον αὐτούς,—
(Reported proposal of the Spartans.)

(v, 42. 1) 'Αθηναίοις ἀποδοῦναι,...καθῃρημένον ηὗρον,—

(Ib. § 2) τῇ καθαιρέσει,...ὀρθὸν παραδοῦναι,...ξυμμαχίαν πεποίηνται,...προσαναγκάσειν.
(Thoughts and words of the Athenians. The endings are to be compared with IV, 118 fin. above.)

(v, 50 fin.) γενομένων τέλος οὐδὲν ἐπράχθη,...διελύθησαν ἕκαστοι ἐπ' οἴκου....καὶ τὸ θέρος ἐτελεύτα.
(End of paragraph.)

(v, 56 fin.) ἐπὶ τὴν 'Επίδαυρον,...βίᾳ αἱρήσοντες· καὶ ἄπρακτοι ἀπῆλθον. καὶ ὁ χειμὼν ἐτελεύτα,...τῷ πολέμῳ ἐτελεύτα.
(End of paragraph. The similarity of the last two cadences is avoided at 81 fin.—χειμῶνος λήγοντος,... πολέμῳ ἐτελεύτα—83 fin.—ὁ χειμὼν ἐτελεύτα οὗτος,... πολέμῳ ἐτελεύτα.)

(v, 61 fin.) οὐδεὶς αὐτοῖς ἐβοήθει, μὴ προαπόλωνται,... Λακεδαιμόνιοι παραδοῦναι.

This Book, like the preceding, is almost entirely narrative, except for the Melian Dialogue (87—111).

The clauses of these chapters, while occasionally running into the heroic pattern—

(Mel. v, 90 fin.) τοῖς ἄλλοις παράδειγμα γένοισθε.
(End of paragraph.)
(Mel. v, 104) ὑμῖν ξυμμαχίαν προσέσεσθαι,—
(Ath. v, 105. 4) ξυμφέροντα δίκαια....τοιαύτη διάνοια.
(End of paragraph.)
(Ath. v, 109) ἔργων τις δυνάμει πολὺ προύχῃ·—
(Ath. v, 111. 4) πρὸς δὲ τοὺς ἥσσους μέτριοί εἰσιν,—

take rather the iambic or trochaic for their few cases of chime, or similarity of beat :—

(Ath. v, 87 fin.) τῇ πόλει, παυοίμεθ’ ἄν· εἰ δ’ ἐπὶ τοῦτο, λέγοιμεν ἄν.
(End of paragraph.)
(Ath. v, 91. 1) τὴν τελευτήν....ἄρχοντες ἄλλων,—
(Ath. v, 93 fin.) ὑπακοῦσαι ἂν γένοιτο,...κερδαίνοιμεν ἄν.
(End of paragraph.)
(Ath. v, 95 fin.) φιλία μὲν ἀσθενείας,...ἀρχομένοις δηλούμενον.
(End of paragraph.)
(So, at 103 fin., the Athenians end a paragraph with μετ’ ἐλπίδων λυμαίνεται.)
(Ath. v, 113) τῶν βουλευμάτων, ὡς ἡμῖν δοκεῖτε,... σαφέστερα κρίνετε,...ἤδη θεᾶσθε,—

The three sentences of narrative which dismiss the affair for the moment end thus :—

(v, 114. 1) περιετείχισαν κύκλῳ τοὺς Μηλίους. (§ 2) τῷ πλέονι τοῦ στρατοῦ, (fin.) ἐπολιόρκουν τὸ χωρίον.
(End of paragraph.)
The same tendency has appeared in speeches of Pericles[1].

[1] I, 142. 7 ; above, p. 258 : II, 37. 2 ; 40. 2 ; p. 259.

(VI, 2. 5) τῆς γῆς ᾤκησαν ἔχοντες, ἐπεὶ διέβησαν,... πρὸς βορρᾶν τῆς νήσου ἔχουσιν.

(VI, 10. 2) σπονδὰς ἔχειν τι βέβαιον,...σπονδαὶ ἔσονται ...τῶν ἐναντίων.

(*Ib.* § 3) ἄντικρυς πολεμοῦσιν,...αὐτοὶ κατέχονται. (Nicias' speech.)

(VI, 18. 6) ἐς τοὺς πρεσβυτέρους ἀποτρέψῃ, τῷ δὲ εἰωθότι κόσμῳ,— (Alcibiades' speech.)

(VI, 28. 2) βεβαίως προεστάναι, καὶ νομίσαντες, εἰ αὐτὸν ἐξελάσειαν, πρῶτοι ἂν εἶναι,...(2 lines) αὐτῶν ὅτι οὐ μετ᾽ ἐκείνου ἐπράχθη,...παρανομίαν.

(Thoughts and words of Alcibiades' enemies.)

(VI, 72. 4) ὅπως ὡς πλεῖστοι ἔσονται, καὶ τῇ ἄλλῃ μελέτῃ προσαναγκάζοντες,—

(Reported speech of Hermocrates. We have noticed elsewhere the regularity of the clauses in this and the following chapter[1].)

(VI, 74. 1) εὐθὺς ἐπὶ Μεσσήνην ὡς προδοθησομένην.... ἐκ τῆς ἀρχῆς ἤδη μετάπεμπτος.

(An effect as of elegiac verse.)

(VI, 80. 2) ὥσπερ τῷ δικαιώματί ἐστιν....καὶ ὁ κρατῶν περιέσται,—

(*Ib.* fin.—4½ lines) μὴ ἐᾶσαι ἁμαρτεῖν. (End of Hermocrates' speech.)

This Book shows, on the whole, an increase of iambic and trochaic endings. In about twenty places[2] the heroic seems to be contrasted with the iambic; in about eight others, with the trochaic. At the same time, we find a dozen or so cases of the heroic in close neighbourhood

---

[1] Above, p. 186.
[2] One of the more obvious is VI, 51. 1—ἐκκλησίαν τετραμμένων,...κακῶς ἔλαθον διελόντες,—

with the pæonic, or something between the two, as in this example :—

(VI, 75, 3) ἀντεπρεσβεύοντο καὶ αὐτοί·...πέμψαι ἃ ἔπεμψαν,...βούλωνται ἀμύνειν,—

(Suspicions of the Syracusans.)

(VII, 5. 3) τὸ ἁμάρτημα ἐκείνων,...ποιήσας ἀφελέσθαι· νῦν οὖν αὖθις ἐπάξειν.

(Reported speech of Gylippus.)

(VII, 22. 1) ἦν καὶ τὸ νεώριον αὐτοῖς,...ἀμφοτέρωθεν θορυβῶνται.

(VII, 27. 2) ὡς ὕστεροι ἦκον,...ἐς Θρᾴκην ἀποπέμπειν.

(VII, 28. 3) μάλιστα δ' αὐτοὺς ἐπίεζεν ὅτι δύο πολέμους ἅμα εἶχον,...ἠπίστησεν ἄν τις ἀκούσας.

(Feelings of the Athenians.)

(VII, 29. 4) καὶ τὰ ἱερὰ ἐπόρθουν καὶ τοὺς ἀνθρώπους ἐφόνευον φειδόμενοι...ἡλικίας,...(2 lines) ἔμψυχα ἴδοιεν·... τοῦ βαρβαρικοῦ, ἐν ᾧ ἂν θαρσήσῃ, φονικώτατόν ἐστιν.

(After some variation, the sentence ends by asserting the previously suggested heroic cadence.)

(VII, 44. 3) ἀήσσητοι ἐχώρουν....τὸ μὲν ἄρτι ἀνεβεβήκει, τὸ δ' ἔτι προσανῄει,...πρὸς ὅτι χρὴ χωρῆσαι....(2 lines) ὑπὸ τῆς βοῆς διαγνῶναι.

(Studied description of fighting in the night. The closing cadence is the same as that noted in I, 23. 6[1].)

Contrasts of iambic or trochaic with heroic and pæonic cadence in this Book are again fairly numerous : the masterly narrative of the later chapters is sprinkled with specimens of these and other kinds of ending, but no single one is allowed to persist. The following is an example of an iambic-dactylic contrast :—

(VII, 75. 2) ναυμαχίας ἐγίγνετο....οὐ καθ' ἓν μόνον τῶν πραγμάτων, ὅτι τάς τε ναῦς ἀπολωλεκότες πάσας ἀπεχώρουν....κινδυνεύοντες,...τοῦ στρατοπέδου ξυνέβαινε—

---

[1] Above, p. 250.

where the heroic cadence comes in, not at the end of ordinary clauses, but of their constituent phrases.

There are however a few striking echoes of iambic metre :—

(VII, 5. 2) μεταξὺ τῶν τειχισμάτων,...χρῆσις ἦν.

(VII, 75. 3) μετὰ φόβου καθίστατο,...(2½ lines) ἀπολωλότων ἀθλιώτεροι.

(*Ib.* 4) ἐς ἀπορίαν καθίστασαν,...ἕκαστον ἐπιβοώμενοι¹.

(VII, 77. 4) ἐστρατεύσαμεν,...τετιμωρήμεθα.
(Nicias' speech.)

(VII, 78. 2) ἐν πλαισίῳ τεταγμένον,...ἡγούμενον τὸ Νικίου,...Δημοσθένους·

(VII, 79. 1) ἐπ᾽ ὀλίγων ἀσπίδων· στενὸν γὰρ ἦν τὸ χωρίον.

(VII, 87. 5) καὶ τοῖς διαφθαρεῖσι δυστυχέστατον.... (2½ lines) οὐδὲν ὅτι οὐκ ἀπώλετο,—

(VIII, 12 fin.) μετὰ Χαλκιδέως τοῦ Λακεδαιμονίου, καὶ διὰ τάχους τὸν πλοῦν ἐποιοῦντο.

(End of paragraph : a suggestion of elegiac verse².)

(VIII, 28. 3) Ἀμόργην ζῶντα λαβόντες, Πισσούθνου νόθον υἱόν,...(2 lines) αὐτῷ προσέταξε,...παλαιόπλουτον γὰρ ἦν τὸ χωρίον....οὐκ ἀδικήσαντες ξυνέταξαν,—

(VIII, 47. 1) ὧν παρ᾽ ἐκείνοις,...(2 lines) εἰ μὴ διαφθερεῖ αὐτήν,...αὐτῷ πείσαντι κατελθεῖν·
(Alcibiades' thoughts.)

(VIII, 48. 4) περιοπτέον εἶναι τοῦτο μάλιστα, ὅπως μὴ στασιάσωσιν· βασιλεῖ τε οὐκ εὔπορον εἶναι καὶ...οὐ τὰς ἐλαχίστας,—
(Reported speech of Alcibiades.)

---

¹ The main flow of this sentence has been considered above, p. 244.
² Cf. VI, 74. 1 ; above, p. 264.

(VIII, 53. 3) ἡμῖν καὶ μεταθέσθαι, ἢν μή τι ἀρέσκῃ,
᾽Αλκιβιάδην τε κατάξομεν,—
(Peisander's remarks.)

(VIII, 86. 8) ὥστε βοηθεῖν·...οὕτως ἀπέπεμπεν.

(VIII, 87. 2) οὐ κατὰ ταὐτό,...οὐκ ἤγαγε τὰς ναῦς.

This Book has a rather less number of combinations
of heroic with pæonic, iambic and trochaic cadences ; and
nothing like the iambic chimes which we have found in
Book VII.

We have thus sixty places[1] in the History where the
familiar close of the epic line can be heard producing, in
a greater or lesser degree, a chiming uniformity at the
end of adjacent clauses. Of these exactly half are cases
where speech or feelings, either direct or reported, have
given a regularly pointed emphasis to the style. In
thirteen examples, this repeated cadence is found at the
winding up of a topic or incident : other single instances
could be shown in the same position ; and we have given
instances of a tendency to chime in other metres for this
final effect, as well as for the emphasis of speech. It is
the evidence of systematic rhythm-effect that has importance, along with antithesis, imagery, assonance and
alliteration, for our study of the aids which poetry
contributed to the formal intonation of prose ; and few
of our instances, which have been impartially collected
from the whole History, cannot be connected with some
analytic or deliberative mood. It is true that such moods
are neither rare nor brief in Thucydides : but it must be
remembered, on the other hand, that we have ignored a
large number of single yet well-marked heroic cadences,
which could be adduced to support our general suggestion
of an oral habit, and which can often be felt to announce,

[1] Counting the formula χειμὼν ἐτελεύτα,...ὃν Θουκυδίδης ξυνέγραψεν—
noted above, p. 256, n. 2.

in the manner illustrated by the Corcyræans' speech[1], the chimes or clusters that seemed chiefly to claim exhibition here.

The signs of this habit are on the whole more distinct in the first four Books than in the last four : while, in watching for the appearance of other metrical systems, we have remarked a growing preference for iambic endings. With this must be connected the fact that there is far less of formal rhetoric in the later Books than in the first three : and we may fairly surmise that if the speeches which are given briefly or indirectly had been worked up to the ample proportions of those delivered, for example, by the Corinthians or by Cleon, we should have had a much larger total of heroic chimes in our record. But, in point of fact, these later speeches are not so worked up ; and in the last Book the voice of rhetoric is scarcely to be heard. It seems likely that in his earlier composition Thucydides felt this metrical tag to be the readiest and most effective means of formal dignity ; that, as he gained a greater mastery of that narrative style which is at its highest power in Book VII, he became aware of a similar utility in iambic and trochaic endings,—perhaps realising it most fully in the contrast with heroic ; and that, in his maturest view, the heroic carried with it more pomp and less natural activity than the others[2]. These we have seen at work in the Melian Dialogue[3] : it is to be noticed that, after their persistent appearance in the sharp give-and-take of

---

[1] Above, p. 251.

[2] Perhaps he may have met with criticism like that of Euripides in the *Frogs*, 1264 foll. (405 B.C.), who exposes the habit of epic cadence in the choruses of Æschylus ; see Rogers, *Intr.* xxv–xxix, and notes ad loc. Cf. Aristot. *Poet.* 4 fin.—'We frequently utter iambic metres in our ordinary conversation, but seldom those of the hexameter, and this is when we depart from the usual tone of talk.'

[3] p. 263.

argument, the first ornamental phrase runs into a heroic cadence :—

(Ath. v, 103) ἐλπὶς δὲ κινδύνῳ παραμύθιον οὖσα—

and we have seen how a change from this cadence to the iambic is brought on by Thucydides' mention of himself, in the Prologue to the latter half of the History[1]. A strong hint of this preference has met us in the Platæans' speech[2].

One interesting case remains,—the Funeral Oration. Strongly as this speech is impressed with the mark of rhetorical fashion, and although here and there its clauses run into a heroic cadence, it does not display this ending in any systematic force. On the other hand, we have observed some iambic chimes[3]; and we have only to glance through the sentences of the speech to perceive that the examples quoted are but a few of the most obvious selected from a large number. This fact, together with the slighter appearances of heroic, pæonic, trochaic and spondaic endings, is of great interest, when we consider that the Funeral Oration is likely to have received careful revision and improvement, from time to time, in accordance with the author's advances in skill and taste, and may be taken to represent his most highly-wrought illumination of the History with splendid though sincere colours of civic eloquence.

§ 4

We must now briefly examine the nature of the cadence which, for convenience, we have called 'heroic.' Taking the point of view of a listener at an ancient recital of the History, and assuming such a person to have been far more sensitive than we are to the time-values in the

---

[1] v, 26 ; p. 262.   [2] III, 53–59 ; pp. 260–1.
[3] II, 37. 2 ; 40, 2 : above, p. 259.

syllables of important words, we have found the orator still relying a little on the appeal of the rhapsode. In discussing periodic form, we mentioned the example offered by the probable duplication of a short ballad-metre for the construction of the epic hexameter[1]. Now this smaller metre, which was continued in the shape of proverbs like—

κακοῦ κόρακος κακὸν ᾠόν

seems to allow, as musical equivalents, a dactyl, a spondee, or a trochee in the penultimate foot :—

Ὦ Λίνε, <πᾶσι> θεοῖσιν
τετιμένε, σοὶ γὰρ ἔδωκαν
πρώτῳ μέλος ἀνθρώποισιν
φωναῖς λιγυραῖς ἀεῖσαι[2].

If we further substitute ᴗ ᴗ ᴗ for – ᴗ before the final spondee in the last line, and steady this lighter cadence by putting – for the preceding ᴗ ᴗ (λιγυρ-), we get the 'pæonic' close which is found in the song from the *Lysistrata*[3]. Thus although this latter cadence may be regarded as a direct development from the cretic and spondee (– ᴗ ‿ – ᴗ), this will only be referring it to another kind of four-time verse. On the other hand, when Thucydides writes—

(IV, 93. 1) ἐπειδὴ προσέμειξεν ἐγγὺς τοῦ στρατεύματος αὐτῶν,—

we seem to have an echo of the three-time 'Glyconic' stanza, with its 'Pherecratean' refrain or close—

γενναίων δ' ἀρεταὶ πόνων
τοῖς θανοῦσιν ἄγαλμα[4].

But we find on the whole such a continuous weight of spondees before the penultimate foot in a very large

[1] p. 106.
[2] Smyth, *Melic Poets*, p. 154.
[3] Above, p. 255.
[4] Eurip. *Herc. Fur.* 357.

number of the Thucydidean cadences, and moreover, so many clauses in which the run of dactyls as well as of spondees is broken by a trochaic or iambic 'basis,'—for example—

(1, 83. 3) καθ' ἡσυχίαν τι αὐτῶν προῖδωμεν—

(1, 86. 1) ὅτι ἀντ' ἀγαθῶν κακοὶ γεγένηνται—

that it is safest to regard these heroic cadences as the final tones of four-time epos, which are occasionally allowed as an accompaniment to the weighty diction of the History. Of the qualities of this diction there is much that might be said, besides what has been said already : but nothing in it is more remarkable than the constant effort to provide at the end of a clause a solid weight of sound to answer the sudden weight of sense at its beginning. Continually we find the half-expected verb bestowing this formal finish on the keen or confident thought, as in these examples :—

(1, 42. 4) μηδ' ὅτι ναυτικοῦ ξυμμαχίαν μεγάλην διδόασι,—

(1, 50. 2) ναυμαχία γὰρ αὕτη Ἕλλησι πρὸς Ἕλληνας μεγίστη δὴ τῶν πρὸ αὐτῆς γεγένηται—

though it often seems a mere matter of chance whether these verbs will produce a heroic or a pæonic cadence. Sometimes, too, the distinction of rarity in the final verb is added to this satisfaction of the ear :—

(1, 33. 4) ἡμέτερον δέ γ' αὖ ἔργον προτερῆσαι,—

or the chief point in the sense will itself be found there :—

(III, 87. 1) ἐγένετο δέ τις ὅμως διοκωχή—

but the general character of the method, in these earlier Books, when it becomes systematic enough to suggest that it was deliberately practised, might be epitomised in the phrases already noticed :—

(I, 101 fin.) τεῖχός τε καθελόντες καὶ ναῦς παραδόντες,... καὶ τὸ μέταλλον ἀφέντες.

As he proceeded in his work, it appears that Thucydides felt and wished to remedy this monotonous swing : for we find an increasing choice and intermixture of iambus and trochee, as in the Prologue to his second Part, or the following emphatic close in the Funeral Oration :—

(II, 41. 4) πανταχοῦ δὲ μνημεῖα κακῶν τε κἀγαθῶν ἀΐδια ξυγκατοικίσαντες.

Nevertheless, it is probable that he would always admit a small heroic cadence for winding up a topic or for marking off a stage of time (ἀνεχώρησαν ἐπ' οἴκου —ὁ χειμὼν ἐτελεύτα—Θουκυδίδης ξυνέγραψεν), and also for rounding off at least a couple of neighbouring clauses which are held on the same level of suspension by the periodic structure. The antithetical and jingling devices of Gorgias gave an individual weight to even the smallest phrases ; and although it was the *clausula*, or finish of the sentence, which afterwards attained the chief metrical distinction, we have recognised, in the formality of this early Attic composition, a stage where the period has not grown so well-liking but that we can tell all its bones at a glance.

These systems of heroic cadence, belonging chiefly to Thucydides' rhetorical and contemplative passages, are probably to be referred to a fashion which dates from an earlier time than the structural divisions of Gorgias. Indeed, it is possible that we ought to regard an epic chime as no less of a protest against mere *prettiness* than the use of long spondaic words which we noted at the

outset[1]. A slight and uncertain hint of this older tradition
has been gathered from Aristotle's remark on *his* citation
of Herodotus' opening words[2]. If we look further into
the first Book of that History, we find a few clear traces
of this feeling for the value of heroic cadence, where
a special dignity of tone is desired. In order not to
encumber our discussion, we shall only pick out a few of
the most striking cases from a large collection :—

(I, 11) αἱρέεται αὐτὸς περιεῖναι. ἐπειρώτα λέγων τάδε·
...κτείνειν οὐκ ἐθέλοντα, φέρε ἀκούσω,...ἐπιχειρήσομεν
αὐτῷ....ἐμὲ ἐπεδέξατο γυμνήν,...ἐπιχείρησις ἔσται. ὡς δὲ
ἤρτυσαν τὴν ἐπιβουλήν,—
(Conversation at the crisis of the story of Gyges.)

(I, 32) πρὶν τελευτήσαντα καλῶς τὸν αἰῶνα πύθωμαι....
ὀλβιώτερός ἐστι,...ἀνόλβιοί εἰσι,—
(Solon.)

(I, 36) ἐξελθόντες ποιέεσκον μὲν κακὸν οὐδέν, ἔπασχον
δὲ πρὸς αὐτοῦ.
(Adrastus.)

(I, 38) παραλαμβανόμενα οὐκ ἀποπέμπω,...ζόης δια-
κλέψαι.
(Crœsus.)

(I, 89) τάδε τοι ἐξ αὐτῶν ἐπίδοξα γενέσθαι· ὃς ἂν
αὐτῶν πλεῖστα κατάσχῃ,—
(Crœsus.)

(I, 91) ἢν στρατεύηται ἐπὶ Πέρσας, μεγάλην ἀρχὴν
[αὐτὸν] καταλύσειν....ἢ τὴν Κύρου λέγοι ἀρχήν.
(Discussion of an oracle.)

More examples could be given, though not many of
the same strength. In the first half of the Book there
are half-a-dozen well-marked chimes, of which four
appear in speeches, one in reported speech, and one in a

---

[1] Above, pp. 241–2.   [2] p. 252.

personal judgement of the author ; the latter half shows
two or three fairly strong chimes in the ordinary narrative.
One chapter has two lively dactylic cadences, at some
distance apart :—

(I, 196) τὸ ἐλάχιστον ὑπισταμένῳ προσέκειτο—
ἐξευρήκασι νεωστὶ γενέσθαι.

Traces of design, then, are very faint and precarious.
We may note some groups which appear in the other
Books :—

(II, 148 fin.) ἁρμοσμένου τὰ μάλιστα....ἐγγέγλυπται·
ὁδὸς δ᾽ ἐς αὐτὴν ὑπὸ γῆν πεποίηται.

(Description of the Labyrinth.)

(III, 64) ὁ μύκης ἀποπίπτει,...Αἰγυπτίων θεὸν Ἆπιν
ἔπληξε, ὣς οἱ καιρίῃ ἔδοξε τετύφθαι, εἴρετο ὁ Καμβύσης ὅ
τι τῇ πόλι οὔνομα εἴη.

(Something like the earlier habit of Thucydides.)

(VII, 104) ἄξιος εἶναι....εἰσι κακίονες ἀνδρῶν,...οὐ
πάντα ἐλεύθεροί εἰσι·...τὰ ἂν ἐκεῖνος ἀνώγῃ· ἀνώγει δὲ
τὠυτὸ αἰεί,—

(Demaratus' speech : these endings are in the space
of seven lines.)

(VIII, 109) τὴν προτέρην κακότητα....(5 lines) καὶ τῆς
Εὐρώπης βασιλεῦσαι,...(3 lines) ἀπεμαστίγωσε πέδας τε
κατῆκε.

(Themistocles' speech.)

The speeches and discussions of Herodotus, then,
afford a few notable repetitions of the cadence. Besides
these, the narrative has one or two, but none so marked
as that in III, 64. We have noticed elsewhere the
epic swing of a concluding period[1]: so Darius ends
a speech with this sonorous roll—

(IV, 98 fin.) ταῦτα δὲ ποιεῦντες ἐμοὶ μεγάλως χαριεῖσθε.

---

[1] VII, 9 ; above, p. 115.

The Persian Debate (III, 76–82) has but sparse examples of the cadence : the third speech ends with— (82 fin.) οὐ γὰρ ἄμεινον, just as Syagrus borrows an epic phrase for the beginning of his—(VII, 159) Ἦ κε μέγ᾽ οἰμώξειε¹. This manner of introducing deliberate reminiscences of poetry suggests that Herodotus intended them to stand out in contrast with his own loose-flowing prose-style. It is important to the freshness of his ambition as a prose-writer that audible hints of traditional verse should now and then arrest the ear. Pieces of oracle-verse have been found sticking out, as it were, from one passage of his prose². A similar suggestion of tragic speech may be felt in another place³. In these and other instances, the transcriptions are partly disguised, but not so as to escape the notice of an attentive listener⁴. But no one could miss the strong epic note of the following forms of address :—

(I, 108) Ἅρπαγε, πρῆγμα τὸ ἄν τοι προσθέω, μηδαμῶς παραχρήσῃ,...ὁ δὲ ἀμείβεται· Ὦ βασιλεῦ,—

(I, 206) Ὦ βασιλεῦ Μήδων, παῦσαι σπεύδων τὰ σπεύδεις· οὐ γὰρ ἄν εἰδείης,—

(VII, 136) Ὦ βασιλεῦ Μήδων,...μεγαλοφροσύνης... Λακεδαιμονίοισι.

¹ The two phrases came from *Il.* XXIV, 52 and VII, 125.
² IV, 163 ; see Rawlinson, ad loc.
³ VIII, 106—ἢ σὲ ἢ τῶν σῶν τινα,...θεοὺς λήσειν οἷα ἐμηχανῶ τότε...νόμῳ δικαίῳ χρεώμενοι. For some gnomic hexameters in VIII, 3, some tragic lines in IX, 16, and some incorporated inscription-verse in VIII, 114, IX, 76, 78 see Verrall, *Class. Rev.* XVII, pp. 98 foll.
⁴ This trick of half disguising a quotation, so as to allow the recognition of an alien phrase while it is roughly fastened into the context, is one of the easy accomplishments of Plato. Perhaps the sudden intrusion of heroic metre upon a passage of the *Phædrus* (267 a) at which we have glanced elsewhere (above, p. 150) may guide us to the cause of the broken construction which Thompson has discussed but not explained. That *metre* is in the air for the moment, is hinted by the sense and also the tragic beat of the remark on

As regards the clause-chime, however, the general conclusion from a comparison of the two historians is that Herodotus admitted, rarely and perhaps accidentally, an effect which stands in the relation of a prototype or pattern to the more anxious formality of Thucydides.

The only distinct traces of the cadence in early Ionian prose appear in two fragments of Heracleitus :—

φάτις αὐτοῖσι μαρτυρέει παρεόντας ἀπεῖναι—
τὸ μὲν ἥμισυ γῆ, τὸ δὲ ἥμισυ πρηστήρ¹—

It makes an occasional but not a striking appearance in the treatises of Hippocrates. Plato's parody of Protagoras in the *Theætetus* has these chimes in a small space—

(166 a) ἐρωτηθὲν ἔδεισεν,...(3 lines) τοῖς λόγοις ἀπέδειξεν.

(166 d) τὸ μὴ φάναι εἶναι,...καὶ λέγω σοφόν, ὃς ἄν τινι ἡμῶν,...φαίνεσθαί τε καὶ εἶναι—

and the speech ends with (168 c) παντοδαπὰς παρέχουσι.

The discourse in the *Protagoras* also has something like a chime of three :—

(321 b) καὶ ὑποδῶν τὰ μὲν ὁπλαῖς, τὰ δὲ θριξὶν καὶ

Euenus :—οἱ δ᾽ αὐτὸν καὶ παραψόγους φασὶν ἐν μέτρῳ λέγειν, μνήμης χάριν · σοφὸς γὰρ ἀνήρ. But at the mention of Tisias and Gorgias we pass to heroic measure :—Τισίαν δὲ Γοργίαν τε ἐάσομεν εὕδειν, οἱ πρὸ τῶν ἀληθῶν τὰ εἰκότα εἶδον ὡς τιμητέα μᾶλλον,...φαίνεσθαι ποιοῦσι διὰ ῥώμην λόγου, καινά τε ἀρχαίως τά τ᾽ ἐναντία καινῶς, συντομίαν τε λόγων καὶ ἄπειρα μήκη περὶ πάντων ἀνεῦρον. The first two cadences seem to announce a quotation which, when it comes, is moulded to fit the large rhythm rather than the grammar. We should suppose an allusion to some verses about Gorgias, which told how he came—

καινὰ μὲν ἀρχαίως ἐρέων ἀρχαῖα δὲ καινῶς,
συντομίαν τε λόγων καὶ ἄπειρον μῆκος ἀνευρών.

On the subject of verse-quotations in Plato, see Vahlen, *Opusc. Acad* 1907, I, pp. 476 foll.

¹ Heracl. (Bywater) fr. 3, 21 ; these and two slight cases are noticed by Norden, *Antike Kunstpr.* p. 44.

δέρμασιν στερεοῖς καὶ ἀναίμοις. τοὐντεῦθεν τροφὰς ἄλλοις ἄλλας ἐξεπόριζε,—

and another of two :—

(322 c) καὶ δεσμοὶ φιλίας συναγωγοί....(2 lines) ὡς αἱ τέχναι νενέμηνται[1],—

The essay *On the Art* has a few slight and isolated cases, which are remarkably scanty considering the length and formality of the work. Like Gorgias' Funeral Oration and Agathon's speech in the *Symposium*, it is too eagerly devoted to the new sort of small word-patterns to leave any room for the heroic cadence, had its presence been desired. The *Constitution of Athens* is inclined rather to groups of iambic and trochaic endings, though it shows the following :—

(II, 1) ὁπλιτικὸν ἄρχειν, εἰ τῶν συμμάχων κρείττονές εἰσι.

Antiphon uses the heroic cadence with some persistence, but more frequently it is in marked contrast with the iambic. His longest speech, *On the Murder of Herodes*, has these systems :—

(10) ἀλλὰ τοῦ σφίσιν αὐτοῖς λυσιτελοῦντος,...τεθνηκότι τῶν εὐνόμῳ [κειμένων].

(20 fin.) ἀνθρώποις ἀπολύσων....τοὺς μάρτυρας παρέξομαι.

(End of paragraph.)

(24 fin.) ἐγίγνετο, καὶ τἄλλα ἀνήγετο πλοῖα ἅπαντα, ᾠχόμην κἀγὼ πλέων. τούτων δ' ὑμῖν τοὺς μάρτυρας παρασχήσομαι.

(End of paragraph : he seems to avoid too much iambic cadence, by altering the formula of 20 fin. and 22 fin.)

---

[1] Also the phrase (324 c) εἴπερ μέλλει πόλις εἶναι, repeated (327 a) and altered to εἰ μὴ οἷόν τ' ἦν πόλιν εἶναι a few lines later.

(35) ἀλλὰ τῶν λόγων·...τῆς τούτων ἐπιβουλῆς,—

(43) τὸν ἄνδρα προυνοησάμην μόνος,...ὁ πᾶς κίνδυνος ἦν,...καὶ συμβούλους ἐποιούμην,...ὡς ὁ τούτων λόγος ἐστίν.

(51) ὁ μὲν γὰρ ἔφησεν, ὁ δὲ διὰ τέλους ἔξαρνος ἦν.
(A neat and apparently deliberate example of the contrast.)

(52) τοιαύτη γεγένηται,...ἀποθανόντα τὸν ἄνδρα.

(69) ᾤχετο φεύγων, ἀλλ᾽ ἐτόλμησε μεῖναι,...ἔνδον ὄντες ἅπαντες·...τολμῆσαί ποτε τοῦτο·...αὐτὸς ὕστερον κατεῖπεν αὐτοῦ.
(Heroic and trochaic.)

(85) ἐγὼ δὲ καθ᾽ οὓς μὲν ἀπήχθην, οὐκ ἔνοχός εἰμι τοῖς νόμοις, ὧν δ᾽ ἔχω τὴν αἰτίαν, ἀγών μοι νόμιμος ὑπολείπεται.

And we find what, in view of the pause, is almost a tragic line:—

(63) τῷ μὲν γὰρ οὐκ ἦν χρήματα, ἐμοὶ δὲ ἦν.

The other speeches of Antiphon exhibit the heroic cadence in rather more strength than these selections would indicate: they are shown here to illustrate his almost monotonous preference for iambic endings; which often, however, throw the others into relief. His most remarkable heroic chime is in the *Poisoning Case*:—

(9–10) ταύτην τε οὐκ οὖσαν ἄπαρνον,...ἀλλ᾽ ἐπὶ φίλτροις....ἠθέλησα ποιήσασθαι περὶ αὐτῶν,—

An obvious instance of contrasted metres has already come before us in some words of the Platonic Hippias:—

φύσει συγγενές ἐστιν,...παρὰ τὴν φύσιν βιάζεται[1].

But whoever first recommended this method, it is clear that the *mature* practice of Thucydides was more in accord with Antiphon's extant speeches than with his own earliest compositions. We have found iambic and

[1] Plato, *Protag.* 337 c; above, p. 147.

heroic endings together in Herodotus, but not such a steady habit as that which gives us an additional link between the other two writers.

Interesting cases of heroic cadence could be quoted from Lysias[1], whose simple eloquence must be remembered as a separate and settled growth beside the later work of Thucydides ; and there is a remarkable frequency of the heroic cadence in Isocrates' fragmentary discourse *Against the Sophists,* which has been described as 'the prologue of his professional life[2].' This short piece of less than six octavo pages has five heroic chimes and twenty-two heroic cadences, interspersed with a good number of iambic, trochaic and pæonic endings[3]: so that, in distinguishing his own methods from those of three sorts of professional teachers whom he attacks, Isocrates has shown that his style, at this date, is not free from the habit or fashion of epic rhythm. A comparison of his other educational essay, the *Antidosis,* which was written about thirty-eight years later, and also of large portions of his mature work, will show that his interest in other metrical schemes has allowed much rarer opportunities to the heroic cadence[4].

We shall not follow any further the traces of clause-chime in Attic prose, except to notice that the fragment of Thrasymachus which we owe to the rather dubious accuracy of Dionysius is marked by four cases of heroic cadence in close proximity :—

τὴν μὲν παρελθοῦσαν ἡμέραν ἀγαπῶσι, τὴν δ᾽ ἐπιοῦσαν

---

[1] E.g. Lysias, *Eratosth.* 40; *De Vet. Republ. Ath.* 5 (both in 403 B.C.: the latter fragment (9) has perhaps a reference to Pericles' speech, Thuc. II, 61); *Mantith.* 3. 6 (392 B.C.). A connection with Thuc. III, 82 is pretty obvious in the Panhellenic tone and the ornate language of *Olymp.* 1-2, 6-7 (388 B.C.). [2] Jebb, *Select Att. Or.* p. 299.
[3] *Contra Soph.* esp. 292 a, c ; 293 a, b ; 294 b ; 295 c (391-0 B.C.).
[4] *Antid.* (310 d-311 a, 316 a) has however some perceptible heroic chimes.

δεδιόσιν, ἀντὶ δ᾽ ὁμονοίας εἰς ἔχθραν καὶ ταραχὰς πρὸς ἀλλήλους ἀφικέσθαι....ποιεῖ καὶ στασιάζειν,...ἐσωφρονοῦμεν, ἐν δὲ τοῖς κακοῖς ἐμάνημεν[1].

Each pair of heroic cadences is separated by endings of a different type : but it is plain that, whatever schemes of pæons or other feet may be detected in the fragment, it undoubtedly contains these repeated echoes of either the epic or the 'Pherecratean' measure. This effect is the more memorable, since we are here in the early, formative stage of prose-style, where the sentence is a diligent array of clauses rather than a perfected organism with humbly subordinate members.

'Hexametric openings and closes of the sentence,' it has been said[2], 'are not so frequent in any later prose-writer as in Herodotus: none of his successors, for instance, would have written—οὐ γὰρ ἐᾷ φρονέειν μέγα ὁ θεὸς ἄλλον ἢ ἑωυτόν[3]: or—ὡς καὶ ἐς τόδε αὐτοί τε ὤνθρωποι καὶ ἡ γῆ αὐτῶν ἐπώνυμοι τοῦ καταστρεψαμένου καλέονται[4].' These sentences are from the speeches of Artabanus and Xerxes, where some other epic endings appear. A record from the whole of this History would probably show that Herodotus was fonder of an epic *opening*, and more frequently allowed a heroic cadence of continuous *dactylic* rhythm, than other writers of prose: but our evidence from Thucydides and Antiphon, and much more that could be adduced from Lysias, Isocrates and others, enables us to dismiss the latter of Norden's assertions as unsupported by fact. Our object here, however, is rather to remark Herodotus' use of the heroic chime in set speeches, and to suggest that the originator of the fashion may have been Protagoras. At any rate, it is clear that Thucydides formed the habit, and seems at

[1] Dionys. *Demosth.* 960-1.
[2] Norden, *Antike Kunstpr.* p. 45.　　[3] Herod. VII, 10. 5.　　[4] VII, 11.

times to use it deliberately for the double purpose—
served also by antithesis—of giving separate weight to
his clauses, and of fitting them into a compact structure.
Accordingly, when Isocrates was looking for an effective
metrical pattern, he had to consider the value of this
fashion, which was followed in some degree by Thrasymachus, and decidedly favoured, at least in his earlier
style, by Thucydides. It certainly appears that the
orator, many of whose Panhellenic notions can be seen
to spring naturally from the History of the War, made
experiments in this method before he became a professed
publicist, and decided—probably from a study of Thrasymachus, Antiphon, and the later Thucydides—in favour
of the trochee and iambus[1].

The search for signs of this metrical mannerism in the
History is only too liable to the accusation of overrating
their importance in the scale of the author's whole artistic
achievement: the zeal of the dissector may cause him to
miss the presence of some ruling nerve, besides disfigur-
ing, and so neglecting, many of the most delicate tissues.
For this reason we dwelt at first on that larger music
which resounds in several places of the book, and
especially in the Retreat from Syracuse[2]; preferring,
however, to spend our chief attention upon a matter of
detail which is both more amenable to analysis and,
when once it is clearly observed, may help to make us
more keenly sensible of those greater and more splendid
intonations.

---

[1] Cf. Isocr. τέχνη fr. 6 (Maxim. Planud. ad Hermog. v, p. 469. 8)—μεμίχθω
[ὁ λόγος] παντὶ ῥυθμῷ, μάλιστα ἰαμβικῷ ἢ τροχαϊκῷ.   [2] Above, pp. 243-4.

CHAPTER IX

INTERPOLATION

§ 1

WE may now suggest in brief the practical use, or rather necessity, of an investigation like the present for any satisfactory treatment of the textual question, which was a part of our original problem[1]. We have followed the course of Thucydides' literary effort through the innovations of 'a time when style was much studied': but the artist whose methods we have watched has been not so much 'a trained stylist' as a writer who, if he forges out, on occasion, a style which is truly his own[2], is far more constantly and remarkably trying his hand at several styles, both old and new, and with various degrees of success. Now it is clear, on the one hand, that no just account of his different modes of expression can ignore this matter of interpolation, at least so far as concerns the larger 'adscripts' which are alleged to have crept into the text,—'those disconcerting trails of comment and explanation which occur on every third page.' But it is equally certain that even the best instructed procedure cannot hope to find one sovereign test for all. It may rather have to recognise that here, as elsewhere[3], we are often faced by a wall of darkness which, the more eagerly we press through it, is the more likely to involve

---

[1] Above, pp. 5–6.   [2] As, for example, in parts of Book VII.
[3] Cf. the case of the scandalous gossip about Pericles, above, pp. 48–9.

us in a night of dreams. And in fact, without attempting
to deal with more than a few of the suspected insertions,
we shall find good reasons for maintaining a Thucydidean
caution in any definite approach towards the trustworthy 'rule of exception' which this problem seems
to require[1]. Much of the matter in dispute will probably
never be settled : but there is some of it on which a
purely literary account of the History should best be able
to pronounce. Just as it cannot be enough to state, once
for all, that 'nations do not go to war on such grounds[2],'
so we may find something useful to say in control of
certain assertions which have been made as to what
Thucydides could or could not have written.

One class of corrections—which would exclude a
number of geographical and ethnological notes—has been
discussed already in our preliminary sketch of the
historian's aim[3]. But besides expecting that he will often
inform us of things with which 'the Greeks must have
been quite familiar[4],' we shall be prepared for other
departures from his habitual brevity. The same purpose
which introduced the larger digressions into his scheme
can be felt at work in some passages where he is
obviously bent on explaining an affair in specially ample
and lucid terms. The deliberate fullness of his opening
words[5] alone should warn us of this occasional liberty.
So, looking at the whole manner of the narrative from
which some critics would excise this note of explanation—

(IV, 25. 2) διὰ τάχους ἀπέπλευσαν ὡς ἕκαστοι ἔτυχον ἐς
τὰ οἰκεῖα στρατόπεδα [τό τε ἐν τῇ Μεσσήνῃ καὶ ἐν τῷ
Ῥηγίῳ][6],—

---

[1] Above, p. 6.
[2] Above, pp. 49 foll.   [3] pp. 18 foll.   [4] Marchant, Bk II, p. xxxviii.
[5] Quoted above, p. 8.   [6] Hude, after Herwerden.

we must refuse to prune away what is only the most obvious among many signs about this place of specially explicit description. Thucydides has invented serious history, but has not arrived at the expedient of referring to separate appendices and notes; his necessary furniture has to be packed into the text itself as his work proceeds. Not that he has always or regularly supplied a note where readers of a later age would be glad to have one. He could not imagine the questions of a Tripos, any more than he could foresee the monks who transcribed him in the Middle Ages. Nor is he always thinking of an audience other than Athenian. Only we must be prepared to find that, as his peculiar brevity exposed him to accretions of scholastic annotation, so his hope of being read by persons remote from his time and outlook has frequently moved him to insert his own explanatory allusions.

Above all, we have to realise that he worked at different subjects in different moods. Yet many modern critics of the text are content to adopt a conservative or a reforming policy, without attending to the variations of the author's manner: whereas it is only when we have obtained from the complexion of the style, as it shifts with the entrance of each new episode or discussion, some sense of the manner which prevails for the moment, that we can speak one useful word on the origin of even an ill-fitting insertion. The arguments of Cobet, for instance, have deserved the most careful hearing, since they work always from the intellectual structure of the style, while relying on a sure knowledge of its *normal* or *frequent* use of particular words : but he would have been more convincing if he had made allowance, as he surely ought to have, for moments of ample detail or sonorous intonation. Thus, in the full-flowing description of the departure of the fleet for Sicily, he would cut down a resonant sentence, so as to relieve it of a comparison which is only apparently inexact:—

καὶ ἐν τῷ παρόντι καιρῷ, ὡς ἤδη ἔμελλον μετὰ κινδύνων ἀλλήλους ἀπολιπεῖν, μᾶλλον αὐτοὺς ἐσῄει τὰ δεινὰ [ἢ ὅτε ἐψηφίζοντο πλεῖν]¹.

If we are going to reduce the whole History to a single habit of abrupt implication, we ought probably to abolish the first five words as well as the last four; just as the mythic theory ought to take account of the Perils which were now winning their way into the popular mind. We recognise the μᾶλλον ἢ τοῦ δέους² in the Funeral Oration as a rather too unapprehensive imitation of Gorgias: but it is fair to expect that rhetoric will have its rightful effect in other elaborate, though more strenuous, performances in the art of Thucydides. On the other hand, a hint from the scholia will sometimes show that the note of a later date has intruded on the brief account of an unimportant affair³.

We have considered the awkward breaks in the narrative for which the 'summers and winters' method is responsible⁴. It is natural, accordingly, to regard phrases like ὥσπερ παρεσκευάζοντο as signs of the author's uneasiness about the conduct of his narrative⁵. So, when we find Βρασίδας δὲ ὁ Τέλλιδος Λακεδαιμόνιος, it is rash to excise the title, on no better plea than that Brasidas was mentioned 'in the first half of the book without any designation⁶.' The whole phrase is intended to start a new episode:—

¹ Thuc. VI, 31. 1; Cobet, Var. Lect.² p. 291; cf. III, 64. 3; Cobet, p. 446: above, p. 101.
² II, 42 fin.; above, p. 159.
³ E.g. V, 83. 1—ἐστράτευσαν ἐς τὸ Ἄργος...ὑπῆρχε δέ τι αὐτοῖς καὶ [ἐκ τοῦ Ἄργους] αὐτόθεν πρασσόμενον: (schol. αὐτόθεν· ἐκ τοῦ Ἄργους).
⁴ Above, pp. 10-11. ⁵ Cf. Rutherford, Bk IV, p. xlix.
⁶ IV, 70. 1; Rutherford, p. xlvii. A more delicate case occurs at VIII, 28. 3 (Πισσούθνου νόθον υἱόν, ἀφεστῶτα δὲ βασιλέως), where although 'Amorges

Βρασίδας δὲ ὁ Τέλλιδος Λακεδαιμόνιος κατὰ τοῦτον τὸν χρόνον ἐτύγχανε περὶ Σικυῶνα καὶ Κόρινθον ὤν,—

and the title serves, first of all, to resume the activities of the Lacedæmonian general after an account of the Athenian operations at Nisæa, and secondly, to dignify the necessary transition with something of an epic manner. When, however, we find the names Λακεδαι-μόνιοι and Ἀθηναῖοι several times repeated in a single sentence or paragraph, our sense of what Thucydides is commonly able to achieve by mere participles, together with the clearest notion we can form of his momentary purpose, may justify excision.

Cobet, and still more those who have freely applied his methods, had to be continually referring the corruption to the carelessness of transcribers. This is a point which the effect of our scanty information too easily exaggerates. 'Monks were the copyists, men of slight learning, which was dangerous to them, men who cared nothing at all about what they did, but only about getting it done[1].' This may be generally true : but after being reminded that by the tenth century the scholia 'had been collected and appended to the text page by page,' we are told that 'the copyists had often mixed up the commentary with the text, and this fertile cause of blunders had been at work now for many centuries, having probably begun to vitiate the original at a time considerably anterior to the Christian era.' Such a statement only gathers clouds. These calamitous monks were not copying texts *before* the Christian era, since the world had not yet made room for their existence. A sharp

has been mentioned before without this addition' (Goodhart, Bk VIII, p. 43) the intention may be to connect two widely severed passages (cf. VIII, 5 fin.) by repeating a description at a point where the pause of the reference will be least awkward.

[1] Marchant, Bk II, p. xxvi.

distinction must be drawn between copyists A.D. and
copyists B.C. ; or rather we should keep this name for
those monks of whom we hear, from the fifth century
A.D. onwards, as having been specially employed in the
work of transcribing ancient texts. We have hardly any
means of knowing to what total extent, or in what
manner, the copying of manuscripts proceeded in Alex-
andrian and Augustan times. One case of deliberate
corruption is mentioned—that of Apellicon of Teos, into
whose hands the works of Aristotle and Theophrastus,
after being injured by damp and worms, at length
arrived ; and who, being 'a bibliophile rather than a
philosopher,' patched up the corroded places, and
'published the books full of errors.' Rome soon afterwards contributed her share of the damage. When Sulla
seized the library of Apellicon in Athens (86 B.C.), these
books were brought to Italy ; and when the book-sellers
produced an edition, 'they employed bad scribes and
omitted to compare the copies with the original. The
same thing happens with other books which are transcribed
for sale both here [in Rome] and in Alexandria[1].' There
is also Cicero's complaint (54 B.C.) of blunders in the
issue of the Latin books of his day[2]. Small mistakes
must always have occurred both before and during the
Augustan age, similar to those which can be attributed
to the mere carelessness of Byzantine or monastic scribes :
but any large amount of interpolation, designed or
accidental, is far more likely to have been a growth
of these later and more ignorant ages.

This point has claimed attention here, since it closely
concerns the question, whether the texts of Thucydides
had suffered much alteration before Dionysius made his

[1] Strabo, XIII, i, 54.
[2] Cicero, *Ad Quint. Fr.* III, 5–6—'De Latinis uero quo me uertam
nescio : ita mendose exscribuntur et ueneunt.'

extracts (38–30 B.C.).   It appears, on the whole, that his
text of the History was not remarkably different from
ours ; after allowing for the faulty condition in which his
own works have been handed down, and his laxity in
quoting from himself[1] or repeating a former quotation[2],
the differences do not suggest anything like a seperate
tradition.   It may of course be argued that this single
tradition had previously passed through many amplifying
hands, so that a number of explanatory notes had
gradually crept in.   The answer must simply be that it
is possible, but very improbable.   At any rate, we have
no sure ground to build on, except such errors as the
ordinary transcriber can hardly avoid[3].

§ 2

A corrective to feverish generalisation was supplied
by a new study of the merits of the different manuscripts[4]:
the best of which were shown to be not seriously corrupt,
even in Book VIII.   Yet there are many points affecting
the sense, ' in which the authority of all the MSS. together
is so little to be trusted that it would often be unsound
criticism to follow them in opposition to external considerations of fitness and probability[5].'   This relates
chiefly to variations in the forms of words : as to large
interpolations, each case for doubt must be considered

---

[1] *Ad Pomp.* ii ; *Ad Amm.* II, ii.   [2] *De Thuc.* 858, 871.
[3] The MSS. of Dionys. *Ad Amm.* II, xi make the critic say that certain
persons had altered a participle in Thuc. VIII, 64 from the masc. to the fem.,
and three other words from the gen. to the accus.   But Herwerden seems
right in making the remark conditional (ἂν ἔζευξαν for ἀντέζευξαν, and
⟨ἂν⟩ ἀντι).   Roberts (*Class. Rev.* 1900, pp. 214–6) holds it just possible that
the MSS. are right, and that Dionys. refers to an 'attempt made to rewrite
the words of Thuc.'   Such attempts were doubtless often made as rhetorical
or grammatical exercises ; Dionys. can hardly be referring to these.   However, it is to be noted that he distinguishes the oddities of the authorised
text from possible or actual improvements.
[4] Goodhart, Bk VIII, *Intr.* (1893).   [5] *Ib.* p. xxvii.

separately. We are to condemn a few additions on linguistic grounds[1]: with regard to parenthetical phrases like ὥσπερ παρεσκευάζοντο—ὥσπερ διενοοῦντο, 'how is any *general* criterion to be established by which such clauses can be rejected?'[2] In fine, 'perhaps there is not much more to be learnt from our existing MSS.'; while the way is left open, as we have seen, for 'external considerations of fitness or probability.' Two years later another critic declared it 'highly probable that some of the passages dealing with geography, customs, constitutional details and the like, which embarrass the commentator, may owe their complexity to accidental insertions, and not to what can only be called clumsiness on the part of the historian.'[3] Thus even a note of nearly three lines' length may have to be excluded[4]. This view, however, discountenances the wholesale rejection of explanatory notes, and requires a plea of 'complexity' or 'clumsiness': though it is unfortunate that such a plea can be urged against other places in the History where excision cannot fairly offer a solution.

Another suggestion which calls for notice is that of a closer study of Thucydidean imitators[5]. But the general effect of this study so far has been to confirm the authority of our text[6]. Moreover, imitations and borrowings of any helpful extent are to be found only in times late enough to have allowed a good deal of contamination of the original. If we look further back, the most likely authors are either now lost to us, or they confined themselves to excerpts or parallels which are of

---

[1] e.g. VIII, 6. 3—ὅθεν...ἐκαλεῖτο ; 77—οἱ δέκα πρεσβευταί.
[2] Goodhart, p. xxx.   [3] Forbes, Bk I, p. v (1895).
[4] e.g. I, 126. 6—ἔστι...ἐπιχώρια.   [5] Spratt, Bk III, p. xii (1896).
[6] See the *testimonia* in Hude's edit. 1898–1901, which however should be supplemented by reference to the fuller collections in Bloomfield's *Transl. of Thuc.* 1829, and his critical edition of 1842.

slight account. Thus, in the first place, Philistus of Syracuse, who wrote a history of Sicily, was 'terse, sagacious, concise—almost a miniature Thucydides[1]': but we are also told that he was more lucid than his master[2]; and that 'he shunned what is most peculiar and curious in the style of Thucydides, and reproduced what is rounded and terse and argumentative; he falls, however, very far behind the beauty of language and wealth of arguments appearing in that writer;...his language is extremely uniform and lacking in variety[3].' It is clear, accordingly, that even if we possessed more than inconsiderable fragments of this most reputed of early imitators, they would have to be used with the greatest caution. Moreover, Dionysius remarks that he knows of no ancient historian who imitated Thucydides 'in respect of the things wherein he is most distinguished from other writers[4]'; though this critic, in spite of his strictures and protests, owes a good many phrases of his own History to the invention or example of Thucydides[5]. Besides the use of single words, he adapts a few expressions like —καὶ παρὰ δύναμιν τολμηταὶ καὶ παρὰ γνώμην κινδυνευταί[6]—to his own purposes. Arrian, who desired to be known to fame as 'the New Xenophon,' found a use nevertheless for a good many pickings from Thucydides. Here we may find either adoption or adaptation; for example, not only δίψει ἀπαύστῳ συνεχόμενοι, but ὕφαλοι κολυμβηταί[7]. Hence this evidence is a good deal less valuable than even the inaccurate quotations of Dionysius.

[1] Cicero, Ad Quint. Fr. II, xi. 4 (transl. Tyrrell). Philistus was born c. 435 B.C.   [2] Quintil. Inst. Or. X, I.
[3] Dionys. Ad Pomp. 781.
[4] Dionys. De Thuc. 943; cf. De Imitat. 427.
[5] See H. Stephanus, cit. Poppo, Proleg. 356—'quorum apud Thuc. μωμητής fuerat, quaedam sunt, quorum postmodo μιμητής esse non erubuit.'
[6] Thuc. I, 70. 3.
[7] Thuc. II, 49. 5—δίψῃ ἀπαύστῳ ξυνεχόμενοι: IV, 26. 8—κολυμβηταὶ ὕφυδροι.

Towards 200 A.D. we find a number of borrowings in Dio Cassius, such as κολυμβηταὶ ὕφυδροι, and ἕως ἂν ἡ αὐτὴ φύσις ἀνθρώπων ᾖ[1] : he has also some dozen passages where the sentiment is obviously derived from Thucydides ; and these larger pieces occasionally throw some light on the merits of a variant reading. Lastly, it is to be observed that the words and phrases which betray all such imitations are for the most part—like the sentiments borrowed from the Funeral Oration by Sallust—memorable rather than difficult or awkward. There is therefore not much further help to be expected from this quarter for the question of interpolation[2].

---

[1] Thuc. III, 82. 2 (see previous note).

[2] Two whole chapters in the text (III, 17 ; 84) may be partly the work of early imitators. III, 17 presents so many perplexities of sense and oddities of diction (Steup, *Rhein. Mus.* XXIV, 350 ; Classen-Steup, *Thuc.* Bk III, pp. 244-9), that it ought probably to be regarded as a patchwork, by a later hand, of rough jottings left by Thuc. for a note on the numbers of Athenian ships. III, 84 is more interesting : its rejection dates from the time of the earliest grammarians, and its ponderous re-handling of the topics of 82-3, though at first suggesting that it is an alternative essay by Thuc. which he discarded for what he preferred to write in a different manner, is more likely —from various hints of language—to be the work of an able imitator (Classen, Bk III, pp. 173-4, 275). His skill is chiefly in compact and well-balanced periodic connection : the first of his three sentences is a lengthy, scientific specimen of a descending period—ἐν δ' οὖν τῇ Κερκύρᾳ...ἀπαραιτήτως ἐπέλθοιεν—which has a good deal of Thuc.'s weighty rhythm.

An important study, with which we are not at present concerned, is that of Byzantine Greek. This has led to the detection and expulsion of language used in a manner alien to the fifth century, and to the distinction of those classical words—though this must be less certain—which required a comment in later times. Yet probably most of the cases in which this knowledge can be of use have been decided ; and considering the number of ἅπαξ λεγόμενα in Thuc. (cf. Goodhart, pp. xxxix-xl), and the difficulty of pronouncing, e.g., whether he could or could not write οἰκία (VIII, 6. 3) in the sense of 'family,' or stretch his grammar to almost any conceivable shape or tenuity for a moment, it is doubtful if this guidance can be followed any further.

It will be well, however, to notice here a fine correction made many years ago, which ought at least to have been mentioned by Goodhart, Tucker and Hude. In VIII, 46. 3 we read :—καὶ οὐκ εἰκὸς εἶναι Λακεδαιμονίους ἀπὸ μὲν σφῶν τῶν Ἑλλήνων ἐλευθεροῦν νῦν τοὺς Ἕλληνας, ἀπὸ δ' ἐκείνων τῶν βαρβάρων, ἢν μή ποτε αὐτοὺς μὴ ἐξέλωσι, μὴ ἐλευθερῶσαι. Hude, on the hint of an omission in one MS. (B), brackets τῶν βαρβάρων, and follows Valckenær in

The most recent English text[1] encloses in hostile
brackets a score or so of phrases excised by modern
critics[2], besides one whole chapter (III, 17), and several
small notes like τοῖς Λακεδαιμονίοις (I, 85. 3) and ἀπὸ
Ταινάρου (I, 128. 1). The editor's principles are conservative : he will only recognise a few interpolations
apart from those which stand condemned on the showing
of the scholia[3]. It is strange, therefore, that although
in one place he discredits three inoffensive words[4]—

(VIII, 94. 1) καὶ πᾶς τις [τῶν πολλῶν ὁπλιτῶν] αὐτὸ
τοῦτο ἐνόμιζεν—

bracketing τῶν Ἑλλήνων likewise. But after these very acceptable excisions
there is nothing but doubtful and perplexing conjecture in the various
treatment of ἦν...ἐλευθερῶσαι. Donaldson (*Pindar*, 1868, Pref. p. xii)
suggested that μή ποτε αὐτούς is a scholiast's note from the margin—'*perhaps
we should insert* αὐτούς': μή ποτε being often used in this way (see
Buttmann, *Demosth. Meid.* 1833, Exc. vii), and the annotator 'not perceiving
that αὐτούς was fully implied in βαρβάρων' (Donaldson had to do without
the encouragement to brevity which is provided by the other two excisions).
The probable reading therefore is—ἀπὸ δ' ἐκείνων, ἢν μὴ ἐξέλωσι, μὴ
ἐλευθερῶσαι, and we translate—'even if they (the Spartans) did not *expel*
them (the Persians), they would at least set the Greeks free from them.'
For Alcibiades is reminding Tissaphernes 'how very unlikely it was that
the Lacedæmonians, whose professed object was to liberate the Greeks from
the tyranny of their countrymen, would not free them from the rule of the
barbarians : to which he adds, in order to terrify the satrap still more, that
in all probability they would not rest contented with merely liberating the
Asiatic Greeks, but would also *expel* the Persians from the country (for this
sense of ἐξαιρέω, cf. Herod. V, 16; II, 30; VII, 106).' Hude alters to
ἐξελάσωσι. The whole passage, as quoted, serves well to illustrate how a
succinct summary of an argument could be swollen and spoilt by the
incorporation of marginal notes.

  [1] Stuart Jones, Oxford, 1898.
  [2] II, 15. 4 ; 19. 1 ; 21. 1 ; III, 21. 3 ; 23. 5 ; 109. 2 ; IV, 45. 2 ; 90. 1 ; V,
32. 5 ; 50. 2 ; 65. 4 ; 116. 1 ; VI, 40. 1 ; VII, 45. 2 ; 58. 3 ; VIII, 44. 3 ; 77 ; 94.
1 ; 99. 1. Only three of these are referred to the scholia, and two more to
Valla's unreliable translation. III, 84 (*in toto*) is bracketed on the evidence
of the scholia.
  [3] *Ib.* Pref. An example of the latter sort has been noticed in ἐκ τοῦ
Ἄργους (V, 83. 1), above, p. 285, n. 3.
  [4] *Secl.* Stahl ; τῶν πολιτῶν Gertz ; τῶν ὁπλιτῶν Hude, after one MS(C).

he ignores an almost convincing correction of Cobet's—

(II, 84. 3) τότε δὴ [κατὰ τὸν καιρὸν τοῦτον] σημαίνει—

while if we are to suspect an insertion in this phrase—

(VII, 45. 2) ψιλοὶ [ἄνευ τῶν ἀσπίδων] οἱ μὲν ἀπώλλυντο, οἱ δ᾽ ἐσώθησαν[1]—

it is hard to be contented with this—

(II, 92. 5) ἔστησαν δὲ καὶ οἱ Πελοποννήσιοι τροπαῖον ὡς νενικηκότες τῆς τροπῆς, ἃς πρὸς τῇ γῇ διέφθειραν ναῦς—

from which Cobet, with much reason, deleted ὡς νενικηκότες, and which would perhaps be a more tolerable and genuine sentence if τῆς τροπῆς were expelled instead[2]. Nor can we fairly pass this incorrect geographical note, especially when it upsets the connection of the language—

(VI, 104. 2) καὶ ἁρπασθεὶς ὑπ᾽ ἀνέμου [κατὰ τὸν Τεριναῖον κόλπον] ὃς ἐκπνεῖ ταύτῃ μέγας κατὰ Βορέαν ἑστηκώς[3]—

This edition, then, not merely recognises a considerable amount of interpolation beyond what is indicated by the scholia, but conducts its practice in a manner which ought to be uncomfortable to its theory: for it admits enough corrections to justify the admission of a good many more; some of which are at least as necessary, but the total effect would show too much favour to the principle of excision. This embarrassment seems to arise from adopting a fixed attitude towards a too confident school of criticism, instead of weighing each accusation, whatever may be its source, on its

---

[1] Secl. Pluygers, Hude; ἀπώλοντο Hude, after Cobet.
[2] This sentence is left intact by Hude; also II, 84. 3 above.
[3] Secl. Hude, after Gœller. The wind is set or standing in the north (cf. Herod. VI, 140. 4), and Gylippus is somewhere not far from Tarentum: Terina is low down on the 'instep' of Italy.

individual merits, and with a sure view of the high though varying merits of Thucydides.

Turning for a moment to 'papyrus ille nobilissimus e ruderibus Oxyrhynchi nuper in lucem prolatus[1]'—on which this editor's theory is partly based—we find the fragment about equal in length to two and a half of his pages[2]. Its differences from our text are slight[3], and the version to which it belongs would have high authority, if the whole had survived. But, as appears by the corrections it has received from either the first or some later hand, its original form did not escape the accidents which befall every transcription ; and how far these and more intentional faults had corrupted the text before this copy was made[4] must remain an open question. Its editors, in treating a small fragment of Book II (94)[5], observe that the removal of grammatical difficulties there and in the fragment of Book IV, by two papyri which are not only nine centuries earlier than the oldest vellum manuscript of Thucydides, but stand above the ordinary rank of classical papyri in point of correctness, 'suggests that the difficulties of Thucydides' syntax may to some extent be the fault of scribes.' Another fragment of the first-mentioned papyrus, containing some more pieces of Book IV, has come to light[6], and still no serious variants appear. Yet these scraps of early manuscript, while tending to discourage an extravagant policy of excision, *may* record a text which has already suffered from omissions and insertions before the first century A.D. A parallel occurs in the case of the papyrus of Bacchyl-

[1] Stuart Jones, Pref.   [2] IV, 36. 2–41. 1.
[3] Two of them are not recorded by Stuart Jones—IV, 38. 4 ; 39 *init.*
[4] It is of the first century A.D. ; Grenfell and Hunt, *Oxyrh. Papyr.* 1898, I, pp. 40–2.   [5] *Oxyrh. Papyr.* 1899, ii, p. 118.
[6] *Oxyrh. Papyr.* 1904, IV, pp. 90–1 (Thuc. IV, 28–35, with considerable gaps). A useful collection of the pieces of the text discovered in Egypt and published up to 1912 has been made by F. Fischer, Leipzig, 1913.

ides, which belongs to the first century B.C. : 'but when
it was written, Bacchylides had been dead for some four
hundred years; and though the manuscript is, on the
whole, of a good class, the text already abounds in
mistakes and corruptions[1].' Further, the abjects and
orts of Oxyrhynchus have given us but brief glimpses of
some of Thucydides' most straightforward narrative : we
must wait for more diverse examples, before we can
argue much from the general import of such evidence.

'Quam mendose,' exclaimed Cobet, 'ad hunc diem
Thucydides editur!'[2] The reproach has been largely
abolished by a Danish scholar[3], whose methods are
according to the highest standards of research and
apparatus. On the question of interpolation, this editor
shows that the two great difficulties are the untrustworthy
character of the manuscript tradition, and the peculiar
licence of the author's style; so that we are frequently at
a loss to tell whether a harsh expression is owing to him
or to the scribes[4]. The procedure of this text is
explained as the middle way of leaving unchanged such
oddities of speech as seem to be countenanced by the
general manner and connection of the passages in which
they occur, or by an affinity to other oddities elsewhere;
while, in cases which admit of ready emendation, the
tradition is freely deserted. 'It is abundantly clear, from
the disagreement of the manuscripts and from a study of
the scholia and the evidence in other writers, that glosses
and scholia have at not a few places crept into the text :
but no adequate account is as yet forthcoming of either
the process or the period at which the author's words
were amplified as some critics would have us believe[5].'

---

[1] Jebb, *Camb. Comp. Gr. Stud.* § 693.
[2] Cobet, *Var. Lect.* 1873, p. 450.
[3] Hude, *Thuc.* I–IV, 1898; V–VIII, 1901.   [4] *Ib.* I, p. viii.
[5] *Ib.* I, p. ix.

Against the methods of Cobet—'princeps ille Batauorum[1]'
—we are to set, first of all, the testimony of Dionysius,
but finally—and this is more convincing and useful—the
variations in the style of the History. The second
Preface finds in the new readings of the papyrus an
encouragement to the further cure of the tradition.
Thus the latest editor, after a careful survey of all that
ancient and modern learning can supply for the correction
of the book, still leaves us to weigh arguments for and
against a considerable number of excisions.

The fluctuating condition in which the question
remains is yet more evident, when we consider some of
the phrases which Hude has or has not seen fit to excise.
He does not notice some probable cases, like two which
we have quoted[2]: yet he accepts this correction of
Krüger—

(IV, 37. 1) εἴ πως τοῦ κηρύγματος ἀκούσαντες ἐπικλασ-
θεῖεν τῇ γνώμῃ [τὰ ὅπλα παραδοῦναι] καὶ ἡσσηθεῖεν τοῦ
παρόντος δεινοῦ,—

in view, apparently, of the τὰ ὅπλα παραδοῦναι which
comes shortly after[3]. Rutherford's argument, that the
words are betrayed by their position (since they belong
to τοῦ κηρύγματος[4]) is unfair both to the collective force
of Thucydides' language, and to his constant habit,
especially in a deliberative moment, of postponing a verb
of this shape to the end of the phrase[5].

---

[1] Perhaps there is here some shadow of that 'αὐτοκοβήτου species mente concepta atque iuxta Heinianum illum camelum producta'; see Badham, *Plato, Euthyd. and Laches*, Epist. Præf. 1865.

[2] II, 84. 3; II, 92. 5; above, p. 293.

[3] The sentence—or perhaps a fresh one—proceeds—ἐκήρυξάν τε, εἰ βούλονται, τὰ ὅπλα παραδοῦναι καὶ σφᾶς αὐτοὺς Ἀθηναίους—

[4] Rutherford, Bk IV, p. xlix.

[5] Above, pp. 250, 256, 257. A stranger excision is that of δι' ἀχθηδόνα
in IV, 40. 4, and διὰ τὸ περιέχειν αὐτήν in IV, 102. 4, on Rutherford's reason,
that the necessary sense 'for the sake of' betrays a late idiom unknown to

§ 3

As a supplement to these views and instances, we shall now inspect a few cases of modern suspicion, to which a careful sense of the prevailing structure and rhythm may be able to offer conclusive advice. The following illustrations will serve at least to indicate the lines on which readers of the modern texts of Thucydides ought to satisfy themselves, as far as possible, that they are aware of his occasional as well as his general artistic intention.

(I, 50. 2) οὐ ῥᾳδίως τὴν διάγνωσιν ἐποιοῦντο [ὁποῖοι ἐκράτουν ἢ ἐκρατοῦντο][1].

The suspected phrase, or at any rate its last two words, may appear to be too explanatory for Thucydides: in his most parsimonious mood, it certainly would be. But in the place where it occurs, it is just in the manner that we ought to expect. The preceding chapter is a piece of direct and rapid narrative : when he comes to reflect and explain, the sentences are more neatly and evenly framed, and the confusion of the fight is emphasised by the balance of the clauses, which work up here to a sort of jingling epigram[2].

Thuc. (Rutherford, Bk IV, p. xxxix). Yet Hude makes no question of διὰ τὴν σφετέραν δόξαν in II, 89. 4, or of διὰ τοῦ θύματος τὴν ἔσπραξιν in V, 53, in both of which the natural meaning of διά is also 'for the sake of.' Cf. Plato, *Resp.* 524 c—διὰ τὴν τούτου σαφήνειαν, 'with the view of making this clear'— and other classical instances given by Graves, Bk IV, 1888, p. 186. δι' ἀχθηδόνα (IV, 40. 4) is perhaps not in its right place, but the reason for cutting it out does not appear to be sufficient, merely from the practice of Hude himself. The point here is a strictly grammatical one : but it illustrates the perplexity in which readers are still left, as to the kind of expression that Thucydides could or could not have used.

[1] *Secl.* Pluygers, Cobet ; mentioned by Hude. Cobet regards ὁποῖοι as 'decrepit Greek for οἵτινες,' and adds that ὁπότεροι is required. But the context ("Ελλησι πρὸς "Ελληνας) gives a good point to ὁποῖοι.

[2] See above, pp. 271-2. The rhythm of this passage has been noticed above, p. 257.

A similar explanation elsewhere is so awkwardly placed, and so needless after the same words have appeared twice within the previous eleven lines, that it probably ought to be expelled :—

(I, 87. 6) ἡ δὲ διαγνώμη αὕτη τῆς ἐκκλησίας [τοῦ τὰς σπονδὰς λελύσθαι¹] ἐγένετο ἐν τῷ...ἔτει—

especially when the only discernible intention is to add a bare chronological note.

(I, 140. 2) βούλονται δὲ πολέμῳ μᾶλλον [ἢ λόγοις] τὰ ἐγκλήματα διαλύεσθαι²—

We have noticed in the earlier part of this sentence an experiment, for oral conviction, in alliterative emphasis, and the consequent sacrifice of brevity³. Hence we have no right to deprive Pericles of the full sound of his antithesis, though the mere intelligence of his hearers might be content with less. The ear, however, demands its toll. The same argument applies to another ample phrase within the next few lines :—

(I, 140. 4) μηδεὶς νομίσῃ περὶ βραχέος ἂν πολεμεῖν, εἰ τὸ Μεγαρέων ψήφισμα μὴ καθέλοιμεν, ὅπερ μάλιστα προύχονται, [εἰ καθαιρεθείη, μὴ ἂν γίγνεσθαι τὸν πόλεμον⁴]—

for it is only if we ignore the earnest, *long-winded* insistence of the whole passage that we can be tempted by even ' the controlled and sane sagacity of Cobet⁵.'

(II, 45. 1) παισὶ δ' αὖ ὅσοι τῶνδε πάρεστε ἢ ἀδελφοῖς ὁρῶ
μέγαν τὸν ἀγῶνα
(τὸν γὰρ οὐκ ὄντα ἅπας εἴωθεν ἐπαινεῖν),
καὶ μόλις ἂν καθ' ὑπερβολὴν ἀρετῆς οὐχ ὅμοιοι,
ἀλλ' ὀλίγῳ χείρους κριθεῖτε.

---

¹ *Secl.* Cobet, Hude: not mentioned by Stuart Jones.   ² *Secl.* Cobet.
³ Above, pp. 257-8.   ⁴ *Secl.* Cobet : cf. above, p. 40, n. 3.
⁵ Rutherford, Bk IV, Pref. p. viii.

It is not too much to say that the parenthesis in the second line was primarily composed or primarily so placed—though by Thucydides, and to the detriment of the connection—for the sake of rhythmical balance ; and primarily for this reason we cannot allow it to be excised[1].

(III, 58. 3) ἑκόντας τε ἐλάβετε καὶ χεῖρας προϊσχομένους (ὁ δὲ νόμος τοῖς Ἕλλησι μὴ κτείνειν τούτους[2]).

The argument from Thucydides' regard for future readers will probably not, but still conceivably may, hold in the case of a speech[3] : to claim that he would not have expressed the matter in these terms[4], is to stop our ears, and miss the tone of simple appeal which runs throughout the Platæans' speech[5]. It is no less in harmony with this than with the explicit connections of the straight-forward thought, that the speaker should pass from ἑκόντας to χεῖρας προϊσχομένους, and so on to this barely worded note of Hellenic feeling[6].

At the end of this chapter there is an equally appropriate tone of earnest pleading in the insistence of —(III, 58 fin.) τῶν ἐσσαμένων [καὶ κτισάντων] and— (59, 1) ἀλλοτρίας ἕνεκα ἔχθρας [μὴ αὐτοὺς ἀδικηθέντας] which again forbids the excisions of Cobet. For in seeking to give Thucydides his due, we must recognise not merely his peculiar brevity, but also the amount of special character which he has purposely bestowed on the arguments and language of the several speeches[7].

---

[1] τὸν γὰρ...ἐπαινεῖν secl. Steup—whose arguments (Classen-Steup, Thuc. 1889, II, pp. 225-6) would be more convincing, if they concerned a piece of narrative like that of VI, 104. 2, above, p. 293.

[2] ὁ δὲ...τούτους secl. Cobet.   [3] Above, pp. 18 foll.

[4] Var. Lect. p. 446—'quasi uero aut Platæenses ista dicere aut Thuc. ea sic dicere potuisset.'   [5] Cf. above, pp. 260-1.

[6] With the simple verb κτείνειν cf. I, 132 fin.—καὶ αὐτὸν ηὗρεν ἐγγεγραμμένον κτείνειν : II, 51. 6—δὶς γὰρ τὸν αὐτόν, ὥστε καὶ κτείνειν, οὐκ ἐπελάμβανεν.

[7] Cf., further on, the distracted intonation of the three phrases—(59. 2) αἰτούμεθα ὑμᾶς—πεῖσαι τάδε—μὴ ἀμνημονεῖν—which Cobet would likewise abolish.

(IV, 4. 2) τὸν πηλόν...ἐπὶ τοῦ νώτου ἔφερον, ἐγκε-
κυφότες τε,
[ὡς μάλιστα μέλλοι ἐπιμένειν,]
καὶ τὼ χεῖρε ἐς τοὐπίσω ξυμπλέκοντες
[ὅπως μὴ ἀποπίπτοι].

The previous sentence, which describes how the soldiers—regarded at first in the mass and, as it were, from a distance—were seized with an impulse of converting the headland˙ into a regular fortress, shows how Thucydides will sometimes so condense his meaning in a few words that its clearness is at once imperilled :—

(IV, 4. 1) μέχρι αὐτοῖς τοῖς στρατιώταις σχολάζουσιν ὁρμὴ ἐνέπεσε περιστᾶσιν ἐκτειχίσαι τὸ χωρίον.

Here by σχολάζουσιν ὁρμή he seems to mean ' an impulse such as commonly falls on men at a time of idleness,' and by περιστᾶσιν ἐκτειχίσαι ' to take each his station, as the rule is, and so build a complete ring of defences[1].' But, as in another case which we have discussed[2], the prefatory, summarising glance is quickly succeeded by the careful detail of analysis, which sets out, in neatly poised clauses, the sturdy zeal of Demosthenes' men in making shift to carry through what they had once begun. This realistic intention is first announced by the mere arrangement of the opening words of the continuation—

(IV, 4. 2 init.) καὶ ἐγχειρήσαντες εἰργάζοντο, σιδήρια μὲν λιθουργὰ οὐκ ἔχοντες, λογάδην δὲ φέροντες λίθους,—

till we are led, by similar even degrees, to their manner of carrying the mud on their backs. If, therefore, we are

---

[1] According to another and less probable interpretation, ἐνέπεσε περι-
στᾶσιν must be taken together, as a violent compression of—' fell upon them in the manner that one knows of, when men veer round (or change their minds).'

[2] Above, p. 170; VI, 24. 3—καὶ ἔρως ἐνέπεσε τοῖς πᾶσιν ὁμοίως ἐκπλεῦσαι κτλ.

to follow Cobet in cutting away the careful amplitude of the two clauses which we have seen in his brackets above, we can only do so by neglecting the descriptive art which informs and directs the whole story, and which is a peculiar product of the author's genius.

That this view of the case is not fanciful, must be granted by anyone who will impartially read the chapter through, observing the further fullness of this explanation :—

(IV, 4. 3) παντί τε τρόπῳ ἠπείγοντο φθῆναι τοὺς Λακεδαιμονίους πρὶν ἐπιβοηθῆσαι· τὸ γὰρ πλέον τοῦ χωρίου αὐτὸ καρτερὸν ὑπῆρχε καὶ οὐδὲν ἔδει τείχους.

(IV, 80. 2) μή τι πρὸς τὰ παρόντα [τῆς Πύλου ἐχομένης[1]] νεωτερίσωσιν.

The strict economy of words in this chapter, and especially in the former half of this sentence—

καὶ ἅμα τῶν Εἱλώτων βουλομένοις ἦν ἐπὶ προφάσει ἐκπέμψαι,—

should be decisive in favour of the correction. The obvious heroic cadence that results would furnish an argument against excision, if this were a passage of Demosthenes ; as indeed it would be an objection in the case of Thucydides, if we trusted the opinion of Norden as to the metrical habits of early Greek prose[2]. This insertion is to be compared with two others already noticed[3].

(V, 10. 5) οἱ ἄνδρες ἡμᾶς οὐ μένουσιν· δῆλοι δὲ τῶν τε δοράτων τῇ κινήσει καὶ τῶν κεφαλῶν· οἷς γὰρ ἂν τοῦτο γίγνηται, οὐκ εἰώθασι μένειν τοὺς ἐπιόντας.

The brilliant acumen of *Variæ Lectiones* might perhaps incite one to cut away the last two clauses, as an

---

[1] *Secl.* Hude. [2] Above, p. 280.
[3] II, 84. 3; VII, 45. 2; above, p. 293.

explanatory adscript supplied by some grammarian who
feared that the point was not intelligible already in
δῆλοι and its clause.   But the idea of such alteration
must be dismissed when we recognise the matter-of-
fact, expansive mood which is occasionally allowed to
the speakers in the History. Brasidas' tone here is
one of light-hearted confidence in the midst of action :
like the distracted Nicias[1], he is drawn by sudden
exertion into a suitably commonplace manner of speech.
This artless manner has appeared at length in the appeal
of the Platæans[2].

(VI, 40. 1) ἀλλ' ἔτι καὶ νῦν, ὦ πάντων ἀξυνετώτατοι, εἰ
μὴ μανθάνετε κακὰ σπεύδοντες, [ἢ ἀμαθέστατοί ἐστε[3]]
ὧν ἐγὼ οἶδα Ἑλλήνων, ἢ ἀδικώτατοι, εἰ εἰδότες τολμᾶτε,
ἀλλ' ἤτοι μαθόντες γε ἢ μεταγνόντες τὸ τῆς πόλεως ξύμπασι
κοινὸν αὔξετε,—

Athenagoras the democrat is rebuking the oligarchical party at Syracuse : his manner is short and sharp,
taking a fresh turn with almost every one of his clauses ;
and therefore we need not hesitate to abolish ἢ ἀμαθέστατοί ἐστε as a late insertion. The reason of that
insertion becomes clear, if we follow Cobet, as we surely
ought, in restoring ὧν ἐγὼ οἶδα Ἑλλήνων to its natural
place after ἀξυνετώτατοι : this dislocation has led to a
clumsy attempt at patching. Cobet would also cut out
the ἀλλ' before ἤτοι μαθόντες γε ; but it ought to be
retained for the office of repeating or picking up the
opening note (ἀλλ' ἔτι καὶ νῦν), and also of separating off
its new pair of alternatives (ἤτοι μαθόντες γε ἢ μεταγνόντες), which briefly answer the double weight of the
former pair (ἀξυνετώτατοι ..ἢ ἀδικώτατοι) and their
appendages.

---

[1] Above, pp. 150-1.   [2] Above, p. 299.
[3] *Secl.* Dobree, Cobet, Madvig, Hude.

The Oxford text, apparently in order to maintain the credit of the manuscripts, follows the old way of putting a full stop after τολμᾶτε, which utterly disappoints the expectation raised by ἔτι καὶ νῦν at the beginning. Yet, when it has thus upset the household, as it were, for the sake of a fraudulent waif, it accepts, in what is at least virtually the continuation of the same sentence, a correction which is only a shade—if at all—more obvious than the other:—

ἡγησάμενοι τοῦτο μὲν ἂν καὶ ἴσον καὶ πλέον οἱ ἀγαθοὶ ὑμῶν [ἥπερ τὸ τῆς πόλεως πλῆθος[1]] μετασχεῖν—

where the inserted phrase most probably comes from the same ready hand. Both phrases must seem about equally fatuous to a proper grasp of *this context*.

VIII, 6. 3 [ὅθεν καὶ τοὔνομα Λακωνικὸν ἡ οἰκία αὐτῶν κατὰ τὴν ξενίαν ἔσχεν· Ἔνδιος γὰρ Ἀλκιβιάδου ἐκαλεῖτο[2]].

In the words preceding these, we are told that Alcibiades was a guest-friend (ξένος) of Endius, one of the ephors at Sparta. The text then proceeds— 'Hence it was that their family[3] got a Laconian name, on the strength of this hospitality: for Endius bore the surname "son of Alcibiades".' The linguistic difficulties of this note (ὅθεν—οἰκία—αὐτῶν—Ἔνδ. Ἀλκ. ἐκαλεῖτο) are over-emphasised by the critics who would cut it out: in any case, it is beside the point to urge that there is a 'want of relevancy in the whole statement[4].' We must put up with some awkwardness of connection, both in sense and in grammar, for the sake of a note, first tightly compressed, and then rather abruptly forced into the narrative. The perilous bareness of the last clause

---

[1] *Secl.* Krüger.
[2] *Secl.* Classen, Goodhart : [κατὰ τὴν ξενίαν] Krüger, Stahl, Hude.
[3] It should be noticed that the use of οἰκία in this sense has had some preparation in the ideas attaching to ξένος. Cf. above, p. 291, n. 2.
[4] Goodhart, Bk VIII, p. 12; Classen, Bk VIII, p. 12.

betrays the anxiety of the writer who has no footnotes[1],
while the concluding verb rounds off the rhythm of his
remark, as if to save the dignity of the text.

These few examples must suffice to show the direction
in which the answer—or rather, the several answers—
to the textual problem should henceforth be mainly
sought. In order to bring out the method as briefly and
distinctly as possible, our illustrations have been selected
from passages where we have to work on the unanimous
tradition of the best manuscripts, and also with a view to
avoiding, as far as possible, the encumbrance of grammatical and historical disputes. Yet the principles here
put forward should obtain a careful hearing at the trial
of many disagreements in the material evidence; for they
are based on the character and habits of the mind which
produced the History. Indeed it is one great merit of
those critics who have been most intent on plucking
weeds from this ancient garden, that their zeal has called
for a clearer understanding of the whole original growth.
Cobet especially has made it impossible for anyone truly
interested in the achievement and fame of Thucydides
to ignore this problem of interpolation, or to rest in the
despair which may come of perusing a vast amount of
indeterminate conjecture. We have shown here in
outline the most hopeful way of advance: in the meantime, a few definite signs of disability in the latest
editions have served to prove an immediate practical
value in our literary estimate of the History.

---

[1] κατὰ τὴν ξενίαν is not strictly necessary in such an emergency, and is
probably a later comment on ὅθεν. Cf. above, p. 284.

CHAPTER X

CONCLUSION

§ I

THE writer whose methods we have followed in both his larger and his smaller applications of form presents the remarkable case of a strict scientific reason endeavouring to realise and bequeath its achievement in a permanent work of art. That such an endeavour was conceived at all, and still more, that it could succeed as far as it did in performance, must have been due to certain fine abilities beyond those that are to be merely termed intellectual. Thucydides was an Athenian of the Periclean age ; and we have been careful to allow that even a man of his severely critical judgement could enjoy the spell of traditional poetry, and to make no surprise of his cultivating a sonorous dignity in his own language. His periodic composition, it is true, shows an industrious energy of analysis which, apart from other signs, should clearly dissociate him from the aim of a dramatist. But the wide range of research, the boldness of experiment in design and manner, and the figurative force of many memorable phrases, have carried our investigation through the noise and glitter of Sicilian rhetoric to a certain rare quality in the nature of this man, who not merely acquired some useful instruments in the market of popular fashion, but endowed them with a strength and a beauty that were all his own. For at the back of

L.   20 his discerning and arranging we meet with a peculiarly vivid sense of things, as they moved around him in their successive groups of persons and events. From the glow of this feeling especially arise the creations of poetry and romance. It is more commonly recognised, of course, where practical reason has had no sway. In Thucydides, it was the secret source of his distinctive power; it gave the edge and brilliance to his keen enquiry. He wanted to know the truth about the things that passed before his eyes, for their own sake, and because he felt their importance. They were a part of one huge and complex but always continuous chain. Profoundly stirred by this main unity, and firmly grasping that section of things which came within his reach, he was eager that others should know and ponder them in times when the chain—into which those others, like himself and his world, must in turn be linked—should be very different in quality and appearance.

So understood, his zeal for the truth must ensure him his place on a level with Socrates. The best intellects of that age were rejecting the authority of both religion and philosophy; and these two men found the road thus opened for work which was to make a new epoch in the functions of literature and thought. The practical enterprise of Thucydides had the advantage of many hints from Hippocrates, Democritus, Protagoras and Antiphon; in whose company he stood aloof from the fantastic elegance of Sicilian speech. But there is another point, connected with that personal concern which we have just noticed, that sets him once more apart with Socrates—his independent daring. For while he could see much folly and harm in the excessive vogue of Protagorean disputation, he could make use of its formal precision for the conduct, in particular, of his terse reflective style. So again, though he scorned the empty ornamentation with

which the 'iatrosophists' and others were chiefly busied,
he detected the real merit of the Sicilian devices. He
saw that Gorgias and his school were working, in their
gay, inconsiderate success, towards an adaptation of the
charm of poetry to the service of truth and right. As we
followed the gradual formalising of Greek prose, from
the first impress of Ionian speculation to the intricate
frivolities of mere phrase-mongers, we remarked how the
question must have arisen, whether poetic words and
expressions—which had flown of old, and still could fly,
with mysterious potency—might not be tamed and trained
to serve the actual affairs of men. The Euphuist could
only pluck a few of the magic plumes, and strut in
ludicrous glory. But Thucydides was able, and boldly
chose, to summon the powers of poetry to support and
recommend the grave discourse of reason ; and thus, in
the figurative and sonorous strength of his language—as
clearly as in his use of digressions and speeches, and in
the sensitive root of his insight—he displays just so
much of the faculty of a poet as may give a rare weight
and value to the witness of historical truth.

The analytical bent of his interest has appeared not
only in the laborious arguments of his speakers but in
his own summary contrasts of leading characters ; while
on every page the antithetical encounters of his clauses
attest the profit that his intelligence derived from the
methods of Protagoras and Gorgias. But in the further
contrasts between the styles of particular speakers, and
again, between the exuberant growth of rhetoric and
the steady progress of military and political events, he
seized an opportunity of subtle artistic treatment ; so
that—if we have viewed the case correctly—in working
up one typical debate, at a juncture when events were
marching to a large and doubtful issue, he laid on some
colours of eristic disputation to suit the momentary

straits of moral dignity. Sophistic studies of the passions
he probably thought impertinent to regular politics and
diplomacy : but here also the schools could help without
hurting his ordinary prose, by directing him to the
luminous force of personification. Another trace of
special treatment is the intonation seemingly concerted
by a metrical chime in occasional groups of clause-
endings; which his later practice, perhaps from the
example of Antiphon, sought to vary. We then argued,
on the question of the text, that the search for these and
even more minute devices can hardly be unimportant, if
it is likely to enlarge our means of recognising the
approach of some deliberate gravity or intensity in the
art of such a finely-gifted observer.

§ 2

As each of these inventions came into view, we cast
a glance at something similar or comparable in the
developement of English prose[1]. These references have
perhaps suggested already the thorough-going infidelity
of the current translations of the History. None of
these bear traces of any adequate attempt to give
Thucydides his proper rank and significance in literature :
they give hardly a sign of his experimental ardour, as it
appears in the chief varieties of his style. Too constantly the translator has endeavoured to set forth, not
the author's taste and dexterity, but his own. Many
years have passed since Gorgias was compared with our
Euphuists[2] : yet no one has ventured to apply some of
the direct results of our own literary Renaissance to the
rendering of even the most striking differences in the

---

[1] Above, pp. 152 (Fuller); 155 (Hobbes); 188 (Meredith); 208 (Raleigh);
239 (Taylor); 244 (Carlyle).

[2] Thompson, *Gorgias*, 1871, p. 177.

formal texture of Thucydides[1]. A version that should
have the continual vigour and occasional crookedness of
Hobbes, but should surpass him in accurate delivery of
both sense and sound, would do much to place the greater
and smaller meanings of the History in their true perspec-
tive. It ought to imitate some 'verbal flourishes which
seem to have little thought behind them[2]' : but they would
be very few, and there, amid the life and main effort of the
composition, they would have something significant, in
each case, to avow. A fresh enterprise in language may
be expected to admit some idle frills, as well as some
awkward wrinkles, in weaving and stitching the noble
garment. Sir Walter Raleigh, in the Preface to which
we have twice referred[3], falls into a tinkling vanity not
unlike that of the Euphuists :—

'To hold the times we have we hold all things
lawfull : and either we hope to hold them for ever ; or at
least we hope, that there is nothing after them to be
hoped for.'

Yet he is able to relinquish his work with that apostrophe to Death, which any age or nation might be
glad to own. The neat precision of the phrases which
have been already quoted is exchanged for a broader
scheme in the conclusion, most admirably enhancing its
small and simple result :—

[1] The choice of *generally* appropriate language was urged and claimed
by S. T. Bloomfield (*Thuc. Transl.* 1829, i, p. xii) who stated that he had
'occasionally *sought*, rather than *avoided*, the rich, nervous and idiomatical
phraseology of the seventeenth and part of the eighteenth centuries'; and
his practice, though too uniformly relying on the Latin resources of our
language, has made the nearest approach to the quality of the author's more
formal manner. The common neglect of this obvious duty is most glaring
in Jowett's version (1881 and 1900 ; see above, p. 241, n. 8): his treatment of
Plato is hardly less damaging to the characteristic styles of speakers in the
Dialogues. Archer-Hind's translation of the *Timæus* (1888) is an example
of what may be done in the right direction. Cf. the excellent Preface to
Twining's *Poetics of Aristotle*, 1812.

[2] Above, p. 5.   [3] pp. 9, 208.

'Thou hast drawne together all the farre stretched greatnesse, all the pride, crueltie, and ambition of man, and covered it all over with these two narrow words, *Hic iacet.*'

We may be inclined to chafe at this elegance in Donne's *Meditations upon our Human Conditions*[1]—

'Instantly the taste is insipid and fatuous ; instantly the appetite is dull and desireless ; instantly the knees are sinking and strengthless ; and in an instant sleep, which is the picture, the copy of death, is taken away, that the original, death itself, may succeed, and that so I might have death to the life.'
Yet shortly after we come to this[2]—

'In the grave I may speak through the stones, in the voice of my friends, in the accents of those words, which their love may afford my memory' ;—
and a hundred reflections might be gathered from his sermons to show that, besides being, as the judgement of Ben Jonson averred, 'the first poet in the world for some things[3],' he is not far from the company of the great masters of English prose. The sophistic incitement which set him and other serious writers in the way of formal power and grace may be illustrated by a passage from Lyly's encomium of England[4] :—

'By whose good endeavours vice is punished, virtue rewarded, peace established, foreign broils repressed, domestical cares appeased. What nation can of councillors desire more ? what dominion, that excepted, hath so much ? when neither courage can prevail against their chivalry, nor craft take place against their counsel, nor both joined in one be of force to undermine their country.'

[1] 1624 : the passage is quoted from Alford's ed., 1839, *Medit.* ii.
[2] *Medit.* iii.   [3] W. Drummond, *Conversations*, 1711.
[4] *Euphues Glasse for Europe*, 1580 (ed. Arber, 1868).

Furthermore, it is precisely the literary aims of the
early Greek sophists that Jeremy Taylor is avowedly
adapting to his purpose when he says[1]—

'The style that I here use, is according as it happens;
sometimes plain, sometimes closer: the things which I
bring are sometimes new, and sometimes old; they are
difficult and they are easy; sometimes adorned with
cases, and the cases specificated in stories, and sometimes instead of a story I recite an apologue,...and in all
things I mind the matter; and suppose truth alone and
reason and the piety of the decision to be the best
ornament.'

His less methodical writings are full of fresh and
generally happy adventure in systems of sound; the
following may serve as an example[2] :—

'In him will be found all the riches of gold, the
delightfulness of the meadows, the brightness of the sun,
the pleasantness of music, the beauty of the heavens, the
comfortable smell of amber, the contentedness of all the
senses, and all that can be either admired or enjoyed.'

The lengthy periods of Hooker, a good while before,
had occasionally resorted to a kind of word-play in the
stress of earnest exposition; and this device, as well as
the continual aim of welding a series of points into round
synoptic masses, can offer a comparison with the artistic
effort of Thucydides.   But the English divine was far
more prolix, and his habit was rather to repeat a word
for the useful connection of an echo than to drive home
the sharp and gleaming wedge of epigram.   Nevertheless, his assonant emphasis comes very near at times to
such an effect, as in this part of one ample sentence[3]—

'When their courts erected for the maintenance of

1 *Ductor Dubitantium*, 1660, Pref. (Bohn, 1850).
2 *Contemplations of the State of Man*, 1684, II, 4.
3 *Eccles. Polit.* 1617, VII, xxiv, 7.

good *order*, are *disordered*, when they regard not the
clergy under them, when neither clergy nor laity are kept
in that *awe* for which this *authority* should serve,'—
which, as an example of the profit gained for serious art
from a late or current extravagance of conceits, might
be classed with some of the less conscious graces of
Thucydides, as for instance[1]—

καὶ ἀπέθανον τῶν Θεσσαλῶν καὶ ᾿Αθηναίων οὐ πολλοί,
ἀνείλοντο μέντοι αὐτοὺς αὐθημερὸν ἀσπόνδους.

There are, therefore, abundant patterns and materials
in English prose for the garment in which the History
deserves to be dressed for its full appreciation. Thucydides might then appear in his proper distinction among
the pioneers of literary art[2].

§ 3

In seeking a true surmise of that position, we have
considered the man as well as his art ; remembering that
he must have conversed, not merely with soldiers and
sailors, but with professors, politicians and men of other
businesses more specialised than his own. Our principal
objective has been the literary craftsmanship of Thucyd-

[1] Thuc. II, 22. 2. With the wider scope for ornament and epigram
provided by the speeches, it may be interesting to compare the words which
Bunyan, one of the least artificial of our writers, has given to Formalist and
Hypocrisy :—'And besides, so be we get into the way, what's matter which
way we get in?' etc. (*Pilgr. Progr.* 1678, p. 42).

[2] The good results of his plainer and more strenuous antithetical structures might be illustrated by the following sentences in which Balzac has
contrasted two sorts of young men :—'Si les uns, semblables à des cribles,
reçoivent toute espèce d'idées, sans en garder aucune ; ceux-là les com-
parent, et s'assimilent toutes les bonnes. Si ceux-ci croient savoir quelque
chose, ne savent rien et comprennent tout, prêtent tout à ceux qui n'ont
besoin de rien et n'offrent rien à ceux qui ont besoin de quelque chose ; ceux-
là étudient secrètement les pensées d'autrui, et placent leur argent aussi bien
que leurs folies à gros interêts.' (*Histoire des Treize*, iii.)

ides : but each advance has manifested the need and use of connecting his work with the discernible endowments and tendencies of his mind. Thus we have further allowed him the æsthetic enjoyment of plays and poetic recitals, and have extended the reach of his intellect to a foresight of new eras of civilisation and the demands of foreign research. It cannot seem accurate now to say that 'he turned away from his main task of narrative to develop the style of his work as pure literature[1].' The probabilities of his daily life in Athens and abroad, the larger and smaller energies of his language, and the rare quality of temperament appearing behind his rational as well as his imaginative powers, all suggest that from an early stage he was stirred and guided by an ambition of memorable phrasing and weighty, rather than brilliant, epigrammatic point. For he seems to have felt that the conflicting polities of Greece, with all their faults and disasters, had earned some right to 'the deathless life that moves and speaks in a deed well told[2].' His exile, it is true, supplied him with new leisure and material for enabling him to include both speeches and disquisitions : but, first and always, his aim was to compose a profitable and lasting record of what was done and said in the War.

Above all, it is not least to the uncompromising keenness and persistence of his observation that we owe those vivid glimpses of persons and passions, which are but the most signal efforts of a linguistic struggle revealed by some of the smallest sinews of his style. For if he threw a certain strength of imagination into these efforts, to provide us with fresh matter for judgement and reflection, we have noticed how sharply the connection of his periodic

[1] Above, p. 13.
[2] Pindar, *Isth.* III, 40 (of 'Homer's praises')—τοῦτο γὰρ ἀθάνατον φωνᾶεν ἕρπει, εἴ τις εὖ εἴπῃ τι.

systems is distinguished by its intellectual fibre from the patch-work—bright and entertaining as it often is—of Gorgias. The same superiority of mind was remarked, when we traced the sincerity and independence of his labour alike in the perplexities and the felicities of particular expressions.

Style, indeed, is like chaff blown about by the wind, if it be severed, either actually or in critical treatment, from the thought which has grown with it and within it to maturity. Because Thucydides has realised so suddenly this relation between the two, and has felt the need of modifying his tone along with the different humours and movements through which his readers are to be carried, it is right to assign him a place of unique importance in the history of letters. If, on the larger lines of his method, the military annals and the imaginative rhetoric have severally risked our blame, it is the duty of sound criticism to estimate his whole intention, after carefully watching the procedure of his work. His building is not to be classified merely by the pattern on the floor, or by the carving on the pediment. There can be no single description of his architecture. Fabric and form are varied to interpret the life of his world. Hence it is rarely possible to be sure that any meaning which we may fairly elicit therefrom is not an effect of his conscious design. His own conception of the History makes him appear almost Roman in his reliance on the power and dignity of literature; more than Roman, however, in his hope that the book will be, not so much a triumphal arch left agape at the wastes of time, as a stately palace wherein civic and national emotions are to be seen assembled for the parliament of truth:

INDEX

For EU product safety concerns, contact us at Calle de José Abascal, 56–1°,
28003 Madrid, Spain or eugpsr@cambridge.org.

www.ingramcontent.com/pod-product-compliance
Ingram Content Group UK Ltd.
Pitfield, Milton Keynes, MK11 3LW, UK
UKHW042148130625
459647UK00011B/1240